WHAT'S IN A NAME?

WHAT'S IN A NAME?

Advertising and the Concept of Brands

Second Edition

John Philip Jones and Jan S. Slater

M.E. Sharpe
Armonk, New York
London, England

Library of Congress Cataloging-in-Publication Data

Jones, John Philip
    What's in a name? : advertising and the concept of brands / by John Philip Jones and
Jan S. Slater.—2nd ed.
    p. cm.
    Includes bibliographical references and index.
    ISBN 0-7656-0973-8 (alk. paper)
    1. Advertising. 2. Brand name products. I. Slater, Jan. II. Title.

HF5823 .J718 2002
658.8′343—dc21

2002030890

Printed in the United States of America

The paper used in this publication meets the minimum requirements of
American National Standard for Information Sciences
Permanence of Paper for Printed Library Materials,
ANSI Z 39.48-1984.

BM (c) 10   9   8   7   6   5   4   3   2   1

To our students, in the hope that throughout their professional careers they will remember that the value of a theory depends on the amount of empirical support it has received.

There must be a personality shining through all the talk about the product. I have overwhelming evidence that one of the reasons why people buy my Mountain Grown Apples is because they take to a character called Old Jim Young, who chats with them in the advertising.

(James Webb Young, *How to Become an Advertising Man*)

James Webb Young was the first person to use the term "added values" to describe the psychological benefits of brands as perceived by their users. Advertising is an important—perhaps the most important—source of these added values. Although this book does not discuss specifically Old Jim Young's Mountain Grown Apples, it attempts to explain what these apples meant to the people who bought and ate them. This relationship with its consumers is a quality shared by every strong brand.

Contents

List of Tables and Figures   xiii

Foreword: Advertising and Brand Planning   xvii
    Don Johnston and Harold F. Clark Jr.

1.   Introduction   3

2.   Brands: What They Are and Why They Emerged   19
    A Shopping Trip and Some Conclusions Therefrom   20
    The Economist's View of Oligopoly—and a Different Hypothesis   23
    Oligopolistic Competition in the Real World   28
    The Emergence of Brands   31
    Oligopoly, Price, and the Consumer   37
    The Argument in Brief   40

3.   Factors That Shape a Brand During Its Conception and Birth   45
    The Importance of Innovation and the Belief in Decline   50
    Five Influences on a New Brand   54
    The Importance of Market Testing   65
    The Argument in Brief   69

4.   Factors That Shape a Brand During Its Growth and Maturity   73
    Initial Growth   74
    Five Influences on a Growing Brand   79
    Beyond the Primary Growth Cycle   101
    The Argument in Brief   103

5.   The Mature Brand and the Consumer: The Nature of
    Repeat-Buying Theory   107
    Consumer Sales Defined in Consumer Terms   112
    Predictive Models in Action   115

Four Myths 124
How Brands Grow 128
How Advertising Strategy Should Be Influenced by
   Repeat-Buying Theory 129
The Argument in Brief 133

6. Advertising Research: A Digression on Recall **136**
Reading-and-Noting: Its Fall from Grace 140
The Twentieth-Century Philosophers' Stone 143
"Learn-Feel-Do" and "Learn-Do-Feel" 145
The Limited Circumstances When Recall Testing Can Be Useful 150
Pretesting Based on Simulating Consumer Behavior 154
Tracking Studies 156
The Argument in Brief—and a Footnote on Aggregated Data 157

7. How Advertising Influences Sales **163**
Advertising's Short-Term Effect and How It Is Measured 165
Medium-Term Effect as a Repetition of Short-Term Effects 170
The Advertising Response Function 177
Continuity in the Marketplace 181
Medium-Term Effects Measured Econometrically 185
The Argument in Brief 185

8. How Advertising Builds Brands **188**
Six Measures of the Long-Term Effects of Advertising 189
Penetration and Purchase Frequency 191
Price and Price Elasticity 199
Advertising Elasticity 202
Advertising Intensiveness 207
Accountability 210
The Argument in Brief 211

9. Giving a Brand Legs: Brands as Collectible Entities **214**
The Case for Collectible Brands 215
Collecting Coca-Cola: It's the Real Thing 217
Hallmark Collecting: When You Care Enough 219
The Loyal Relationship with Collectible Brands 220
Building Brand Loyalty 222
Linking the Collectible to the Company 223
The Argument in Brief 228

10. The Contribution of Advertising Strategy to Brand Building   **230**
Putting Advertising in Perspective   231
What Advertising Cannot Do   232
What Advertising Can Do   234
The Development of a Strategy   238
Formulating the Strategy   239
The Brand Audit   240
The Strategy Itself   242
Target Group   244
Proposition   248
Role of the Advertising   250
Can an Old Brand Be Reintroduced with a New Strategy?   253
The Argument in Brief   254

11. From Advertising Strategy to Advertising Campaign   **257**
The Campaign   258
The Contribution of the Media   263
The Campaign for Louisiana: "Come As You Are.
    Leave Different."   266
The Argument in Brief   269

12. How to Develop and Expose Better Advertising   **270**
First Recommendation: The Case for More Market
    Experiments   271
Second Recommendation: How to Close Some of the
    Gaps in Our Knowledge   282
The Argument in Brief   287

Index   291

About the Authors   309

List of Tables and Figures

Tables

F.1	Leading Advertised Brands in 1913	xix
2.1	Growth of Consumer Expenditure and Advertising	26
3.1	Manufacturers' Market Shares	57
3.2	Manufacturers Operating in Different Market Segments	58
3.3	Five-Year Changes in Manufacturers' Market Shares	58
3.4	Success of Brands with Umbrella Names and New Names	61
4.1	Development over Time in Ratio of Sales to Distribution	76
4.2	Comparison of Share of Market and Share of Advertising Voice	88
4.3	Progress of Share of Market and Share of Advertising for Two Brands	89
4.4	Price Premium and Market Share	96
4.5	Range of Price Elasticity	96
4.6	Range of Advertising Elasticity	98
5.1	Patterns of Consumer Purchasing	110
5.2	Analysis of Sales in Consumer Terms	113
5.3	Example of Analysis of Sales in Consumer Terms	113
5.4	Four-Week Penetration	116
5.5	Penetration Growth	117
5.6	Average Purchases per Buyer: Sugared Cereals	117
5.7	Purchases per Buyer: Shredded Wheat	118
5.8	Growth in Purchases per Buyer: Shredded Wheat	118
5.9	Frequency Distribution of Purchases: Shredded Wheat	119
5.10	Average Product Purchases of Gasoline Brands	122
5.11	Average Annual Product Purchases: Sweetened Cereals	122
5.12	Average Annual Product Purchases: Standard Cereals	123
5.13	Hypothetical "Leaky Bucket" Buyers	126
5.14	The Importance of Large Brands	132
6.1	Findings of DEMOS Study	143
6.2	Aggregated Reading and Noting Data	159
7.1	Decile Analysis of STAS	169

7.2 Three-Country Decile Analysis of STAS Differentials   170
7.3 STAS and Medium-Term Effects Compared   172
7.4 Matrix Relating STAS Differential to Advertising Intensity   173
7.5 Matrix Relating Advertising Effort to Promotional Intensity   174
7.6 Growing Brands: Medium-Term Growth Compared with
     Combined Marketing Stimuli   175
7.7 Relative Effectiveness of TV Schedules Based on Different
     Combinations of Continuity and Weekly Weight   184
8.1 Average Share of Market and Penetration, Cold Breakfast
     Cereals, 1991   192
8.2 Average Share of Market and Penetration, Regular
     Domestic Beer, 1997   192
8.3 Average Share of Market and Penetration, Laundry
     Detergents, 1998   192
8.4 Average Share of Market and Penetration, Brands in Twelve
     Categories, 1991   193
8.5 Depth of Purchase by Quintiles   196
8.6 Marketplace Prices of 142 Brands in Twelve Product
     Categories, 1991   200
8.7 Effect of 10 Percent Price Reduction on Sales   200
8.8 Profit and Loss from 10 Percent Price Reduction   201
8.9 Price Increase and Profit   202
8.10 Price Elasticity Compared with Advertising Expenditure:
     Eighteen Typical MMA Brands   202
8.11 Effect of Extra Advertising on Sales of Four Brands with
     NSV of $100m, During the Advertised Period   204
8.12 Incremental Costs for Brand EAA   204
8.13 Incremental Costs for Brand EAB   205
8.14 Incremental Costs for Brand EAC   205
8.15 Incremental Costs for Brand EAD   205
8.16 Medium-Term Plus Long-Term Effects of Advertising:
     Seventeen MMA Brands, 1997   211

Figures

4.1 Dynamic Difference Format   91
4.2 Dynamic Difference: Four Brands   92
4.3 Dynamic Difference: Powerful Brands   93
4.4 The Elliott Extension   95
4.5 The Corlett Shift   100
7.1 Ad Households and Adless Households   167

7.2 STAS Measures for Brand AL   169
7.3 Schematic Diagram of Sales Gains and Losses for Brand
     AAA over the Course of a Year   171
7.4 STAS Differential and Medium-Term Sales Effect for
     Brand ZAA   171
7.5 Quintile Analysis of Thirty-nine Brands Showing
     Medium-Term Growth   176
7.6 Advertising Response Function with Threshold   177
7.7 Advertising Response Function without Threshold   177
7.8 Response Function: McDonald's 1966 British Pure
     Single-Source Data Recomputed with the Jones Method   180
7.9 Response Function: Nielsen 1991 American Pure
     Single-Source Data from Seventy-eight Brands   180
8.1 Long-Term Effects of Advertising   189
8.2 Share of Market and Penetration Relationship: Cold Breakfast
     Cereals, 1991   193
8.3 Share of Market and Penetration Relationship: Regular
     Domestic Beer, 1997   194
8.4 Share of Market and Penetration Relationship: Laundry
     Detergents, 1998   194
8.5 Share of Market and Penetration Relationship: Brands in
     Twelve Categories, 1991   195
8.6 Purchase Frequency by SOM Quintiles: Cold Breakfast
     Cereals, 1991   197
8.7 Purchase Frequency by SOM Quintiles: Regular Domestic
     Beer, 1997   197
8.8 Purchase Frequency by SOM Quintiles: Laundry Detergents,
     1998   198
8.9 Purchase Frequency by SOM Quintiles: Twelve Categories,
     1991   198
8.10 Profit and Loss for Brands with Different Advertising
     Elasticities   207
8.11 Share of Market and Share of Voice Advertising–
     Intensiveness Curve   208

Foreword: Advertising and Brand Planning

Adapted from the Foreword to the First Edition of *What's In a Name?*

Those practitioners deep in the business of creating advertising are all too aware of the changing environment in which we operate. Media structure is changing everywhere. New forms with seductive promises are attracting advertiser investment away from traditional media. Yet, some of the breakthroughs in the technical revolution have already proved illusory. What change is permanent and what is merely a blip on the conventional media screen?

The emergence of super marketers who will, and must, challenge the growing dominance of the super retailers is already changing the agency scene. Problems of conflict and exclusivity will require these new mega-marketers to concentrate their budgets in very few agencies, to hire a large number of smaller agencies, or to start their own in-house agencies (an experiment that has never worked on a small scale in the past). The fact remains: there is an insufficient number of large agency networks to provide exclusive service for these dominant marketers.

The fallout of the recall battle, so definitively described and decried in this book, has yielded some damaging anomalies in the agency business. Increasingly, we have become embroiled in the battle of creating outstanding advertisements. Clients look for the "big idea," the "breakthrough execution," the winner of the Clio. Creative resources are applied to solve specific short-term problems with short-lived executions. A campaign may last as long as a year. Agencies and clients become obsessed with advertisements; the critical question of how a long-range, three- to five-year "advertising" strategy can benefit a brand is widely overlooked.

A further indication of this emphasis is the great premium placed on creative people. Agencies bemoan the dearth of creative talent; there simply are not enough top writers, art directors, and producers to fill the demand for outstanding advertisements. Salaries escalate proportionately. More and more time and dollars are spent looking for that award-winning advertisement.

What does it look like when it finally appears? Do consumers recognize a "big idea"? Do users of a brand respond differently, or in greater numbers? How is "breakthrough" measured anyway? The copy in these advertisements is frequently written in some mythical language, "advertisingspeak," which purports to be "slice of life" but which, in fact, is totally alienating to the very people whose life is supposedly being sliced up.

Not surprisingly, then, readers and viewers of advertising become increasingly skeptical and cynical about the value of advertising.

With this apparent loss of consumer acceptance on one hand and growing market pressures on advertisers on the other, how then can one account for the fact that overall the advertising industry when viewed from a long-term perspective, appears to be growing? The rate of growth was powerful during the 1990s, and most analysts believe that the cyclical downturn of the early twenty-first century will lead before too long to a recovery.

Closer analysis of this long-term growth, as will be seen in the most detailed discussion of packaged goods in this book, demonstrates that certain historically dynamic subsegments are not participating in the overall growth rate. Indeed, there is not only a real decline in share, there is, more critically, a decline in potential. The importance of advertising in the minds of certain traditional advertisers is diminishing at the same time the target groups of the advertising are questioning its very relevance.

The growth in the industry is coming from new kinds of advertisers and new product categories that have entered the arena. Both the importance and the frailty of the new advertising budgets from the electronics industry in various Silicon Valleys have been well documented in the recent past. Looking at the overall industry statistics, then, may not in itself be a heartening exercise but rather another means of masking what is really taking place.

The marketplace is perilous. Times change quickly. There are signs that the industry has lost its growth potential and that consumers are turning off to advertising in ever greater numbers. A very compelling case can be made that the practitioners of advertising have lost touch with the very reality of which they are allegedly the custodians. One could argue that we overstate the case for dramatic effect; to a degree we accept this point. The professional advertising community, however, will recognize the dull reality behind our allegations.

Now consider for a moment the ten largest advertisers in the year 1913 (see Table F.1). If we were to double or triple this list, it would have pretty much the same characteristics. These are mostly names you still recognize, companies with known brands that command a significant market share today. As perilous as a changing marketplace can be, there must be some way to survive.

Table F.1

Leading Advertised Brands in 1913

Advertiser	Some of the advertised brands
1. Procter & Gamble	Ivory Soap; Crisco
2. Quaker Oats	Quaker Oats; Puffed Wheat; Puffed Rice
3. Postum Cereal Co.	Post Toasties; Grape Nuts; Regular and Instant Postum
4. Victor Talking Machine Co.	Victor Records; Victrola Players
5. Willys-Overland	Overland Coupe
6. Colgate & Co.	Colgate Dental Cream; Colgate Cold Cream; Cashmere Bouquet
7. Eastman Kodak	Kodak cameras; Kodak film
8. P. Lorillard and Co.	Zubelda; Egyptian Deities; Mogul; Murad
9. Steward Warner Speedometer Co.	
10. American Tobacco Company	Pall Mall; Bull Durham smoking tobacco

If brands have survived this long—through two world wars, a major economic depression, and (potentially most damaging of all) some decades of well-meaning brand managership, then something is at work that will help us overcome the problems in today's "real world." Familiar brands will continue to prosper. New brands—as long as they are demonstrably better and demonstrably different—will succeed in the marketplace. They can be brought to life, nourished, and allowed to grow and survive.

Early in this book, there appears a very valuable metaphor of a complex machine that describes how brands function. Another useful metaphor, of course, is to compare a brand to a person. In the preceding paragraph, all of the verbs just as aptly describe a person. For years, we have known that consumers respond comfortably to the invitation to compare a brand to a person. The metaphor is helpful in this context as well. To survive as a child in an urban neighborhood today (the milieu to which the packaged goods marketplace most readily can be compared), an individual must have savvy, street smarts, a certain degree of acknowledged power, strong parentage on which to rely, and considerable luck. Most children survive and some prosper and succeed in life well beyond the most hoped-for dreams of their anxious parents.

The conditions are no different for brands—except that far fewer survive. (Whether this is the result of the obvious fact that brands have no life of their own—they are managed—is outside this discussion but is not an irrelevant question.)

Key for a brand are the elements of parentage (who the manufacturer is), acknowledged power (the appropriate level of resources for the launch), and luck. What we want to focus on, however, is the importance of savvy and street smarts—knowing what it takes to survive and then using the knowledge in a flexible, tactical plan. It is in these areas that we will discover the keys to maintaining and building major brands for the balance of the twenty-first century.

There is a great deal about how brands and advertising work that we do not know. This volume examines the state of our knowledge in detail and makes a fervent and timely plea to all marketers to begin to build a better base on which to make decisions. We would agree that we need more solid and reliable information.

We would also add, however, that we must make better use of the information we already have.

Much of the accumulated wisdom and expertise lying in the files and archives of agencies and marketers is not known, understood, used, or passed down to the generations of new young brand personnel. Quantities of data which are assembled about the marketplace, the consumer, and social and economic trends are simply not brought to bear on the decisions affecting individual brands. The results of specific brand research, diligently carried out, are unused because earnest, smart advertising people simply do not have the time or resources to wring them dry for every important nuance and clue. We are not providing the marketing savvy we have because we have no mechanism or budget with which to do so.

A communications revolution is at hand. At times one feels rather as people must have felt in Paris in 1789: we know the revolution is going on but we do not have the time or perspective to see who is winning. One winner will clearly be the person who can harness the accumulated expertise about a brand, its history, its properties, and its marketplace and use that expertise to carry it forward.

The process of carrying it forward is the second element of the survival kit. Street smarts, the marriage of instinct and intelligence, translate into a plan for survival. A brand, which requires a more explicit plan, depends no less on the instincts and intelligence of its creators. The plan must encompass all that is known about and all that is relevant to the brand:

- the broad social and economic issues,
- marketplace factors,

- brand and category developments,
- company data,
- advertising data—competitive and noncompetitive,
- media trends and opportunities.

The plan fuses all of this into a long-term strategy. A long-term strategy is not concerned with advertisements—how to make the sales target in the next quarter—it is concerned with advertising and the role it must play in the survival of the brand over the next twenty years. Only when one knows where one is going can one make the first decisions about how to get there.

The development of a long-term strategy, you may respond, has always been the responsibility of the advertising agency. Isn't that what they have been doing all along? Isn't that the primary function of account management? Of course, the agency assumes responsibility for this role whenever and however it can in all client–agency relationships. The problem is that in an already fractured marketing world, the various aspects of this function have also become fractured and dispersed. Some of the responsibility lies in the agency research department, some in the client research department, some in account management, some in brand management, some in media planning, some (even) in media buying, and some in research and development (R&D), and some has simply fallen between the cracks because no one has the time or budget for the synthesis it requires. The demands of today's marketplace come first. The pressures that public companies feel on their quarterly earnings statements are carried into the advertising and sales departments, which must "make the numbers" this quarter. The plan is not thought through or written down. The best street smarts we can give to the brand for its own survival are sacrificed on the expedient altar of time and dollar pressure.

There has to be a new dimension in the advertising–marketing mix—a function that pulls together all that is known and, in a meaningful, relevant, and helpful manner, sets it down in the common plan. This role is called "account planning." It is not really a new function. It has existed in some agencies in Britain and the United States for almost four decades. The need for it is becoming more acute, however, and this volume is, in itself, a testimony to the urgent need for some new systemic solution.

The genesis of account planning, some maintained at the time, was the "weaknesses in the training of . . . account executives" (referred to in chapter 12). Regardless of its cause, account planning enables the agency to do what it has always done *better.* The account planner does it better simply because he/she combines the functions that have become distorted by separation. That combination becomes the primary responsibility of an individual in the account team who is not its leader.

There is nothing novel in what the planner does (except that it is largely not being done by anyone else). The planner provides the basis on which the advertising for a brand can be developed, executed, and evaluated. The creation, maintenance, and modification of the advertising strategy summarizes in a coherent model the way in which advertising in an ongoing way might help the brand to grow. To fulfill this role, the planner

1. interprets data—which may be desk research, commissioned research, or simply introspection and common sense;
2. makes advertising judgments—because strategy necessarily involves judgment about how advertising might work within the overall framework of how marketing principles in general might work;
3. communicates these interpretations and judgments to the rest of the agency team and client product group, in a way that is both objective and stimulating.

It is the combination of objectivity and involvement that makes the role of the account planner unique. The traditional split between account management and research functions prevents these two essential elements from coming together systemically. Research remains dispassionately objective (insofar as it can), and account management, heavy in the day-to-day thick of things, displays incredible involvement. Both functions remain critical (although it can be argued that the research element per se no longer needs to be inside the agency). Account management continues to lead the charge. It is only that it has an additional competitive weapon at its disposal—account planning.

The addition of account planning to traditional agency structures will inevitably alter how agencies function as well as how they are perceived and valued by their clients. Their service will change. The nature of their counsel will change. They will become tougher, more realistic and more demanding in their analyses and recommendations. We know this because of those instances where account planning has been successfully operating in the service of our clients over a significant period of time.

Will account planning overcome all of the problems that the industry may be facing? Can account planning suddenly make it possible to undertake the kind of market experimentation that will be demanded? Obviously, account planning is not a panacea; it merely assures us (and our clients) that we are making a conscientious effort to use the best of our expertise and resources in the most innovative and constructive way possible to solve brand problems. As long as an advertising agency can make this claim to its clients, it can fairly claim to represent the real world.

The way to provide a client with a neat and simply arranged plan to get from the Wonderland of brand strategic planning to dull reality is merely to make someone accountable for doing it, and to provide the resources and information bases and the requisite thinking time apart from, yet committed to, the specific brand problems of the moment. There are no guarantees that all problems will be solved. At the very least, however, we will be out of the business of creating advertisements and back in the business of providing advertising counsel for our clients. And maybe the brands we are serving today will make the top ten list in the year 2013.

Don Johnston
Chairman, 1976–86, J. Walter Thompson Company

Harold F. Clark, Jr.,
Executive Vice President, 1984–87, J. Walter Thompson Company

WHAT'S
IN A NAME?

1

Introduction

We are addressing this book to people who want to learn something about brands in the real world. Such people may already be in the marketing and advertising business as entrepreneurs, as brand managers in manufacturing companies, as executives in advertising agencies; or they may be planning to build careers in such organizations. The book should also be of value in universities, and we have every intention of using it to teach our own students. Academic readers are warned, however, that the book severely and directly disputes the validity of certain widely held notions, such as that competitive brands in a market are functionally indistinguishable from one another; that the decline phase of the so-called brand life cycle is inevitable and irreversible; and that advertising is in general a powerful persuasive force in overcoming resistant attitudes. The extent of this book's use in academe will depend on how much professors wish to protect their students from the dangerous heresies propagated here.

This book is devoted to the marketing and especially the advertising of what are referred to most commonly as repeat-purchase packaged goods (or sometimes as fast-moving consumer goods, FMCG for short). This is rather a large field; its more important categories are packaged, canned, and frozen foods; proprietary drugs; tobacco products; toiletries and cosmetics; wine, beer, and liquor; soaps and cleaners; gum and candy; and soft drinks.[1] This mixed collection of categories has considerable homogeneity from a marketing standpoint. They all have six common general characteristics, and in most of these they differ at least in degree from other categories of products and services (such as automotive, travel, retail, direct response, financial, and entertainment). Each of these characteristics will now be briefly described as a logical starting point for the argument of this book, although the reader will find them discussed more fully in the main body of the text.

1. Women are the most important category of buyers

Repeat-purchase packaged goods are sold predominantly in supermarkets. In about 70 percent of cases, the buyers are women, although such goods are of course used by all members of the family in addition to the homemaker. Despite recent changes in the individual roles of women and men (which may cause the 70 percent estimate to fall), many manufacturers of packaged goods continue to refer to their target consumer as "she," and this useful convention will occasionally be followed in this book. The only other advertising category in which a female target group is comparably important is the retail one.

2. Buyers buy repeatedly and have a repertoire of brands

Brands are bought not once but repeatedly, in many cases in predictably regular patterns; hence the truth of the saying that when we build brands we are making customers and not just sales. In marketing jargon, we are building a long-term franchise.

In virtually every category examined empirically, it has been found that at least 80 percent of buyers normally buy (with varying degrees of irregularity) more than one brand. This introduces the extremely important concept of the repertoire of brands, the collection the homemaker buys in varying proportions, often (again) in predictably regular patterns.

The uniformity of such patterns will be a surprise to some readers, but they will find it plentifully illustrated by the factual data in chapter 5. This element of constancy—or the inertia of habit—in most markets for repeat-purchase goods partly explains the manifest difficulty of breaking into such markets with new brands.

It also suggests the large role for advertising aimed at reinforcement and protection for the majority of established brands. Indeed, much advertising is addressed to existing regular and irregular users of such brands. We advertise to these people in order to hold as well as to increase our market share. We talk to them with the intention of reinforcing their loyalty to our brand, to compliment them on their wisdom in using it so that they will remain friendly with us, and to encourage them to use it more than before. If we look upon advertising in this way, our approach becomes different from what conventional wisdom suggests, which is that advertising is a means of converting people, persuading them to switch from brand A to brand B. There is much evidence that brand advertising as it is practiced in the real world is substantially based on continuity and not conversion. This is quite a different way of looking at the subject. Here the phrase "looking at the subject" should be emphasized. We are talking about a fresh standpoint, a mental sidestep. In a very apposite phrase originally used in a different context, this way of looking at the subject is "an apparatus of the mind, a technique of thinking."[2] Because of the large role of habit in the purchase decision, such decision making is often described as "low involvement."

These factors of repetition and multibrand purchasing are of generally greater importance with packaged goods than in most other categories because of characteristics endemic to such markets, notably the high rate of product use.

The importance of repeat buying means that in advertising repeat-purchase packaged goods, it is not only ethical but also good business to be truthful, because if the advertising overpromises, the customer will punish the manufacturer by not buying the brand again. It is surprising that this argument appears so infrequently in debates about truth in advertising.

3. Competitive brands differ from one another in functional terms

Many readers of this book will be stopped by this statement. It may very well disturb a deep-seated and rather remarkable belief held by numerous people, especially individuals without first-hand experience of brand marketing, that competitive brands in any market are indistinguishable from one another in functional terms. The widespread prevalence of this belief has caused products in such markets to be referred to as "parity products" or "homogeneous package goods,"[3] and product improvements in them to be described as "cosmetic changes,"[4] or "induced product differentiation" created by advertising.[5] Since this issue is important to the development of the argument in this book, it is necessary to take the time to discuss it and present some additional views before continuing with the mainstream discussion.

One point should be made first. Most consumer goods markets are oligopolies dominated by a small number of large competitive manufacturers. (This type of market organization will be discussed in chapter 2.) It is substantially true that the nature of oligopolistic competition and the relative ease with which functional improvements can be copied are forces that cause functional innovations in new and restaged brands to be widely and sometimes rapidly diffused through markets. It is both wrong and dangerous, however, to infer from the force and characteristics of oligopolistic competition that all brands are (or become) functionally interchangeable. It is wrong because it flies in the face of the facts, some of which will shortly be presented, and dangerous because such a line of thinking can persuade marketers to introduce new brands that offer a mere functional parity with their competitors, with a subsequent rate of failure that is in most cases only too easily and dishearteningly predictable. Success almost always requires differentiation.

The writings of researchers, advertisers, and workers in advertising agencies—people who have a day-to-day operational knowledge of brands—make it quite clear that competing brands in any market tend to be functionally different from one another. Their evidence of differences between brands in functional terms comes mainly from blind product tests, in which the names of the brands being compared are not disclosed, in order to focus exclusive attention on their functional properties. Although such tests suffer from a number of practical imperfections, we have never come across a single manufacturer of packaged goods who does not employ them on a regular basis for evaluating consumer responses to the functional delivery of his own and his competitors' brands.[6]

Although product tests normally provide fairly clear-cut results, it is not always wise to interpret them in an equally clear-cut way. Brands with a "minority appeal" should not always be rejected by manufacturers, since these are often able to attract small groups of users interested in specific attributes, on which such brands might score well. In fact, in most markets, there is a "tail" of profitable brands with individual market shares of less than 5 percent, all of which sell steadily to relatively small numbers of consumers.

Now, what do knowledgeable practitioners have to say about functional product differences? Here are the views of five of them.

James O. Peckham, a researcher with forty years of experience with the A.C. Nielsen Company, wrote

> Based on a composite trend of eighteen new and/or improved brands marketed nationally prior to the start of our study, we see that consumer purchases of these new brands are up 51 percent in the two-year period. If we examine the individual brands making up this fine sales trend, we find that they all had a "consumer plus" readily demonstrable to the consumer.

Again:

> The board chairman of one of the leading manufacturers of a household product recently stated in a speech before the National Industrial Confer-

ence Board that the company's top brand had had fifty-five product improvements in the twenty-nine years of its existence.

Again:

> On a blind product test of your new brand versus leading brands already on the market, you should not ordinarily consider trying to build a consumer franchise unless you have a 60–40 preference—and 65–35 would be preferable.[7]

J. Hugh Davidson, a senior executive in a major international marketing company, published an empirical examination of successful and unsuccessful new products, with the conclusions that

> Fully 74% of the successes I studied offered the consumer better performance at the same or higher price. . . . My study revealed a close correlation between a brand's success and its distinctiveness.[8]

David Ogilvy, one of the most distinguished practitioners in the advertising agency field, referred to statements by the former chairman of Procter & Gamble:

> Says [Ed] Harness, "The key to successful marketing is superior product performance. . . . If the consumer does not perceive any real benefits in the brand, then no amount of ingenious advertising and selling can save it."

To which Ogilvy responded

> The best of all ways to beat P&G is, of course, to market a *better product.* Bell brand potato chips defeated P&G's Pringles because they tasted better. And Rave overtook Lilt in less than a year because, not containing ammonia, it is a better product.[9]

Bill Bernbach, who, like Ogilvy, was one of the luminaries of the post–World War II advertising scene, was clear on the point:

> I think the most important element in success in ad writing is the product itself. And I can't say that often enough. Or emphasize it enough. Because I think a great ad campaign will make a bad product fail faster. It will get more people to know it's bad. And it's the product itself that's all important

and that's why we, as an agency, work so closely with the client on his product—looking for improvements, looking for ways to make people want it, looking for additions to the product, looking for changes in the product. Because when you have that, you are giving the people something that they can't get elsewhere. And that is fundamentally what sells.[10]

Rosser Reeves, a scarcely less distinguished figure in the field than Ogilvy and Bernbach, observed

The agency can induce the client to change his product, improve his product. We have done this on numerous occasions. . . . A great advertising man of three decades ago once said: "A gifted product is mightier than a gifted pen." How right he was! This is not a secondary road. It is often the first, and the best road, to travel.[11]

During our own professional careers, we have studied the reports of scores, perhaps hundreds, of blind product tests on our clients' brands. From this experience we found it so normal to expect different preferences for different brands that it never occurred to us or our colleagues to expect anything else. The result of a pair of such tests will be given in chapter 2. This comes from a manufactured food category in which some of the perceptible taste differences between the brands are the result of different ingredients and manufacturing processes, but some are also there because certain manufacturers are able to get fresher stocks to the retail trade as a result of their superior shipping systems.[12]

Despite the informed opinions and the evidence quoted here, we still believe regretfully that the myth of "artificial" product differentiation[13] is so well established in the academic and journalistic worlds that this and related notions will continue to be a picturesque feature of the literature. However, our studies of the facts leave us in no doubt that functional differences between brands are as important with packaged goods as with any other category: indeed probably more so, because of the relatively large number of competitive brands that are available in such markets, as a result of the rapid pace of oligopolistic competition.

Incidentally, it might be considered reasonable to expect the proponents of the "homogeneous package goods" school to subject their hypothesis to empirical examination and to publish their evidence. This evidence, if it existed, would demonstrate in effect that consumers are fools, or at least that their clearly expressed preferences among brands are based on capricious and frivolous considerations. To the best of our observation, no such evidence has ever been presented for evaluation.

4. Brands are enriched with added values

In addition to the functional rewards that consumers get from using brands, there are further benefits to the consumer that are substantially psychological. Often referred to as added values, they are built by consumers' experience of using brands, and by the advertising and the packaging. The existence of added values will be easily demonstrated in chapter 2. Added values are important to all products and services, especially to repeat-purchase packaged goods, but their importance relative to functional benefits varies according to product category; for instance, added values are relatively more important with toiletries than with food products. Packaged goods almost certainly include those categories in which added values are of the most substantial importance.

The result of added values is that successful brands are preferred to their competitors in named product tests by a higher margin than in blind product tests since the latter screen out added values and force respondents to react exclusively to functional performance. But it is important to appreciate that added values are added on top of functional performance and do not substitute for it. A misconception of this point is the main reason why unsuccessful marketers have sacrificed fortunes in new brand ventures, by trying to use advertising as a substitute for product superiority.

This matter is exceptionally important in the discussion of advertising. Here there is a real role for intuition and imagination, which are regarded by many people as predominantly feminine qualities, as well as for the logic, precision, and drive sometimes seen as predominantly masculine virtues.[14] The reader will note how the feminine associations of intuition and imagination are consistent with the first characteristic of repeat-purchase packaged goods in the present analysis: the importance of women as target consumers.

5. The field is relatively advertising-intensive

By "advertising-intensive" we mean that a brand's advertising, when expressed as a proportion of the value of its sales, is a relatively high figure. *Advertising Age* data (published annually on a company and not on a brand basis) show an average figure in the categories of repeat-purchase packaged goods of above 8 percent.[15] (The published figures cover both "measured" and "unmeasured media." A more realistic figure, based on media advertising alone, is approximately 5 percent of the net value of sales. This in turn represents a formidably large dollar sum.) The comparable ratios in categories other than packaged goods are mostly much lower. For instance, those for the automotive, airline, and retail categories are all about 2 percent.

The obvious inference from this observation is that advertising is a relatively important sales-generating activity in packaged goods marketing, or rather that it is perceived as such by the manufacturers, whose expenditures measured in real terms are relatively constant year by year. This consistency suggests that companies have experience-based guidelines for the marketplace effectiveness of certain levels of advertising expenditure, which is in accord with our professional experience. Certain companies, however, have much greater knowledge of the effects of advertising weight, as a result of econometric investigations of the marketplace results of their advertising. This difficult procedure calls for the screening out of advertising as a separate variable in the marketing mix, but manufacturers' increasing ability to do this is an important matter that will be examined in some detail in this book, in particular in chapter 8.

Although the conclusion that the field of repeat-purchase packaged goods is relatively advertising-intensive may be based on the simplest possible processes of observation and deduction, an analysis of six complex pieces of empirical evidence bearing on this subject reaches strongly similar conclusions.[16]

6. The field is very large

Advertising investments in the various categories of repeat-purchase goods are consistently extremely large and account year after year for well over one-third of the aggregate advertising investments of the hundred largest advertisers in the United States.[17] The combined category of repeat-purchase packaged goods is still the largest among American advertisers. (Nevertheless, its share of the total has come down from 60 percent in the mid-1980s, to 37 percent in 2000. This is a point that will be discussed in chapter 4.)

The size of the total category and its special importance with large advertisers have significant additional related effects. For instance, television is the most important advertising medium for the largest advertisers (except those in the tobacco industry, for the obvious reason of government prohibition). It is not a coincidence that it is with packaged goods that television has developed its ability both to show the functional characteristics of brands by demonstrating them and to generate nonfunctional added values largely through the communication of mood and emotion.

Manufacturers of repeat-purchase packaged goods have also become the most important clients of the largest and most sophisticated advertising agencies. Improvements in the techniques and skills of writing and scheduling advertisements almost invariably take place with packaged goods, and we are accustomed to associating most of the advances in the marketing field with names such as Coca-Cola, Procter & Gamble, Kraft General Foods, Nestlé, and Warner-Lambert, and with the advertising agencies employed by such companies.

What we have attempted to demonstrate so far is that packaged goods differ from most other product categories in six distinct ways. These six differences in degree are so great that they almost add up to a difference in kind. This is why packaged goods justify being examined and analyzed on their own, or at least being given a special emphasis to differentiate them from the advertising field as a whole. Let us now examine how they are handled in the literature of advertising, including marketing works that embrace advertising.

Books and articles in this field fall into three categories: primary, secondary, and tertiary works.

Primary works. These are writings by people with the highest professional credentials and are based on their first-hand experience. There are not many such works. We do not include in this category the writings of all the top professionals, but we would certainly include those of Bill Bernbach, Leo Burnett, John Caples, Claude Hopkins, David Ogilvy, and James Webb Young.[18]

Primary works are easy to read. But despite their unique and unquestioned value, they tend to be intellectually rather slight, giving a true but regrettably faint and impressionistic flavor of how advertising works in the real world. They are not therefore in themselves adequate as textbooks for university courses, but they are nevertheless indispensable to people interested in advertising. The works of Bernbach, Burnett, Ogilvy, and Young are informed by profound knowledge of the packaged goods field, but their treatment of it is regrettably too little focused on specific cases for the instruction of people who really want to learn what it is all about.

Secondary works. The extremely important category of secondary works must be carefully defined. Secondary books and articles are written by both professionals and academics: the books in roughly equal proportions, the articles more by the former than by the latter. We define secondary works as generally having the following four characteristics:

1. In almost every case they deal with parts of the field and not the field as a whole.

2. They are empirical rather than theoretical, and in this they publish, or republish and interpret, original source material.
3. They admit the existence of controversies surrounding the subject and make a consistent effort to steer a path through these. In other words, they are judgmental and interpretative, although the reader may not fully accept all of the interpretations. But with most of the works we have in mind, the sure impression remains that the discussion is informed, embracing analysis and synthesis often of a high order, and supported in many cases by the authors' direct experience in the field.
4. They are well written. This in itself is unusual, and we shall return to the question of lucidity.

Good secondary works are relatively rare. In our belief there are about twenty books and two hundred articles in professional and academic publications that fall into the category. We do not intend to list them here, but we have made extensive use of secondary works in writing this book, and the reader will see the names of many of them in the endnotes. Despite the fact that many of these books include packaged goods in their argument, there is little serious empirical (as opposed to theoretical) examination of the field, the only work based exclusively on facts being Ehrenberg's magnificent but narrowly focused study.[19]

Readers would be correct in concluding that there is a respectable corpus of serious secondary literature on advertising, including marketing works with an advertising focus. They should remember, however, that these works represent only a minuscule fraction of all the books and papers written on the subject, the vastly greatest proportion of which fall into our third category.

Tertiary works. The category of tertiary works is a catch-all for everything else written about the field. Much is simple descriptive work. Many of the books rely on what is said in other tertiary works and in the trade press.[20] Most of the books make no attempt to be empirical, and many of the theories enunciated are highly questionable in the light of modern research. In professional and academic magazines, there is some empirical work, but it is often bedeviled with mathematical examinations (many based on inadequate data bases) of problems for which mathematical analysis is an inappropriate tool. In such works, repeat-purchase packaged goods are not looked upon as in any way special and are accorded a fairly cursory descriptive treatment if they are mentioned at all.

As far as we have been able to find out, tertiary literature is not used at all by practitioners.[21] However, its use is fairly widespread in universities.

We have tried very hard indeed to write a book that would qualify as a secondary work.

The first characteristic of our book is that it deals with a single aspect of the subject: the marketing and advertising of repeat-purchase packaged goods and how advertising contributes to the building of brands, a process we believe to be more a matter of repetition and reinforcement than of impact and conversion. We intend that the book should be a work of practical value; and it will be fairly easy to estimate the extent of this by the simple test of how much it is actually used by practitioners in the field. (This is not a bad criterion for evaluating the worth of anything written about any aspect of advertising.)

The second characteristic of this book is that it is based substantially on facts. These facts have been interpreted, angled, as it were, for the light they throw on various aspects of the subject. In many instances, our supporting material is in the public domain or can at least be found with a little difficulty; the reader is encouraged to study it at leisure. Chapters 3 through 5 rely on aggregated data from the A.C. Nielsen Company and Market Research Corporation of America, sources of incomparable quality and authority. Later chapters examine many studies of the marketplace effectiveness of campaigns, some of the research described and evaluated having been executed with the use of the most sophisticated techniques available in the United States or abroad.

However, although the book is empirical, we have lightened the writing by a selective use of anecdotes from our professional experience, anecdotes carefully chosen to highlight principles for which there is a substantial factual basis. Telling "war stories" is a favorite habit of former marketing and advertising people, and a serious attempt has been made to restrain our self-indulgence in this regard.

The third point is that the book is uncompromising in its examination of advertising controversies caused by gaps in what we know for certain about advertising and its effects. The reader will find significant debate about the following topics, about which there are and will continue to be great differences between practitioners, although it would be wrong to say that significant advances in our knowledge have not been made:

- the generation of advertising ideas,
- the value of the creative contributions to campaigns,
- advertising response functions,
- how advertising works in psychological terms,
- advertising research,
- the effects of the agency commission system.

In all these controversies, we have not shied away from drawing hypotheses or, in some cases, even from making recommendations for policy, which we hope will generate much debate and further empirical work, because these are the only ways in which we shall seriously advance our knowledge. Writings that do not at least describe these controversies are not only inadequate, but seriously misleading.

Our fourth point about this book concerns the style in which it is written. The subject matter is not always easy, but this is never an excuse to be turgid or obscure. No matter what may be the subject of any piece of writing, we believe that all good writing strives for lucidity and that no pains should be spared to achieve it.

Only the readers can tell whether our efforts have achieved the slightest success. But we can assure them that we have not followed advice that has seriously been offered that books such as this should be written in a deliberately difficult or obscure way, lest students "pass them by." (This remarkable sentiment explains a great deal about academic literature in general.)

What we have attempted to do in this book is to analyze and synthesize what we know about brand advertising, with the intention of instructing the curious about both what we know and what we do not know. But it must not be thought that what we have learned is enough to construct a general theory with anything like universal application. Still less is it possible to draw up laws that will predict certainly and precisely what results will follow certain courses of action. But we have learned some things with pretty fair certainty: separate or related pieces which add up to a little over a third of the total corpus of existing and potential knowledge about advertising. These elements of knowledge are individually quite small and some way removed from the all-embracing theories that we sometimes hear.

British market researcher Colin McDonald uses an extraordinarily elegant analogy to show how the study of advertising can only be empirical, and piece by piece, in order to examine "how patterns of response vary between markets and, on that basis, guess at what will happen in similar cases." Thus advertisements should be classified in a way similar to how an entomologist classifies insects, "where one looks for common factors linking thousands of different species."[22] McDonald is himself a major contributor to studying advertising in this way.

As mentioned already, we shall be devoting quite a lot of attention to describing and evaluating what we know about the underlying patterns of consumer behavior as revealed by empirical studies. This is an essential preliminary to understanding how advertising can contribute to developing brands. Knowing how a brand fits into a market and how this may resemble how other brands fit into other markets helps us to set limits to the contribution that advertising can make to brands. But once we set, acknowledge, and understand these limits, advertising can be shown to make a large contribution indeed.

McDonald's comparison of the study of advertisements to the study of insects is strikingly apt, but the more we have dwelt on it, the more we have come to the view that it lacks the important element of movement. All markets are in a state of flux, despite what may appear to be surface stability, apparent stasis. This flux is caused by the way markets are made up: of transactions resulting from a multitude of buying decisions that take place every minute of every hour of the day. We should like therefore to suggest an analogy, which, although not as unexpected and original as McDonald's, may be a little more useful in describing an untidily changing world.

We suggest that we can compare the process of marketing a brand to a large and complex piece of mechanical equipment. As with most machines, the speed of the machine bears some relation to the energy applied to make it work. We can half see and half infer (because we cannot see everything) that all parts of the machine are connected to other parts by a complex system of pulleys, levers, and cogwheels. But although we can observe much of the functioning of the machine with our eyes, and we can evaluate the input and output, the parts we can see represent only a small proportion of the total, because of things blocking our view. Some people observing the whole apparatus believe that they can explain its workings in some general, overall way, following what we might call the "macro" approach (which, if it oversimplifies, is likely to mislead). On the other hand, some people, like us, prefer to follow the "micro" or inductive approach, which attempts to build up knowledge by looking at the mechanism piece by piece. This latter approach can at least explain discrete parts and can provide the hope (although not the firm expectation) that a general theory might eventually be built up to explain the whole.

There is one important feature of the large machine: in its very center, we can make out quite clearly a much smaller apparatus that is connected with most of the parts of the bigger machine and on occasion even appears to be controlling them. We can see the small machine reasonably clearly; when we look at it, we are struck by its extraordinary precision, delicacy, even fragility. The more we look at it, the more the thought strikes us that this little apparatus was constructed by a different sort of person, by an artist perhaps, rather than by one of the engineers and craftspeople who made the larger machine. And although we can see the smaller machine whirring harmoniously, some of the visible details of its construction make no sense to the engineers and craftspeople and the rest of us observers whose education has taught us to think along rational, logical, and, of course, predictable lines.

It will be no surprise to the reader that the small machine within the large machine is, in our analogy, advertising, one of the main sources of a brand's added values. The analogy will reappear throughout this book. As is the case with our small machine, some elements of advertising are visible (although only some of the elements that can be seen can be understood), but some things are completely concealed. Let us clarify this point.

All advertisements are by their nature visible or audible. The scripts, copy, film sequences, and pictures; the number of insertions and the number of subjects in a campaign; and their scheduling and seasonality are all more or less available for study by the outside observer. It is, moreover, normally possible to make reasonable guesses at what an advertisement was intended to accomplish, although we might have in no way been privy to the advertising strategy. We can with little trouble compare how much money is spent on a particular campaign with expenditures on other campaigns. Finally, by studying how long individual campaigns are exposed and how much money is spent on them, we can draw realistic conclusions about their effectiveness or lack of effectiveness in the marketplace, although we cannot always explain their impact.

This point was made by James Webb Young, the most sagacious of all writers about advertising and one of the most successful practitioners of the art. He wrote:

> Advertising education must rest on the close observation and study of actual cases.
>
> The raw material for such case studies is all around you, in print and on the air. . . . Through these, by persistent accumulation of data, study and analysis, you will begin to grasp the application of basic advertising concepts.[23]

But this technique of observation and reflection, valuable though it is, will not reveal everything, still less explain it. The central process in constructing our small machine, which is the generation of the idea behind the advertisement, remains concealed from sight. And the harder we look for it, the more maddeningly elusive it becomes. There are, however, other things to consider first. In particular we must examine some of the visible parts of the large machine. This is the concern of chapters 2 through 5; but a few words first about the structure of this book.

The second edition is substantially different from the first edition, which was published in 1986. This second edition comprises twelve chapters. Chapters 1 through 5 deal with brands in a general sense and describe many factors of permanent importance to brands during the various stages of their development. Chapters 6 through 12 are focused on advertising's specific contribution. Chapter 6 covers the important but controversial question of pretesting advertisements before they are exposed in the marketplace, as background to the remaining discussion of advertising methods and effects. Chapters 7 and 8 describe what became known during the 1990s about how advertising actually works to build brands. Chapters 9 through 11 give practical guidance to building advertising strategy, including thoughts on an unexpected aspect of line extension: brands as collectible phenomena. Chapter 12 is devoted to the significant matter of how we should extend our knowledge of advertising's effects with a view to improving its present indifferent record of success.

About half of the book (chapters 1 through 6 and chapter 12) represents material adapted from the first edition, but the text is amplified to include descriptions of the findings of much recent research. The other half of the book (chapters 7 through 11) comprises totally new material that reflects the advances that have been made in our knowledge of advertising and brands since the first edition was written in the mid-1980s.

Notes

1. This categorization is used by *Advertising Age* in its annual estimates of the advertising expenditures of the hundred leading advertisers in the United States. These are published in the September following the year to which the data apply.

2. This phrase is taken from a celebrated description of economic analysis by John Maynard Keynes in the original introduction to the series of *Cambridge Economic Handbooks.* D.H. Robertson, *Money* (New York: Harcourt, Brace, 1922), p. v.

3. Julian L. Simon, *Issues in the Economics of Advertising* (Urbana, IL: University of Illinois Press, 1970), pp. 269–285.

4. Mark S. Albion and Paul W. Farris, *The Advertising Controversy* (Boston, MA: Auburn House, 1981), p. 71.

5. Ibid., p. 88.

6. These tests are thoughtfully discussed by Stephen King, *Developing New Brands* (London: Pitman, 1973), pp. 137–139.

7. James O. Peckman, Sr., *The Wheel of Marketing,* 2d ed., 1981 (privately published but available through A.C. Nielsen), p. 92. (The first two quotations come from the first edition, published in 1978, pp. 50–51.) Peckham provides a primary source of exceptional importance, based on a massive aggregation of Nielsen data in a number of product fields.

8. J. Hugh Davidson, "Why Most New Consumer Brands Fail," *Harvard Business Review* (March–April 1976): 117–122.

9. David Ogilvy, *Ogilvy on Advertising* (New York: Crown, 1983), pp. 156–157. For a description of the operating policies of Procter & Gamble, see Bill Saposito, "Procter and Gamble's Comeback Plan," *Fortune* (February 4, 1985): 30–37. Also

see John Smale and Priscilla Hayes Petty, "Behind the Brands at P.& G.," *Harvard Business Review* (November–December 1985): 79–80.

10. Denis Higgins, ed., *The Art of Writing Advertising* (Chicago: Advertising Publications, 1965), p. 23.

11. Rosser Reeves, *Reality in Advertising* (New York: Alfred A. Knopf, 1961), p. 55.

12. This statement is based on first-hand evidence of a senior food chemist with extensive experience when employed by a number of leading food manufacturers in the United States.

13. Albion and Farris, *The Advertising Controversy,* p. 88.

14. We are reminded of an aphorism attributed to Kipling (one with which we do not completely disagree): "A woman's guess is much more accurate than a man's certainty."

15. *Advertising Age,* September 24, 2001, S14.

16. Albion and Farris, *The Advertising Controversy,* pp. 117–136.

17. *Advertising Age,* September 24, 2001, p. S14.

18. Of these famous writers, Bernbach is the only one who did not leave us a book describing his views on the art. A number of his speeches can be found, however, if one searches for them in anthologies and monographs.

19. Andrew Ehrenberg, *Repeat Buying: Theory and Applications,* 2d ed. (New York: Oxford University Press, 1988).

20. A good example is a recently published and widely reviewed book that attempts to debunk brands (devices that are viewed by the author as tools of American economic imperialism). Since the book contains not a shred of first-hand information about brands themselves, but is a potpourri of the strongly expressed but not very well-informed views of other journalists, the trenchant opinions of the author herself cannot be taken too seriously. Naomi Klein, *No Logo: Taking Aim at Brand Bullies* (New York: Picador USA, 1999).

21. This conclusion is based on personal observation, supplemented by information from senior executives in thirty leading U.S. advertising agencies about their own training programs.

22. Colin McDonald, "Myths, Evidence and Evaluation," *Admap* (November 1980): 546–555.

23. James Webb Young, *How to Become an Advertising Man* (Chicago: Advertising Publications, 1963), p. 12.

———— 2 ————

Brands: What They Are and Why They Emerged

This chapter is concerned with defining the meaning of a brand and describing how and why brands emerged in the marketplace. It is important to spend some time on this historical progress because there are issues here beyond purely technical ones, issues that touch on aspects of social and economic welfare. The time to consider these broader matters, albeit briefly, must be at the beginning of this book.

Brands developed out of trademarks, a longstanding means of providing legal protection to an inventor's patent. But even with the earliest brands that emerged more than a hundred years ago, the branding process developed a purpose and importance beyond this simple legal role in that it suggested a guarantee of homogeneity and product quality to buyers of a brand, who might otherwise know nothing about its manufacturer. Even more importantly, it provided an unmistakable means of differentiating one manufacturer's output from another's, a matter central to oligopolistic competition (the type of organization most typical of consumer goods markets today).

To examine these points more fully so as to be able to evaluate the branding system for its implications for general economic welfare, we must make a brief incursion into economic history. The reader should be warned that there are differences between our interpretation of the economic history of brands and the conventional one. Opinions vary a great deal about the broader effects of oligopolistic competition, but the majority view interprets oligopoly as an anticompetitive force, a force certainly less socially and economically desirable than the supposed alternative of atomistic competition. We take issue with this view, not on the grounds of its theoretical validity or invalidity, but on the grounds of its relevance to the real world past or present.

The argument that we shall develop in this chapter is, first, that conditions of atomistic competition never existed in many, perhaps most, consumer goods markets and, second, that oligopoly emerged as a competitive, not as an anticompetitive force. The pioneer manufacturer in most product fields was substantially a monopolist who used his brand as a device to demonstrate the legal protection of his product. The monopoly profits attracted competition from firms that had to grow large quickly to compete successfully. This process involved the launch of new brands that competed with varying degrees of directness with the original one, a process which changed the organization of the market to oligopolistic competition. If our view is correct that most consumer goods markets have during their history been only either monopolistic or oligopolistic (a very restricted range of competitive options), then our judgment about the welfare effects of oligopoly, compared with other types of market organization, is going to be quite different from what our view would be if the alternatives were to include anything approaching atomistic competition.

It will be apparent to readers with some training in economic analysis that we are in effect attempting to stand conventional theory on its head. They will discover, however, that we approach economic history from a totally empirical point of view. A comfortable and relevant starting point is to look at some facts that any observant person would be able to collect by making a visit to a grocery store.

A Shopping Trip and Some Conclusions Therefrom

One of the largest grocery stores in Syracuse is Wegmans supermarket in Dewitt. It is a large, well-laid-out store with an impressive range of merchandise, and although many people prefer it to others in Syracuse, we know at least half a dozen stores comparable in size and style. On a Friday evening during the 1980s we decided to spend some time in the cold breakfast cereals aisle to examine as many packs and check as many prices as we could. We concentrated on the ready-prepared cereals, excluding all breakfast foods that need cooking, all prepared "complete breakfasts," and all of the compressed "muesli" products made of grains, nuts and fruit. The main findings were as follows:

- There were seventy varieties of cold cereal sold under different names, with the exception of a few flavors sold under a common brand name, which we counted separately. The seventy different varieties came in 107 different pack sizes.

- The brands appeared to be substantially different from one another in functional terms. (We counted a difference in taste or ingredients as a functional difference.) Specifically, the brands differed from one another in sweetness, in type and proportion of the various ingredients, and in shape and appearance of the product. The functional properties were clearly illustrated on the packs, and of course the surface design of the packs differed as much as their names.
- Most brands came from one of six manufacturers: General Foods, General Mills, Kellogg's, Nabisco, Quaker Oats, and Ralston Purina. By the end of the twentieth century, the number of major manufacturers had been reduced to four as a result of amalgamations. However, the aggregate market share of the four at the beginning of the twenty-first century was no different from the total share of the six in the mid-1980s.
- The 107 different pack sizes were sold at a wide variety of prices. The cheapest pack sold for $0.43 (Malt-O-Meal Puffed Wheat and Malt-O-Meal Puffed Rice); the highest price pack for $1.97 (eighteen-pack Kellogg's Variety). The ratio between the prices of the cheapest and most expensive was therefore 100:458. (This range, of course, refers to packs of all sizes, which accounts for some but by no means all of the variation.) This range of prices was reasonably evenly spread, the median price ($1.19) being fairly close to the unweighted average ($1.23).
- Wegmans indicates clearly on the shelf price tickets the price per pound of most goods. Prices can be compared directly so the careful shopper can see at a glance what value for money the various packs are offering, irrespective of the different sizes.
- We noted a price range from $0.79 per pound (Wegmans generic corn flakes) to $2.11 per pound (Quaker Puffed Wheat). The ratio of bottom price to top price was, as can be seen, fairly large (100:267), although not quite so large as in the previous analysis, for the reason already given. The prices per pound were (like the pack prices) uniformly spread, something demonstrated by the closeness of the median ($1.38) to the unweighted average ($1.36).

What lessons can we draw from this brief exercise in observation and analysis? The object of this exercise was simply to confirm and illustrate some things we knew already, mainly from a knowledge of Nielsen data.[1] But it is always useful on these occasions to have some undisputed facts available, no matter how commonplace they may be.

Before conducting our investigation, we were pretty sure that the breakfast cereal market had six easily confirmed characteristics:

1. The market is oligopolistic, being dominated by a relatively small number of manufacturers.[2] In the 1960s, the six main firms accounted for 97 percent of total sales, the remaining 3 percent was mainly accounted for by private labels.[3] The overall shape of the market was virtually the same in the 1980s and in 2001. The fact that there is a relatively small number of competitors, each of which is a substantial manufacturer, means that oligopoly can represent a heightened type of competition because it brings an advanced degree of consciousness of one's competitors and the influence of one's actions on them.

2. There are many different brands and pack sizes, and each firm has a number of brands that, although in general complementary to each other, also compete with each other to some degree. The different brands reflect different functional characteristics of the products, mainly different taste. The number of brands and varieties has *increased significantly* since the 1960s, as confirmed by Nielsen data and Jules Backman's classic investigation of advertising and competition.[4]

3. All of the brands on sale have significant added values. This chapter is concerned with added values, but before we take any serious steps to describe their features and importance, a number of different but related notions will have to be introduced into the argument. Added values are essentially psychological and subjective to the user of the brand, and they come in the main from two sources: a person's firsthand experience of a brand and its presentation in the packaging and consumer advertising. We can be sure that consumers have experience of all of the brands on sale in Wegmans, for the simple reason that efficient stores evaluate punctiliously and continuously the store traffic generated by all brands on display. It is also certain that such brands receive significant advertising support (a normal condition of stocking by larger stores). We can therefore reasonably assume the brands on the shelves to have added values. Another quite graphic way of describing such brands might be as "bundles of functional and nonfunctional benefits."

4. We expected the range of prices to be large and to have increased over time for a number of reasons, mainly active and continuous price competition among both manufacturers and retailers. This competition can take two forms: strategic or long-term, representing the corporate policy of the manufacturer or retailer; and tactical, by means of temporary promotional actions with specific short-term objectives. The latter are typical of many packaged goods markets (for instance,

bar soaps) where a major share of total tonnage sales is made through temporary reductions, most indicated on the pack.[5] As a general rule, promotions are by far the most important and aggressive expressions of price competition in oligopolistic markets. But for breakfast cereals, price promotions are uncommon; extensive and permanent price differentials are an important feature of the market.

5. We would have drawn approximately similar conclusions from an investigation carried out ten years before the one reported here and the same from one conducted ten years after.

6. Most importantly, our general conclusions from breakfast cereals apply *mutatis mutandis* to most consumer goods markets. Indeed, what can be learned from professional experience and illustrated by our visit to Wegmans regarding price competition and product differentiation applies to most of the packaged goods that shoppers buy regularly and that account for the largest proportion of household consumer expenditure. The truth of this statement can be confirmed by checking any family's shopping list even if the reader does not have access to the vast amount of Nielsen data on the subject.

There is nothing in any way original in these observations. We would have expected any sensible, observant shopper to have drawn the same sorts of conclusions without even the benefit of an hour's store check.

The Economist's View of Oligopoly—and a Different Hypothesis

After the description of the visit to Wegmans supermarket with its plentiful evidence of price competition as well as significant and objectively perceptible product differentiation, it comes as rather a surprise to learn what some economic observers have to say about oligopoly. Here are two examples, neither of them outrageously extreme:

> [Under oligopoly] the characteristic form of industrial system eschews price competition as too dangerous and channels its rivalry into ever-changing strategies for winning customers away from one another.[6]

> In markets dominated by a small number of large corporations, both price and product competition decline. Such products as are on offer tend increasingly to resemble one another, and scope for consumer choice diminishes. . . . A comparison between advertising in the competitive era and today brings out clearly the virtual disappearance of price and product competition.[7]

The idea that the organization of markets changed because of a large reduction in competition is common in economic literature. On a related subject, more than one economist has associated the growth in consumer advertising with the decline of the wholesaler, a supposedly powerful participant in the market who is considered once to have maintained competition among manufacturers by subjecting them to the necessity of bidding for wholesalers' patronage.

Neil Borden of the Harvard Business School mentioned the point in his examination of the economic effects of advertising, published in 1942.[8] Borden listed conflict within the distributional chain as one of nine factors that he claimed had contributed to the growth of consumer advertising in the United States. When the debate passed from Cambridge, Massachusetts, to Cambridge, England, the role of the wholesaler was given a greater, indeed, a central importance among the factors leading to the growth of advertising.

The most extreme expression of this view was made by Nicholas Kaldor in an influential paper published in 1950.[9] Kaldor claimed that price competition among manufacturers was once maintained by the power of wholesalers, but that manufacturers found a way of breaking out of this confinement by branding and advertising their output and "speaking over the heads of the wholesalers to the ultimate buyer."[10] This led to the growth of manufacturers until they began to dominate markets, creating the general conditions of oligopoly we see today. In this situation, the consumer has to pay higher prices because there is much less competition than in the era that supposedly preceded it; the higher prices under oligopoly are used, of course, substantially to fund advertising. The reader will note that Kaldor's argument is not devoid of political implications.

But to put this point into perspective, it is important to understand the historical progress, not so much from a purist's desire for historical accuracy (although this is not a completely unimportant reason) but more because a misunderstanding of history can lead to false conclusions, which can lead in turn to dangerously misleading policy recommendations.

Neither Borden nor Kaldor produced any evidence. There have been, however, a number of serious examinations of the development of the wholesale trade in the United States.[11] From these studies, the unmistakable conclusion emerges that *from the beginning* it was manufacturers who were the dominant partners and wholesalers the weaker ones. Indeed, wholesalers appear to have been called into existence by the need of manufacturers to sell large volumes of production, although in most cases wholesalers were unable physically to service a multitude of retail accounts.

But as the sales of consumer goods grew, wholesalers were often unable to keep up with the demands of manufacturers, and in particular were unable to make an effective job of new product introductions. Manufacturers increasingly found themselves selling directly to the retail trade, especially as the retail trade itself became more and more concentrated. (This process has continued to this day, with important effects on the balance of power in the marketing world.) An even more significant development was that manufacturers found it necessary to appeal directly to the public by advertising to maintain the impetus of demand. But the reader should note that the driving force in this first expansion of advertising was not conflict between supposedly small manufacturers and supposedly large wholesalers, but the simple and pressing need to sell rapidly the burgeoning output of mechanized production, which is essentially a large manufacturer's problem.[12] Before illustrating this point statistically, we must describe and comment on market concentration as it is conventionally described in the microeconomic literature.

The concentration of markets has long been studied by economists. Karl Marx and his disciples were specifically interested in it. As shown by the Sherman Antitrust Act of 1890, the Clayton Act of 1914, and the Federal Trade Commission Act of 1914, the idea had emerged from theory and entered the realm of government policy well before World War I. The interwar period saw vigorous development of the theoretical study of monopolistic competition in the two Cambridges.[13] The trend toward concentration was assumed to move progressively from perfect competition to monopoly, unless impeded by strong legislation. In general, this development was seen to coincide with growth in the size of the market, where growth of output and continuous growth in concentration were seen to proceed in step.

What is striking about the classic studies of the growth of industrial concentration is that they were concerned essentially with a limited number of special cases: transport and heavy (mainly extractive) industry, economic activities in which consumer advertising has never played a large role.[14] The hypothesis that we shall develop is that, in the markets in which advertising *has* been important—where demand had to be forced up rapidly to mop up increasing output—the path toward market concentration has been quite a different one. And if such a hypothesis can be validated, it would explain the dissonance between what we found during our visit to Wegmans supermarket and the conventional microeconomic description of oligopoly.

Let us now return to studying the historical growth of advertising. If we start by looking at statistical data, the most striking fact is that the first substantial absolute increases in advertising were during the decades of steeply rising manufacturing output. In the United States, although advertising appears to have begun to rise immediately after the Civil War, until 1880 it was still at a very low level in absolute terms (with an annual volume of advertising in newspapers and other periodicals the equivalent of only $0.78 per head of the population). In about 1880 the increase really began.

Table 2.1 demonstrates trends in two sets of data: aggregate consumer expenditure (which is closely related to the aggregate value of manufacturers' sales of consumer goods) and print advertising (an activity mainly directed at the consumer).[15]

There is an unmistakable relationship between the rate of increase in consumer expenditure and that in print advertising. This is not a mere statistical correlation. There is real cause and effect here, because the size of advertising budgets has almost invariably been governed by the volume of sales. This seems rather illogical because advertising is supposed to *cause* sales, not the other way around, but it must be remembered that advertising is a residual expense, that is, it is committed after the fixed and more important variable costs have been paid. We are not denying that advertising is in general planned to achieve certain sales objectives, and that manufacturers have built up crude but useful experience-based guidelines from the results of different levels of advertising expenditure. But the parameters effectively determining this expenditure are the likely earnings of the brand at different levels of sales, after the payment of fixed and main variable costs. If sales go up, advertising is almost invariably increased (normally the next year); and if they go down, it is reduced (generally immediately). This procedure means of course that the prime determinant of the amount spent on advertising, es-

---

Table 2.1

Growth of Consumer Expenditure and Advertising

| | Estimated consumer expenditure[a] | | Estimated print advertising[b] | |
	$M Current	Index	$M Current	Index
1880	5,331	100	39	100
1890	9,810	184	71	182
1900	12,349	232	96	246
1904	17,460	327	146	347
1909	25,982	488	203	520
1914	33,019	620	255	654

[a]Robert R. Doane, *The Measurement of American Wealth* (New York: Harper, 1933), p. 39.

[b]Frank Spencer Presbrey, *The History and Development of Advertising* (Garden City, NY: Doubleday, Doran, 1929), p. 591.

pecially in the early days before manufacturers had built up their experience in using it, is the sales of the brand. With refinements, the situation remains the same today, at least for ongoing brands.

If we look at the early histories of a sample of large advertised brands, we will discover that most advertising today is for brands and even products that did not exist a hundred years ago. The basic staple commodities accounting for most household expenditure in the nineteenth century were not then advertised; nor are they today, when they account for a much smaller proportion of the household budget. The growth in standards of living in the past hundred years has led us to spend our incomes on new types of merchandise, especially on discretionary goods and services for which branding and advertising have been the characteristic marketing devices from the first day of their introduction.[16]

For example, let us take one product field as typical of the whole: the sizable market for safety razors with disposable blades.[17] Before this product was invented by King C. Gillette, the safety razor market simply did not exist. But in the second year of production, 1905, the Gillette company's sales totaled 250,000 razor sets and 100,000 blade packages.[18] What had happened was that a total market had been created overnight, essentially by a monopoly. This was the natural result of the legal protection provided by the inventor's patent.

In the market for safety razors (as in the markets for toothpastes, deodorants, shampoos, nonsoap detergents, breakfast cereals, margarines, prepared salad dressings, frozen foods, and manufactured pet foods, to pick a few examples at random), there were simply *never* any conditions remotely resembling atomistic competition. These markets are all of enormous size and heavily advertised. They once accounted for two-thirds of the expenditures of the hundred largest advertisers in the United States, although this proportion is now reduced because of the emergence of important new advertised categories.[19]

What seems generally to have happened in these and most other markets for manufactured consumer goods is that an inventor had an idea for some sort of product that no one was making already. The first thing he or she did after inventing and patenting the product was to name it and almost invariably to employ a trademark or brand. The word "brand" supposedly originated in the identifying marks burned onto wooden whiskey casks during the early nineteenth century, but trademarks themselves are much older than this, having their origins in the medieval trade guilds in Europe.[20]

The inventions that were to become successful caught the public favor, and advertising demonstrated to the satisfaction of the manufacturers its ability to

increase sales far beyond the unsupported efforts of the retail trade. Manufacturers and final consumers almost immediately lost firsthand contact with one
another, which made the use of brand names doubly essential: as a means of
identifying and guaranteeing to consumers the homogeneity and quality of the
advertised goods and, in addition, to provide legal protection to the manufacturer—their original purpose. Typically, for a short while the manufacturer had
a monopoly, which helped sales and profits grow. But competition would arise
through fair means or foul (such as attempts to infringe trademarks). The competitors who survived were those able to achieve competitive economies of
scale, so that they grew large too. This is nothing but the emergence of oligopoly as a natural result of competitive forces—hence our hypothesis that the
paths of concentration in the advertising-intensive markets for packaged consumer goods led generally *from* monopoly *to* oligopoly—the direct reverse of
the path plotted by conventional economics.

What has emerged so far from this analysis is, first, a serious doubt about
the relevance of the wholesaler in the growth of advertising and branding
and, second, an equally serious doubt about the path of concentration in the
markets where advertising is an important force: the markets for packaged
consumer goods. In these markets, our hypothesis suggests oligopoly to be a
competitive and not (as it is conventionally perceived) an anticompetitive
force. This is a key part of the argument, and we will endeavor to develop it
by looking at oligopolistic competition as viewed by economic theory and as
viewed from a close focus on the real world.

Oligopolistic Competition in the Real World

The starting point of most investigations of competition is an analysis of price
in the most extreme conditions conceivable: conditions of atomistic or perfect competition. For this type of competition to operate, three conditions are
necessary: a homogeneous product, many small buyers and sellers with free
entry into the market, and perfect communications and knowledge between
buyers and sellers. These are breathtaking assumptions, and it is not surprising that they apply only to a tiny minority of cases: in the markets for company stock, some agricultural commodities, and industrial raw materials, where
there is a uniformly graded product, where worldwide communications exist,
and where buyers can bid against one another in the exchanges. In discussions of most other markets, the concept is nothing more than a theoretical
abstraction.

Despite this, there is, however, often a lingering feeling that perfect markets were once normal, or at the very least that there was once much more competition than at present, a change that has led to a loss of social and economic benefits. The worrisome aspect of such a feeling is that politicians and economists often express the wish to employ management techniques to turn the clock back, but even in such a theoretical activity, there is a difference between wanting to turn the clock back to a world that once existed and wanting to turn it back to one that never existed outside the realm of economic theory. This is why it is so important to get the historical record straight and to understand how and why advertising actually emerged.

There is also the point, expressed with considerable logical force by Friedrich von Hayek and based on his observation of real competitive processes, that the notion of atomistic competition is a grossly flawed way of describing *any* competitive mechanism.[21] His arguments are complex and interrelated, but they hinge on the fact that the model of atomistic competition is one of an equilibrial state. Competitive markets, on the other hand, are almost by definition dynamic, and their dynamism is expressed in a striving to overcome *imperfections in knowledge* and, even more important, in a continuous urge to steal business from competitors by means of product *differentiation.* (The reader will remember that these central processes are excluded by the assumptions of atomistic competition.) Product differentiation is what branding, advertising, and in particular added values are all about.

Oligopolists, like any other businesspeople, will endeavor to price their products at what the market will bear. What the market will in fact bear depends on how easily the output of competitive oligopolists can be substituted for theirs. In practice, their ability to force up their prices is limited, because the price elasticity of demand of most brands is rather high—indicating a fairly high degree of substitution between brands, because if the price of A goes up, people will tend to buy more of a substitute, B or C. We know that the prices of advertised brands do not rise at a faster rate than those of other goods.[22] This is due to the fact that competition among oligopolists is very real.

As anyone with first-hand experience of oligopolistic markets can testify, there is normally a burning urge on the part of oligopolists to capture their rivals' markets by functional innovation, by a rapid copying of the functional benefits of competitive brands, or by an equally rapid reinforcement of the added values of the oligopolists' own brands (not to mention tactical price competition). There is a great deal of anxiety about this type of competitive situation, but this anxiety affects the oligopolists (and their advertising agencies) more than consumers, for whom oligopoly is by no means devoid of benefits.[23]

In the first place, since oligopolists are by definition large producers, oligopoly production reaps the benefit of scale economies, significantly reducing costs. Much of this point is conceded by Kaldor, although he concentrates on production economies to the exclusion of economies in purchasing (which are especially important in the food trade) and in marketing (which are important to all manufacturers once they pass a minimum size).[24] In the second place, the real competition among oligopolists commonly affords consumers a number of direct benefits connected with the dynamics of the market; such advantages include a rapid rate of product innovation and improvement, and more price reduction than is immediately obvious because promotions are the normal mechanism of price competition. (Lower prices are of course a general reflection of the scale economies of large output.)

It is not universally agreed that oligopoly provides these advantages, but there is good evidence to substantiate them, over and above personal observation. It is possible on the basis of Nielsen data to make an empirical analysis of the rate of innovation in typical oligopolistic markets. This rate is usually rapid, although the speed with which markets normally "shake down" to accommodate a successful new brand (with adjustments to the shares of existing brands) leaves a residual impression of not much change overall.[25] And critics would be well advised to read the statements of leading manufacturers when they speak about the number of improvements that take place in brands on a routine basis.[26] In one instance, a well-known industrialist details the number of product improvements over a five-year period in the formulas of a number of major specified brands and, examining the experience of twenty-nine different brands sold in one or more of eight different countries, demonstrates that for more than twenty brands, consumer prices had fallen significantly in real terms over a twenty-year period.[27] These were long-term and not just tactical reductions. Product quality had also improved.

The amount of competition in oligopolistic consumer goods markets—those in which advertising is an important force—is also a factor that may well inhibit market concentration. Aggregated Nielsen data indicate the wide prevalence of stable market conditions measured in terms of combined market shares of leading brands, although this apparent overall lack of movement conceals increases in some brands' shares that are balanced by other brands' losses.[28] On the evidence of Backman, there is a broad balance between the markets showing evidence of increasing concentration and those showing diminishing concentration.[29] Most importantly, the role of advertising can be isolated. On the basis of a number of different empirical studies, Backman concluded that there is no relationship between high advertising and either high or rapid concentration.[30] Concentration is a result of factors other than advertising; and advertising is indeed one of the more important expressions of competition, which in general acts against concentration.

The Emergence of Brands

If the first purpose of branding was to confirm the legal protection afforded by the inventor's patent, and the second was to guarantee quality and homogeneity after sellers and buyers had lost face-to-face contact, a third purpose stems directly from oligopolists' need to differentiate their products. They quite rightly see branding as a device to enable them to control their markets better, by preventing other people's products from being substituted for theirs.

It is unlikely that oligopolists have ever felt the need to rationalize these purposes; their responses are quite instinctive in most cases. It seems that in the makeup of more successful marketing men and women there is the innate knowledge that branding is the key to protection and an important contributor to growth.

Generally speaking, oligopolists will compete on price, normally by means of active and continuous price promotions. But competition among them is not confined to price. The strength of oligopolists' brands and in particular the added values that enrich them move the field of competition from price reduction to product and brand improvement, progress in the latter tending to reduce the need for the former (although it is never eliminated). Margins are at least maintained, but not all are put into profit, because building brands costs a great deal of money. Kaldor, who makes the point clearly, calls these expenses "selling costs," although this seems a confining definition, "brand-building costs" is rather more precise.[31]

Before we look at the costs and prices of brands, it is essential to pause to define a brand simply, comprehensively, and objectively. Objectivity is not universal in discussion of this rather emotional subject. For instance, Joan Robinson, one of the economists who pioneered the analysis of oligopolistic markets in the 1930s, argues that "various brands of a certain article which in fact are almost exactly alike may be sold as different qualities under names and labels which will induce rich and snobbish buyers to divide themselves from poorer buyers."[32] This is not untrue, but it leaves rather a lot out of consideration.

The important distinction is between a product and brand. A product is something with a functional purpose. A brand offers something in addition to its functional purpose. All brands are products (including brands such as Hertz or American Airlines, which are technically services) in that they serve a

functional purpose. But not all products are brands. It follows that our definition of a brand should be something along the following lines:

> *A brand is a product that provides functional benefits plus added values
> that some consumers value enough to buy.*

Added values form the most important part of the definition of a brand. By
way of introduction, two general points must be discussed briefly.

First, the strongest brands are often the most distinctive. But in their distinctiveness they are generally well balanced between motivating benefits—
those (generally functional) benefits that prompt the consumer to use any
brand in the product field—and discriminating benefits—those prompting
the consumer to buy one brand rather than another. All brands are different
from each other in the obvious sense that the names and packaging are different. But distinctiveness over and beyond this is highly desirable, although a
distinctiveness based so much on discriminators that it neglects motivators is
a recipe for a weak brand. This all sounds extremely theoretical, but if the
reader will think about successful brands in the real world with these points
in mind—if he or she will think of Ajax, Birds Eye, Crest, or Dove—the idea
of balance between motivating and discriminating benefits will make sense.

Second, the reader will note the emphasis in the definition on "some consumers." Tastes differ so widely that no brand can be all things to all people.
Moreover, a manufacturer who strives to cover too wide a field will produce
a brand that is number two or number three over a wide range of attributes,
rather than number one over a limited range of attributes (which might enable it to become first choice to a limited group of consumers, the normal
route to success). Many marketing professionals contend that it is more attractive to go for a limited part of the market rather than move head-on against
the entrenched competition in the largest sector; the general validity of this
point has been demonstrated on logical grounds, though there are exceptions
to it.[33]

We now come to the matter of added values, a subject of the highest relevance to the techniques, economics, and ethics of advertising. There is no
doubt whatsoever that added values play a role in almost all purchasing decisions. These values are over and beyond the prime functional benefits for
which the brand or product is bought. The idea of added values is not a new
one and was described succinctly by James Webb Young in a book based on
his teaching at the University of Chicago seventy years ago, although only
published in 1963: "The use of advertising to add a subjective value to the
tangible values of the product. For subjective values are no less real than the
tangible ones."[34]

What are these added values and where do they come from? Some marketing professionals claim that every factor from a brand's early history to the distribution of its competitors has a bearing on them, but while this is not completely untrue, some factors are clearly more important than others. All of the most important added values are nonfunctional, although we would include as an added value the unexpected functional uses we sometimes find for some brands (such as the way Arm & Hammer baking soda can be used to sweeten a swimming pool or deodorize a refrigerator). But this is by and large an exception. Most brands have a known and restricted range of functions, and added values are the nonfunctional benefits over and beyond them.

By "known and restricted range of functions" we mean for a motor car its ability to move us from place to place safely, reliably, and economically; for a suit of clothes, its warmth and appearance; for a packet of cornflakes, its taste and nutrition; for a bottle of scent, its smell; and for a power drill, its ability to produce holes of a range of uniform sizes reliably, safely, and quickly. The added values beyond these that seem to us to be important are

1. *Added values that come from experience of the brand.* These include familiarity, known reliability, and reduction of risks. A brand becomes an old friend. This introduces the centrally important notion of brand personality, which can on occasion be interpreted as the voice of the manufacturer: Betty Crocker or Old Jim Young (see the epigraph at the beginning of this book). But it is more frequently interpreted as the personality of the brand itself—its functional and nonfunctional features as they might be described in quasi-human terms, a device used by some advertising agencies to map a brand's position in relation to its competition.[35] But this personality must be interpreted broadly, a point we once discussed with the head of research of a leading Madison Avenue agency. His agency makes a distinction here between personality and character; the former is a quality a person looks for in a girlfriend or boyfriend; but the latter is what is required of a wife or husband!

2. *Added values that come from the sorts of people who use the brand.* Rich and snobbish (as in Joan Robinson's definition) or young or glamorous or masculine or feminine. The reader can find examples of brands that have these user associations, most of which are fostered by advertising.[36]

3. *Added values that come from a belief that the brand is effective.* This is related to the way in which some medicines, even placebos, work on people's beliefs, and sometimes even makes them do their job. There is good evidence that the branding of proprietary drugs affects

the mind's influence over bodily processes. "Double-blind trials demonstrated that branding accounts for a quarter to a third of the pain
relief. That is to say, branding works like an ingredient of its own
interacting with the pharmacological active ingredients to produce
something more powerful than an unbranded tablet."[37] Belief in effectiveness also plays an important role with cosmetics, with their
ability to make their users *feel* more beautiful, with generally beneficial results.

4. *Added values that come from the appearance of the brand.* This is
the prime role of packaging. And lest it be thought that this matters
only to brands sold to impressionable adolescents, the reader is advised to look at Theodore Levitt's essay "The Morality(?) of Advertising," in which, as part of a well-reasoned discussion of added
values, he recounts the following anecdote.

A few years ago, an electronics laboratory offered a $700 testing device for
sale. The company ordered two different front panels to be designed, one
by the engineers who developed the equipment and one by professional
industrial designers. When the two models were shown to a sample of laboratory directors with Ph.D.'s, the professional design attracted twice the
purchase intentions that the engineers' design did. Obviously the laboratory director who has been baptized into science at MIT is quite as respon-
sive to the blandishments of packaging as the Boston matron.[38]

The reader may be surprised that we have omitted from the list the added
values that come from a manufacturer's name and reputation. This omission
is deliberate, for three reasons. First, consumers do not know who manufactures many of the brands they use. (Try and think of who makes the leading
brands of laundry detergent, bar soap, or shampoo.) Second, brand names are
sometimes used as "umbrella" devices to help launch new but related brands
(like Ivory Shampoo, which follows Ivory Soap), and in examining such strategy, Nielsen has provided powerful evidence that the umbrella name has little
influence on the success of the new brand.[39] Third, a familiar brand name is
no longer needed as a guarantee of a new product's homogeneity and quality.
Branded goods are known to be homogeneous and to perform their function
reasonably well. It is doubtful whether flagrant deceit was ever common, and
it is rare indeed today for no better reason than the legal penalties, although
some observers believe that this attention to quality is more the result of
manufacturers' policies and in particular their interest in consumers' repeat
purchase, than the letter of the law or the efforts of Ralph Nader.

The contribution of added values to consumer choice is easily demonstrated by the familiar technique of matched product tests. In these tests, a sample of consumers uses and judges brands in coded but unnamed packages, and a second and similar sample of consumers uses and judges those same brands in their normal containers. The invariable pattern is that the preferences among identified brands are quite different from preferences among those same brands in coded but unidentified containers. A leading breakfast cereal was preferred to two competitors in blind tests in the ratios of 47:27:26. When the test was repeated with identified packages, the preferences changed to 59:26:15. The proportion of people preferring the leading brand was therefore 47 percent blind and 59 percent named, a difference of twelve percentage points that can only have come from the added values in the brand that were not in the product alone.[40]

The subject of added values is alluring. Readers who want to dwell on examples can extend their knowledge by observation and analysis, in the way recommended by James Webb Young.[41] But let us recapitulate that added values arise mainly from people's use and experience of the brand, from the advertising, and from the packaging. It follows that added values are not immediately available to a manufacturer of a new brand but are built over time. A brand enters the world naked and must rely almost solely on its functional properties for its initial survival.

There is good empirical support for this belief. The majority of the large number of new brands that do not succeed fail precisely because of their functional weaknesses.[42] It also follows that old and successful brands build up a large stock of added values in the goodwill of their users, so a new brand whose manufacturer has ambitions to overtake them must start off with a generous margin of functional superiority if it is to make any progress. The opinion of James Peckham was discussed in chapter 1; remember that the recommended preference for the new brand over the existing brand in blind product tests should be on the order of 65:35.[43] Peckham does not describe the empirical basis for this generalization, but his views are always worth hearing. This margin of superiority in blind test is rare indeed. But so also are successful new brands.

The importance of nonfunctional added values is greatly emphasized by John Kenneth Galbraith, who, in his well-known book *The New Industrial State* maintains with great style that the farther we get from a subsistence standard of living, the more important become both the psychological rewards of using products and the role of advertising in providing these rewards. "The further a man is removed from physical need the more open he is to persuasion—or management—as to what he buys. This is, perhaps, the most important consequence for economics of increasing affluence."[44]

But Galbraith takes his argument much too far. In his view, since the oligopolist's ability to manage consumer demand is complete, a reduction in sales needs only a change of selling strategy for the situation to be corrected and management of demand reasserted. "It is the everyday assumption of the industrial system that, if sales are slipping, a new selling formula can be found that will correct the situation," he says in a passage concerned largely with the U.S. automobile industry.[45] Written in the mid-1960s, today his words read strangely indeed, after all that happened in Detroit during the years that followed.

Equally remarkable in its own way is a passage from Theodore Levitt's 1960 article "Marketing Myopia": "The fact that the new compact cars are selling so well in their first year indicates that Detroit's vast researches have for a long time failed to reveal what the customer really wanted. Detroit was not persuaded that he wanted anything different from what he was getting, until it lost millions of customers to other small car manufacturers."[46] After Detroit's noteworthy inability for so many years to produce the sorts of small car that consumers have made it clear they want (and despite the spur of spectacular resultant operating deficits in the industry), Levitt's prescient words are all the commentary necessary on Galbraith's claims that such troubles can be met by a simple change in selling strategy.

The car industry remains perhaps an exceptionally unhappy example of the inefficiency of the capitalist system in managing consumer demand. But these passages from two well-known academics only confirm our belief that the first step in the satisfaction of consumer demand must be the manufacture of a product with a functional performance the consumer requires and therefore might with luck be persuaded to buy. If there is management in this process, it is not quite in the sense that Galbraith means demand management. The second step in the satisfaction of consumer demand—the building of added values—is much more what Galbraith means. But added values are not a substitute for functional performance. And the stronger a brand becomes, the stronger the added values become, with great long-term benefit to the brand. But it is also possible to think of brands (not excluding brands of motor cars) that concentrated on added values to the neglect of functional improvements and found themselves vulnerable to competitive assault.[47] In the packaged good field, Nielsen can provide a good deal of evidence that brands lose leadership generally because of weaknesses in relative functional performance—a failure to keep up.[48]

Because added values stem from use of the product plus packaging and advertising, building these values takes not only time but money. It is in this sense that advertising people commonly refer to advertising expenditures as investments—money spent to achieve a return. This is a defensible definition, but there is one aspect of it that must be clarified. Advertising works by stimulating sales in the short term. This stimulates brand purchase by consumers, brand use, and the long-term buildup of added values, which stems from brand use. Thus the long-term effect of advertising is via long-term use of the brand, and not so much from the advertising itself. There is much professional disagreement about this, with some people believing that advertising on its own has both short- and long-term effects (stimulating sales not only tomorrow but also in a week, a month, or a year's time, presumably because advertising sticks in people's conscious or unconscious minds). We personally find it difficult to accept this view on both commonsense and empirical grounds. Readers who think that the distinction is an unimportant one are urged to consider the possibility that this matter may well have the greatest single influence on the frequency of advertising and hence on the economics of the advertising process. The whole matter is reviewed in detail in chapters 7 and 8.

Whether or not advertising, together with other brand-building costs, works in the short term, the long term, or both, it cannot be denied that it is an expensive process. Branded goods are almost always sold at some premium over unbranded goods, a practical manifestation of a brand's added values,[49] although there are limits to oligopolists' ability to push up the prices of their merchandise.[50] The question we are left with is whether people prefer a near-substitute item at a low price or something different at a higher one. The higher price rules in most markets because of the real but imperfect competition among oligopolists' brands; the something different reflects the added values bought by time, by use, and by the advertising and other brand-building expenses that oligopolists can afford to pay because of the higher prices they can generally get for their brands.

As usual, there are some surprises.

Oligopoly, Price, and the Consumer

Let us assume that an item at a low price offers an acceptable functional performance. Let us also assume that a second product at a higher price offers a somewhat better functional performance but, most importantly, also has added values that are substantially responsible for the higher price. These assumptions are reasonable and accord well with how buyers of generic products and many store brands seem to view their purchases.[51] The question then boils down to whether people would knowingly pay the extra money mainly for the added values.

The evidence points to the fact that they *will* normally pay the premium; we need look no further than the relatively small market shares of generic brands to confirm this. In Wegmans supermarket, a packet of "price-brand" cornflakes sells for $0.79 per pound; Kellogg's Corn Flakes, in a box of similar shape and size (but not surface design) sells for $0.97 per pound (23 percent more). In Wegmans, price-brand cornflakes have only four box facings on the shelf compared with eighteen for Kellogg's, which suggests that Kellogg's sells a good deal more than four times as much as the generic.[52] This is the normal situation in most countries and most product fields. But why?

The fact is that human value systems encompass more than strict rationality. "No one contends that a bottle of old wine is ethically worth as much as a barrel of flour, or a fantastic evening wrap for some potentate's mistress as much as a substantial dwelling-house, though such relative prices are not unusual."[53] Advertising has not of course been blameless in the encouragement of such oddities, and advertising people should not be pleased that the "invisible hand" whose movements they influence is capable of such unexpected sideswipes.

But advertising is not the main culprit. In comparison with the influence of society as a whole (not to speak of education), advertising's importance is small indeed. Knowledgeable advertising people know that their best efforts can only either reinforce or slightly modify attitudes that are built into people's psyches. Advertising is rather a weak force when it is expected to persuade people to change existing attitudes radically. This is not commonly understood, but many advertising professionals can attest to it from direct experience; it is evidenced for instance by the shockingly high failure rate for new brand introductions. In some cases, this is a result of deficiencies in advertising; in all others, it is an illustration of the inability of advertising to overcome other inadequacies in the marketing mix.

It is also generally accepted by the more objective observers of the scene that competitive capitalism, despite all the waste and distortions it causes, offers advantages in efficiency that many of these observers believe greatly outweigh the distortions and waste. But the latter represent the world as it is, and no matter how much we may deplore consumers for their lack of education and objectivity, and their reluctance to make the sorts of rational decisions that atomistic competition and other abstractions of the real world suggest they should, there is nothing we can do about it. If Levitt's laboratory directors with Ph.D.'s are so strongly influenced by the physical appearance of the $700 testing machine, it is hardly realistic to expect the Boston matron or the Syracuse grocery shopper to behave more rationally.

One way in which the value system of the real world differs from that of simple models of the price mechanism is in the matter of price itself. The assumption of marketplace knowledge is, for a start, pretty wide of the mark.

Studies of specific markets have found that the proportions of consumers who could recall actual prices varied widely from market to market, and nowhere was there anything like general accuracy. In one investigation of fifteen markets, "The variation in the percentage correct ranged from 44% to 80% with an average of 59%. With a 5% margin of error, the average was 65%; with a 10% margin, it rose to 73%."[54] In other words, an average of 27 percent of consumers in this particular study were unable to remember to within 10 percent the actual prices they were paying.

However, despite this unquestioned (and surely not unexpected) haziness in consumer knowledge, the attempts made to construct demand curves on the basis of purchase intentions or figures of actual purchases have shown such curves to have the generally downward slope associated with classical economic theory, although degrees of elasticity vary and there are odd shapes here and there.[55] The most pronounced quirk falls at the extreme low-price end of certain demand curves, reflecting an association of low price with low quality; thus demand is in absolute terms sometimes *less* at low prices than at higher ones. There is also evidence of a price–value relationship at the higher-price end, a point made by Andre Gabor and C.W.J. Granger by means of a delightful example: "What we have in mind here is . . . the case of gin, which was not considered a gentlemanly drink and even less a ladylike one until successive increases of the excise duty brought its price closer to that of whiskey and other, formerly more expensive, alcoholic beverages."[56]

Gabor and Granger's evidence on this point is anecdotal and not statistical, but it supports the likelihood that at the upper levels of price, the value connotation reduces the elasticity of demand, although to nowhere near inelasticity. This reduction in price elasticity is serendipitous for the oligopolist, who should be grateful for it. If people buy higher priced merchandise in reasonably large quantities in the belief that it is better than lower priced items partly by the very fact of its higher price, they will presumably get greater satisfaction from the more expensive article than they would have gotten from the cheaper ones; and if this situation is deplored, people's psychological makeup is surely more at fault than the actions of oligopolists. As already suggested, the latter are not entirely blameless, but other features of oligopoly, notably the aggressive attitude of oligopolists toward one another, are not devoid of social and economic benefits. The present system has good as well as bad points, and if we are honest enough to consider the different types of economic organization in the real world as limited choices among imperfect alternatives, we can judge our present system by *realistic* criteria; and if we are concerned to improve matters, we will be aware of our rather constricted area of maneuver.

Manufacturers have, in any event, only unconsciously encouraged perceptions of a high-price/high-value relationship, for instance by the indirect effect of added values. In building added values, oligopolists rarely touch on the argument that if something is expensive it must be good. Even on the occasions when scenes of gracious living appear in advertisements, the advertiser is often uncomfortable about them and the advertising agency is blamed for being out of touch with the real world. In this and certain other matters the agency is not always wrong, as some of the more successful agencies (and their clients) have on occasion demonstrated.

This brings us to a point which, if it is to be developed, would probably interfere with the basic structure of this book. But having come some distance in the argument in this chapter, it is more appropriate now that we should try to summarize the points made.

The Argument in Brief

This chapter has questioned the validity of certain theories that are widely and uncritically believed.

First, there is the idea that advertising emerged historically as a response to conflict between weak manufacturers and powerful wholesalers. An examination of historical data does not support this hypothesis, insofar as the markets for packaged consumer goods are concerned. On the contrary, it seems that the driving force in the development of advertising was the upward pressure of manufactured production. Getting the facts right is not just a matter of historical truth; it can impinge on policy recommendations for economic management. The notion that there were once perfectly competitive consumer goods markets (to which some people may wish to return) is substantially illusory.

Second, there is the contention that the path from competition to concentration that had been followed in many heavy industries was followed also by modern consumer goods markets. An examination of cases strongly suggests the hypothesis that such markets began as monopolies, and *oligopoly emerged as a competitive force.*

The third point (one related to the first) is that the abstraction of atomistic competition is relevant to an examination of competition in the real world. The very actions of competition are a denial of the assumptions on which atomistic competition is based.

Oligopolistic competition (assuming the absence of any restriction to market entry or collusion between oligopolists) is always real and intense and brings significant social and economic benefits despite its costs. But these costs include waste and a distortion of value systems to which all members of society (including marketing people) should address themselves.

We also argue that brands are an essential manifestation of oligopolistic competition, that they are a combination of functional and nonfunctional values (the functional ones being the more important), and that the contribution of advertising is mainly to encourage use of a brand that in turn helps build nonfunctional added values. In the eyes of the consumer, added values are often seen as the justification of the premium prices commonly charged for branded merchandise. Despite what is claimed by some of its protagonists, advertising is in general a weak force, except when it is used to reinforce and occasionally modify existing attitudes. In doing these things, however, it sometimes has considerable power, and it is one of the key influences on the building of brands.

Notes

1. For readers unacquainted with the marketing field, the A.C. Nielsen Company is the world's largest market research company specializing in the measurement of retail sales. In the United States, it is also the leading firm in the field of television audience measurement.

2. There is a technical distinction in the economics literature between oligopolistic competition and monopolistic competition. Monopolistic competition means more competitors than oligopoly but with generally more differentiated products. However, we shall avoid this distinction here and use the word "oligopolistic" in a general sense to describe a market with a relatively small number of competitors.

3. Jules Backman, *Advertising and Competition* (New York: New York University Press, 1967), p. 109.

4. Ibid., p. 77.

5. For some brands of soap, this proportion only rarely drops below 40 percent of brand sales. (This estimate is based on unpublished research.)

6. John Kenneth Galbraith, *The New Industrial State* (Harmondsworth, Middlesex, UK: Penguin, 1978), p. 209.

7. Graham Bannock, *The Juggernauts: The Age of the Big Corporation* (Harmondsworth, Middlesex, UK: Penguin, 1973), pp. 72, 79–80.

8. Neil Hopper Borden, *The Economic Effects of Advertising* (Chicago: Richard D. Irwin, 1942), pp. 49–51.

9. Lord Kaldor, "The Economic Aspects of Advertising," *Review of Economic Studies* 18 (1950–51), 1–27; reprinted in *The Three Faces of Advertising* (London: Advertising Association, 1975), pp. 103–145.

10. Kaldor, "The Economic Aspects of Advertising," in *The Three Faces of Advertising*, p. 129.

11. Paul Terry Cherington, *Advertising as a Business Force* (Garden City, NY: Doubleday, Page, 1913, reprinted 1919); Harold Barger, *Distribution's Place in the American Economy Since 1869* (New York: National Bureau of Economic Research;

Princeton: Princeton University Press, 1955); Louis P. Bucklin, *Competition and Evolution in the Distributive Trades* (Englewood Cliffs, NJ: Prentice-Hall, 1972).

12. In case the reader thinks that Kaldor's point might relate exclusively to the British experience, there is evidence that the wholesale trade followed the same patterns in Britain as in the United States. See Ralph Harris and Arthur Seldon, *Advertising in a Free Society* (London: Institute of Economic Affairs, 1959), pp. 9–10.

13. Two important works covering startlingly similar ground were published at the same time at the two universities: Edward Hastings Chamberlin, *The Theory of Monopolistic Competition* (Cambridge, MA: Harvard University Press, 1933, reprinted 1948); Joan Robinson, *The Economics of Imperfect Competition* (London: Macmillan, 1933, reprinted 1950). Chamberlin was not pleased with the coincidence of the timing. It was said apocryphally that a student could get a degree at Harvard in Chamberlin's day by abusing Robinson.

14. See, for instance, Alfred Marshall, *Industry and Trade* (London: Macmillan, 1920), book 3, chaps. 3–10.

15. The difference between the value of consumer expenditure and manufacturers' sales of consumer goods is accounted for by trade margins and adjustments to inventories. These remain more or less constant from year to year.

16. Data in indirect but general support of this contention can be found in Borden, *The Economic Effects of Advertising,* pp. 204–205.

17. Net sales value in the United States of $1,182 million in 1997. *Census of Manufactures* (Washington, DC: U.S. Department of Commerce, Bureau of the Census, 2001).

18. *The Gillette Company 1901–1976* (Boston: Corporate Public Relations Department, Gillette, 1977), p. 4.

19. According to figures published in the late summer or early fall of every year by *Advertising Age.*

20. Borden, *The Economic Effects of Advertising,* p. 22.

21. Friedrich August von Hayek, "The Meaning of Competition," in *Individualism and Economic Order* (Chicago: University of Chicago Press, 1948), pp. 92–106.

22. W. Duncan Reekie, *Advertising and Price* (London: Advertising Association, 1979). Among the factors that inhibit rises in the prices of advertised brands is the reduction in retail margins that such brands carry, a significant scale economy. This conclusion was first drawn by the American economist Robert L. Steiner, and the phenomenon became known within the Federal Trade Commission as the "Steiner Effect."

23. This topic was explored some time ago with great perception by Frank Hyneman Knight in the title essay in *The Ethics of Competition and Other Essays* (New York: Harper, 1935), pp. 41–75. The whole discussion in this chapter is of course based on the premise that there is no restriction to entry into the market or any other collusion between oligopolists. Although in the past entry restriction and collusion have not been unknown, it is reasonable to assume their absence in modern circumstances, largely on the grounds of legal sanctions.

24. Kaldor, "The Economic Aspects of Advertising," in *The Three Faces of Advertising,* pp. 131–132.

25. James O. Peckham Sr., *The Wheel of Marketing,* 2d edition, 1981 (privately published but available through A.C. Nielsen), p. 75.

26. Ibid., 1st edition, published in 1978, p. 50.

27. Lord Heyworth, "Advertising," chairman's annual company speech, 1958 (London: Unilever Ltd., 1958).

28. Peckham, *The Wheel of Marketing,* 2d edition, p. 74.

29. Backman, *Advertising and Competition,* pp. 82–114.

30. Ibid., p. 113.

31. Kaldor, "The Economic Aspects of Advertising," in *The Three Faces of Advertising,* pp. 135–141.

32. Robinson, *The Economics of Imperfect Competition,* pp. 180–181.

33. See the interesting description of the "majority fallacy" in Alfred A. Kuehn and Ralph L. Day, "Strategy of Product Quality," *Harvard Business Review* (November–December 1962): 100–110.

34. James Webb Young, *How to Become an Advertising Man* (Chicago: Advertising Publications Inc., 1963), p. 73.

35. See, for example, Stephen King, *What Is a Brand?* (London: J. Walter Thompson, 1970), pp. 10–11.

36. One of the most famous of the earlier analyses of the brand concept made persuasive use of the notion of user associations. See Burleigh B. Gardner and Sidney J. Levy, "The Product and the Brand," *Harvard Business Review* (March–April 1955): 33–39.

37. Judie Lannon and Peter Cooper, "Humanistic Advertising: A Holistic Cultural Perspective," *International Journal of Advertising* (July–September 1983): 206.

38. Theodore Levitt, "The Morality(?) of Advertising," *Harvard Business Review* (July–August 1970): 89.

39. Peckham, *The Wheel of Marketing,* 2d edition, pp. 89–91.

40. There were different consumer preferences for the various physical attributes of the three brands, so that the preference ratios of the lowest rated brands (27:26) should not be construed as evidence of parity in functional performance.

There is another important point regarding blind versus named product tests. On occasion, when such tests have been carried out, the preferences between the brands have been analyzed into their component parts, and it has been found that the preference for a particular brand on functional grounds (e.g., taste) is greater in named than in blind tests. The reasons for this are psychological. The findings are of more than hair-splitting importance. For instance, in 1985, Coca-Cola was relaunched nationally with a sweeter flavor similar to that of Pepsi-Cola. This followed blind product testing that supposedly demonstrated consumers' preference for the new Coca-Cola flavor. In the marketplace, the new flavor was not liked and not bought, which demonstrated clearly that when the brand was named, consumers' flavor perceptions were altered. The astonishingly myopic decision of the Coca-Cola Company to change their formula on the basis of such inadequate research stemmed from the greater attention the company was paying to its competitor than to its consumers.

41. Young, *How to Become an Advertising Man,* p. 12. Note the author's advice about collecting case studies of print and television advertisements.

42. J. Hugh Davidson, "Why Most New Consumer Brands Fail," *Harvard Business Review* (March–April 1976): 117–122.

43. Peckham, *The Wheel of Marketing,* 2d edition, p. 92.

44. Galbraith, *The New Industrial State,* chap.18, sect. 2.

45. Ibid., p. 212.

46. Theodore Levitt, "Marketing Myopia," *Harvard Business Review* (July–August 1960): 51.

47. It may surprise some readers that added values are in any way important for "high-involvement" products like motor cars. As long ago as 1984 the General Motors Intercollegiate Marketing Competition threw up a reasonable amount of qualitative data that suggested that potential car buyers were well aware that the various General Motors "A" Body cars were functionally very similar to one another; nevertheless the added values embodied in the name of the different marketing division of General Motors represented powerful brand discriminators.

48. Peckham, *The Wheel of Marketing,* 2d edition, pp. 73–74.

49. Paul Clark, "Reaction to Recession: The Case History of Margarine," *Admap* (December 1980): 612–614. Note particularly the author's remarks about premium prices.

50. Reekie, *Advertising and Price.*

51. Beth Axelrad, Bruce G. Vanden Bergh, and Dean M. Krugman, "Risk, Quality and the Generic Item Phenomenon: Implications for Retail Advertising and Promotion," *Proceedings of the 1982 Conference of the American Academy of Advertising,* University of Tennessee, March 27–30, 1982.

52. This is because of a tendency for small brands to have a share of display space slightly above the proportion suggested by their market share. See Peckham, *The Wheel of Marketing,* 2d edition, p. 45.

53. Knight, "The Ethics of Competition," p. 56.

54. Andre Gabor and C.W.J. Granger, "Price Sensitivity of the Consumer," *Journal of Advertising Research* (December 1964): 42.

55. Ibid., and some unpublished examples.

56. Andre Gabor and C.W.J. Granger, "The Pricing of New Products," *Scientific Business* (August 1965): 141–150.

3

Factors That Shape a Brand During Its Conception and Birth

The visit to Wegmans store described in chapter 2 was a device used to relate some of the principles of microeconomics to the everyday experience of the consumer. We are now going to visit another store to examine another market. Here the emphasis of the investigation is going to change: we are going to attempt by simple observation to uncover some of the facts about this market that manufacturers would need to know if they wished to compete successfully in it. The product category that will be examined is cat food. Published data can serve as a check on the accuracy of our estimates. The store visited was Peter's, in the Syracuse suburb of Nottingham.

The investigation was carried out during the 1980s, and the lessons remain relevant today. It was conducted in a very simple manner: by counting the packs on the shelves, working on the assumption that the number of packs on display would lead to an approximation of the rates of sales of the various brands and pack sizes. The process took about an hour, and this is what we found:

1. Brands of cat food occupy about 150 feet of shelf space. This suggests a relatively large category, although it is only about half the size of the breakfast cereals market, because of the relatively smaller size of the user base.[1]
2. The market is segmented into three parts (canned, dry, and moist cat food) that differ from one another in functional characteristics.

Canned food is the largest segment; the number of packs on the shelves suggests that it represents a bit under half the total value of sales. The display of the dry product indicates that it represents rather more than a third of the total sales value. Moist cat food accounts for the remainder, about 20 percent.

3. The largest brand in the canned sector appears to be Nine Lives (with more than 20 percent of the market), followed by Buffet, Kal Kan, and Purina. We estimated the combined shares of the four to be about 60 percent. The largest brands in the dry sector were Cat Chow, Meow Mix, Friskies, Special Dinner, and Nine Lives, which are not dissimilar in sales and between them account for about 60 percent of the market. The moist sector seems to be dominated by Tender Vittles, which alone probably accounts for 60 percent of sales value.

4. There is a great deal of commonality in pack sizes. We estimated that at least 70 percent of sales of canned cat food are in the 6-oz size. The dry market is dominated by the 18-oz boxes and 56-oz bags. The moist food is more fragmented by pack size, but a third of sales appear to be accounted for by the 12-oz size and another third by the 18-oz size. As in the breakfast cereals market, commonality of pack size is not accompanied by uniformity of price.

As in the description of the breakfast cereals market in chapter 2, there is nothing in any way original about the features just described. However, from what had been published at about the same time about the cat food market, the estimates seem to be pretty close to the mark. This should act as a reminder of something extremely important, something that ought to be in the bloodstream of every marketing professional: the central importance of the retail store in consumer goods marketing. In their day-to-day work, advertising agencies invariably think exclusively of the final consumer (when they are not worrying about their client!); whereas on the client side, "consumer orientation" is considered the mark of the more sophisticated type of manufacturer. But both agencies and advertisers should remind themselves that the retail store is the battleground on which much of the competitive struggle takes place. An equally important point is that the most readily accessible information on both consumer purchasing and competitive activity is information gathered from retail outlets.

The way to get this information is by properly conducted retail audit research, the mechanism of which will shortly be described. But even with data collection that makes as little claim to scientific accuracy as our visits to Wegmans and Peter's stores, it is demonstrably easy to get an impressionistic picture of a market, as long as the investigator observes the brands in a studied way and knows what to look for.

Much of this chapter and the next concerns generalized patterns of retail sales and the large number of different aspects of brands that can be revealed by these patterns. We were at first inclined to treat each of these separately, with chapters devoted to describing each in detail. The five main topics we had in mind were, first, the importance of innovation in packaged goods markets and, on the other side of this coin, the belief in the inevitability of decline that often accompanies a belief in the importance of innovation. The second subject was factors influencing the initial and continued progress of a brand: functional performance, positioning, name, price, distribution, trade promotions, consumer promotions, and advertising. The third topic was the importance of market testing and (a related matter) the success rate of new brand introductions. The fourth was the initial growth cycle of a brand, and the fifth, the importance of restaging. But we eventually decided against the original plan of treating each topic separately because of the importance of emphasizing the interconnections.

It therefore seemed better to structure the examination by looking briefly at the most important factors operating during a brand's conception and birth, and then at those operating during its growth and maturity. This led us to omit some of the topics in the above list from the present chapter and postpone them to the next one. The extremely important matters of promotions and advertising are among the things being deferred; and it is by no means suggested that these have no role during a brand's conception and birth, merely that their long-term continuous role makes it more appropriate to discuss them in the context of ongoing brands. Promotions are the most important expressions of continuous oligopolistic price competition. Advertising builds added values to achieve repeated brand use.

Our purpose in these early chapters is that the reader should get used to facts about normal patterns in order to develop a deeper understanding and perhaps to acquire the quality so esteemed by the Germans, the "feeling at the tips of the fingers," a practiced ability to discern what is viable and what is not. Let us consider for instance the manufacturer who plans to enter a market with a new brand in the wake of a successful pioneer brand marketed by a competitor (a quite common strategy, sometimes known as "me-too"). The newcomer should understand first of all that a mere functional parity with the pioneer will probably mean that the me-too brand will fail. On the assumption, however, that it is able to offer a degree of functional superiority at least to some consumers, the manufacturer will not be beaten before he begins, and a knowledge of generalized patterns will immediately give him a proper sense of how realistic (rather than how desirable) his sales targets will be.

The newcomer may wish to achieve a sales level equivalent to two-thirds of that of the pioneer brand, but he will have learned that the normal share of market of a me-too brand after three years is only 47 percent and not 66 percent of the level of the pioneer.[2] This does not mean that he will not in any circumstances make 66 percent in three years; just that if the new manufacturer is to succeed, both his brand and the support he puts behind it must be very much above the normal. Knowing his resources, the newcomer might also of course conclude that the 66 percent is unrealistic and look for a viable business at a lower level of sales. But note that the firm is able to draw these conclusions, which are of direct operational value, without having sold one pack, even before inventing the product and designing the brand.

Since this chapter and the next are devoted substantially to patterns of retail sales, they must inevitably be based in the main on the work of the organization that is the best informed objective observer of the retail scene, the A.C. Nielsen Company. We are relying heavily in particular on Peckham's historical studies, to which reference has already been made in chapters 1 and 2. His is one of those rare contributions to the marketing literature to which we can constantly refer, and from which we can always learn something new.

We must, however, say a word first about the retail audit mechanism, so that the reader can appreciate its advantages and limitations. The most important data provided by Nielsen are estimates of consumer sales. Nielsen works with panels of shops. In Peckham's day, in each shop, by the simple arithmetical process of counting deliveries of goods over the checking period (two months), adding inventories at the beginning of the period, and deducting inventories at the end, sales out of the store during the period could be accurately measured. Information was provided for all brands and pack sizes in a market. By adding the findings from all of the shops in the panel, a large accumulation of data could be assembled that could be grossed up to estimate total sales in the market, the share of each brand and pack size, and how these change over time. Long- and short-term trends could be exposed, as could specific strengths and weaknesses of brands, varieties, and sizes. As well as consumer sales, Nielsen provided data on distribution and display and on retail deliveries and inventories (from which consumer sales were in turn computed). One ever-refreshing feature of Nielsen data is that they are an observed measure of sales based on aggregated consumer behavior and are not a monitor of people's memory or opinions, with the notorious problems that such research entails.

Retail audit data are now collected more simply with the use of scanners, but the characteristics of the system described above still apply.

Yet some important limitations to Nielsen data should be borne in mind. First, the classes of stores audited by Nielsen may cover only a limited proportion of the sales of the brands in a particular product field. Remember that the retail trade is a dynamic business, and the changes are sometimes greater and subtler than imagined. This points to the wisdom of using consumer panel data to supplement those from retail audits. (Consumer panels once relied on pencil-and-paper diaries, but they also now employ scanners.) A consumer panel, which monitors what homemakers actually buy day by day, does not count as large a volume of sales as a retail audit, but the data collection covers purchases from all types of stores and not just the store types monitored by Nielsen. A consumer panel therefore has a wider but weaker data base than a retail audit. The two types of research complement one another.

But there is another reason why consumer panels are important. Measurement of consumer sales by retail audit is from shop sales, which are the result of an aggregation of a large number of individual consumer purchases. Internal movements inside the aggregates are concealed. The actual people buying in one period could very well be different, or the same, or partly different and partly the same as those in a second period. A retail audit cannot provide any means of tracking down these differences; it cannot analyze whether individual consumers continue to buy the same as, or less than, or more than before. When we further study the inner workings of our big machine (notably how the little apparatus in the middle—advertising—seems to be a motive force disproportionately important for its size), we shall need to find out how advertising influences consumers, the people to whom it is primarily addressed. For this, we shall need the sorts of research discussed in chapters 5, 7, and 8: consumer panel data in particular.

In the meantime, we shall be studying aggregated information mainly provided by Nielsen. This does not mean that in these earlier chapters we shall be ignoring the effects of advertising. But aggregated data will only tell us *what* is likely to happen as a result of certain advertising strategies (in particular as a result of the application of defined advertising pressures, i.e., changes in the size of the budget). These data will not tell us either why or how such results happened. Nevertheless, the *what* is undeniably important to us.

Let us then start with the workings of the most visible parts of the machine, in particular those parts that appear to be the most directly relevant to the establishment of a new brand. This will lead us to chapter 4, which looks at a brand growing toward maturity. Here, some of the factors discussed in this present chapter will still be relevant, but trade and consumer promotions and advertising will be coming into their own, so that it is in the next chapter that we will begin the first major discussions of these important matters.

The Importance of Innovation and the Belief in Decline

The reader will remember from chapter 1 the notion of apparent stasis as a characteristic of most consumer goods markets. By this is meant a surface stability: if not equilibrium, at least a strong tendency toward equilibrium. Viewed over short- and medium-term periods, most markets appear to be stationary when we measure both total sales (with established and predictable seasonal patterns) and brand shares. New brands do not normally succeed, but the rare occasion when one does causes little overall disturbance; competitors' shares normally settle down rapidly, with a few share points clipped here and there to accommodate the newcomer.

But this picture can be misleading in two respects. First, it does not recognize the ferment of new brand activity, most of which has no lasting effect on the marketplace. Second, viewed over the long term, markets often change markedly in three separate ways. The changes appear small in the short term, but their cumulative effect is often large in the long term.[3]

1. There are sometimes substantial long-term increases and decreases in the absolute size of products or groups of products, because of the influences of technological improvement and social change. A dramatic instance quoted by Nielsen concerns convenience products. This is not a single category but a mini-aggregation of ten different product groups, from tea mixes to disposable diapers; their aggregate growth over a typical two-year period was 52 percent, which was almost seven times the increase for grocery store sales as a whole during the same period.
2. There can be large increases in the absolute size of *individual categories* resulting from the introduction of clusters of new and improved brands. Nielsen analyzed 23 product classes where dynamic new or improved brands with a demonstrable improvement over the competition had been introduced, and compared these with 31 product classes where there had been no such improvements. The categories with the innovations grew by 34 percent in a typical three-year period, compared with a growth of 3 percent in the categories without major innovations.
3. The pace of innovation within product categories causes significant *shifts of share,* with pressure on existing brands from new and innovative ones. This type of movement can be demonstrated by studies of seven different product categories over longish periods (10 to 22 years) ending in 1977. In these categories, there were 37 major ad-

vertised brands at the beginning, accounting for a total of 74 percent of the market. During the years that followed, this share was pressed down to 43 percent as a result of a flurry of new brands, which by 1977 themselves accounted for a total of 35 percent of the market.

This same point can be made even more dramatically if we look at longer periods. By examining a single but typical product category of household goods over a forty-four-year period, 1936–80, it can be seen that

- Only two of the five most important brands in 1936 were still on the market at the end of the period, and they had severely reduced market shares.
- Of the thirteen most important brands introduced since 1949, seven had disappeared by the end of the period.
- Brand leadership had changed hands five times, the losing brands having in the main failed to keep themselves up to date.

The first conclusion concerning such changes that are apparent only in the long term is that oligopolists innovate very widely indeed. This must be true because the changes described were brought about by the minority of new brands that succeeded; the majority of new brands always fail. And consumers respond favorably by buying the successful minority of new brands and new product types because these items satisfy their needs. Habit and inertia play a major part in purchasing decisions in the short term, but most mutations in consumer buying behavior have substantial long-term effects because of repeat purchase.

The second conclusion is that it is mainly the pressure of competition that dictates the pace of innovation. This should be seen against a background of more general pressures on the oligopolist. One of the most important of these pressures is a virtually universal although mistaken belief in the inevitable cyclical decline of existing brands. Other pressures include the demands of technological change and the need to grow.[4] In our observation, however, the trigger for action—sometimes precipitate action—is almost invariably the competition. This expresses itself in a number of ways: in the need to preempt, bearing in mind that second and third brands in markets will achieve shares significantly below those of the innovators; in the need for manufacturers to follow competitors' innovations for fear of erosion of their existing brands; or (a common strategy with multinational organizations) in the opportunity to steal a competitor's ideas in one country and apply them in an amended form in a second country, thus preempting the originator's entry in that second country.

Without a great deal of competitive effort (much of it self-canceling), it is extremely difficult to maintain the status quo in oligopolistic markets over long periods.

British analyst Stephen King has devoted much attention to the belief in the inevitability of cyclical decline. Since it widely affects oligopolists' actions in the marketplace, it must be considered briefly here.

The central tenet, which is believed equally widely in business and academic circles, is that brands resemble those things studied by the zoologist and botanist, and inevitably go through the stages of birth, growth, maturity, and decline. We are talking here about long-term irreversible decline, not short-term controllable cyclical movements, which we shall consider in chapter 4. There is no shortage of examples of brands that have gone through these various stages from birth to final decline and extinction, although the actual shape of the curve up and down has varied a good deal in particular cases.[5] The empirical evidence for life cycles, however, is dangerous and misleading for two closely related reasons.

For a start, there is also a good deal of evidence pointing the other way: to brands that have reached maturity and maintained relatively constant levels of market share over long periods in the face of competition. The large number of examples that could be quoted includes the leading brands in nineteen American consumer goods markets, brands that kept their leadership for fifty years.[6] But this is not really the central point, because the question cannot be decided by weighing the examples on both sides with so many demonstrating the existence of a life cycle and so many not, for the simple reason that anyone *can cause* a brand to go into decline by simple inaction. Decline is very much within the manufacturer's control and is not by any means entirely governed by external influences.

This leads to the second and key point: the life cycle is a self-fulfilling concept, which is what makes it so dangerous:

> Not long ago, a leading manufacturer was promoting a brand of floor wax. After a steady period of growth, the sales of the product had reached a plateau. Marketing research suggested that an increase in spot television advertising, backed by a change in copy, would help the brand to regain its momentum. Feeling that the funds could be better spent in launching a new product, management vetoed the proposal. But the new product failed to move off the shelf despite heavy marketing support. At the same time, the old brand, with its props pulled out from under it, went into a sales decline from which it never recovered. The company had two losers on its hands.[7]

In this instance, the manufacturer was clearly torn by a typical conflict of priorities. There is also sometimes an obsessive fear of the competition. When, in the late 1960s, Warner-Lambert was faced in Canada with aggressive new competitors (including Procter & Gamble), whose activities reduced the market share of its mouthwash Listerine, it seriously considered removing advertising support from the brand and milking it for profit, although Listerine was still significantly the market leader, was still used on the most recent occasion by a third of all mouthwash users, and still kept a clear lead over all of its competitors in virtually all image attributes when the various competitive brands were rated by consumers. Warner-Lambert's attitude toward the brand gives a remarkable insight into the psychological pressures of oligopolistic competition, although here wiser counsels prevailed. Support for the brand was increased and not decreased, with generally beneficial results.[8]

Much of the difficulty regarding life cycles stems from a failure to distinguish between the product and the brand. Products can become obsolete. Brands need not become obsolete if they are adapted functionally to remain competitive. (This sometimes requires launching product variations: Tide powder and Tide liquid; Budweiser and Bud Light; Campbell's soup and Campbell's Low Sodium soup.)

It is, however, rather more common to find examples of the opposite: of once substantial brands whose popularity has dwindled. This should immediately prompt us to ask how many reductions in the market share of existing brands following the launch of new brands are *caused by a conscious transfer of resources* from the old to the new. This often represents tragic misjudgment, because the growth of added values in an old brand represents a genuine investment that is all too often sacrificed through a misplaced belief in the inevitability of the brand's decline. To make matters worse, the new investment for which so much is sacrificed produces in many cases an unsuccessful or mediocre new brand. Remember that most new brands *are* unsuccessful.

One of the temptations to milk a brand (to turn it into a "cash cow") is the fact that the withdrawal of support means an immediate increase in profit. But this is temporary, because sales invariably decline, so that the brand after a time yields not only a much reduced profit, but also often a drastically reduced contribution to the general overhead.

Observation of oligopolistic markets demonstrates unambiguously the rapid pace of innovation. But for the oligopolist to survive, the qualities of balance and judgment that should lead him to nurture the old and extract the maximum return from past investments are second only in importance to the urge to participate in the forward thrust of innovation that the competitive nature of the market demands. It is by no means uncommon for an established manufacturer to have more than 25 percent of sales accounted for by brands that were not on the market five years before.[9] But the intelligent manufacturer who plans for the long term invariably accompanies this internal shift with a rising total market share, so as not to pay for new successes by undersupporting established and almost certainly more profitable brand properties. Procter & Gamble, from its observed behavior in the marketplace, is clearly an organization that accepts this philosophy. "One former brand manager notes 'the first thing they tell you is, "Forget product life cycles and cash cows!" One of the soaps has been reformulated over eighty times and is thriving.'"[10]

Five Influences on a New Brand

This section mainly concerns describing effects and interconnections. The data presented are factual. They are aggregated to make generalizations possible. Individual brands are disguised only to preserve confidentiality.

1. Functional performance

Think again of the point made in chapter 2 that a brand comes naked into the world. Unless its competitive functional performance is superior in at least some respect, it has little chance of succeeding; a person who buys it on a trial basis or who receives a free sample will not be persuaded to buy it again. One of the roles of the pack design, the introductory promotions, and the advertising is to communicate this functional performance clearly and forcefully.

The pack (an extremely important advertising medium) and the advertising itself should also begin to build those added values that are vital to protecting the brand's often rather fragile franchise once competitors have moved toward functional parity with it. In other words, the new brand needs the edge of added values to maintain its position when, as often happens, it loses *within months* the advantage of its initial functional lead. If when it enters the market the brand is to be bought more than once, the decision is essentially based on its functional properties.

Nielsen once examined the fifty-three most successful new brands launched over a two-year period, finding that the most important of eleven reasons for success was clearly functional performance. Among the reasons for failure, functional performance was even more important. Peckham, in summarizing the data, draws an important conclusion here. He believes that the functional superiority of a potentially successful brand also provides underpinning and support for the other factors contributing to success, notably the efforts of the sales force. So if the first and most important thing, the brand's functional performance, is recognized, synergy will lend a hand to boost its effect. But when a brand is *not* going to succeed, efforts of the sales force alone are not enough to compensate for its functional weaknesses.[11] British Nielsen data add a time dimension and suggest that functional weakness as a cause of failure is becoming even more important with the passage of time.[12]

An analysis by Davidson of 100 new grocery brands in the United Kingdom provides data that closely confirm and supplement the Nielsen findings.[13] Of these brands, fifty succeeded and fifty failed, a rate of success better than the general average. Of the successes, thirty-seven offered better performance than the competition, and twenty-two of these offered significantly better performance. Of the failures, forty offered the same or worse functional performance than the competition.

Competitive functional performance is not something that is important to new brands and unimportant to mature brands, because the added values that these brands have acquired over the years cannot provide a permanent bulwark against functionally superior newcomers.

The large British food manufacturer Brooke Bond Oxo has published evidence that the repeat buying of its brands correlates highly with product performance, as evaluated by the blind product tests it carries out skillfully and repeatedly (itself an unusual procedure). The conclusion of the analysts who published this case is that since repeat purchase is essentially determined by consumer satisfaction concerning the functional performance of a brand, advertising does not have much role in this process and "may find its greatest potential at the periphery of the user group."[14] This interesting suggestion will be evaluated in chapter 5, when we look in some detail at repeat purchase.

Aggregated Nielsen information supports the data from Brooke Bond Oxo on the importance of a competitive functional performance to existing brands. During the fifteen-year period 1946–61, leading brands in a third of thirty-four different product classifications in the United States lost their leadership. In two-thirds of these cases, the cause of the loss was competitive technological advances. In the six years 1965–71, well over half of the brands losing market leadership in major product fields in the United Kingdom lost it for this same reason. "It is a cardinal fact that a consumer franchise will not protect a brand against a well-advertised technical breakthrough by competition."[15]

There is a further point to be made about the functional properties of a brand. They help to describe the competition and thus become a tool to specify the best target group for advertising: the users of defined competitive brands. What makes this such a relatively efficient planning device is the looseness of alternative (demographic and psychographic) descriptions and their general inability to discriminate between competitive brands.

Paradoxically, users of a brand are best defined by that very fact of usage. This is not as circular a definition as it appears, because once a brand joins the homemaker's repertoire, inertia and habit begin to play a role. Repeat purchase comes about at least in part because it saves the homemaker trouble, although of course a new brand with functional superiority will always pose a threat to the brands already in the repertoire. This is why it is so important for a manufacturer of a new brand to target it specifically at existing competitive brands with the intention of elbowing them out, so that inertia will work for the new item instead of for the others (unless it is breaking new ground: creating a new market or building one from a low existing level, both of which are now the exception and not the rule in economically developed countries).

The first question for the manufacturer of a new brand to ask is, "From which brand do we want to take business?" Once this question has been answered, the firm can direct research and development efforts at the specific functional characteristics for which it must provide superior performance with the new brand. But it is impossible to provide the right answers unless it asks the right questions in the first place.

2. Positioning

There is so much talk in advertising circles about brand positioning in terms of demographic groupings of the users of brands and more recently of their psychographic or life-style groupings, that it still causes some surprise when we look at hard data on the characteristics of actual users (for instance standardized brand penetration data such as those published by Simmons or Mediamark) and see that there is nothing like a neat differentiation of usage between any important competitive brands. They are all used in the main by the same types of people, with only differences of *emphasis* in the importance of the various demographic and psychographic groups. And as brands grow, which invariably happens as a result of growth of their user base, the overlap with other brands becomes even greater, because of the increase in multibrand purchasing. If the buyers of Kellogg's Corn Flakes are similar to buyers of Nabisco Shredded Wheat, this can be explained by the fact that they are often the same people. During the course of a year, a large proportion of buyers of Kellogg's Corn Flakes will also be buyers of Shredded Wheat. These two unsweetened brands are positioned in the same market segment.

It follows that if Kellogg's is to introduce additional brands to compete against Shredded Wheat, it would be in danger of competing with itself by cannibalizing its own Corn Flakes. Some manufacturers will follow this strategy in the partially correct belief that to have two brands in one market segment will provide a larger total share than one brand alone, although the first brand will inevitably be cannibalized to some degree by the second. But most manufacturers will search for a slightly less self-destructive strategy for growth.

The most fruitful policy would in fact be to introduce a new brand into a different subdivision of the market on the assumption that the market is already segmented or can be segmented with the help of advertising and promotion into recognizably different although not necessarily completely self-contained parts. This can often be done, but the only segmentation of a market that is reasonably common in the real world is one based on *functional differences.* This in turn leads to psychographic and demographic segmentation (as people with active life styles will use deodorant bar soaps and mothers of young children will buy presweetened breakfast cereals), but the principal motivating argument for buying these products or brand groups is the functional one, as in the examples of deodorancy and presweetening.

It is possible to examine the details of a precisely relevant real-life example of a manufacturer's use of segmentation to create the opportunity for an important new brand. The market in question is for an important personal product bought with the greatest regularity. The market is large, static, and mature; it is also organized oligopolistically, although the leading manufacturer has a larger share than is normally the case in such markets. In 1975, the four main manufacturers (all nationally known names) had the following shares on an equivalent case basis (see Table 3.1).

Brands in this category can be classified into four functional segments, named with code words *red, blue, green,* and *yellow.* Typically enough, these are not absolutely self-contained. The first two segments (*red* and *blue)* overlap with one another; in fact *red* grew out of *blue* in the 1930s. The remaining segments (*green* and *yellow*) also overlap with one another, with *yellow* having grown out of *green* in the 1970s. *Yellow* is the newest, its development initially having taken place in Europe.

Table 3.1

Manufacturers' Market Shares

Manufacturer	Share (%)
A	42
B	20
C	14
D	9
Other manufacturers	15
Total	100

In 1975, each manufacturer had a number of brands and was represented in more than one market segment, but their individual patterns were different (see Table 3.2).

Manufacturer A was in much the strongest position, with the largest market share in total, the largest average share per brand, and the best coverage of the market segments (although this was not quite complete). By way of contrast, manufacturer C had four brands, each with a small market share, with three of these in fact clustered uncomfortably into a single segment. Manufacturer A was in such a powerful position that in any other circumstance, he or anyone else with a 42 percent market share would have been happy to preserve the status quo. But A's awareness of an opportunity in the *yellow* sector supported his natural aggressiveness: such is the nature of the competition between oligopolists. And A's expansion-based strategy was indeed successful, as can be seen from the market shares five years later (see Table 3.3).

Manufacturer A had added 4 percent of market share, taken directly out of competitors B and D. He had in fact done this by introducing a new brand aimed at the *yellow* segment and had managed to gain 7 percent in the process for the new brand, cannibalizing his own existing brands by 3 percent

Table 3.2

Manufacturers Operating in Different Market Segments

Manufacturer	Total market share (by volume) (%)	Number of brands	Average share per brand (%)	Segments in which they operated
A	42	4	10.5	Red, blue, green
B	20	2	10.0	Red, green
C	14	4	3.5	Red, green
D	9	2	4.5	Blue/green (two variants), yellow

Table 3.3

Five-Year Changes in Manufacturers' Market Shares

Manufacturer	1975 (%)	Mid-1980 (%)
A	42	46
B	20	17
C	14	14
D	9	8

but more importantly taking 1 percent from manufacturer D and 3 percent from manufacturer B.

This is a neat, opportunistic, and successful piece of positioning. But to put it into perspective, we should go back to the point that the new and attractive market segment, *yellow,* had originated in Europe. Of our four oligopolists, three are multinationals (the exception being B, who lost most to A's new brand). The success stemmed unquestionably from A's awareness of European trends and his ability to move quickly into the U.S. market with a well-conceived brand, capitalizing on them.

But do not assume that manufacturer A's analysis of market trends and subsequent new brand entry were a simple sequential process that anyone could have followed. It so happens that the growing importance of the fourth market segment had been known from European experience for more than ten years. And all this time manufacturer C had been trying to break into the segment. Manufacturer C, it will be remembered, had a total of four brands, with three crowded into one market segment. C was acutely aware of the need to broaden his base by moving into new parts of the market. And yet the brands directed at the *yellow* segment that C had introduced into tests since 1968 had invariably failed, despite C's track record of successful innovation in Europe, considerable resources, and no lack of energy on his own part or that of his advertising agencies. The success of manufacturer A just says a great deal for A's greater overall competence.

3. Name

It might strike the reader that the choice of a name for a brand is a less substantial matter than the concerns we have discussed so far: making sure that the brand is functionally effective and is properly positioned in the market. Many people believe, however, that the added values of a brand are in some way embodied in its name, and that these values can be transferred to another product by using the brand name as a common property. This is the rationale for the strategy of using an umbrella name for a number of different products (a strategy often described as line extension).

The first and most obvious point is that the danger of cannibalization is likely to be greater where the products with the umbrella name are in competition with one another (Tide powder and Tide liquid) than when they are not (Ivory bar soap and Ivory shampoo).

In one published case, a manufacturer introduced a new brand on top of an existing successful entry. In the fifth year, the new brand was about a third the size of the first, which had by then been cannibalized to a significant degree, so that overall share of the two brands together was only 18 percent ahead of the company's former share with one. This is not a disastrous achievement, but a second case of a similar type shows a much better performance. Here, by the fifth year the manufacturer of the new brand had virtually doubled sales. The original brand had remained at its previous level, but the second brand had put on additional sales almost as large as these again. How can we account for this much better performance?

In view of the earlier discussion in this chapter, it will be no surprise that much of the difference stems from functional performance. In the less successful of the two cases, the existing brand was not improved, thus leaving it vulnerable to cannibalization, while the new brand was slightly disappointing in performance, thus inhibiting its growth. In the more successful case, the existing brand was improved so that it was protected, and the new brand performed up to expectations. Moreover, in the less successful case, the existing brand was milked in the way normally expected of manufacturers who believe in life cycle theory. In the more successful case, support was maintained for the existing brand. The findings thus far underline the principles discussed in this book. This is not the whole story, however, because before getting to these causes, a more obvious one suggested itself. Very simply, in the first case the *names* of the old and new brands were similar to one another, which tended to attract an undue proportion of the second brand's customers from the first rather than from the field as a whole.[16]

But what about the more obvious *advantage* of umbrella naming: that people who use one product under a brand name can presumably easily be persuaded to sample a second, perhaps different category of product using that same brand name? We are talking here about extending a franchise across product categories.

Nielsen can provide interesting aggregated information. The data base is 167 new brands in a variety of packaged goods categories and shows their market share levels at the end of their first two years. New brands using an existing or umbrella brand name are compared with new brands using a completely independent brand name. At first glance there are big differences (see Table 3.4).

On the basis of these facts, a good case can be made for using new brand names rather than existing ones, emphatically so in the household and food categories. However, this is not the end of the story. There is also strong evidence that manufacturers pursue an umbrella naming policy largely because *they think that they can save money* by doing so, presumably by relying on the added values of the other products carrying the umbrella brand name. This seemingly plausible argument has tempted academics and journalists to

Table 3.4

Success of Brands with Umbrella Names and New Names

Market	Median market share at end of second year (%)		
	Number of examples	New brand with new names	New brand with umbrella names
Household (U.S.)	28	6.7	3.3
Food (U.S.)	36	6.5	1.9
Food (U.K.)	26	14.0	7.6
Health/toiletries (U.S.)	51	2.7	2.6
Health/toiletries (U.K.)	26	8.8	8.2

speculate, quite wrongly, on the supposed scale economies of using joint trademarks for different products.[17]

When in fact the Nielsen figures just quoted are weighted to take into account the different levels of advertising investment behind each new brand, the performance of new brands with umbrella names is brought almost exactly into line with that of new brands with new names. In other words, the generally lower level of performance of new brands with umbrella names is a result of a generally lower level of advertising investment put behind them. "[M]any marketing executives who have seen these results seem to feel that it is largely a matter of marketing psychology: realizing that marketing a new brand under a new name is tough, manufacturers gear up their marketing efforts proportionately. On the other hand, since it is commonly (and erroneously, as it turns out) believed than an established brand name is already pre-sold, less money and effort is directed at the brand and a smaller market share results."[18]

The data in these examples lead us to draw a clear but negative conclusion. The economic advantages of umbrella naming are substantially illusory in the short and medium term. Umbrella names are in general no worse and no better than completely new names. As a general rule the level of success of a new brand is much more dependent on support levels than on the name per se. It is possible that umbrella names provide greater staying power, by enabling a greater addition to added values, which is an essentially long-term process; the examples of Ivory, Palmolive, Hershey, Kellogg's, and Kraft support this contention. But the payoff is likely to be protracted and not really discernible in the analysis of a two-year sales effect, which we have just seen. In the longer term, umbrella naming is really a part of a manufacturer's corporate policy—especially as a way of reinforcing his long-term position vis-à-vis the retail trade—an act of faith, and one of the basic elements on which his business is based and to which the firm might be inclined to attribute its long-term success in the marketplace.

4. Price

In perhaps two-thirds of all cases, a new brand enters an existing market at a premium price. The firm, if it feels the need, justifies this to itself and (it hopes) to the consumer on the basis of the innovation and functional superiority of the new brand over the competition. In reality, the premium price is necessary to fund the high cost of achieving sampling by expenditures above and below the line. These expenditures must be at a high or "investment" level to compensate for the established position of existing brands with their stock of added values that have been acquired over the years. And while a new brand rarely makes a profit during its first two years or so, deficit budgeting puts an automatic upward pressure on the consumer price. Of course, the negative effect of the premium price is often concealed by the use of temporary price reductions and other promotional methods to encourage sampling, but the wise manufacturer will be careful about the widespread use of such devices because of the destructive effect of price reductions on the consumer's perception of a brand's value.

There is also a good deal of evidence that, although new and different brands will normally command a significant price premium, this premium tends to narrow during the first few years of a brand's life. William T. Moran, formerly a senior Unilever executive, has published analyses illustrating this trend in prices of new brands of deodorants, mouthwash, cough syrups, and sandwich bags.[19] A simple observation of the retail scene can add confirmation.

There are also facts to support the contention that premium prices are reasonably well accepted as a justification for functional improvement, although consumers are hearteningly skeptical about manufacturers' attempts to charge a premium price for no obvious functional advantage at all. Davidson, whose investigation was quoted earlier in this chapter, examined fifty successful new brands and fifty failures. Of the fifty successes, more than half were sold at a premium price, and in virtually every case the higher price was accompanied by a better performance than those of competitive brands. Of the fifty failures, thirty-five were sold at a premium price, but twenty-five of them were accompanied by a similar or a worse performance than competitive brands.[20]

These analyses and their lessons are useful as far as they go, but this is of course not far enough to provide operational advice for a manufacturer who wishes to launch a new brand. King, whose treatment is based partly on academic studies and partly on practical experience in the United Kingdom, suggests a useful investigative and pragmatic approach to the question of initial pricing, working on the basic assumption that the best price for the manufacturer to charge must be based roughly on what consumers will accept. The technique recommended is research into consumers' attitudes based on direct and indirect questions, which will provide guidance to the feasibility of "skimming" or "penetration" pricing (aimed respectively at skimming the cream from the market by pricing high, and opening up the market by pricing much lower).[21] On the other hand, basing prices on a derivation of production costs will tell the manufacturer whether he will cover costs at a given level of output, but it will give little idea about whether the company will in fact be able to sell that output.

It is also true that econometric techniques are helpful in pricing, although they are essentially a fine-turning device for the period after a brand is launched. The most useful such device is a calculation of price elasticity. It is by no means impossible to estimate this within limits for ongoing brands, as demonstrated by Broadbent, whose work will be considered in chapter 4. The trouble with this type of analysis is that it is constructed from historical data, which take some time to build for any brand. But a useful procedure in a brand's early planning stage is to make guesstimates of the price elasticities of competitive brands in the market; any internal consistency could well be valuable to note.

As the reader can infer from this discussion, the role of judgment in establishing an individual price is especially important. Once a brand is launched and progressing, the sensible manufacturer will take steps to estimate price elasticity as soon as a range of data becomes available. (Sales data from different regions and in different types of stores provide a surprisingly large amount of information quickly.) The range of elasticities for brands is quite wide (from virtually zero to beyond -2.0),[22] and the average elasticity is quite pronounced, as confirmed by Broadbent and a number of Nielsen studies.[23]

With an ongoing brand, the manufacturer will obviously wish to protect a price premium insofar as it is practicable to do so, and there is good evidence that consumer advertising can make a major contribution here. But this brings us to the part that price plays with an established, ongoing, mature brand, a matter to be discussed in chapter 4.

5. Distribution

One key factor influencing the immediate success (or failure) of a new brand is the ability of the manufacturer's sales force to get it into distribution.

A glance at Nielsen data suggests that manufacturers in general have little trouble in achieving quick distribution. This is a result of the efficiency and concentration of the American retail trade, with its relatively small number of buying points. This significant scale economy is also evidence of the muscle exercised by the sales force of the average large manufacturer.

In 1971, Peckham investigated all new brands in seventy product categories and estimated that three-quarters of these achieved the extraordinarily satisfactory weighted distribution level of 70 percent within eight months of launch.[24] What the analysis does not show, however, is the different growth patterns for successful and unsuccessful brands. King, using British Nielsen data, draws this distinction and shows differences in degree between the United States and Britain, particularly in the absolute distribution levels in the United Kingdom, which are much lower. For example, successful brands reach a weighted distribution of well under 60 percent within the first eight-month period, and unsuccessful brands achieve much less than this. The differences between Britain and the United States are probably connected with differences in manufacturers' and retailers' attitudes to new brand activity, with American retailers being more optimistic than those in Britain.

King shows us that both successful and unsuccessful brands make noticeable distributional headway during their first four months, although even in this short period the successful brands do rather better. But it is at this point that their paths seriously diverge. This distribution of successful brands continues to climb, to the 60 percent weighted level and beyond. The unsuccessful ones remain static and eventually begin to fall. Is this a reflection of differences in the effort of the sales force? Or a result of the initial acceptance of the product by the consumer, a matter influenced primarily by the brand's functional performance? The latter is almost certainly the more important cause:

> [D]istribution is a result of success. If the brand goes well in the early stages, the public demands it, retail branches hear from head office, the word gets around and more retailers want to stock it.[25]

But functional performance is not important to the consumer alone. Retailers themselves, and even more importantly the sales force, are conscious of functional superiority and its contribution to a brand's success. Functional superiority will provide conviction to the salesman and draw commitment from the retailer. When Nielsen executives actually sat in as observers on new brand presentations to chain and independent supermarket buyers, they found that evidence of saleability made a considerable difference to the degree of retail acceptance of a new brand.[26]

Retail distribution is not only a concern for a brand during all stages of its development (as will be discussed in chapter 4). It should also influence the initial decision about the case size for a new brand, because too small a size brings the immediate danger of shops running out of stock before the end of the manufacturers' sales cycle. Changing the case size is obviously more difficult and troublesome once a brand is under way than at the beginning. It is at the earliest stage that the manufacturer should do the necessary home-work (which means making a careful estimate of likely rates of sale in differ-ent outlets), introduce the optimum size from the outset, and explain to the retail trade exactly why this particular size was chosen.[27]

The Importance of Market Testing

Testing Mechanisms

The manufacturer of a new brand will almost invariably test its functional performance on some consumers. Various test techniques are employed, some of them extremely sophisticated. But before being sold to the public in quan-tity, the brand will also almost invariably be introduced first into a test mar-ket: a restricted geographical area (or two or three areas), where the public will—it is hoped—respond to the brand and its advertising in a way repre-sentative (or not too unrepresentative) of what would happen if the brand were to be sold nationally. The procedure is in a sense an insurance policy, a way of spending a relatively modest amount of money in order to prevent the manufacturer from losing a large amount of money in the all too common event of failure. A test market also permits improvements to be made in the details of the plan before national launch. The advantages of the procedure are therefore considerable, but there are two immediate tactical disadvan-tages: first, a test market takes time and alerts competitive manufacturers, who during the course of the test will have the opportunity to take retaliatory action in the classic oligopolistic fashion. Many cases have been known of competitors who have ruined test markets for new brands, because (in Stephen King's words) "If one is faced with a potentially dangerous new competitor, what better than to try to strangle it at birth?"[28]

Even more serious is the second point. There is a fundamental structural problem about test markets, which is that they can only be representative of the country as a whole in a crudely approximate sense. This problem has been much discussed in the professional literature. Jack Gold, a senior adver-tising agency executive who was formerly on the client side, examined this issue by analyzing sales for a number of Mennen brands in different com-monly used test areas in the United States and grossing these sales up to give estimates of national sales, with pretty inaccurate final results.[29] (For instance, predictions from sales in a single area overestimated the national picture by at least 25 percent in about a third of all cases.) On the basis of this and many other examples, it is difficult not to conclude, in the words of John Davis, another informed practitioner: "Test marketing then tends to be statistically invalid from the start."[30]

But the more we study the niceties of the statistical representativeness of test areas, the more we depart from the way they are actually employed in the real world, which is to provide a result that might approximate in a directional way to a national outcome to help the manufacturer make a reasoned decision. They are also used widely for the different purpose of what King calls "pilot marketing."[31] The idea here is to allow all of the details of the brand, production and physical distribution as well as marketing, to be tested in practical conditions. The brand can then shake down in a realistic fashion, and detailed problems can be solved before a national launch.

Bearing these points in mind, test marketing is not only useful; it is really indispensable. Nielsen can provide interesting data on how test markets are used in actual cases and what sort of results they provide. In an analysis of fifty test markets in the United States, Nielsen found that the eventual national share of market came within 5 percent of the test level in fourteen of the cases, within 10 percent of the test level in twenty-five of the cases, and within 20 percent of the test level in forty of the fifty cases. "[L]ooking at it another way, the odds turned out to be about four to one that national performance will match test results within plus or minus 20%."[32] This level of accuracy is nowhere near perfection, but it is a good deal better than Gold's and Davis's conclusions would have led us to expect. In general, these results, and the conclusions drawn from them, can be understood in light of the probable care and common sense used in planning, executing, and interpreting most test markets, of which Nielsen monitored a reasonably representative sample.

One important general observation that Nielsen makes is that, as a rule, conditions are *less* favorable in the national introduction than in a test area, a factor that is probably related to the retaliation of competitors. Researchers also have in their armory a number of statistical techniques to make for more sensitive interpretation of test market results. One of the most useful is the simple arithmetical technique of standardizing test data described by Davis.[33] This means that normally in a test market, the test brand will take market share from existing brands, and retail audit and consumer panel data will provide accurate estimates of how much each existing brand loses. On a national basis, the initial shares of the competitive brands will probably be different from their shares in the test market, but the amounts they lose in test can be used to predict what they will lose nationally. This is done by standardizing or applying to the national shares the same *relative* losses that the competitive brands suffered in the test market. As a consequence surprisingly accurate predictions of national results can be made.

There is a further aspect of testing on which Nielsen throws valuable light: the question of the time necessary for tests to provide reliable answers. From data provided by 100 tests in the United States and forty-one in the United Kingdom, it is clear that the longer a test runs, the greater becomes its ability to predict the final outcome accurately. After two months, there is a very small chance indeed of a reliable prediction; after six months the chance is 50–50; after a year, the reliability is 94 percent.[34] There is of course nothing here that should surprise us, but as usual it is satisfying to have factual validation of what common sense leads us to expect.

Success Rate for New Brands

Anyone with the smallest practical experience in marketing and advertising is aware of the part that myth plays in a business whose practitioners sometimes make considerable scientific claims for it. Even if observers of the scene are not themselves practitioners, they will get a good idea of the role of myth by studying the literature, certainly if they accept the view of that ever perceptive observer Colin McDonald, "What is a model but a myth with numbers?"[35]

One of the most deep-seated myths in the whole of marketing is the high failure rate of new brands, but for once, here is something that seems to be true. An examination of this will form a fitting end to this chapter, as well as make a bridge to chapter 4. A commonly mentioned statistic for the average failure rate of new brands is 80 percent.[36] Davidson gives his own estimate of 70 percent.[37] King reviews various empirical studies and gives different estimates of 54 percent, 60 percent, 40 percent, and 49 percent.[38]

Based on 100 studies, a 1972 Nielsen investigation in the United States disclosed an overall failure rate of 55 percent, which compares closely with the British Nielsen experience. Of these fifty-five failures, forty-seven were failures in test that were not extended nationally, and eight were national failures of brands that had apparently succeeded in test market. (Comparing these eight national failures following the test with the forty-five national successes following the test market gives us odds of about 6:1 in favor of a test market predicting national success.)[39]

There is then a good empirical basis for suggesting that half or more of new brands turn out to be near-immediate failures. These brands presumably had been designed by competent and imaginative people, and the management of major manufacturing companies had been persuaded to spend money on development and test marketing. The outcome of all this effort is if anything worse than the 50–50 result of the toss of a coin. This is not an encouraging picture; and its most important cause is almost certainly a lack of functional superiority in the test brands, as is obvious from the data discussed in the earlier parts of this chapter. Insofar as the marketing aspects of the launch plans can be blamed, most of them were in our experience unspecific about the brands used at present by the target users ("from what brands do we want to take business?"), with the result that priority was not given to achieving superiority *over the functional attributes of those specific brands.* This is the heart of the problem of achieving the first repurchase of a new brand, the truly nodal point in the whole path of a new brand's development.

As a result of a widespread awareness of the extraordinary failure rate of new product ventures, there was a major change after 1968 in relative expenditures made by American business in exploration, screening, and the development of new products, in comparison with commercialization of them.[40] But the key importance of comparative functional performance is still not universally understood by the marketing profession, which is why the matter is given such prominence in this book.[41]

The picture regarding the initial success and failure of new brands is clear. But it brings us to a point of comparable importance that is discussed much less frequently; and where it is discussed, it leads to conclusions that are generally even more discouraging. Of our 45 percent of new brands that are considered initial successes, how many grow to anywhere near market leadership, and how many limp along as neither real successes nor real failures? American and British figures provide distressingly similar answers.

Peckham made an analysis of forty-nine new brands launched nationally in seven product categories since 1955 and concluded that only eleven did well enough to get at least a 10 percent market share measured by Nielsen on an ongoing basis. Remembering that only half the brands entering test markets are introduced nationally, these eleven brands represent only about 10 percent or so of all new ventures.[42] An investigation by John Madell, of the British advertising agency (then named) Boase Massimi Pollitt Univas, examined 730 new brand launches in the British food market, and came up with an even worse finding:

> I have chosen to define a successful new brand as one which achieved a turnover of at least £4 million sterling in 1978.

> This is a fairly rough-and-ready measure and takes no direct account of profitability. However, on the whole, most major fast-moving packaged

goods manufacturers would regard this as the minimum turnover necessary to sustain marketing support and show a reasonable return.

Using this criterion, I found only 31 new brands had achieved this in the
last ten years. In other words, only 4 percent of the 730 new brand launches
that occurred across that period.[43]

Madell's analysis adds something to Peckham's beyond the important
matter of crude but general confirmation. Madell names all of the brands in
his successful 4 percent, and these are, as could be expected, familiar to anyone who has been a regular observer of the British scene. What strikes the
observer about these really successful brands is not simply their functional
superiority. An observer in the market would also be conscious of the added
values that have been built, sometimes in quite short periods of time. Ongoing success becomes then more a matter of brand building on a continuous,
long-term basis, and the major factor that contributes to this is unquestionably advertising. This, as suggested, is the reason for our having deferred the
discussion of advertising until we came to consider the brand as a growing
and mature entity, a proper matter for the next and subsequent chapters.

The Argument in Brief

This chapter has concerned the retail trade and how, by research and even
simple observation of competitive brands in retail stores, it is possible to
obtain a clear and accurate picture of a market.

Viewed over short periods, most consumer goods markets appear to be
relatively stationary. Yet there are large long-term changes. This chapter has
attempted to explain this phenomenon. Two factors are at work. The first is
that most new brands fail, so that the ferment of new brand innovation leads
to no *effective* change in the makeup of markets. The second point is that,
even with successes, there is a strong equilibrial tendency within markets,
which causes them to shake down quickly to accommodate a new brand. In
the long term, however, small changes lead to large cumulative effects, and
these are mainly due to repeat purchase adding a dynamic to product and
brand innovation. To a substantial degree also, the decline of many mature
brands is brought about by underinvestment caused by a virtually universal
but mistaken belief in the inevitability of cyclical decline. This is one of the
most grievous myths of the marketing profession.

Five factors are most important to a brand during its conception and birth:
functional performance, positioning, name, price, and distribution. These all

have great weight, but the first, functional performance, has an influence on virtually all of the other factors, and this makes it in effect the key to successful new brand activity.

New brands are almost always tested in the marketplace. Test mechanisms, while they have the disadvantages of being technically imperfect and giving competitors advance notice of a manufacturer's intentions, nevertheless act as an insurance policy. What makes such an insurance policy essential is the high rate of failure in new brand launches. Testing reduces this somewhat.

The most common reason for this high failure rate is functional deficiencies. Realizing this, American business has in recent years increased significantly the amount of relative effort applied to planning (as opposed to exploiting) new brands. But the failure rate remains so high that new product ventures remain the most hazardous feature of the entire marketing process.

Notes

1. Sales estimates relating to 1982 were published in *1984 Advertising Age Yearbook* (Chicago: Crain Books, 1984), pp. 248–252. The total value of the cat food market was estimated to be $1.6 billion.

The 1982 market shares of the different segments of the cat food market were as follows: canned, 51 percent; dry, 36 percent; and moist, 13 percent. (In 1982, however, moist was the fastest growing sector, which means that our estimate of 20 percent may not be unreasonable for some years later.)

In 1982, Nine Lives, Buffet, Kal Kan, and Purina together accounted for 61 percent of sales value in the canned sector. Cat Chow, Meow Mix, Friskies, Special Dinner, and Nine Lives accounted for 67 percent of the dry market value. Tender Vittles alone accounted for 67 percent of sales value in the moist sector.

Government estimates of the net value of sales always lag by some years. That for breakfast cereals was put at $2.5 billion in 1977. *Census of Manufactures* (Washington, DC: U.S. Department of Commerce, Bureau of the Census, 1981).

2. James O. Peckham, Sr., *The Wheel of Marketing,* 2d edition, 1981 (privately published but available from A.C. Nielsen), p. 77.

3. Ibid., pp. 72, 74, 75.

4. Stephen King, *Developing New Brands* (London: Pitman Publishing, 1973), pp. 2–6.

5. R. Polli and V.J. Cook, "Validity of the Product Life Cycle," *Journal of Business* (October 1969): 385–400; R. Polli, *A Test of the Classical Product Life Cycle by Means of Actual Sales Histories* (Philadelphia, PA: privately published, 1968).

6. *Advertising Age,* September 19, 1983, p. 32.

7. Nariman K. Dhalla and Sonia Yuspeh, "Forget the Product Life Cycle Concept," *Harvard Business Review* (January–February 1976): 102.

8. Stephen A. Greyser, *Cases in Advertising and Communications Management,* 2d edition (Englewood Clifs, NJ: Prentice-Hall, 1981), pp. 148–167.

9. Peckham, *The Wheel of Marketing,* p. 80. The 3M Company requires each of

its forty operating divisions to generate 25 percent of any year's sales with brands introduced during the previous five years. Thomas J. Peters and Robert H. Waterman, Jr., in *In Search of Excellence* (New York: Harper and Row, 1982), p. 233.

10. Peters and Waterman, *In Search of Excellence,* p. 233.

11. Peckham, *The Wheel of Marketing,* p. 30.

12. *Nielsen Researcher* (Oxford, England: A.C. Nielsen Company) 14, No. 1 (January–February 1973): 10–11.

13. J. Hugh Davidson, "Why Most New Consumer Brands Fail," *Harvard Business Review* (March–April 1976): 117–122.

14. Peter Carter and Roz Hatt, "How Far Does Advertising Protect the Brand Franchise?" *Admap* (May 1983): 261–280.

15. Peckham, *The Wheel of Marketing,* p. 73.

16. Ibid., p. 86.

17. Julian L. Simon and Johan Arndt, "The Shape of the Advertising Response Function," *Journal of Advertising Research* (August 1980): 23.

18. Peckham, *The Wheel of Marketing,* pp. 90–91.

19. William T. Moran, "Why New Products Fail," *Journal of Advertising Research* (April 1973): 5–13.

20. Davidson, "Why Most New Consumer Brands Fail."

21. King, *Developing New Brands,* pp. 161–167.

22. See for example Simon Broadbent, "Price and Advertising: Volume and Profit," *Admap* (November 1980): 532–540; also chapter 4, note 33.

23. Peckham, *The Wheel of Marketing,* pp. 31–38.

24. Ibid., p. 15.

25. Stephen King, *Advertising as a Barrier to Market Entry* (London: Advertising Association, 1980), p. 14.

26. Peckham, *The Wheel of Marketing,* p. 23.

27. *Nielsen Researcher* (September–October 1972): 7–9.

28. King, *Developing New Brands,* p. 172.

29. Jack A. Gold, "Testing Test Market Predictions," *Journal of Marketing Research* (August 1964): 8–16.

30. John Davis, *The Validity of Test Marketing* (monograph) (London: J. Walter Thompson, 1965).

31. King, *Developing New Brands,* pp. 169–170.

32. Peckham, *The Wheel of Marketing,* p. 95.

33. Davis, *The Validity of Test Marketing,* pp. 8–12.

34. *Nielsen Researcher* (January–February 1968): 4–7.

35. Colin McDonald, "Myths, Evidence and Evaluation," *Admap* (November 1980): 546–555.

36. This figure is mentioned on a number of occasions by A.S.C. Ehrenberg and G.L. Goodhardt in their seventeen essays in *Understanding Buying Behavior* (New York: J. Walter Thompson and Market Research Corporation of America, 1977–80).

37. Davidson, "Why Most New Consumer Brands Fail," p. 117.

38. King, *Developing New Brands,* pp. 1–2.

39. Peckham, *The Wheel of Marketing,* p. 96. Note that the odds on a test market predicting national success as given here (6:1) are more favorable than the odds quoted in the text referred to in note 32 (4:1). The reason for the difference is technical, in that the quotation referred to in note 32 calculated the number of times test market predictions came within 20 percent of the eventual national outcome. These could be

20 percent overestimates or 20 percent underestimates. In the later quotation, the underestimates have been ignored, to give better odds on predicting success. They have been ignored for the simple and practical reason that a national outcome exceeding the test market prediction does not indicate an unsuccessful test!

40. Booz Allen Hamilton, *New Product Management for the 1980s* (privately published, 1982).

41. Two examples, one from the professional literature and one from the popular press, show this:

(i) "An annual trek through the product development practices of thirty to seventy [sic] firms has given the University of Michigan Graduate School of Business Administration a unique opportunity to assess the 'state of the art'." The report of these treks discloses that the "state of the art" does not include any form of recognition of the importance of functional efficiency for a new brand (C. Merle Crawford, "Product Development: Today's Most Common Mistakes," *University of Michigan Business Review* 29, No. 1 [January 1977]: 6).

(ii) In the *New York Times,* March 3, 1985, the head of a major advertising agency, a securities analyst, a Miller distributor, a marketing professor, and a bartender commented on the new Miller High Life Beer advertising campaign. The first four people were concerned exclusively with the marketing and advertising reasons for Miller's problems and how these had influenced the new campaign. Only the bartender referred to the functional performance of the beer: "I think High Life is very bland. It has no significance at all. No character. It is a little watery." The difference between this comment and the statements of the other four observers was raised in a letter by a James Rudolph published in the *New York Times,* April 7, 1985.

42. Peckham, *The Wheel of Marketing,* p. 76.

43. John Madell, "New Products: How to Succeed When the Odds Are Against You," *Marketing Week,* February 22, 1980: 20–22.

— 4 —

Factors That Shape a Brand During Its Growth and Maturity

This chapter concerns growth; and it is substantially concerned with the long term. But we must reach the long term via the short term, and there is often a severe dissonance between long-term and short-term objectives when it comes to planning the growth of a brand. It is important for the reader to appreciate this dissonance before we get into the main argument of this chapter.

In the mid-1980s, while conducting qualitative research among advertising decision makers on how they selected media, we reported the views of the marketing vice president of a large American-based international food company, one whose advertising budget then exceeded $60 million. He talked specifically about the relative value of above-the-line (theme advertising) and below-the-line (promotional) expenditures, and long-term trends in the marketplace, which even then were demonstrating strong relative movements from the former to the latter.

Afterward he wrote a letter. Its points are acute, having extra force because they come from a successful advertiser. A manufacturer is a much more objective observer than, say, an advertising agency or media executive, whose views might be colored by the self-interest of dependence on clients' advertising expenditures.

> The real problem is the same one which pervades other aspects of corporate behavior today: an overemphasis on the short term with short term defined, at best, as "this year" just as often this "quarter."

Trade deals generate *measurable* volume *now.* It can be seen, tabulated, and included in current financial statements. Advertising, on the other hand—and marketing practitioners and scholars know this well—cannot be tied directly to volume, except possibly over the long term (two to five years), and even then only imprecisely.

So when we need extra volume this quarter, or this year, whatever the reason, we do not increase advertising, we increase trade deals. And since short-term budgets tend to be filed, we naturally shift relative monies from the imprecise area of advertising into the more easily measured area of trade deals.

Note the emphasis on the problem of reaching sales goals, a problem caused mainly by competitive pressure. Note also the long-term value implicitly attributed to advertising. It is indeed not difficult to demonstrate that a syphoning of funds from advertising to promotions may increase sales, but it does so at the expense of long-term damage to brands. There is persuasive empirical evidence of this.[1] Judgment suggests, however, that such evidence is not likely to have much influence on individual advertisers, no matter how strong and enlightened they may be, in the all too common pressures of the marketplace, specifically when tonnage targets are in jeopardy but simply have to be met. Advertising is normally a matter of strategy aimed at the long-term objective of increasing the number of customers and their loyalty to the brand. Promotions are essentially a matter of tactics, aimed at increasing sales in the short term. With the increasing strength of the retail trade, the ferocity of tactical battles will not lessen in the future.

Initial Growth

The first problem a manufacturer faces with a new brand is to achieve consumer trial. Various techniques are used to bring this about: in the main, consumer promotions of different sorts, although advertising also has some part to play. As a result of the initial activity, a consumer base is built: people who have tried the brand once. The critically important stage now is first repurchase. It should again be emphasized that the brand must offer some type of functional superiority to achieve repurchase; the consumer will be aware of how well the brand performs after having used the first package. But naturally, not all trial purchasers will make a repeat purchase. First, because in functional performance a new brand cannot be all things to all people, any brand will have functional weaknesses as well as functional strengths. It follows that the brand will not be bought again by those people who were more disappointed by the weaknesses than satisfied by the strengths. It is also likely that some people are going to be wedded to their existing brands, which may have added values that are particularly strong and personally relevant to these consumers, so that the new brand will need to offer considerable functional superiority indeed to compensate.

The largest increases in the sales of a new brand will be those accompanying the growth in its distribution, although when the brand has achieved a high level of distribution, growth must then come from increasing sales in the average store. It is surprising, incidentally, how low a level of sales is achieved by even a major brand. In a fairly large supermarket, three-quarters of all brands sell a maximum of twelve packs per week; a third of them sell only four packs or even less.[2]

As a brand becomes accepted by the consumer, distribution grows at a continuous and often rapid rate. As we saw in the previous chapter, it is by no means uncommon for a new brand to achieve a 70 percent weighted distribution level after about eight months. But the growth is often slower than this. In observing the growth of distribution, we can normally discern a relationship between distribution and sales that can help us to predict the eventual sales level when the brand has reached its long-term stability. This is a modeling procedure, and the mathematics are no more complicated than the standardization of test market data described in chapter 3.

The first thing to do is to look at a new brand's sales and weighted distribution in test market, and compute the ratio between them. This shows sales volume per percentage point of weighted distribution. With sales of 61,000 units and a weighted distribution of 41 percent, this ratio is 61,000:41, or 1490 units per percentage point of weighted distribution. This is more simply expressed as 1.49 thousand units per distribution point.[3]

As the brand grows, so the sales and distribution grow, and we can calculate this ratio of sales to distribution for each period. We will immediately see that this ratio steadily increases. In other words, sales are going ahead faster than the number of shops stocking our brand, because the sales per shop are increasing because of the brand's growing popularity. The actual progression of the ratio over the course of the first year in our example is as follows: 1.49, 1.51, 1.76, 2.13, 2.27, 2.50. As the ratios are calculated for further periods, the rate of increase, however, is seen to be slowing up. Here are the data for the second year, with a calculation of the increase over the same period in the previous year, showing how this progressive increase is being reduced (see Table 4.1).

Table 4.1

Development over Time in Ratio of Sales to Distribution

Second year	Period 1	2.65	78 percent above a year before
	Period 2	2.26	50 percent above a year before
	Period 3	2.48	41 percent above a year before
	Period 4	2.88	35 percent above a year before
	Period 5	3.02	33 percent above a year before
	Period 6	3.28	31 percent above a year before

We now have a series of figures from which three specific predictions can be made.

1. The future ratios of sales to distribution can be predicted on the basis of the declining rate of growth, projecting forward the trend in increases over the year before (the figures on the right of the preceding table).
2. Distribution growth can be separately forecast, or at least targeted. It is, after all, substantially under the manufacturer's own control, in that it is directly influenced by promotional and sales force activity.
3. By applying the projected ratio to the targeted distribution, we can make a forecast of sales. This tool is of day-to-day value to the brand manager. (This book and indeed this chapter contain others.)

Another pronounced pattern about which generalizations can normally be made is the primary growth cycle for a brand. We are talking here about a medium-term period (of an average length of two years or so) and a sales pattern showing a peak of initial sales followed by noticeable decline. This decline can be explained partly by the loss of some initial users: those who are not sufficiently convinced of the new brand's functional superiority to repurchase it. It is also partly the result of a slowing in the growth of new trial users following the normal reduction in promotional and advertising expenditures from an initial peak to a more normal ongoing level. And it is also commonly the result of competitive retaliation. The reader will note that this primary growth cycle (something finite, predictable, and to some extent within the control of the manufacturer) is a concept totally different from the long-term, supposedly uncontrollable life cycle discussed in chapter 3, where it was argued that final and irreversible decline is normally the result of a manufacturer's policy of draining resources out of a mature brand because of a belief in the inevitability of its eventual extinction.

The concept of the primary growth cycle is relatively straightforward, and it is a useful tool that can help us plan the recycling that is normally necessary to maintain a brand's long-term strength, thus prolonging its mature life. At the end of this chapter, we will take a look at the recycling process, but let us first examine the primary growth cycle. The data quoted are based on a Nielsen examination of a large number of newly introduced brands in scores of different product categories.[4]

Nielsen's observation of these brands suggests that the normal pattern is for a brand to grow to its peak and then decline to a relatively stable level of 80 percent of that peak. The primary growth cycle is defined as the time between the brand's introduction and the point when it drops to this 80 percent level. The first thing to examine is the length of the cycle. The average figure calculated from an examination of 86 cases is twenty-eight months, with a spread from less than a year to more than four years, the average brand taking slightly longer to peak (fifteen months) than to decline to the 80 percent level (thirteen months).

Four points can be made about this cycle as it affects different types of brands.

1. There is a direct relationship between a brand's share of market and the length of the cycle. The brands with the longest cycle are those with the highest achieved market shares.
2. Brands in the health and beauty fields have longer primary cycles (an average of thirty-four months) than brands in the household and food fields (averages of twenty-three and twenty-four months, respectively).
3. Brands with long primary cycles tend to have high levels of advertising support and innovation, but a low level of new brand activity in their markets.
4. Brands with short primary cycles tend to be in large, crowded markets with a high degree of new brand activity, but a low degree of innovation and relatively low advertising support.

These characteristics point to the likelihood of the cycle becoming shorter over time, as markets become more densely crowded with brands and as it becomes increasingly difficult for new brands to gain large market shares. Additional analyses demonstrate that this has indeed been happening, with cycles falling to as little as eighteen months in many cases. An interesting sidelight is that in a less developed market like the United Kingdom, the share of market for a new brand is on average two or three times greater than in the United States. This suggests that overall economic development may be leading to progressively lower average market shares and shorter primary cycles.

Because of the characteristics of the primary growth cycle, the operational lesson from this analysis is the importance of regular restaging, and that plans for the first restage should be developed in the period following the initial launch of a brand. Increasingly long lead times will be required to develop and implement product innovations and all of the other changes that restages always call for, while the initial growth cycle itself may be growing shorter.

A rather different illumination of the primary growth cycle is provided by a classic investigation by John Davis of British test market experience.[5] Davis examined forty-four test markets, both successes and failures. Although he does not make direct comparisons with Nielsen's analyses, which are mainly American, his observed primary growth cycle

- is of much shorter duration (as little as eight months in most cases);
- shows a pronounced drop from peak to relative stability (on average about 40 percent reduction);
- is associated with generally lower levels of distribution than in the United States (a point discussed in chapter 3).

The differences from the mainly American experience of Nielsen are not too easy to explain. Some of these differences must stem from the fact that Davis's examples include a large number of test market failures, which probably cause both the extent and speed of the drop to be exaggerated. The Nielsen data appear to exclude early failures, although some of the analyses do not make this absolutely clear. It is also probably true that the differences between the American and British findings are a reflection of the differences between the two markets, with the likelihood of a greater general volatility in Britain, as evidenced by the larger initial market shares there.

The thing that makes Davis's study so interesting is a supplementary investigation into the levels of the drop from peak to stability. Davis's conclusion has not been tested in the United States, but there is no intrinsic reason to believe that it would not operate here. What he suggests is a *consistency* in the extent of the drop from peak to stability for individual brands, as they are moved from test to national distribution. In other words, regardless of whether the initial peak is different between the test and the national launch, the ongoing level can be predicted.

Here we have the making of another simple model with which it should be possible (on the assumption that American and British experiences are similar) to forecast the extent of the drop in the ongoing national sales level, on the basis of the percentage drop in test market when that is applied to the initial national peak.

Five Influences on a Growing Brand

It is time now to look at some more visible parts of our large machine. As in chapter 3, the approach will be analytical rather than descriptive, as we take our first look at trade and consumer promotions and at consumer advertising. After this, we will enjoy a new perspective on two factors discussed in the previous chapter, price and distribution. This chapter will conclude with a brief look at the restaging process, which brings us back yet again to the factor of functional performance, the first and most pervasive of the factors influencing a brand's initial success and continued growth. But now, functional performance will be shown to work much in tandem with advertising.

1. Trade promotions

Trade promotions, which normally take the form of either explicit or indirect rebates to wholesalers and/or retailers, are costly but are generally considered important for both a new brand and an ongoing one. They are an essentially defensive tactic dictated by what competitors are doing. Their main effect is a loading of inventories in wholesale and retail establishments. The success of trade promotions in achieving this makes them popular with manufacturers' sales forces, who use them as a lever to sell what they believe to be significantly higher-than-average volumes of merchandise. In contrast to consumer promotions, which act on the consumer to pull goods through the distributional pipeline, trade promotions are aimed at the trade, to *push* the stocks through this same pipeline, mainly by encouraging retailers to put the goods on display and perhaps pass on some of the benefit of the promotional rebates in reduced selling prices to the consumer.

There is little doubt that trade promotions can have a demonstrable short-term effect in moving goods out of the factory, but two considerable qualifications must be made about them.

In the first place, they are extremely expensive in absolute terms. Indeed, the whole matter of promotional as compared with advertising expenditure calls for some comment. Nielsen estimates the average proportion of a manufacturer's marketing budget that goes into various trade promotions to be on the order of 23 percent, a figure larger than that for consumer promotions (18 percent) or consumer advertising (15 percent). This gives a promotion-to-advertising ratio of 41:15 (the residual 44 percent represents all other marketing costs, which are mainly sales force salaries and expenses).[6] Expressed more simply, this ratio is 73:27. Such an estimate gives rather more weight to promotions than did many of our former clients, although they all tended to spend more money below than above the line. An estimate by Donnelley Marketing of 56:44 is more in accordance with our own clients' practices. But the proportion going below the line is clearly growing.[7] Interestingly enough, Procter & Gamble used to be well known for spending more money on advertising than promotions as a general rule. However, the pressures of business conditions have caused a change in this policy, so that even Procter & Gamble now spends a minimum of 60 percent of its total budget on promotional activities.

From some points of view the traditional advertising–promotion distinction is artificial. Robert Prentice, a consultant to the Marketing Science Institute, makes a good case for creating a new category, "consumer franchise building" expenditures, which should include advertising, sampling, certain coupons (manufacturers' coupons that include a selling message), demonstrations, and service material (such as recipes). In his opinion, these expenditures should account for 55 percent of the advertising and promotion budget; we do not disagree with him, except to wondering whether his figure is too low. This analysis suggests, incidentally, that if his 55 percent is to include such expensive items as sampling and most manufacturers' coupons, the advertising element alone is likely to come down to something as low as Peckham's figure of 27 percent.[8]

What makes promotions so expensive is that they are substantially a means of price reduction, which, at either the retail or the consumer level, must come out of the manufacturer's contribution to overheads and profit. Indeed direct costs will actually go up as a result of the larger volume of goods sold on promotion. A 10 percent trade rebate can commonly mean a 20 percent reduction in contribution. In these circumstances, the manufacturer would need to increase sales by 25 percent simply to cover the costs of the deal and break even. In most cases, promotions do not achieve this.

This brings us to the second important point about trade deals, which is that although it is by no means impossible for a trade deal to boost sales by 25 percent in the short term, this may not be quite what it seems, because much of the spurt may represent a pulling forward of sales that would have been made anyway during a later period. The all too common effect is therefore to transfer goods from the manufacturer's to the trader's inventory without bringing about a very noticeable increase in sales through the pipeline to the consumer. Additionally, there is frequent evidence of trade promotions syphoning business away from varieties of a brand (like flavors of a food) that do *not* carry the offer, to those varieties that *do,* leaving total sales more or less unchanged.[9]

These unquestioned difficulties prompt us to ask why manufacturers continue with these expensive and sometimes destructive tactics. The answer must come back again to the nature of oligopolistic competition, which forces manufacturers to go on with an activity that is in the last analysis nothing more than implicit price competition. And as retailers grow in strength vis-à-vis manufacturers, the pressure on the latter to grant substantial, increasing, and even permanent overriding discounts will unquestionably become greater, with interesting effects on the balance of power in the marketing world. Indeed, an analysis of trade promotions based, among other things, on information from marketing managers and promotional specialists in manufacturing companies indicated strongly that "trade promotion expenditures are rising at the same time as their productivity is declining."[10]

As with consumer promotions (as we shall shortly see), trade deals tend to be a more effective device for a growing or stable brand than for a declining one. But for all types of brands there are basic problems. A Nielsen analysis of a typical brand showed that over a ten-month period, a substantial trade promotion at the beginning boosted volume by 22.5 percent over the 10 months, but with an overall *reduction in profit of 7 percent.*[11] It would be interesting to know how many manufacturers would willingly pay the cost involved to achieve this self-destructive result if they were not forced to do so by the competitive climate in the markets in which they were operating.

Display is an important motive for trade promotions. Sometimes promotions are specifically geared to achieving it. This is the most important way in which trade promotions can be said to act on the consumer, and most manufacturers are conscious of the problems that arise for growing brands, because of the strong tendency for larger brands to receive *fewer* shelf facings than their market share justifies, while smaller brands receive more. This is for simple mechanical reasons, shelf stocking being generally done in multiples of a case, which provides rather a large minimum display for the smaller brands, thus squeezing the display space available for the larger ones.[12] But even if increased display results from promotional actions, there are problems that could cloud the effects. For a start, very few lines are on mass display in a supermarket at any time—perhaps twenty in any week out of a total of many thousand different items. This means that the display of the brand on offer is neglected at other times. Peckham writes: "One district manager I know kept a two-year record of his sales separately for stores which occasionally featured and mass-displayed his merchandise and also for comparable sized stores which stocked his brands normally. You know what he found: the annual sales trend was better in the stores with normal but year-round support."[13] Much of the effect of mass display must be to enable users of the brand to fill their own store cupboards, so that these promotions bring about a transfer of inventories from manufacturer to retailer and from retailer to customer, with only a modest increase in final consumption.

The value of a brand's display is of course influenced by its pack design, which must be neatly balanced between what is required by the brand's endogenous characteristics (packaging being a means of communicating functional performance and added values) and what is required to make it stand out on the shelf from possibly more aggressive rivals. Not all brands have aggressive personalities. It will of course encourage considerable dissonance to use powerful colors and lettering for the packaging of brands whose underlying character calls for a quieter outward impression.

One further type of trade promotion, cooperative advertising, deserves brief consideration, although positive evidence of its prolonged beneficial effects on the standing and sales of brands is just as scarce as with other types of trade promotion. A distillation of Nielsen experience suggests that although cooperative advertising is often associated with increasing sales of mature brands, it is difficult to untangle the specific effect of cooperative advertising from other stimuli that may be contributing to the increased offtake, not least of which is the manufacturer's own consumer advertising.[14] As with other types of trade promotion, it is doubtful whether manufacturers would allow themselves to be forced into this sort of activity were it not for the presence of competitors who would step in if they were to drag their feet. We should remember also that with the strength of the retail trade, cooperative advertising provides some protection to small manufacturers from being delisted, an ever-present danger for the third, fourth, and lower brands in a market. The advantage of cooperative advertising may then lie in its influence on the retail buyer rather than the ultimate customer, especially since the average cooperative advertisement, with its hard-selling, relentless, almost exclusive price orientation, can add little to the average brand's store of added values.

One simple but necessary recommendation is that manufacturers should keep much fuller and more carefully compiled records than many of them do at present of the results of their trade promotions (and their consumer promotions too). Trade and consumer data should be included in both cases. As some additional return for the huge expenditures on these activities, manufacturers should assemble a constantly growing portfolio of promotional ideas that work (or do not work), including information on how well they perform and why.[15] To my knowledge, Procter & Gamble is the only firm that has done this consistently.

2. Consumer promotions

We have already seen from Nielsen's broad data aggregation that consumer promotions take a smaller proportion (18 percent) of the average manufacturer's marketing budget than trade promotions (23 percent). Consumer promotions are nevertheless a large and dynamic influence on a brand, with an importance that differs according to whether the brand is expanding or contracting and also according to the type of promotion itself.

The logic of consumer promotions is that they provide an incentive (normally price-oriented) for the consumer to sample a brand. Sales will rise sharply, always going down after the end of the promotion, but (the manufacturer hopes) still settling at a slightly higher level than before, as some buyers will like the brand enough to add it to their repertoire. This might be called the ideal pattern, and only if this happens can promotions be said to be building the consumer base. In most circumstances, however, the main emphasis is only on short-term sales. Nielsen provides empirical illumination, with conclusions of considerable operational importance. In studies of fifty-one different promotions, the brands with an *increasing* sales trend can be shown clearly to follow the ideal, with sales before the promotion indexed at 100, sales during the promotion at 112, and sales in the period after the promotion at 110. Brands are of course more commonly in a stationary position in the short and medium term; in these cases, the Nielsen data show sales in general coming down to the prepromotional level at the end of the promotion. With brands on a *declining* sales trend, however, the sales in the period after the promotion are usually lower than those in the period before it, presumably a reflection of general disappointment in the brand's performance, and evidence of erosion of—rather than addition to—the customer base.

Consumer promotions can be seen then as a sampling device, something extremely important for a new brand, and an extra dynamic to the short- and medium-term sales trend of an established brand, speeding the success of the growing ones but hastening the failure of those going down. The empirical basis of Nielsen's generalization is European as well as American, with the sole difference that promotional sales peaks tend to be higher in Europe, a point connected with the greater volatility of the less sophisticated markets.[16]

As with trade promotions, consumer promotions are essentially defensive, competitive tactics for an ongoing brand; the manufacturer finds himself forced into them to protect his position. Like trade promotions, they are expensive and operate as a deduction from the manufacturer's contribution to overhead and profit. A sales gain would have to be large indeed to compensate for the reduction in revenue necessary to fund the promotion. There is substantial merit in the argument of British analysts King[17] and Roberts[18] that price rebates (the most popular type of consumer promotion[19] as well as virtually the sole type of trade promotion) should not actually be considered as marketing expenditures at all. They are hardly investments in the sense of money staked out to achieve a return. They are *reductions in income,* or a variant on the theme of price competition. The more regularly they are carried out by manufacturers, the more they take the form of long-term price cuts, which are effectively subsidies to existing buyers, in whose eyes the brand is likely to be devalued, a counterproductive side effect.[20]

This is really another way of saying that consumer promotions do not help declining brands. Growing brands, with their increasing base of contented repurchasers and accumulation of added values, have less need to be rebated, with the concomitant danger of debasing the value of the brand in the opinion of its users. One slight qualification to this generalization is that consumer promotions can to some extent buy time for a normally successful brand that may be under immediate threat from new brands with product improvements. But the role of promotions here is a "holding" or short-term one, to provide a breathing space for the manufacturer to improve his own brand's formulation in line with the new market entrants and thus protect his own long-term position.

Some types of price promotion are more efficient and beneficial than others. Some types of nonprice promotion can even add to a brand's stock of added values, although promotions that combine a short-term sales stimulus with added values are rare. There is sometimes a genuinely creative element here, but creative specialists—and often also other members of account groups—in advertising agencies are generally not too interested in generating promotional ideas, although those same people may do the most distinguished work in developing consumer advertising campaigns.

Of the different type of price promotion, couponing (the most rapidly growing although not the largest type in volume terms) has distinct advantages over direct rebating by the use of such devices as price-off packs, banded packs ("buy three and get a fourth pack free"), and other explicit ways of flagging cheapness. Absolutely the most effective, but also the most expensive promotional device is house-to-house sampling in conjunction with a coupon for follow-up purchase. Procter & Gamble's use of national sampling in Britain in the 1960s for Fairy Liquid dishwasher has become a marketing legend; Fairy Liquid has never subsequently lost its market leadership. In an example quoted by Peckham, a new brand launched in half the United States with a home sample and coupon achieved a market share of 5.3 percent in the fifth check period (i.e., ten months). It was launched with a conventional introductory price-off in the other half of the country and achieved 3.1 percent in that same period.[21] But this Nielsen analysis does not give details of the vastly greater costs of the sample and coupon.

The particular advantages of coupons are fourfold. First, regular buyers are limited to one reduced-price pack, so that the element of subsidy to existing buyers is reduced. Second, a coupon does not erode brand values by introducing the idea of cheapness quite as explicitly as specially printed bargain packs. Third, with rebate packs, the customer tends to resist paying the normal price again after the rebate has come to an end. And fourth, competitive retaliation is not triggered quite so directly by couponing as by rebating.

All of the generalizations made here about consumer promotions are based on facts. Evidence is also available that diminishing returns set in rapidly with promotions for even well-established and growing brands. Peckham recommends, again on the basis of his long experience, that consumer price rebates should not be used more often than once every twelve to eighteen months. Yet, despite this rapid fall in efficiency plus the longer-term danger of devaluing brands in the eyes of consumers, manufacturers are sometimes led by competitive pressures to self-destructive orgies of rebates. Stephen King documents one well-known case of an established brand, Kimberly-Clark's Delsey toilet tissue in the United Kingdom, which was for all intents and purposes destroyed by continuous promotions funded by stopping all consumer advertising.[22] There is one complete product field in which competitive price cutting extinguished the profit for all manufacturers. This took place in a small country, Denmark, but the market was a large one: washing powders.

Nevertheless, in spite of these extraordinarily dramatic and by no means isolated examples, consumer promotions of the most direct and ultimately most self-destructive variety continue seemingly unchecked by any second thoughts by even the most well-trained brand management. This can only be because consumer promotions, like trade promotions, enable the manufacturer to buy short-term tonnage irrespective of the longer-term consequences.

Not all consumer promotions are like this, especially those for new brands and those with rising sales trends, and most particularly those few consumer promotions with sensible long-term as well as short-term objectives. There are cases that demonstrate that synergy can result from promotions run *coincidentally* with periods of advertising if the campaign itself is intrinsically strong. But such examples are rare. As a general rule, Nielsen evidence suggests that consumer promotions—like trade promotions—bring no long-term benefit to a brand's sales trend.[23]

3. Advertising

Much the most important aspect of advertising—and one receiving a good deal of attention in this book—is the creative content of campaigns, an essentially qualitative consideration. But there is also another aspect that will receive much attention in this chapter: the quantitative element, or the effects of the weight of money put behind campaigns. There are relationships here between advertising volume and sales that will be looked at in some detail. This is a productive study, although it took considerable time for the advertising industry to come around to examining these relationships. Early explorations of campaign effectiveness concentrated almost exclusively on campaign content, using simple techniques derived from direct response. Even Albert Lasker, one of the small handful of really powerful personalities to come out of the advertising agency business, once admitted that "it took him years to learn that mere volume of advertising could be as important as the copy message."[24] In this statement he goes too far, but volumes in themselves have a quantifiable effect in many circumstances, and these will be illustrated.

One thing to bear in mind is that (as already mentioned) advertising does not account for as large a share of the average manufacturer's marketing expenses as trade and consumer promotions. This does not mean that the effect of advertising is eventually not large. Its effect is as large as it is because over and beyond its short-term influence there is an additional long-term effect. Because advertising contributes in this way to building a customer base, we made the point in the analogy of the large machine that the small apparatus in its middle appears to have an effect disproportionate to its size. But in the early stages of a brand's life, the cumulative effect of advertising on brand use has not had time to be built. Indeed from strong evidence in the British market, "shop display and word-of-mouth are thought to be much the most important channels of communication for a new brand," with advertising a much less important initial influence.[25] Over longer periods, however, advertising moves steadily to a position much more comparable in importance to that of the functional performance of the brand. Indeed, as discussed in chapter 3, advertising has an important role, during the growth of a successful new brand, in building added values quickly to protect it if and when competitive brands have been improved to reach functional parity with it.

Nielsen and other sources provide a good deal of information on the generalizable relationships between volume of advertising and volume of sales for ongoing brands. We should be careful, however, to avoid drawing exaggerated conclusions from these, because (as discussed in chapter 2) the prime determinant of the absolute size of the advertising appropriation for an ongoing brand is normally the absolute level of sales. This means that it is misleading and possibly dangerous to interpret the relationship between *absolute* advertising volume and *absolute* sales volume as cause and effect, except in rather special circumstances.

There are three such circumstances. The first is the case of new brands, for which the advertising appropriation is always established at an "investment" level, influenced by the ongoing expenditures of competitive brands, and determined by the client's and agency's judgment on what needs to be spent to ensure a successful launch in a competitive marketplace. The best Nielsen evidence of the success of such launch expenditures comes from thirty-four new brands, indicating a marked degree of response to advertising pressure. "New brands having the highest share of sales also have the highest share of advertising and, conversely, those having the lowest sales shares are at the bottom of the share-of-advertising list." The degree of advertising investment in the new brand can be described by its share of all advertising in the category (share of voice); Nielsen evidence suggests that this needs to be a good deal higher than the anticipated brand share for success in the market (e.g., by a 3:1 multiple).[26]

The second circumstance is the case where advertising budgets are set with the help of econometric techniques, for instance, using knowledge of the brand's advertising elasticity (discussed later in this chapter). But this is a relatively rare procedure, and there are not enough cases available to enable us to draw any generalized conclusion about advertising volumes so determined and resultant sales volumes.

The third circumstance is the case where a comparison is made between year-by-year changes in advertising and year-by-year changes in sales. This focuses on short-term adjustments that are not necessarily dictated by projected sales increases and decreases, although total advertising expenditures in the medium and long term continue to be governed by the brand's earnings and therefore its sales. The change in advertising for a given year (measured in comparison with a norm) is calculated from the advertising budget, which is set and agreed upon before the beginning of the year. In the majority of circumstances, the sales result in that same year does not influence the level of advertising, most of which is spent before the year's overall sales have been made anyway. But a good sales performance will probably cause the budget to be increased the next year, while a poor performance will cause a cutback next year or even in the last quarter of the present year.

Such a comparison of changes in the two variables makes it reasonable to expect a causality from advertising to sales, and not vice versa. If the assumed relationship between the two variables is able to *predict the effect on sales* of advertising increases and decreases, then the exercise gains much credibility.

Before we begin to examine a number of readings of this relationship between change in advertising and change in sales, let us return to the concept of measuring a brand's advertising by its share of voice. There is a simple mathematical aspect of this share that must be clarified. This stems from the fact that not all brands in a market are advertised; in a typical category there could be ten important advertised brands, plus twenty others in fairly broad but patchy distribution that are sold only on price and promotions, these being almost invariably the smallest brands. In such a market, ten brands account for all the advertising, but thirty brands account for the sales. Therefore, the average *advertised* brand will have a larger share of advertising than the average *brand's* share of market, because there are ten of the former and thirty of the latter.

These are 1979 figures for a major packaged goods market (the market used to describe positioning in chapter 3). The ten largest brands are ranked by market share in Table 4.2.

Certain things are clear about this table. First, seven of the ten brands follow the normal pattern that has just been explained, in that for each, the share of advertising exceeds the share of market. The amount by which one exceeds the other depends on the degree of investment spending. Brands G and N, for instance, are relatively new and aggressive brands, which the reader can see reflected in their advertising expenditures.

Table 4.2

Comparison of Share of Market and Share of Advertising Voice

Brand	Share of market by volume (%)	Share of advertising voice (%)
G	3	8
H	3	5
J	4	6
K	5	6
L	6	8
M	7	10
N	8	11
P	10	10
Q	15	12
R	17	13
Other brands	22	11
Total market	100	100

But it will immediately also strike the reader that there is something different about the three largest brands at the bottom of the table. For P the two shares are equal; but for the two largest of all, Q and R, the share of advertising is significantly *smaller* than the share of market. This is an almost universal tendency with big brands and a demonstration of *measurable scale economies* that can be calculated in terms of advertising expenditures. This phenomenon receives general confirmation in Lambin's analysis of 107 European brands.[27]

These scale economies are very real, yet there is a limit below which it is dangerous to reduce the advertising budget. For the largest brands, this limit has to be carefully judged. This can be demonstrated by an examination of five years' figures for brands Q and R (see Table 4.3).

The reader can see from this table how the manufacturer of brand R kept the brand in generally better repair than the manufacturer of brand Q. The latter's share of advertising was on occasion reduced a little too much for safety, and losses of share resulted. Brand R, on the other hand, was advertised at a slightly higher average level. It is a much older brand than Q and, as a result of the manufacturer's marketing skills, has yielded enormous profits over a long period. The brand is a household name, and its profitability must be considerable indeed, with a 17 percent market share financed by a 13 percent advertising share. But from the evidence of the table, expenditure on R is rather carefully evaluated, and the manufacturer is not so greedy for profit that he eschews large absolute advertising investments. The 13 percent in 1979 represents an expenditure well in excess of $10 million—money well spent. Brand R is in fact an excellent example for demonstrating the general invalidity of the life cycle theory; the brand is more than a century old.

Brand Q is an equally instructive example, although for a different reason. Brand Q comes from the same manufacturer as Brand G. The briefest glance

Table 4.3

Progress of Share of Market and Share of Advertising for Two Brands

| | Brand Q | | Brand R | |
	Share of market by volume (%)	Share of advertising voice (%)	Share of market by volume (%)	Share of advertising voice (%)
1975	18	11	18	11
1976	17	9	17	10
1977	17	11	16	9
1978	16	8	16	12
1979	15	12	17	13

at their advertising expenditures will show clearly where the funds for G's investment have come from. The manufacturer has in fact maintained high investment spending for five years on G. Its 1979 market share of 3 percent must have been disappointing and some way below what was necessary for profitable operation. So here we have yet another example of the classic pattern of a disappointing new brand G funded in the main from a large and successful brand Q, which is now also suffering from this unproductive syphoning of expenditure.

This relationship—of large brands as advertising underspenders and small brands as advertising overspenders—has been confirmed by extensive aggregated data. This is discussed in chapter 8, where the relationship is described statistically with the use of the Advertising Intensiveness Curve (AIC).

We now come to a formal exposition of the *long-term* relationship between advertising changes and sales changes. This will be done by means of the important concept of the *dynamic difference,* designed ("discovered" is perhaps a better word) by Unilever analyst Michael Moroney, the author of a well-known textbook on statistics.[28] His book does not mention the dynamic difference, because this device has been used over the past thirty years on a more or less confidential basis by Unilever marketing companies. But ten years after Moroney's original work, it so happened that the model was independently discovered by James Peckham Sr., of A.C. Nielsen and named the Marketing-Advertising Pattern (MAP). Many of the Nielsen findings have now been published, and we shall be quoting these extensively, while at the same time continuing to pay tribute to Moroney's original work.

The mathematics of the model are simple. The reader is advised, however, to dwell on them and to go back over the description until it is understood. The model itself employs a simple diagram in the form of a cross. The data applied to the diagram are based on readings for one brand over two-year periods. What is measured is the *change* between the second year and the first (see Figure 4.1).

On the horizontal axis, we measure the advertising level change. This is represented by the difference between the share of advertising in year 2 and the share of market in year 1 (the dynamic difference). The principle here is that the share of market in year 1 should dictate a "normal" advertising expenditure level. (In fact this would be a slightly subnormal expenditure because, as we have seen, most brands have a share of advertising slightly greater than their market share; hence, if their advertising share is only the same as their market share, they are spending below the norm. This difference is substantially technical, however, because we are examining *changes* and not absolute levels.)

Figure 4.1 **Dynamic Difference Format**

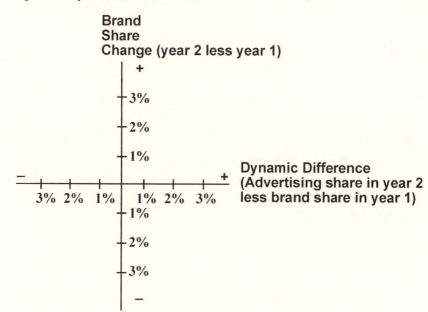

On the vertical axis, we measure the difference in the brand's market share between year 2 and year 1. The diagram is cruciform because movements can be either positive or negative, and positive and negative parts are on different sides of the point of intersection.

Now for each brand, a number of years' experience can be plotted. Based on the experience of more than three hundred brands in five countries, a line can be fitted in about 70 percent of the cases.[29] This 70 percent figure is important. It coincides with the best estimate, discussed in chapter 7, of the proportion of advertising campaigns that have a measurable short-term effect on sales. If the campaign is not effective, the dynamic difference obviously cannot apply to it.

The dynamic difference will rise from left to right (southwest to northeast) if the regression has a normal fit. It will not necessarily cut the center of the cross. And most importantly, the lines will be quite different for each brand in a market: a total category will look something like what we see in Figure 4.2. Peckham makes clear on the basis of substantial empirical evidence that the pattern "is different for every brand in just the same way as human thumbprints differ."[30]

Figure 4.2 **Dynamic Difference: Four Brands**

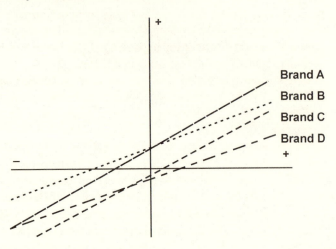

But what does the diagram mean? It exemplifies five major points.

1. The relationship between advertising and brand share is essentially long-term, needing perhaps five years of data to establish. But it is built from year-to-year changes, representing short-term/medium-term sales effects.
2. The slopes for individual brands have the same general shape, rising from bottom left to top right. This should reassure the more skeptical advertisers and afford their agencies fewer sleepless nights, because these slopes indicate a general rule that increases in advertising pressure are associated with increases in market share, and reductions in advertising pressure with reductions in market share. As indicated, the model fits in 70 percent of the cases examined by Nielsen.
3. The model can be of considerable predictive value to a manufacturer. The company must of course be able to estimate what the total advertising expenditure will be in its market in the next year to determine its own share. But on the assumption that it can do this reasonably efficiently, the firm can predict with fair accuracy what market share will result from a given advertising investment. It will also be apparent to the reader that the responsiveness of market share to change in advertising pressure is measured by the slope of the curve. The steeper the slope, the higher the degree of response. Nielsen, by using the model in a total of 500 actual cases, made accurate predictions of market share changes following advertising

pressure changes in 77 percent of the cases in the United States, 71 percent in the United Kingdom, and 68 percent in Germany. Even if they were not precisely accurate, the model's predictions were in the correct direction in 92 percent in the United Kingdom, 86 percent in Germany, and 83 percent in the United States.

4. One important conclusion concerns the best established and most profitable brands. For these, the dynamic difference slope cuts the horizontal axis to the left of the point of intersection, in the way indicated in Figure 4.3.

   In effect a brand such as that in Figure 4.3 is able to hold its market share constant even though its share of advertising is reduced below its market share level. This is precisely the situation for brands Q and R in our earlier example; they could afford to have an expenditure well "below the odds," yet it was possible in many years for them to hold their market shares despite expenditure reductions. The dynamic difference model provides here a quantifiable expression of those brands' added values, which can be seen to provide a benefit that for other brands without such added values costs substantial advertising dollars. This important demonstration and conclusion will be the foundation of an argument concerning pressure reduction experiments we shall make at the end of this book, one addressed directly to large advertisers.

5. The last point is not so positive, and it brings us back to the matter of campaign quality. Thirty percent of campaigns do not work. And of the campaigns that do, more than half have rather a weak effect (see chapter 7). The weak ones are likely also to show a low response to incremental budgetary pressure.

Figure 4.3 **Dynamic Difference: Powerful Brands**

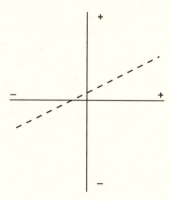

The only too common existence of weak campaigns is a criticism of the advertising scene, and an extra dimension can be added to the dynamic difference to help us quantify the effect of campaign changes. Work carried out in the United Kingdom by Jeremy Elliott of J. Walter Thompson suggests how to do this. Figure 4.4 depicts the Elliott Extension, and it describes the dynamic difference for Kellogg's Rice Krispies for the years 1971–77. It can be seen that the line provides a reasonably good fit for the seven years in question. The line is, of course, upward sloping and cuts the horizontal well to the right of the point of intersection of the axes. The brand shows the effect of a rather weak campaign—one without built-in advertising-related scale economies—since it needs increases in the share of advertising above the market share to maintain the status quo (see Figure 4.4).

But in 1978, the campaign was changed. The new campaign, according to a number of other measures, was highly successful in the marketplace. This success can also be expressed in the dynamic difference model by a new observation that is clearly incompatible with the old regression. What this almost certainly means is an upward shift in the dynamic difference line, although it would need more years of data to confirm the permanence of the new relationship.

A rather dramatic way of using the former regression to evaluate the effect of the new campaign is by estimating that the 1978 sales increase would have needed a dynamic difference of plus or minus 8.5 percentage points of advertising share in excess of brand share if the former advertising–sales relationship had still been in operation. The difference between such an advertising investment and what was actually spent on the brand is equivalent to approximately a million dollars at 1978 media prices—a sharp reminder of the cash value of the creative content of an advertising campaign. It is also a reminder of the value of the dynamic difference model and its versatility in accommodating and quantifying the importance of an unexpected variable.[31]

This is by no means the end of our consideration of advertising weight. Indeed, there is another way of expressing a brand's response to change in pressure: by direct estimates of advertising elasticity. But this procedure is best viewed when compared with estimates of price elasticity, because there can be interesting links between the two. This is the substance of the next section of this chapter.

4. Price

Remember from chapter 3 that although it is difficult to estimate the price elasticity of a new brand for lack of historical data, it is common practice to

Figure 4.4 **The Elliott Extension**

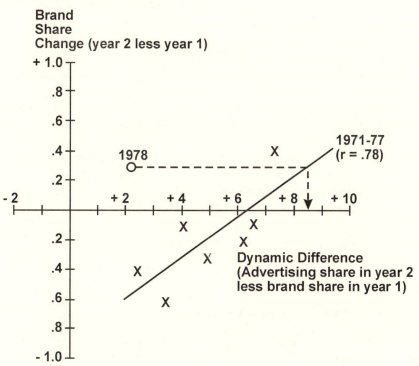

do so for an ongoing brand. We are measuring here the immediate or short-term effect on consumer purchasing of an increase or decrease in price; the elasticity is a calculation of the change in sales resulting from a 1 percent change in price. Manufacturers normally have a lot of information to help them with the calculations because they can use regional as well as national retail audit figures. National data alone are sometimes enough—even a simple series like the following Nielsen data for a real brand. In this particular instance, we can judge by eye that the brand has a pronounced price elasticity.[32] Note that as the price premium is reduced, the market share goes up, whereas in the single occasion (Year 4) in which the price premium is increased, market share goes down markedly.

The prices stated in this example are expressed as price premium above other brands, because by doing this we can eliminate the overall influence of inflation, which can be assumed to affect all brands in a more or less similar way (see Table 4.4).

Empirical studies tend to show quite a high degree of price elasticity for most brands within the limits explored. This qualification is important, because it can be dangerous to extrapolate the figures too far. However, since the operational value of price elasticity is to help to make marginal price adjustments, the limited span of the data does not matter too much. Simon Broadbent, former head of research at the London office of Leo Burnett, has published the following distribution of elasticities for 105 brands (some taken from other published studies), which show a relatively uniform progression. Broadbent's average is fairly close to other published estimates (see Table 4.5).[33]

As a general confirmation of the relatively high degree of price elasticity for most brands, it has been estimated by econometric techniques that anything between 65 percent and 85 percent of the short-term variability of sales of most consumer brands can be explained by price alone.[34]

Table 4.4

Price Premium and Market Share

Year	Price premium (cents)	Market share (%)
1	7.3	19.9
2	5.6	21.1
3	3.9	23.6
4	6.6	20.0
5	5.8	22.8
6	5.1	25.5
7	5.0	26.6
8	4.6	26.5
9	3.9	28.1

Table 4.5

Range of Price Elasticity

Price elasticity range	Number of brands
0 to −0.49	22
−0.50 to −0.99	20
−1.00 to −1.49	26
−1.50 to −1.99	16
−2.00 and over	21
Average −1.32	105

Another important related concept is the break-even elasticity, or the amount by which volume sales could be reduced before a 1 percent price increase reduces *profit*. In an examination of twenty-three brands handled by the London office of (then) D'Arcy, MacManus, and Masius, the agency's operations director, Andrew Roberts, tabulated the distribution of both their actual price elasticities and their break-even elasticities. His actual price elasticities show a reasonably broad spread with an average figure of –1.67, a marginally higher figure than Broadbent's. But Roberts's calculation of break-even elasticities yields a most important conclusion: "Overall, these results suggest that half of the brands are seriously underpriced."[35] In this range of examples, the price could be raised without any great effect on sales, and the higher price would of course go virtually entirely into increased profit. Naturally, most of the brands to which this applies have the lower levels of elasticity. Thus, although price elasticities as a whole tend to be quite pronounced, the range is so great that there are many brands at the inelastic end that provide their manufacturers with significant opportunities for profit improvement by price increases.

These analyses should provide most manufacturers with food for thought and encourage them to take a hard, objective look at their present prices and the way they are set. But there is still more that can be done, because advertising is also an activity to which the elasticity concept can be applied. What is measured here is the short-term sales response to a change in advertising pressure (again within fairly narrow limits). The elasticity measure is the percentage change in sales following a 1 percent change in advertising. The reader should note that the relationship here is direct, with an increase in one leading to an increase in the other (unlike price elasticity, where the relationship is inverse).

Broadbent's data for eighty-four brands show a range that is very broadly representative of the field as a whole (see Table 4.6).[36]

As is obvious from this table, advertising elasticity tends to be less pronounced than price elasticity. But the break-even advertising elasticity is generally quite close to the actual advertising elasticity, so that in most cases manufacturers do not have the opportunity to boost profit simply by increasing advertising within the present parameters of the brand's response to marketplace stimuli.

The operational value of Broadbent's and Roberts's work is the way in which price elasticity and advertising elasticity can be treated together, with the intention of guiding manufacturers toward optimizing their profits. This parallel calculation is an especially good way of estimating the extra profit

Table 4.6

Range of Advertising Elasticity

Advertising elasticity range	Number of brands
0 to 0.09	27
0.10 to 0.19	27
0.20 to 0.29	12
0.30 to 0.39	5
0.40 to 0.49	4
0.50 and over	9
Average 0.20	84

provided by a price increase, and the further extra profit provided by applying some of the price-related extra profit to increased advertising. All that Broadbent and Roberts claim for the technique is the ability to set directions with limited objectives. But even in this, they are talking of profit optimization in a greatly more calculated and precise way than is done at present in the vast majority of businesses. It is regrettable but generally true that manufacturers and their advertising agencies make insufficient use of historical information in their possession. This is mainly due to a lack of experience in handling such data; they simply are not conscious of its potential operational value. This lack of experience is compounded by shortages of time and of statistical skills.[37]

There has also been a good deal of work in the United States in the exploration of advertising elasticity. Elasticities for a number of unspecified American brands have been published by Nariman Dhalla, formerly of J. Walter Thompson.[38] Dhalla's range of twenty-one short-term elasticities is not dissimilar to Broadbent's, with an average of 0.23 (compared with Broadbent's 0.20). But what makes Dhalla's analyses especially interesting is that he calculates for each short-term elasticity a long-term or cumulative elasticity as well. This is generally a good deal higher than the short-term figure, especially for cigarettes, liquor, gasoline, and proprietary drugs. What Dhalla is saying is that advertising has a measurable cumulative effect on sales in the long term over and beyond its immediate effect on sales in the short term. "Advertising may lead directly to sales; and many new buyers, being satisfied with the brand, may repeat the purchase. Or, the advertising stimulus, instead of winning fresh converts, may increase brand usage per customer; and this habit may persist far into the future."[39] This describes neatly the beneficial effect on sales, first, of favorable consumer experience that comes from use of the brand, and second, of the added values that come from advertising. These are topics discussed in chapter 8.

A consideration of such long-term effects brings us to the final and most dramatic demonstration of the use of market data to illustrate the workings of advertising. This analysis relates strictly to price. The technique, which was pioneered by Tom Corlett, formerly of J. Walter Thompson, London, and confirmed by further empirical work by his colleague Jeremy Elliott, demonstrates a clear operational distinction between the short and long term. It will be remembered that the dynamic difference, although it is built from a series of short-term changes, is really an examination of a long-term relationship. Similarly, what Corlett's work demonstrates is a short-term situation and how this changes in the longer term.

Corlett's starting point was to build a demand curve for a brand. He chose a major British brand in a large packaged goods category. This calculation was possible because the brand is sold at various price premiums above other brands in different geographical regions, with resultant differences in the brand's market share. Thus a range of data could be provided for a fairly short time period. The demand curve follows the normal descending slope we would expect from a study of microeconomics.

The price is expressed as the premium over other brands, thus eliminating the effect of inflation (the practice followed by Nielsen in the example quoted at the beginning of this section). This also means that what is measured on one axis—the price of one brand compared with others in the market—is entirely consistent with what is measured on the other axis—the sales of one brand compared with others in the market.

The second stage in Corlett's work is the construction of a similar demand curve for a later period, after the exposure of advertising. The campaign had initially been judged to be highly successful on the basis of all available objective measures: ex-factory sales, market share, attitudinal and other qualitative research, and popularity polls. But the best demonstration of the campaign's success is Corlett's analysis of the brand after the campaign's exposure, because his demand curve had moved quite significantly to the right (seen in Fig. 4.5); this is described as the Corlett Shift.

Figure 4.5 clearly shows that, after the advertising:

- At a given price premium, the brand could now command a quantifiably greater brand share.
- At a given brand share, the brand could now command a quantifiably greater price premium.

This enables us to make estimates of marginal sales revenue added by the campaign—estimates that can also be compared with the cost of the campaign to indicate its marginal profitability to the manufacturer.[40] Jeremy Elliott shows a parallel movement of the demand curve in his description of the

Figure 4.5 **The Corlett Shift**

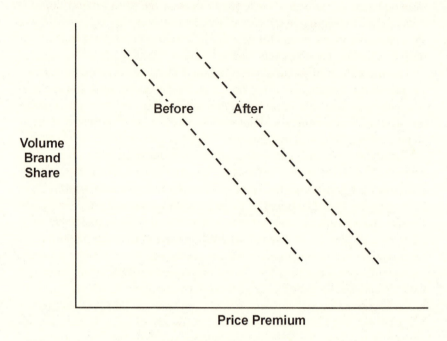

Kellogg's Rice Krispies case.[41] And Eskin's work in the United States, although more complex, has similarities of method.[42]

5. Distribution

The reader will remember from chapter 3 that even for a new brand with growing distribution, shops running out of stock can be a problem, in that they can cause widespread switching away from a brand to its competitors during the period just before the end of its sales cycle. With an ongoing brand, although the absolute level of distribution is generally steady once the distributional base has been built, the disappearance of retail stocks remains a real and continuous problem.

This can put consumers in a dilemma. They will normally buy a substitute brand if the brand they are looking for is not available (i.e., changing brands within the store). This will happen in 58 percent of cases, according to Nielsen data. If the size they seek is not on the shelf, they will buy another size of the same brand in 52 percent of cases or buy a different brand altogether in a further 30 percent of cases. Retailers should realize that in the case of the missing brand, 42 percent of customers will leave the store with no purchase in the product category. In the case of the missing size, 18 percent will leave (i.e., changing stores within the brand).[43] These represent absolute losses of business, in most cases to other stores.

This dilemma is by no means uncommon. Extensive Nielsen data describe the product categories in which homemakers are more loyal and those in which they are less loyal to the brand they are looking for. Among the categories in which homemakers will not readily accept a substitute are dentifrice, instant coffee, floor wax, and detergents. Among the categories in which substitutes are more readily acceptable are toilet tissues, crackers, ready-to-eat cereals, and canned beans. During the course of a year, homemakers will buy a number of different brands, but on many individual shopping trips they will be looking for a specific brand (perhaps for use by a particular member of the family) and will not buy another if this first choice is not available. Interestingly enough, Nielsen shows a degree of correlation between the long-term level of advertising investments and the product fields in which customers are unwilling to substitute. This is but one example of the many beneficial side effects of advertising: its long-term effect on brand loyalty.

Retailers running out of stock remain a stubborn problem, with dangers of marginal but real losses of business. A normal out-of-stock level is considered to be 3 percent. With computerized stock control linked to the checkout, there is no reason for manufacturers and retailers to accept even as much as this. But 6 percent and more is by no means uncommon. With the resultant level of sales loss (which is as much as 6 percent of case sales over a year in a specific and typical Nielsen example), manufacturers, even more than retailers, will continue to pay a significant penalty for their inability to solve what is in essence a relatively simple mechanical problem, and one that it is in the interests of manufacturers and retailers alike to solve.

Beyond the Primary Growth Cycle

Now that we have reviewed the factors that matter most to an ongoing brand, we can direct our attention to the future and the path that a brand will normally take if it is to be a long-term contender in a market. Whether its long-term sales trend is going to be upward, static, or even declining, its path will commonly ebb and flow in accordance with regular planned and announced improvements, a process known as restaging or recycling (commonly known in Europe as relaunching). This is a normal and indeed necessary strategy for companies in competitive markets. There is strong Nielsen evidence from

both the United States and Great Britain that recycling is a much more efficient means of increasing market share than attempting to maintain the impetus of brands without the novelty and incentive for consumer reappraisal that
recycling provides. In fact, for a brand that is *not* restaged, odds are about 3
to 1 that it will not increase its long-term market share.[44]

A restage covers a shorter period than the primary growth cycle for a brand,
perhaps one year compared with two for the primary cycle.[45] This does not
mean that a brand is recycled every year; but the recycle stage, which occurs
once every three or four years, itself lasts for about a year. In view of the lead
time for the necessary change in product, packaging, and advertising, planning is needed at least a year in advance of the beginning of the recycle. As
suggested at the beginning of this chapter, the manufacturer of a new brand
will need to be thinking about the first restage as soon as an initial launch is
under way. In this process, continuous product testing of the brand in comparison with competitors (a topic discussed in chapter 3) provides valuable
guidance for desirable functional improvements.

Although with restaging there is still a continuously important role for
functional improvement, advertising now joins functional performance in the
front-running position, becoming one of the two dominant influences on the
development of a brand, cementing the loyalty of early users, and working
with other stimuli to extend the consumer franchise. By this time the added
values will have begun to accumulate.

Nielsen data from the history of 320 different brands make it clear that 61
percent of the vehicles for recycling are connected with advertising. We are
talking here about the 41 percent of recycles that involve product innovation
plus increased advertising investments and new campaigns, a further 10 percent involving merely increased advertising expenditure, and a further 10
percent again involving more expenditure and new campaigns. The question
of a new campaign for a restage is a matter of careful judgment. Although the
task of advertising during the primary growth cycle is mainly to contribute
(together with consumer promotions and packaging) to meeting the first object of consumer trial, these introductory advertising campaigns often quite
rightly contain first indications of the added values that will become more
important during the subsequent life of the brand. The added values to be
built up in the long term will also be expressed in the pack designs, which
should be planned sensitively to promise more for the brand than functional
performance alone.

During a brand's long-term development there will be a continued and
growing advertising emphasis on those added values that soon become its
unique property. With progressive restaging, product improvements can be
evaluated alongside the established and accepted battery of functional and

nonfunctional benefits that the brand provides. Recycling is thus the opportunity for the manufacturer to bring a brand now and again quite sharply to the attention of existing users and potential new users alike. By this time these people will probably know quite a lot about the brand, but this is the opportunity for the manufacturer to encourage them to look at it with fresh eyes and be made aware that it is not falling behind in functional performance, but instead is being improved to meet the challenge of newer brands.

Restaging, however, is not only a means of introducing functional improvements. It is also extremely useful for the introduction of new variants (types, flavors, colors, and so forth), which, if the manufacturer judges the situation well, can add market share to a brand without cannibalizing its existing sales. The word *new* is of great value in all matters of communication (packaging and display as well as advertising) in which the consumer is encouraged to reappraise a brand. *New* has always had a special connotation in advertising circles; most experienced copywriters attest to its continued value and the way that it should be used for as long a period as possible after the beginning of a restage.[46] There is also a group of related words (*now, announcing, introducing, improvement,* for example) that offend the fastidious because of their overuse. But successful writers of advertisements harden their hearts to such niceties. David Ogilvy is such a one: "Don't turn up your nose at these clichés. They may be shopworn but they work."[47]

The Argument in Brief

The initial sales of virtually all successful brands of packaged goods follow a similar pattern in that they rise to an early peak and then settle down to a lower, steadier level. The rise is partially influenced by increasing distribution, but more heavily by increasing sales per store, an indication of consumer repeat purchase. Simple models based on test market experience can be applied to the earliest retail audit data measuring national sales and distribution, and these can be used to forecast the path of sales during the period (which averages rather more than two years) before a brand reaches its stable national level. This period is tending to shorten as markets become more crowded and competitive. This puts increased emphasis on the importance of early plans for restaging.

Trade and consumer promotions account for more money than advertising, out of the average manufacturer's total expenditure above and below the line. There is a significant dissonance between the short-term demand for promotions to increase sales and the long-term (but normally less insistent) demand for advertising to increase the numbers and loyalty of consumers.

This dissonance is frequently expressed by budgetary adjustments—a move of funds from above to below the line—during the last quarter of any year, under unplanned and often crisis conditions, to enable tonnage sales targets to be met. The pressures to increase promotions are increasing over time because of the growing strength of the retail trade.

Advertising, expressed as a share of advertising voice in a market, can be viewed in parallel with the market share of an individual brand. For large brands, the market share normally *exceeds* the advertising share; for smaller brands, the opposite is true. This general relationship is strong evidence for the existence of advertising-related scale economies for large brands.

This chapter has examined the influence of advertising share on market share, allowing for the possible contamination of the reverse influence of the sales level on the advertising level. In the cases of about 70 percent of ongoing brands, there is a relationship between advertising and sales that is both linear and causal. This figure is harmonious with what we know from other sources about the success rate of ongoing campaigns. The dynamic difference regression describing this relationship can be used for two purposes: first, to predict the effect on market share of a change in advertising weight within the regression; and second, to demonstrate the financial productivity of any campaign change having effects beyond its limits.

The marginal extra productivity of a new campaign can also be estimated approximately by the use of the shifting demand curve. Another productive device, the use of advertising and price elasticities, can be used not only for sales maximization, but also for sales optimization, with the aim of pushing profit to its peak. Although the data needed to compute these elasticities are difficult to put together, the technique of manipulating them operationally is relatively simple to understand and apply. The other mathematical methods discussed in this chapter are in general easier to compute, and they are quite simple in their application.

Notes

1. See, for example, Don E. Schultz and William A. Robinson, *Sales Promotion Management* (Chicago: Crain Books, 1982), pp. 469–480; and Robert M. Prentice, "How to Split Your Marketing Funds Between Advertising and Promotion," *Advertising Age* (January 10, 1977): 41–44.

2. James O. Peckham Sr., *The Wheel of Marketing,* 2d edition, 1981 (privately published but available from A.C. Nielsen). The data here came from a study produced by *Progressive Grocer.*

3. Ibid., p. 18.

4. Ibid., pp. 78–80; and *Nielsen Researcher* (May–June 1967): 3–7.

5. John Davis, *The Sales Curves of New Products* (London: J. Walter Thompson, 1965).

6. Peckham, *The Wheel of Marketing,* p. 5.

7. F. Beaven Ennis, *Marketing Norms for Product Managers* (New York: Association of National Advertisers, 1985), p. 81. But estimates made in the late 1990s show an increased percentage going to promotions, more in line with Peckham's figure. John Philip Jones, "Trends in Promotions" in *The Advertising Business. Operations, Creativity, Media Planning, Integrated Communications,* John Philip Jones, ed. (Thousand Oaks, CA: Sage, 1999), p. 321.

8. Prentice, "How to Split Your Marketing Funds," p. 42.

9. Peckham, *The Wheel of Marketing,* pp. 46–47, 49–50.

10. John A. Quelch, "It's Time to Make Trade Promotions More Productive," *Harvard Business Review* (May–June 1983): 130–136.

11. Peckham, *The Wheel of Marketing,* p. 48.

12. This point was raised in chapter 2 in connection with the displays of generic cornflakes and Kellogg's. See chapter 2, note 54.

13. Peckham, *The Wheel of Marketing,* p. 44.

14. Ibid., pp. 43–44.

15. Quelch, "It's Time to Make Trade Promotions More Productive," pp. 135–136.

16. Peckham, *The Wheel of Marketing,* pp. 58–59.

17. Stephen King, *What Is a Brand?* (London: J. Walter Thompson, 1970), p. 5.

18. Andrew Roberts, "The Decision Between Above and Below the Line," *Admap* (December 1980): 588–592.

19. *Nielsen Researcher* (July–August 1973): 4.

20. Peckham, *The Wheel of Marketing,* p. 57.

21. Ibid., p. 63.

22. King, *What Is a Brand?* pp. 5–7.

23. Peckham, *The Wheel of Marketing,* pp. 61–62.

24. James Webb Young, *The Diary of an Ad Man* (Chicago: Business Books, 1944, reprinted 1990), p. 230.

25. Stephen King, *Advertising as a Barrier to Market Entry* (London: Advertising Association, 1980), p. 15.

26. Peckham, *The Wheel of Marketing,* p. 101.

27. Jean Jacques Lambin, *Advertising, Competition and Market Conduct in Oligopoly Over Time* (New York: American Elsevier, 1976), pp. 127–129.

28. M.J. Moroney, *Facts from Figures* (Harmondsworth, Middlesex, UK: Penguin, 1951).

29. Peckham, *The Wheel of Marketing,* p. 108. The regression can be described algebraically or geometrically. The latter has been chosen because it makes for easier exposition.

30. Ibid., p. 113.

31. Jeremy Elliott, "Kellogg's Rice Krispies: The Effect of a New Creative Execution," in *Advertising Works: Papers from the I.P.A. Effectiveness Awards,* Simon Broadbent, ed. (London: Holt, Rinehart and Winston, 1981), pp. 86–87.

32. Peckham, *The Wheel of Marketing,* p. 32.

33. Simon Broadbent, "Price and Advertising: Volume and Profit," *Admap* (No-

vember 1980): 536. See also Gerard J. Tellis, "The Price Elasticity of Selective Demand: A Meta-Analysis of Economic Models of Sales," *Journal of Marketing Research* (November 1988): 331–341.

34. Tom Corlett, "Anyone for Econometrics?" *Admap* (August 1978).

35. Roberts, "The Decision Between Above and Below the Line," p. 592.

36. Broadbent, "Price and Advertising: Volume and Profit," p. 536. See also Gert Assmus, John J. Farlet, and Donald R. Lehmann, "How Advertising Affects Sales: A Meta-analysis of Econometric Results," *Journal of Marketing Research* (February 1984): 65–74.

37. Simon Broadbent, "Practical Economics and Computing at Brand Level," *International Journal of Advertising* (January–March 1983): 3–15.

38. Nariman K. Dhalla, "Assessing the Long Term Value of Advertising," *Harvard Business Review* (January–February 1978): 87–95.

39. Ibid., p. 87.

40. Tom Corlett, "How to Make Sense of Market Analysis," *Campaign* (May 26, 1978).

41. Elliott, "Kellogg's Rice Krispies," pp. 84–85. Both Corlett and Elliott put the price on the horizontal axis and quantity on the vertical, the opposite of how they are plotted in normal diagrams describing price theory. But this does not affect the analysis.

42. Gerald J. Eskin, "A Case for Test Market Experiments," *Journal of Advertising Research* (April 1975): 27–33.

43. Peckham, *The Wheel of Marketing,* p. 27.

44. *Nielsen Researcher* (May–June 1967): 6–7.

45. Peckham, *The Wheel of Marketing,* pp. 82–83.

46. This period has been set rather arbitrarily by the Federal Trade Commission at six months. Samm Sinclair Baker, *The Permissible Lie* (Cleveland: World Publishing, 1968), p. 24.

47. David Ogilvy, *Confessions of an Advertising Man* (New York: Atheneum, 1963, reprinted 1984), pp. 105–106.

5

The Mature Brand and the Consumer: The Nature of Repeat-Buying Theory

This chapter concerns uniformity and regularity. The reader may be surprised that such words could ever be used to describe matters as naturally erratic and subject to the vagaries of competition as the marketing and advertising of a brand. The previous two chapters were devoted to the most important factors that shape a brand from its conception to its maturity; and although there are a respectable number of consistent and generalizable underlying patterns, these are far short of anything deserving to be described as uniform and regular.

This chapter will demonstrate that the mature brand that has joined the user's repertoire and has its position in a mature market acquires some of the stasis of that market. When this happens, the role of advertising changes from aggressively promoting growth to a more restrained protection of the status quo.

There are many circumstances in which a manufacturer may indeed not give much priority to increasing the sales and market share of his brands. Four of the most obvious are

1. If the marginal extra profit yielded by the extra sales is less than the advertising and other costs required to achieve these sales.
2. If the growth in the market share of one brand carries the danger of

clipping a share point or two off other brands the firm markets, with the result that the overall share is not much increased.

3. If the resultant total increase in company market share will make the firm vulnerable to investigation by the Federal Trade Commission (or its equivalent in other countries).

4. If the company has other priorities for funds and management time.

The larger a manufacturer becomes, the more these circumstances will operate; the greater will be his stake in the market and his interest in its preservation; and the more the firm will act protectively—especially in product, marketing, and advertising strategies—to maintain the existing situation.

The reader may wonder whether the regularity and uniformity to be described shortly might in any way be created by manufacturers' strategies, particularly by the repetition of strong advertising. The answer is probably no. Manufacturers' strategies, in particular those for their advertising, do not have strong force in a world of free choice. They cannot create demand dynamically or radically alter beliefs. This fundamental limitation is the ultimate reason why so many new brands fail: manufacturers are inefficient at discovering things that have real potential interest to consumers, and they cannot build business with anything less. The consumer *always* has the upper hand.

Consumer behavior itself shows regularity. Consider the response to advertising stimuli. Where the influence of an advertisement can be isolated from the other variables in the marketing mix, there is an invariable regularity of patterns—if advertisements A, B, and C yield different results from one group of consumers, they will almost certainly yield the same differences among other groups of consumers. The evidence for this statement comes from the field of direct response. Indeed, there is first-hand unpublished evidence that consumers in one *country* respond to advertisements in a way that is closely similar to that of consumers in another country.[1] Facts of this sort are normally lacking in debates on the controversial and much misunderstood subject of international advertising.

If readers remain skeptical about this uniformity of response to campaigns (or about the separate question of whether direct response can provide a reliable measure of trends in nonspecialist fields), they should consider the vast worldwide use of well-known advertising strategies and campaigns in the most substantial and competitive consumer product fields. And although there is a scarcity of hard facts on the testing of such procedures in an experimental, scientific way, the overwhelming *opinion* of advertisers and agencies, based on their direct and often extensive experience, is that such strategies and campaigns are effective in most circumstances. And they work with a sometimes surprising uniformity of effect in countries that are far apart geographically as well as in culture, income, and sophistication.[2]

Response to advertising is not, however, the main subject matter of this chapter. We are concerned here with patterns of consumer buying and their relevance to a brand's advertising strategy. An individual's purchasing behavior may at first glance appear erratic and haphazard. But the more we study such behavior over time, and the more we look at the aggregate behavior of large numbers of consumers, the more regular and predictable it all appears to be.

Previous chapters used retail audit data to study total volumes of sales. These data, of course, are the result of the accumulation of many individual buying decisions. But we have not begun to study the purchasing process itself, only its overall effects. We have seen, for instance, that changes in advertising pressure can lead to differences in sales. But the problem with using these data is that they tell us the "what" but certainly not the "how." If we wish to explore the "how," we must work from the assumption that the consumer sees and/or hears the advertising and responds in some way. To examine this process, we are forced to look at parts of the mechanism of our large machine that are well below the surface. And to make such an examination, we shall need research information that is different from the aggregated data we have used in the analysis so far.

We shall now need to look at the purchasing behavior of individual consumers over time. We can do this only by studying data, collected with the use of diaries or by continuous electronic tracking of buying, that expose what brands are bought, on what occasions, and by whom.

There is a second problem with concentrating on aggregated data, one that will be important when we study specifically the effects of advertising exposure. Aggregated data can create a misleading appearance of a direct association between a brand's advertising and its sales, when in fact the advertising and sales might be separately influenced by an unconnected third factor. A well-known example of this is the presence of children, which causes a household to use more of certain brands and to watch more television. It is therefore often misleading to attribute high sales of brand A to heavy television advertising for that brand. The household heavily using brand A may also be exposed to considerable advertising for competing brands, just because the television may be on for longer periods than the average. There is therefore no certainty that it is the brand A advertising that has the decisive effect.[3]

These problems are avoided if we concentrate on the study of individual consumers' diary records. If we are examining the influence of a brand's advertising on its sales, we can relate individual buyers' purchasing to their exposure to advertising and thus establish real rather than spurious relationships. Diary studies, because of the way they track data through time, are sometimes described as longitudinal. They produce large quantities of data that are extremely cumbersome to handle. Researchers, however, have developed the techniques and the patience to interpret the information, and this chapter is illustrated virtually exclusively by data collected by this means. The technique is also used in chapter 7.

Let us start by looking at typical purchasing patterns. Remember the points made in chapter 1 that the average homemaker buys a brand not once but repeatedly, and that she or he normally buys more than one brand in any product field. Individual purchasing patterns, when viewed longitudinally, can look something like the following. The letters refer to specific brands and to real homemakers. There are different patterns that occur regularly, and these can be described in the following ways (see Table 5.1).

The patterns are commonly much more complex, with one type superimposed on others, as in the following example of one homemaker's purchases of different brands of tea:

BOOcGBOCOBGBGABBGBBcBGBCBBGGBBB

This customer "shows a trend toward brand B and a cycle in buying brand G, which recurs on average every 4.4 times."[4] This housewife made thirty-one purchases in the product category. She bought her favorite brand, B, on fifteen occasions and her next favorite, G, seven times.

This complexity may surprise readers not familiar with why homemakers need to buy a number of different brands. At least three factors are at work. First, there is the need for more than one functionally different brand for different purposes; brand choice is determined here by the homemaker's judgment of the different brands' functional performance for these different purposes. Second, the consumer is normally buying for other members of the household and for visitors, who in turn have different functional needs. Third, homemakers want variety as such, a factor that makes it easier than might first appear for a manufacturer to get people to try a new brand once. These

---

Table 5.1

Patterns of Consumer Purchasing

Cyclical:	AEAEAEA
Trend:	AAACCAACBABBB
Conversion:	AAABBBBBB
Spasmodic peak:	EEEEEBBBBBEEEE

three explanations, provided by the British analyst John Treasure, are amplified by a battery of data demonstrating the degree of multibrand purchasing in different markets. Treasure examines fifty different product fields over a six-month period and finds multibrand purchasing in every one of them, although the number of buyers who buy more than one brand varies greatly, from a low of 17 percent for starch to a high of 87 percent for butter and margarine. Typically 50 percent of buyers in a market buy two brands or more.[5]

But only rarely do homemakers split their patronage equally between brands. "For most housewives a brand either accounts for a high proportion of her purchases or for a very low proportion . . . although there may be several brands on the housewife's shopping list, she tends to have one particular favorite."[6] This introduces the notion of the homemaker's major and minor brands, which will be important to us when we consider advertising strategy. But to put a major brand into proper perspective, it must not be thought that it is by any means a dominant purchase in any product field for normal homemakers. On the contrary, an individual's combined purchases of other brands will usually be greater than purchases of her major brand. A homemaker is likely to have a single major brand in a product field plus a handful of minor brands, and these various brands will all be bought at different regularities. "A major characteristic of frequently bought goods is that consumers vary greatly in how often they buy them."[7]

However, despite the complexity and seeming irregularity of purchasing patterns, there is a large degree of underlying consistency. To illustrate this we shall be referring extensively to the work of Andrew Ehrenberg, the British academic now recognized as the most informed student of the *facts* of consumer purchasing behavior and a major contributor to our understanding of the role of advertising in influencing this behavior. We shall be referring to the underlying theory described in his classic monograph, *Repeat-Buying: Theory and Applications,*[8] and to data from various American markets published in *Understanding Buying Behavior,* a series of essays he wrote in cooperation with his colleague G.L. Goodhardt. The data base is wide, covering more than thirty product fields, leading brands in each field, different pack sizes, the United States and various European countries, a thirty-year time span, various demographic subgroups, and periods of time ranging from one week to twelve months.[9]

The work of Ehrenberg and other analysts on this enormous data base disclosed patterns of consumer behavior consistent enough to form the basis of mathematical models. With their use, predictions of behavior patterns in other markets were compared with observed behavior, and prediction and reality generally more or less coincided, thus providing validation for the models. This procedure was carried out so extensively that we are able without exaggeration to talk of generalizable patterns.

The assumption underlying these patterns is that the market in which they hold must conform to the stable conditions described in chapter 3. As a specific illustration of these conditions, we shall describe some other features of the real market used for the discussion of brand positioning in chapter 3 and advertising weight and share of market in chapter 4.

In this particular category, the data show an 8 percent advance in total volume in the five years 1974–79, or an average growth of under 2 percent per annum. In the most recent two years, the total size of the market did not change by a fraction of a percentage point. As far as individual brands are concerned, the reader will remember from chapter 4 that the market shares of the ten leading brands totaled 78 percent in 1979. Their combined shares in 1974 had totaled 72 percent, but in 1974 only nine of the ten had been on the market. The tenth brand, introduced in the intervening period, reached a market share of over 7 percent in 1979. None of the remaining brands, however, gained or lost brand share by more than a point or two, except for brand Q, described in chapter 4, which lost three points of share, from a high of 18 percent in 1975 to a low of 15 percent in 1979, mainly because its manufacturer did not sustain the necessary volume of advertising support.

This typical market exhibits then only modest mutation over the years, and nothing resembling strong trends that in Ehrenberg and Goodhardt's definition would make a market nonstationary. The assumption of stability, or normal conditions, provides only the underlying conditions for the model. The assumption of these conditions has a further use, because exceptions that they sometimes throw up can be explained in terms of nonstationary elements. For instance, if consumer purchasing of a brand does not appear to be happening as predicted, this is probably happening because there is something abnormal about that brand: it is following an upward or downward sales trend. It is normally possible to isolate the reasons for this trend, assess the relative importance of such reasons, and thereby draw operational conclusions.

Consumer Sales Defined in Consumer Terms

We are now in a position to get much closer to what sales actually represent than are the earlier aggregate figures, which were based on either a manufacturer's shipments or retail audit estimates. We need now to approach consumers more closely to obtain details of their behavior so as to understand more adequately how this behavior can be influenced by advertising. A single example of the available alternative choices would be to increase sales either by getting new customers to make a first purchase or by getting existing buyers to buy more often. We cannot tell which is the better alternative until we understand more about consumers and their buying habits.

In consumer terms, sales of a brand in any period can be calculated from the equation in Table 5.2.[10]

Looking at one fairly important brand in the U.S. breakfast cereal market, Nabisco Shredded Wheat, we can estimate sales over a particular four-week period at 3 million lbs. This is calculated from our equation as done in Table 5.3.

Of the five elements on the right-side of the equation, two are more or less constant, varying little between brands (or between time periods of the same length in the short and medium term). These are the size of the household population and the average number of packs per purchase. A third point is that, in most categories, pack sizes tend to be uniform. The remaining two factors are the penetration (proportion of households buying a brand) and the number of purchase occasions per buyer. These *do* vary between brands, especially the proportion of households that buy (the brand's penetration).

As explained, the equation relates to a four-week period, but a similar figure could be worked out for any purchasing period, although the shortest one that is worth looking at is normally a week. Remember, purchasing be-

---

Table 5.2

Analysis of Sales in Consumer Terms

Sales = number of households in the country
          × proportion of households buying the brand at least once
          × number of purchase occasions per buyer
          × number of packs per purchase
          × weight or price per pack

Table 5.3

Example of Analysis of Sales in Consumer Terms

Sales of 3.0 million lb. = 85.4 million households in the United States
                             × 0.034 (the 3.4 percent who bought in four weeks)
                             × 1.3 purchase occasions per buyer
                             × 1.05 packs per purchase
                             × 3/4 lb. (12 oz.) per pack

havior takes more regular forms as we consider longer periods of time. Behavior that may seem erratic on a week-by-week basis looks very regular when looked at over months, quarters, or years. We shall therefore confine ourselves to periods of four weeks, thirteen weeks, and fifty-two weeks.

Returning to the equation, we can see that sales in a period can be determined from the penetration and the purchase frequency, on the assumption that we also know the three other factors, which is normally possible in practice, since they are mostly constants. Ehrenberg's models can now be used to extend our knowledge. From the facts of penetration and purchase frequency, it is possible to predict three other important measures: frequency distribution, repeat buying, and multibrand buying. This is enough information to enable us to understand consumer purchasing in a market clearly and precisely. Here are the five key variables:

Penetration: percentage (normally of households) buying at least one pack of a brand during a defined period;

Purchase frequency: number of times the average buyer buys the brand during that period;

Frequency distribution: number of buyers who buy a brand at different frequencies (once, twice and so forth) during the period;

Repeat buying: percentage of buyers who continue to buy the brand during the *next* period;

Multibrand buying: percentage of buyers who also purchase another brand or brands during the period being measured.

All these factors must relate to time periods of the same length. But the mathematical models (whose workings will be illustrated) function equally well no matter what time period is chosen, so long as it is constant. We can compare week with week, month with month, quarter with quarter, or year with year.

Note that the word *penetration* has a special and precise meaning for the percentage buying at least one pack of brand in a particular period. Confusingly enough, the word is used in at least three other senses in the marketing literature. In the Bates advertising agency it is "the number of people who remember your current advertising." The unpenetrated are those who do not remember.[11] In the automobile market, it means the market share of a single make of car. It is also sometimes used to mean the percentage of people who have ever bought a brand.[12] The reader must be careful not to be misled by these different meanings, but to concentrate on the precise meaning used in the present context: the proportion of buyers in a stated and limited time period.

Of these five factors, the key ones are *penetration* and *purchase frequency*. Their importance is such that all other variables in some way stem from them. In fact the main use of the mathematical models is to make projections of the other factors on the simple basis of estimates of penetration and purchase frequency in one period.

Predictive Models in Action

This chapter concerns typical applications of the models described by Ehrenberg. Mathematically inclined readers should note the technical background and the algebra he uses to discuss these models.[13] We have attempted to write this chapter in simple English.

Ehrenberg's work is based on three main models. First is the negative binomial distribution (NBD), and the second, a simplified version of this, the logarithmic series distribution (LSD). These relate to the purchase of a single brand in a stationary market. They have a strong empirical base and have been extensively validated. "Given the value of the brand's penetration and average purchase frequency in some specific 'base period' like a particular quarter of a year, the models can predict all the detailed aspects of buying frequency in that time period and also in any other periods of any length."[14] Third is the Dirichlet model (named after a nineteenth-century German mathematician) dealing with multibrand buying. It fits well with the observed data, but the empirical base and the amount of validation are not as extensive as with the NBD/LSD models. The Dirichlet model can predict penetration and average purchase frequencies for different brands on the basis of the market share of each and certain characteristics of the product category as a whole: the percentage of households that bought any brands in the category in the period in question, the average frequency of purchase of the buyers, and the average frequency of purchase of the average brand.

We are now going to examine some applications of these models. The data relate to real and typical brands. But the models are not just illustrative. They are capable of providing precise estimates for any brands and markets in which a reader may be interested and can provide the appropriate data inputs.

The original analyses frequently provided two sets of data—the theoretical figures provided by the model and the observed data provided directly by consumer research (collected and tabulated to verify the predictions of the model). The two series are mostly closely similar to one another. But when we have had a choice of data, what was observed has been selected in place of what was predicted, and this is what we shall mainly see in the following tables. This procedure does not imply any lack of confidence in the models' predictions. But we always see a value in approaching the real world as closely as possible.

1. Penetration

Penetration varies a good deal between brands, and indeed most clearly differentiates one brand from another when we try to explain sales differences.[15] But it remains consistent for any one brand in different time periods, as long as they are of equal length (see Table 5.4).

The very uniformity of these figures is rather misleading, however, because the people who buy a brand in one period are *not* all going to be the same as those who buy it in the next. The table must not be misread as implying that they will. In fact, as we move from the first to the second period, some buyers will drop out (they will mostly be lost only temporarily, not forever), and some new buyers will come in. The penetration in two periods (we might say "net penetration") will therefore always be greater than that in one period. Of course this net penetration grows with the length of the period examined (see Table 5.5).

From Table 5.5, readers can easily see how the net penetration for each brand is progressively growing; but they can also make out that it is growing at a *somewhat diminishing* rate. If the growth had been at a uniform rate, the penetration figures for Shredded Wheat, for example, would have been 1, 4, 13, 52 (in direct proportion to the number of weeks) instead of the actual 1, 3, 7, 17. This deceleration in growth is caused by a slowing down in the percentage of *new* buyers in each new period. The percentage of buyers who have bought before must therefore be increasing. This is a reflection of the

---

Table 5.4

Four-Week Penetration (%)

Weeks	Kellogg's Corn Flakes	G.M. Wheaties	Nabisco Shredded Wheat	Quaker Cap'n Crunch	Post Sugar Crisps
1–4	11	6	3	3	2
5–8	11	7	3	3	2
9–12	10	6	3	4	2
13–16	11	7	5	3	2
17–20	11	6	4	4	3
21–24	12	6	4	4	3

Table 5.5

Penetration Growth

Percentage of households buying in	Kellogg's Corn Flakes	G.M. Wheaties	Nabisco Shredded Wheat	Quaker Cap'n Crunch	Post Sugar Crisps
1 week	3	2	1	2	1
1 month	11	6	3	3	2
1 quarter	22	12	7	6	5
1 year	41	23	17	16	14

reappearance of the infrequent purchaser who, to paraphrase Alice's friend the White Queen, buys jam last month, next month, but not this month.

2. Purchase frequency

There are five important points to be made about average purchase frequency.[16] In the first place, it tends to be low. Over the course of a year it is rarely much more than six purchases for even large brands of packaged goods, and it is commonly much smaller than that. (The single notable exception to this rule is purchases of brands of cigarettes, but this market exhibits a number of exceptional patterns.) This fact of low purchase frequency is another way of saying that most major brands do not account for the majority of people's purchases. No matter how attached a housewife is to her major brand, she will generally buy a larger total quantity of other brands.

The second point about average purchase frequency is that, surprisingly enough, although it varies between markets, it does not vary very much *between brands in any market*, as seen from the average quarterly purchase frequencies in Table 5.6 for presweetened breakfast cereals. (These figures

Table 5.6

Average Purchases per Buyer: Sugared Cereals

	Average purchases per buyer in 13-week period
Frosted Flakes	2.2
Life	2.7
Cap'n Crunch	2.4
Froot Loops	1.9
Sugar Crisps	1.8
Lucky Charms	2.1
Trix	1.8

are all rather high because they reflect the consumption levels of households containing children.)

In this category Frosted Flakes has a much larger market share than Trix, yet the average buyer of Frosted Flakes buys only slightly more often than the average Trix buyer. But if the difference in the number of purchase occasions will not explain the difference in market share, the relative penetration of the two brands will. The quarterly penetration figures are 12 percent for Frosted Flakes and 5 percent for Trix; this relationship between penetration and market share is evidence that penetration is the key variable in describing consumer buying behavior.

The third feature of a brand's average purchase frequency is that it varies very little between periods of equal length (see Table 5.7).

The consistency in these frequency figures resembles the consistency in the penetration figures for periods of equal length.

The fourth point also suggests a parallel between average frequency and net penetration, because, like penetration, average purchase frequency grows over time, but at a diminishing rate (see Table 5.8).

However, the rate of growth here is *very much slower* than the penetration growth (for which, it will be remembered, the comparable figures were 1, 3,

Table 5.7

Purchases per Buyer: Shredded Wheat

Weeks	Average purchases per buyer of Nabisco Shredded Wheat
1–4	1.3
5–8	1.3
9–12	1.3
13–16	1.3
17–20	1.3
21–24	1.3

Table 5.8

Growth in Purchases per Buyer: Shredded Wheat

	Average purchases per buyer of Nabisco Shredded Wheat
In one week	1.1
In one month	1.3
In one quarter	2.0
In one year	3.8

7, 17). This is a reflection of decelerating penetration growth accompanied by the entry of increasingly infrequent buyers.

Our fifth and final point about frequency concerns its direct relationship with penetration. In fact, when a brand reaches a high absolute level of penetration, this is likely to be accompanied by an *increase* in the purchase frequency. This double effect is akin to an economy of scale, and indeed there is more than one type of scale effect associated with high penetration. We shall coin the phrase *penetration supercharge* to describe these effects, the importance of which will be considered later in this chapter.

3. Frequency distribution

The normal frequency distribution of purchases of a brand is (as common sense might lead us to expect) extremely skewed. The pattern is a regular one. Given normal penetration levels, much the largest figure will be in the "no-purchase" category. As we progress upward in terms of purchase frequency, there is a relatively high figure in the "one-purchase" category, but thereafter the figures trail away.[17] The following distribution is for purchases of Nabisco Shredded Wheat in one quarter. Although the data come from the observed readings, the predicted readings are (as usual) close to them. The predictions were drawn up on the basis of two simple inputs: the brand's penetration in the quarter (which the reader will remember from the discussion of penetration growth to be 7 percent—to be precise, the figure is 7.3 percent); and the average purchase frequency of 2.0 (from the discussion of frequency in the previous section) (see Table 5.9).

The widespread existence of this type of skewed distribution has led to the formulation of the well-known "80:20 rule," which is normally a reasonable

Table 5.9

Frequency Distribution of Purchases: Shredded Wheat

Number of purchases in thirteen weeks	%
None	92.7
One	4.3
Two	1.1
Three	1.0
Four	0.2
Five	0.4
Six or more	0.3

approximation of the concentration of heavy purchasing in any market. This can be expressed in one of two ways: either that the 80 percent lightest and 20 percent heaviest users of a brand each account for about half of its sales; or that if buyers are divided into three groups, the 50 percent lightest, 30 percent medium, and 20 percent heaviest buyers, then these groups often account for about 20 percent, 30 percent, and 50 percent of sales, respectively.

It is salutary to realize from a table like the previous one that even fairly large brands have such low levels of purchase: almost one-third of all Shredded Wheat purchases in this thirteen-week period were made by buyers who bought only once. There is also a significant technical point connected with this "once only" figure: although in most respects frequency distribution patterns are regular, and observed distribution coincides with the model, the model frequently underestimates one figure, the amount of single purchasing (probably in most cases trial purchasing). In the same way, the model commonly slightly underestimates long-period penetrations because it fails to take account of the frequent presence of trial purchasers appearing for the first time. This is a nonstationary element—the model therefore cannot cope adequately with it—but it opens a most interesting avenue for exploration, because it is the very element that leads to brand growth. Net penetration growth almost invariably takes place with the addition of a small number of low-frequency buyers. The manufacturer hopes that some of these can be persuaded by the functionality and the added values of the brand, reinforced by its advertising, to use it more often. We shall shortly look at this point in detail.

4. Repeat buying

It is a relatively simple matter for the models to predict the percentage of purchasers of a brand in one period who will repurchase in a subsequent period. It is also simple to predict their frequency of purchase in that second period.[18]

If again we use Shredded Wheat as our example (with its 7.3 percent penetration and average frequency of 2.0 in one thirteen-week period), the model predicts that 58 percent of the buyers in this quarter will repurchase in the next. (The actual figure observed was 59 percent.) Making the normal assumption that there will be no significant change in the total number of purchasers between the two periods, then in the second quarter 59 percent of purchasers will be repeaters from the first quarter and 41 percent will be new purchasers (much the majority being very infrequent purchasers from earlier periods). Thus the increase in net penetration in the second quarter will be by the addition of 41 percent: from the actual net level in the first quarter of 7 percentage points to a new net level of 10 percentage points in the two quarters. (This was the actual figure observed.)

From the discussion of frequency, the reader will remember that the higher levels of penetration in a particular period are associated with higher general levels of purchase frequency in that period (a phenomenon contributing to the penetration supercharge, the tendency of a large brand to have a higher frequency of purchase than a small brand). But the effect does not stop there, because higher penetration is also associated with higher *repurchase* rates in the next period. If a brand is in the 5 percent to 10 percent penetration range (Shredded Wheat, for example), an average purchase frequency of 2.0 will predict (as we have seen) a repurchase rate of 58 percent. But if a brand's penetration is as high as 20 percent, predicted repurchase goes up to 60 percent, with further increases in frequency causing predictions of even further increases in repurchase. Again, this is a scale effect for a brand expressed in consumer terms.

Among repurchasers in a second period, frequency of purchase will tend to be higher than in the earlier one, in the Shredded Wheat case, at 2.52 purchases compared with the earlier period's 2.0. But among *new* purchasers in the second period, average frequency will be at a much lower level, an approximately constant level of 1.4.

Sole purchasers (people who use only one brand and are therefore by definition repeat purchasers if they are regular buyers of the product field at all) are normally a small group, especially if we confine the definition to buyers of just one brand over a reasonably long time period. Again using Shredded Wheat as our example, only about 18 percent of buyers are sole buyers over the course of one month, 6 percent over a quarter, and less than 1 percent over a year. When these purchasers are analyzed by their frequency of purchase of the brand, they do not appear to be different from the much larger number of multibrand purchasers, so that there is no particularly heavy usage to justify special attention being paid to these buyers. Therefore, for operational purposes, the small group of sole users is generally neither large nor attractive enough to justify any special marketing effort to exploit it.

5. Multibrand buying

From the definition of multibrand buying (more than one brand will be bought in a given period), it follows that the rate of product purchasing must be higher than the rate of brand purchasing, and this will be more marked in long than in short time periods.[19] For instance, in the case of breakfast cereals, the average Shredded Wheat buyer will purchase 1.1 packs of the brand in a week but will buy an average of 1.9 packs of breakfast cereals as a whole. Over the course of a year, the average Shredded Wheat customer will buy about four packs, but from the product field as a whole he or she will buy as many as forty-two packs. In fields where there is less variety than in breakfast cereals, the homemaker's weekly purchase of one brand will represent the total of product purchasing; but the consumer soon begins to buy other brands, so that after a time the normal relationship of greater product buying than brand buying begins to assert itself.

Product purchase rates are similar within markets or within defined functional market segments. In a market such as gasoline in the United Kingdom, which has no functional segmentation by brand, the average buyer of each of the major brands will make the following number of product purchases (purchases of all brands) in a four-week period (see Table 5.10).

Similarly, where there is functional segmentation by brand (as in the American breakfast cereal market), the average annual purchases of all products in the same segment will be similar. *But they may be different in different segments.* Table 5.11 lists the annual figures for the presweetened segment. For buyers of unsweetened brands, the figures are as in Table 5.12.

The internal consistency between these sets of figures is obvious. A moment's thought will tell us why purchase levels are significantly higher for the presweetened segment than for the unsweetened one: the large size of

Table 5.10

Average Product Purchases of Gasoline Brands in Four Weeks

Esso	5.8
Shell	5.8
National	6.2
Mobil	6.1
BP	6.1
Texaco	6.0

Table 5.11

Average Annual Product Purchases: Sweetened Cereals

Cap'n Crunch	55
Life	55
Sugar Crisps	55
Froot Loops	54
Lucky Charms	60

Table 5.12

Average Annual Product Purchases: Standard Cereals

Kellogg's Corn Flakes	34
Rice Krispies	39
Grape Nuts	37
Shredded Wheat	42
All Bran	38

the average household using sweetened cereals due to the presence of young children (as pointed out in the introductory discussion in this chapter).

An important feature of product purchase rates is that although they are generally consistent from brand to brand, there is a tendency for them to be slightly lower for larger brands. We have seen that there is an opposite tendency for *brand* purchase rates, in that these are higher for large brands. Thus, *the buyer of a larger brand will show generally greater brand loyalty than the buyer of a smaller brand,* because she or he will be making more purchases of the larger brand out of a smaller total number of purchases in the product field as a whole.

Having looked at the differences between brand buying and product buying, we can now examine the duplication of buying between brands. This is yet another aspect of buying behavior that shows regularity and consistency, at least within categories (or between functional market segments). This consistency is in fact so great that the relationship has been formulated as a rule called the *duplication of purchase law.* This states simply that the buyer of one brand will buy a second brand in direct proportion to the penetration of the second brand. For example, over thirteen weeks, 11 percent of Kellogg's Corn Flakes buyers will also buy Shredded Wheat, 11 percent of Kellogg's Rice Krispies buyers will also buy Shredded Wheat, and 11 percent of Kellogg's Bran Flakes buyers will also buy Shredded Wheat. The duplication figure between these different brands and Shredded Wheat remains fairly constant, and this duplication is essentially related to Shredded Wheat's penetration, which is (of course) a single figure, 7 percent.

The duplication is not exactly the same as Shredded Wheat's penetration, however, but rather a *multiple* of it, about 1.5. This figure is called the *duplication coefficient* and remains reasonably constant over a whole market, about 1.5 for breakfast cereals in the United States, but only 1.2 for gasoline in the United Kingdom.

Significantly, the higher values of the duplication coefficient (including exceptionally above-average figures we sometimes see for two or three brands in individual markets) relate to groups of brands that consumers regard as particularly similar to one another. The brands have a lot of users in common because of their similarity. The values we are talking about here are much higher than those we have seen so far for breakfast cereals and gasoline, where the average duplication between brands is uniform but at a low level. But there are exceptions even within these markets, such as between Kellogg's Raisin Bran and Post Raisin Bran. For these two brands, 35 percent of Kellogg's buyers buy Post (3.5 times the Post penetration and much higher than the market duplication coefficient of 1.5). This high degree of duplication is simply explained in terms of the two brands' functional similarity. But the reader should also bear in mind that the duplication between these two brands is by no means complete, because although 35 percent of Kellogg's buyers buy Post, 65 percent of them do not, so that as a general rule, home-makers' purchasing patterns are much less self-contained than preconceptions of market segmentation would have us believe.

Four Myths

We shall now use empirical studies and mathematical models to illustrate some commonly held conceptions (or misconceptions) about how markets work. Three of these illuminations are general and apply over the whole marketing field; the fourth is a special case with a limited empirical foundation, although judgment suggests it to have a quite general application. (The reader is urged to examine the source material for more detailed explanations.)

1. Demographic and psychographic positioning

Ehrenberg's work confirms chapter 3's points on positioning and the weaknesses of demographic and psychographic measures as means of segmenting markets and determining brand positions.[20]

As the reader knows from the (above) discussion of multibrand buying, there is little evidence in the real world of any clear-cut segmentation by *consumers*. However, there is often a segmentation of brands on the basis of their functional performance. In the market for ready-to-eat cereals, the clustering that takes place is of brands having particular functional characteristics, such as

- the two bran flakes, Kellogg's and Post;
- the two raisin brands, again Kellogg's and Post;

- the range of presweetened brands: Frosted Flakes, Froot Loops, Cap'n Crunch, Trix, Sugar Crisps, Lucky Charms, and Life;
- Rice Krispies and Cheerios (both expanded products).

But even such unusually clear functional segmentation will not enable a manufacturer to reach anything like exclusive groups of consumers. "Instead, there is a general mass market, with buyers of each brand buying the other brands in about the same proportions. Superimposed on this is the high substitutability of brands of the same sub-type."[21] Finding a market segment where such substitution takes place, however, can provide opportunities to a manufacturer as alert as the one discussed in chapter 3, who was imaginative and aggressive enough to launch a new brand that achieved a 7 percent brand share (4 percentage points of which came from competitors). The secret was to target potential consumers in terms of their brand usage. This was not exclusive usage, but it was large enough for the firm to come in and seize (and build) a substantial business.

2. The hard core of loyal buyers

There is a prevalent idea that when sales of a brand decline, they reach and maintain a rock-bottom level that represents the use of the brand by a hard core of old and loyal users.[22] We have observed at first hand manufacturers who have developed and implemented marketing strategies based on this idea, on more than one occasion and in more than one country. The underlying assumption is that the loyal group repurchases the brand at an above-average rate (hence the above-average loyalty). Although their numbers may dwindle, they make up for this decline by their high level of repurchase.

Empirical studies illuminate this question in two ways. First, the word "loyalty" itself can be seen to have a special meaning. What we know of the buyers is that these people are not so much *less loyal* to the brand as *less frequent buyers* of it. Although they may not buy in one particular period they will return in later periods, since most brands have a long tail of irregular purchasers who are not lost forever (as described in the next section). Second, when we look again at the average frequency of purchase of a brand and the frequency distribution around this average, we will note the remarkable and predictable similarity between such averages and such distributions for different brands.

There is therefore no factual basis for the notion of a hard core of loyal buyers, whether these are for a declining brand, store brand, generic brand, or any other type. The only brands that have a regularly above-average rate of purchase are those brands with high absolute levels of penetration. This has nothing to do with any special characteristics of the brands, but is simply a result of their high penetration per se. It is essentially a function of their large size.

Generally speaking, when a brand declines, it is the result of falling penetration, and when sales reach bottom level, it is because the penetration has been stabilized. Frequency of purchase has not come into the matter at all.

3. The "leaky bucket"

There is also a prevalent theory, which is even subscribed to by that normally impeccable observer Peckham, that the users of a brand, like the contents of a leaky bucket, are constantly dripping away, disappearing from the market in significant numbers, accounting perhaps for the loss of a fifth of a brand's sales during the course of a year.[23] Such losses would make it necessary for the manufacturer to devote much attention to recruiting new users simply to compensate for the natural wastage.

We have seen in the analysis of repeat buying that 59 percent of all Shredded Wheat buyers in any one quarter will come back to buy it in the next quarter. The average purchase rate for *any* brand of breakfast cereal is 54 percent (i.e., 46 percent not repurchasing). If there were a "leaky bucket," we should expect the normal repurchase to waste away to nothing after a few further quarters. If, for instance, it were to decline by 46 percent on a continuous basis, the repurchase by the original buyers would be very low in less than a year and would be close to disappearance in eighteen months (see Table 5.13).

But this does not happen in practice. The actual repurchase in the fourth quarter is not 16 percent, but three times that—an observed figure of 48 percent.

Table 5.13

Hypothetical "Leaky Bucket" Buyers

1st quarter	100%
2nd quarter	54
3rd quarter	29
4th quarter	16
5th quarter	8
6th quarter	5

This means that as a general rule infrequent buyers remain infrequent, but do not drop away altogether except in marginal cases (which might eventually be reflected in an erosion in a brand's market share). This erosion will in any event not happen if the slight loss in repurchase is matched by a modest compensating entry into the market of new trialists (as discussed in the case of Shredded Wheat's frequency distribution). The way in which market share will actually trend up and down is in most circumstances a reflection of these modest marginal changes in penetration between periods. And although these are real movements, they are not of an order of magnitude to justify manufacturers' diverting effort simply to influence them.

4. Promotional sales increases and season uplifts

We now come to the meaning of two types of short-term sales increases, those caused by promotions and by seasonality, which are commonly thought to be brought about by increased usage by existing users.[24] It is not possible to generalize widely from the data, although judgment suggests strongly that the patterns discussed here are widespread.

In a successful consumer promotion for a brand of laundry detergent in Britain, sales increased during one February by 30 percent, thereafter coming down in the way expected of all consumer promotions for steadily selling brands. The promotion employed a banded pack, offering more powder for the same price, a type of offer thought to be much more interesting to existing users of the brand than to new users.

On the basis of January sales, Ehrenberg's model predicted that without the promotion, 210 packs per 1,000 households would have been sold in February; and of these, 60 would have gone to people who did not buy in January. In fact, the promotion boosted February sales to 272 packs per 1,000 households, and 101 of these went to households that had not bought in January. Thus, contrary to expectations, the promotion appealed to a considerable degree to new trialists. But if this suggests some long-term effect for the promotion, this was denied by the almost immediate reestablishment of normal repeat-buying rates as soon as the promotion was over. The promotion gained some extra sales, mainly from new trialists, but these people did not appear to have selected the promoted brand to add to their repertoire. The effect of the promotion in this case was to increase penetration by the entry of some extra once-only buyers, but this was of little long-term value to the brand.

A similar conclusion was drawn from an instance of a seasonal sales increase for a brand of packet soup in the United Kingdom. The sales level was

480 packs per 1,000 households during the three winter months of peak sales, compared with 360 packs during the three summer months of lowest sales. Food manufacturers believe that the winter increase in soup sales is always due to people using more soup, rather than to new buyers coming into the market. But the facts of this case showed the opposite to be true. The model predicted that repeat buying by off-season purchasers accounted for 320 sales per 1,000 households in the peak season. The remaining 160 purchases (the seasonal uplift) has to be coming from new purchasers. "Getting winter-only buyers of soup also to buy in the summer is a different task than getting all-the-year-round buyers to buy *more* in the summer." [25]

How Brands Grow

After considering and digesting all of this evidence, in particular the examples of consumers buying in regular and unchanging patterns, you are probably wondering, what in fact is the mechanism that causes the market share of a brand to increase or decrease?

Two clues in this chapter will help us understand changes in market share. First, a brand's penetration is the consumer measure that has the greatest influence on a brand's sales; big brands always have a higher penetration than smaller brands. Second, in the discussion of frequency distribution, the point was made that models of stationary market conditions slightly underestimate the amount of once-only purchasing by brand trialists. The percentage movements need only be marginal to represent substantial numbers in absolute terms. This is how stationary markets become a little less stationary.

But might the emergence of one-time trialists upset the normal patterns of skewed frequency distribution? In practice, the reestablishment of the normal frequency distribution is more likely to be achieved with a growing brand by the trialists remaining infrequent purchasers, *but with some of the former infrequent purchasers becoming more frequent purchasers.* Everybody moves up a rung. Some nonusers become minor users; some minor users become major users. Thus the normal frequency distribution will now hold for the higher level of penetration. In this rather special sense, advertising can be seen to boost frequency of purchase; in totally stable markets this is much more difficult to do.

When a brand is declining, the opposite happens. Some major users become minor users, and some minor users become nonusers. The brand eventually settles down to the same frequency distribution pattern at a lower level of penetration. British analyst Tom Corlett first worked out this hypothesis to explain growth and decline in consumer terms. It accords with common sense.[26] There is also a well-documented unpublished case of a medium-term decline of a major brand of packaged goods on the British market, which is explicable precisely in the terms just outlined. In this case, analysis of the trouble enabled the manufacturer to take successful corrective action.

The powerful tendencies toward equilibrial regularity in markets give a brand an inbuilt momentum once it crosses that first and most difficult hurdle of early establishment of penetration and repeat purchase. Once a brand becomes a "goer," the tendency toward regularity is as much in its favor as it was an obstacle to be overcome during its initial market entry.

How Advertising Strategy Should Be Influenced by Repeat-Buying Theory

The concepts described in this chapter and the rather complex relationships between them should prompt further reflection, and they should suggest that what has been described ought to have a major influence on the way a manufacturer draws up advertising strategy. We shall identify twenty factors.

Factors Influencing the Choice of Target Group

1. Demographic and psychographic measures are imprecise descriptors because

- There is generally a large common usage of functionally different brands within demographic and psychographic population groups.
- Users of different brands are often actually the same people because of everyday multibrand purchasing. This factor becomes more important as any brand grows in size.

2. A target group can be precisely described in terms of brand usage. But a decision must be made about how much the manufacturer is targeting his own users (for repeat purchase); how much he is targeting users of competitive brands; and *which* competitive brands are being targeted. Generally speaking, the larger the advertised brand, the greater the emphasis that should be placed on existing users.

3. Figures for penetration tend to be large. Over a year, for instance, the figure for penetration is much bigger than the figure for market share. This is

due to the continuous growth of net penetration, through the increase in the numbers of infrequent buyers. These factors suggest that

- Although the route to increasing market share is mainly via increasing penetration, this strategy should be accompanied by a secondary strategy;
- That since a brand has an enormous number of infrequent buyers, the secondary strategy should be addressed to them to increase their purchase frequency.

4. Data from a source other than Ehrenberg suggest that advertising has a consistently greater effect on users of a brand than on nonusers.[27] This is probably connected with the fact that users of a brand notice its advertising because of selective perception.

5. Over periods of six months to a year, there are normally very few sole buyers of a brand, except in the case of cigarettes. Absolute brand loyalty is therefore a rare phenomenon.

6. Heavy users of a brand represent a small proportion of total users. Twenty percent of users use half the volume, according to the 80:20 rule.

7. Purchasers of a brand, when measured by how often they buy, are distributed in a skewed fashion, but the average purchasing level is low in general. With a typical brand, a third of all purchasing in a thirteen-week period is made by people who buy only once.

8. Overall levels of brand purchasing are also low. Nielsen shows that in a fairly large supermarket, three-quarters of all brands sell only a dozen packs a week.[28]

9. Points 6, 7, and 8 are mutually supporting and suggest that the best target group for a brand (heavy users of the product category and the brand) represents a relatively small proportion of the homemaker population: in many cases under 25 percent. This in turn means that the advertising has to influence only a relatively small number of people to have an effect. Unfortunately no way is known of finding these people accurately and without waste, by media selection. This is because of the overall lack of selectivity of television, although magazines are not quite so inefficient. Therefore they must be located by means of the content of the advertisement—the creative appeal, which should be sharply angled to catch them. For higher priced merchandise, database marketing (e.g., of existing users) offers possibilities of reducing waste despite its high cost per contact in reaching consumers.

10. Point 3 suggests that the secondary target group (irregular users of the brand, who might be persuaded to increase their purchase frequency) is probably much larger than the primary target group. Irregular users should also be located by the creative appeal of the campaign, although the larger size of

this group means that attempts to locate it by the use of media are less wasteful than attempts to locate the primary group.

Factors Influencing the Argument and Tone of Voice of the Advertising

11. Since much advertising effort is directed to the maintenance of the status quo, the tone of voice of such advertising should be unaggressive, protective, and reinforcing. Selective perception means that a brand's advertising will often be noticed by existing users, which means that it is not required to be strident to attract attention. In parallel with this, the brand's budgetary policy should be highly disciplined to shore up profit. The evidence on advertising weight presented in chapter 4 suggests strongly that the advertising of larger brands tends to be more cost-efficient than that of smaller ones.

12. Regular product use means that homemakers are familiar with the motivating arguments (those aimed at primary demand in any market). Brand advertising should concentrate on discriminating arguments, emphasizing in particular the brand's added values.

Factors Influencing the Role of Advertising

13. The role of the advertising directed at the primary target market should be to increase penetration. This is a tough task for a large brand, and consumer promotions should work alongside the advertising to accomplish this. This whole argument is consonant with the Brooke Bond Oxo experience described in chapter 3, with its recommendation that the most fruitful area for development is "at the periphery of the user group."

14. The role of advertising during seasonal sales peaks should be to encourage a temporary increase of penetration rather than usage.

15. The role of promotions in most circumstances should also be to increase penetration rather than usage. If a brand's sales trend is slightly upward, a permanent increase in penetration could take place, although this would probably be proportionately smaller than the temporary increase in sales.

16. There is no permanent loss of users in stable market conditions. There is no "leaky bucket." Advertising should not therefore be addressed to people who are thought to be quitting a brand.

17. There is no hard core of loyal buyers. Advertising should not therefore be addressed to such a group.

General Considerations

18. Multibrand buying means that homemakers will continually appraise competing brands. This is yet another confirmation of the importance of maintaining competitive functional performance. Multibrand purchasing is the norm between functional segments as well as within them. Segmentation is virtually never brand-exclusive.

19. There are scale economies for large brands connected with the penetration supercharge: economies explained essentially in terms of consumer usage. This means that such brands should be punctiliously nurtured and certainly not sacrificed on the altar of the life cycle theory!

- Large brands tend to have a higher purchase frequency within a purchasing period. This can be quite large within long purchasing periods (see Table 5.14).[29]
- Brands with a higher penetration tend to have a higher repurchase rate (higher repurchase frequency in the next purchasing period).
- Brands with a high penetration tend to have slightly lower than average *product* purchase rates. Since they also have slightly higher *brand* purchase rates, this means that they generate greater than average brand loyalty.

20. Data on penetration, purchase frequency, frequency distribution, repeat buying, and multibrand buying can be collected for a brand and its competitors from analysis of a couple of years of consumer panel data, which many manufacturers may already possess but not fully use. These data will provide a more enlightening basis for developing strategy than the simpler (and often syndicated) information most commonly used.

Table 5.14

The Importance of Large Brands

	Brand A	Brand B
Share of market	46%	12%
Average observed purchase frequency		
in 1 week	1.0	1.0
in 4 weeks	1.8	1.5
in 12 weeks	3.7	2.5
in 24 weeks	6.0	3.3
in 48 weeks	10.1	5.0

The Argument in Brief

Patterns of buying in stable markets (such as are normal in the world of repeat-purchase packaged goods) disclose a remarkable degree of underlying uniformity and regularity. These can be described with the use of mathematical models constructed by Ehrenberg and other analysts from a wide data base, with virtually universal application to such markets.

To understand a brand fully, we need to know a number of facts about its consumers and its competitors. These include penetration, purchase frequency, frequency distribution, repeat buying, and multibrand buying. Knowing the first two of these variables is enough to be able to predict the remaining ones from the models.

A knowledge of the facts of purchasing behavior has considerable operational value. For instance, it enables us to examine the validity of commonly held beliefs about markets. It can also help us understand how brands grow, normally by an increase in the number of once-only purchasers, which is enough to disturb the existing stationary pattern of a market. Such an increase is often accompanied by an increase in the frequency of purchase by existing buyers, which in turn leads to a continuation of the normal pattern of frequency distribution, although the brand as a whole is now slightly larger.

The facts of consumer buying carry many implications for advertising strategy. Some of the most important are that with many brands (certainly large ones), a good deal of advertising effort should be directed at the maintenance of the status quo in a market. The primary target group for advertising should normally be heavy buyers of a product field, many of them users of the brand advertised. The secondary group should always be users of the brand, but infrequent ones, the purpose of the advertising being to increase their frequency of buying. In many circumstances, both creative and budgetary policies should be protective and unaggressive.

Brands with high penetration and market share benefit from the scale economies associated with the penetration supercharge. This is itself a strong reason for manufacturers to nurture such brands, and not encourage decline by inaction, notably by allowing investments of all types to dwindle.

The facts of consumer purchasing behavior can be assembled relatively easily for any ongoing brand and its competitors. This procedure provides a battery of information for developing a strategy that is more direct, stimulating, and productive than the rather jejune data normally used for this important purpose.

Notes

1. This experience dates from 1966–67 and was derived from the European advertising for the Famous Artist Schools, a substantial direct-response advertiser. The campaign ran fully in six European markets and experimentally in two others.

2. The authors' experience in the international field has been derived from Chesebrough-Pond's, Gillette, Nestlé, PepsiCo, and more than twenty brands from Unilever. Outside the FMCG field, their experience came from the Champion Spark Plug Company, the Ford Motor Company, and Pan American.

3. Six specific examples are quoted by Colin McDonald, "What Is the Short-Term Effect of Advertising? The Relationship between Frequency and Advertising Effectiveness," in *Effective Frequency,* Michael Naples, ed. (New York: Association of National Advertisers, 1979), pp. 86–88.

4. Michael Barnes, "The Relationship between Purchasing Patterns and Advertising Exposure," in *How Advertising Works* (London: J. Walter Thompson, 1974), p. 55.

5. J.A.P. Treasure, title essay in *How Advertising Works,* pp. 77–91.

6. Barnes, "The Relationship between Purchasing Patterns and Advertising Exposure," p. 57.

7. A.S.C. Ehrenberg and G.L. Goodhardt, *Seventeen Essays on Understanding Buying Behavior* (New York: J. Walter Thompson and Market Research Corporation of America, 1977–1980), pp. 5.14, 5.5.

8. A.S.C. Ehrenberg, *Repeat Buying: Theory and Applications*, 2d edition (New York: Oxford University Press, 1988). Additional data are also to be found in John Philip Jones, *When Ads Work: New Proof That Advertising Triggers Sales* (New York: Simon and Schuster, Lexington Books, 1995), chap. 12.

9. Ehrenberg and Goodhardt, *Understanding Buying Behavior,* pp. 1.3, 5.15.

10. Ibid., pp. 6.2–6.3.

11. Rosser Reeves, *Reality in Advertising* (New York: Alfred A. Knopf, 1961), p. 10.

12. Ehrenberg and Goodhardt, *Understanding Buying Behavior,* pp. 6.12, 6.5.

13. Ehrenberg, *Repeat Buying,* chaps. 7 and 8; and Ehrenberg and Goodhardt, *Understanding Buying Behavior,* essays 11 and 12.

14. Ehrenberg and Goodhardt, *Understanding Buying Behavior,* p. 12.1.

15. Ehrenberg, *Repeat Buying,* pp. 33–40; and Ehrenberg and Goodhardt, *Understanding Buying Behavior,* pp. 6.7, 7.7.

16. Ehrenberg, *Repeat Buying,* pp. 37–40; and Ehrenberg and Goodhardt, *Understanding Buying Behavior,* pp. 6.7, 7.4, 8.5–8.7, 11.7, 12.14.

17. Ehrenberg, *Repeat Buying,* pp. 53–55; and Ehrenberg and Goodhardt, *Understanding Buying Behavior,* pp. 10.5–10.6, 12.10.

18. Ehrenberg, *Repeat Buying,* pp. 17–28; and Ehrenberg and Goodhardt, *Understanding Buying Behavior,* pp. 3.4–3.8, 12.4–12.5.

19. Ehrenberg, *Repeat Buying,* pp. 170–173; Ehrenberg and Goodhardt, *Understanding Buying Behavior,* essay 9.

20. Ehrenberg and Goodhardt, *Understanding Buying Behavior,* essay 4.

21. Ibid., p. 4.9.

22. Ibid., essay 3.

23. Ibid., pp. 2.14–2.15. See also James O. Peckham Sr., *The Wheel of Marketing,*

1st ed., 1978 (privately published but available through A.C. Nielsen), p. 80. This source is a good example of the occasional problem associated with using aggregated retail audit data.

24. Ehrenberg and Goodhardt, *Understanding Buying Behavior,* essay 2.

25. Ibid., p. 2.13.

26. Tom Corlett, "Consumer Purchasing Patterns: A Different Perspective," in *How Advertising Works,* pp. 111–119.

27. "Major Advertiser Ad Tel Scheduling Study, 1974," in *Effective Frequency,* pp. 44–56.

28. Peckham, *The Wheel of Marketing,* p. 22. The data came from a study produced by *Progressive Grocer.*

29. Ehrenberg, *Repeat Buying,* p. 36. Many additional examples could be given.

6

Advertising Research: A Digression on Recall

Before proceeding with the mainstream argument in this book, and in particular to the important matters of advertising quality and campaign effects, a digression is necessary to describe methods of evaluating advertising, all of which require market research. This chapter mainly concerns one particular type of research: recall testing.

Market research was originally made possible by the discovery of techniques of sample selection and is virtually the only scientific tool available to marketing and advertising practitioners. Over the years there have been continuous improvements in the way it is carried out, particularly, in the recent past, in methods of analyzing data. But while we cannot deny the increasingly important contribution of research to marketing and advertising, we must also be aware of four endemic concerns with all research (in ascending order of importance): the sample, the sample frame, causality, and the questions. And most emphatically, we must also remember that research is to be an aid to judgment, not a substitute for it.

1. The sample

The reliability of research results depends on the size and representative nature of the sample. A great deal is known about both sample selection and the margins of error. It is nevertheless common practice to use small samples of about 100 for quantitative surveys and even smaller ones of about twenty for qualitative investigations. Although such samples can be usefully employed, researchers do not always make it explicitly clear that the range of error is extremely wide and, in the case of qualitative investigations, that the data are not capable of any type of quantitative extrapolation at all.[1]

2. The sample frame

This means that we should decide whether we are questioning the right type of people: are we selecting the sample from the correct universe (a technical word describing what the sample is drawn from)? This decision is often heavily judgmental; for instance, in researching advertising, should we talk to users or nonusers of a brand? If this is in turn decided by the target group described in the brand's advertising strategy, it begs the question of whether that is in fact the most suitable group for the marketing plan and therefore for the research.

3. Causality

There is a fundamental question that is particularly important in continuous tracking studies: which of two variables is the cause and which is the effect? Does A cause B, or does B cause A? Or are they both perhaps caused by C? Do increasingly favorable attitudes toward a brand *cause* the brand to be bought increasingly? Or are they really the *result* of increasing purchase?

4. The questions

This is the worst problem of all, because people are only rarely capable of responding to possibilities outside their range of direct experience. (It was once said that if the development of household lighting systems had depended on market research, houses would be lit today with highly sophisticated kerosene lamps.) The problem is exacerbated by researchers' almost universal habit of framing questions in ways that may be easy to tabulate and present, but often provide a blocked conduit when it comes to providing insights into consumers' beliefs and attitudes. All too often, instead of asking people a range of direct and oblique questions for them to answer in their own way, researchers make startlingly bald statements, many concerned with matters of questionable importance, and expect people to respond, according to varying degrees of agreement or disagreement, on a five- or seven-point scale. The user of such research should beware.

In discussing these central problems, we have ignored common solecisms in the description of research findings, since the practiced user of research will immediately notice these. One of the most common and irritating mistakes is the habit of percentaging data on the basis of totals much smaller than 100. The person who does this needs to be reminded that he or she is in effect making projections. Before such projections can be accepted, we need evidence that when the smaller total is projected up to the larger, the internal composition of the figures is not going to be changed in important ways.

This chapter will concentrate on one specific variety of research: the measurement of advertisement recall. We are going to examine the measures used to test the effectiveness of individual advertisements, and later briefly discussing recall measures used to evaluate the cumulative effect of campaigns. Research into individual advertisements is most commonly and succinctly (but not most elegantly) described as copy testing. Depending on the technique, such testing can take place before an advertisement is exposed, after it has been run on a trial basis, or after it has been exposed before a substantial audience. Of all types of advertising research, recall testing has the longest history. Until the mid-1980s, it also had the widest popularity, certainly in the evaluation of finished campaigns.[2] It also has a most pervasive aura of controversy surrounding it.

The earliest types of advertising research were developed by George Gallup and Daniel Starch in the 1920s. They were originally and continue in the main to be concerned with print media. The "reading-and-noting" method, originally developed by Gallup, has been used in a regular syndicated service by Starch since 1931 and is run in Britain by the British Gallup organization. The research aims to find out whether members of the public can recognize advertisements in specific issues of newspapers and magazines that they claim to have read. Readers are taken through the appropriate issue and asked about each advertisement in it. Recognition is assessed at three levels: first, whether the advertisement in question has been noted (whether the respondents remember having seen it); second, whether they associate the advertisement with the advertiser's name; and third, whether they have read at least half the copy. Starch, it should be emphasized, is concerned with *recognition* of something supposedly seen in the recent past.

The method used by Gallup and Robinson in the United States is based on a different and more searching technique. Here, the publication is not opened for inspection, and people who have read it are asked whether they can remember (and what they can remember about) advertisements for particular brands, with emphasis on sales points. This technique can correctly be described as recall rather than recognition, although the methodological problems that apply to an extreme degree to recognition also apply to some extent to the various types of recall. (Gallup and Robinson's work provides typical examples.)

For many years, Starch was looked upon as a service that provided, if not diagnostic insights, at least a general confirmation that particular campaigns were working. The findings were rarely regarded as critical discriminators between advertisements, but were widely read by creative people in agencies, who used them in a general way to improve their skills.

Some interesting experience dated from the late 1950s, a time when J. Walter Thompson, London, handled the advertising of two generic commodities, butter and cheese. (The role of the advertising was to stimulate overall consumer demand to boost the producer price. The campaigns were funded by levies on each ton of imports and home production.) During this time some of the most interesting campaigns for these commodities were editorial in style and devoted to recipes. In the media buying, the agency took particular pains to ensure that they appeared on women's pages in national newspapers.

These campaigns consistently achieved remarkable reading-and-noting scores. Some of the smallest advertisements (four inches across two columns) received levels of copy readership normally expected of advertisements ten times as large. The copywriters were suitably gratified, but this research evidence did not prevent the campaigns from being abandoned—on the grounds of their supposed dullness—before they had run their full course. This decision was made jointly by representatives of the client and the agency account management, who were, needless to say, all men. The decision was also made against the advice of Stanley Resor, the man who in all essentials had created the J. Walter Thompson Company, and who was then coming to the end of his long reign. It is presumed that he was thought at the time to be past his best.

This anecdote is used to illustrate the way in which this type of research was then treated and used by clients and agencies: it was an interesting but essentially peripheral matter. Decisions about which campaigns to run were made on the basis of different arguments—essentially subjective judgments.

This was about the time that television was establishing itself, in the eyes of most clients and agencies, as the most glamorous medium for advertising consumer goods. And it was the arrival of television, with its exciting opportunities but also its massive unknowns, that caused advertising research to be extensively reconsidered by advertisers. This triggered the biggest development in its use, together with an extensive exploration of ideas borrowed from different scientific disciplines, a widespread experimentation with different testing techniques, and a still active current of professional controversy about the meaning of the different sorts of research. It had been estimated that by the 1970s, the number of reported research studies was doubling every five to eight years.[3] Today, the literature is vast although variable in quality, very piecemeal, and to an extent contradictory. The progress toward enlightenment has been extremely slow and painful, but few people would deny that some steps have in fact been made.

Reading-and-Noting: Its Fall from Grace

In 1955, in a burgeoning spirit of enquiry, the Advertising Research Foundation (ARF) embarked on a rigorous validation of recognition and recall research as it was then carried out. A Committee on Printed Advertising Rating Methods (the PARM Committee) was set up to plan and carry out this research. They concentrated on a single issue of *Life* (May 16, 1955) and paralleled the investigations of both Starch, and Gallup and Robinson, but with a much larger and more carefully controlled sample.

There were differences between PARM and Starch findings, and between PARM and Gallup and Robinson findings; and a modest amount of debate took place on the reasons for these differences. Suggestions for improvement were made, but nowhere was there a feeling that the scientific basis for these two research methods had been destroyed or even called seriously into question.

However, some years after the PARM investigation had been published (after a period in which there had been surprisingly little serious comment in either academic or industry circles on PARM and what it had brought forth), Darrell B. Lucas, who had been associated with the PARM Committee since 1955, began some fruitful speculation about the implications of the research.[4] When examining recognition scores researched over a two-week period from the publication date of a sample issue, he found that the scores at the end of the two weeks were no lower than at the beginning. In other words, recognition scores did *not* erode over time, as memory has always been thought to do (and indeed as Gallup and Robinson recall scores were found to behave). This disturbing finding caused Lucas to try and puzzle out what recognition scores really measured; the more he thought about them, the more he concluded that they could not have much to do with what they purported to measure: whether or not a person had seen that particular insertion before. "Certainly the evidence does not justify the projection of recognition ratings to the actual number of noters or readers per dollar."[5]

On both sides of the Atlantic, much speculation and experimentation then began to take place. This was of two main sorts. First, work was done on factors that were likely to contaminate recognition and recall findings. Second, fundamental exploration took place into the nature of perception, in particular the automatic prescreening processes that appear to be built into the human senses and brain. The concept of selective perception had long been familiar in the study of psychology. This new research was about to demonstrate its relevance to advertising.

The studies of contaminating factors, although they were extensive and fairly comprehensive, are easy to summarize because they generally pointed in a single direction. Experiments eventually isolated at least nineteen factors that could be shown to influence recognition scores.[6] Some of these, as expected, relate to the content of the advertisement itself (size, use of color, pictorial content, attractiveness, meaningfulness, interest level generated, and the product field). Some, also as expected, relate to the medium (position of the advertisement, size of the issue, surrounding material, and interest in the editorial). Some, not as expected, relate to the respondent (interest in the product, product usership, closeness to brand purchase, demographic characteristics, and response "set" of the individual). Some, also not as expected, relate to the research itself (the training of the interviewers, the length of the interview, the research procedure).

The fundamental assumption of the Starch technique is that the scores reflect partly the creative content of the advertisement and partly the particular medium in which the advertisement appears. The fact that exogenous factors relating to the respondent and the interview also have a strong influence on recognition scores means that these scores cannot be taken at their face value. Moreover, detailed improvements in the research technique—a number of which were suggested and tested—do not appear to shake the validity of this broad conclusion, although they may reduce the imperfections marginally.[7]

The investigations into the physical processes of perception provided even more disturbing hard data. The hypothesis set up for investigation was that the eye, in scanning a printed page, picks up impressions in very short time periods less than a quarter of a second each. In these short periods, the hypothesis continues, the eye can see and the subconscious mind can reject some things as being of no interest. If a subject (such as an advertisement because of the creative content, but also because of the brand advertised or the product field) is registered by the individual's subconscious as interesting, more time is spent on this advertisement, which then enters the individual's memory and is presumably reflected in the recognition and perhaps also in the recall. But if this hypothesis is valid, the recognition and recall scores are not a reflection of whether the individual has seen the particular insertion; they mean that the ad (or brand or product field) is something that caught his or her interest. This information is not irrelevant, but it is not what recognition and recall are supposed to be about.

This may appear to be a complex concept, but it proved remarkably easy to test by the use of an apparatus designed by the Institute of Market Psychology in Mannheim, Germany. A similar machine had been used in the United States in 1940, in the psychology department of Purdue University, and some interesting findings had been published in the fall of 1941, which (not surprisingly in view of the timing) failed to trigger any academic debate.[8] The European system is known as the direct eye movement observation system (DEMOS); its experimental and validation work was carried out in London by the British Market Research Bureau from 1966 to 1968.

Each person who was to be interviewed was asked to spend time in a waiting room. Here, he or she saw a (prepublication) copy of a newspaper or magazine on a lectern. Since there was nothing else to do, the respondent would begin to read. As this happened his or her eye movements were, without the subject being aware of it, filmed with continuous individual exposures of one-quarter of a second so as to establish exactly what pages and portions of pages were looked at, and for how long.[9] The people were then interviewed to establish normal reading and noting scores, which were compared with the precise, scientific DEMOS measurement to confirm (or otherwise) the reading-and-noting findings.

The main validation study can be summarized in a single uncomplicated statistical table (see Table 6.1). In the magazine study, the average percentage of respondents who claimed to have looked at the advertisements was 13 percent (although only 8 of the 13 percent actually did so), while the actual number who looked at the advertisement was 43 percent. The ratio of claim to reality was therefore 13:43 or the equivalent of 100:330, a gross underreporting of 230 percent!

This startling finding dramatically confirms the hypothesis of selective perception, a phenomenon that has of course been known instinctively by advertising practitioners since the days of unregulated advertising for proprietary medicines a century ago. The tiny advertisement with a headline such as "Painful Hemorrhoids" would indeed be noticed by the small but vulnerable target group of sufferers from this distressing condition. But for the majority of readers, the advertisement would of course be easily and simply screened out. The advertiser could safely employ small spaces, which were the only size he could afford in view of the relatively small size of the target audience.

Table 6.1

Findings of DEMOS Study

	Magazine study: average for all advertisements in *Woman's Own* (%)	Newspaper study: average for all advertisements in *Daily Mirror* (%)
Looked at and claimed	8	6
Not looked at and claimed	5	1
Looked at and not claimed	35	35
Not looked at and not claimed	52	57

Recognition scores may indeed measure something, but that something has little to do with whether a specific advertisement has been seen in a particular issue of a publication. Recall scores are perhaps a purer measure than recognition, since they are more concerned with whether or not a person can recall an advertisement with his or her conscious mind—leaving open the question of whether selective perception might have taken place. But recall measures, like recognition, are by no means free of contaminating factors (as we shall examine in detail in connection with twenty-four-hour recall of television commercials). Remember that all research—and advertising research in particular—is like a minefield. Things that seem firm and safe are often not what they appear, so actions based on them can have unexpected and dangerous consequences. We shall try to chart a course through this minefield.

The Twentieth-Century Philosophers' Stone

When we referred at the beginning of this chapter to the popularity of recall testing, this mainly meant its use not with print but rather with television advertising. Here, the most prevalent variety takes the form of twenty-four-hour recall or DART (day-after-recall test). Most large advertisers have used it. The pioneer research organization in the field, Burke Marketing Services, had its headquarters, appropriately enough, in Cincinnati, location of Procter & Gamble, originally its most important client.

The DART technique is simple. A television commercial is screened once. The next day (within twenty-four hours of the advertisement's exposure) a sample of people is contacted by telephone, asked whether they viewed the television show at about the time the commercial was on the air, and asked to recall verbal and visual elements of the advertisement's contents. The aim is to contact a sample of about 200 people who saw the television program. (This takes time for shows with small audiences, a fact that distorts the findings to a significant degree).[10] The recall scores are then compared with a substantial battery of normative data in similar product fields, and the findings, which are delivered promptly, are crisp, businesslike, and eminently operational.

It will be no surprise to readers, however, that experimental work has uncovered a substantial number of contaminating factors that influence the recall levels, so that (as with press advertising) what is measured is a good deal more complex than recall of the particular advertisement under scrutiny. The issue is examined most succinctly in a paper by Shirley Young, formerly director of research services for Grey Advertising in New York.[11] Examining ten examples of test and retest of the same commercial, she demonstrates recall levels in the second test to be significantly different from those in the first in half of the cases. (This is typical of investigations of the technique.) Differences in recall levels have been attributed to a miscellaneous collection of external factors, such as differences between test cities, whether the program is liked, brand usage, time of the program, the ad's position in the program, whether the entire program is viewed, various demographics of the respondents, and when within the twenty-four-hour period the interview takes place (reflecting the impact of fading memory).

Sonia Yuspeh, who formerly directed all research and planning in J. Walter Thompson, New York, published convincing evidence to demonstrate that significant differences in recall scores take place as a result of different program environments. In thirty-six tests (six of each of six different commercials), different programs affected the outcome significantly in fourteen cases.[12]

The literature suggests even more fundamental problems concerned with recall testing. For instance, there is evidence that the *type of claim* will influence the level of recall. Young states unambiguously that recall testing discriminates in favor of explicit copy, "which communicates concrete, product-related benefits," and again, implicit copy, "which communicates less tangible or more psychological benefits."[13] In most circumstances, with increases in a brand's store of added values, implicit copy will become relatively more important as it takes on some of the prominence that was held by explicit copy during a brand's introduction.

There is another point of great significance indeed. A powerful body of evidence has established that there is no simple and direct connection between factual recall on the one hand, and preference and buying behavior on the other. The point was first established by Jack B. Haskins in a seminal paper published in 1964, which was based on a total of twenty-eight empiri-

cal studies. His conclusion has been widely propagated: "[R]ecall and retention measures seem, at best, irrelevant to the ultimate effects desired, the
changing of attitudes and behavior."[14] Much further evidence has been collected during the intervening two decades, but Haskins's central conclusion
has never been seriously disputed.

The question that immediately suggests itself is why ready-made research
techniques, in particular recall testing, are so widely and apparently uncritically
employed by many demonstrably successful manufacturing companies as a
quality control over their advertising. Perhaps these advertisers have learned
special and sensitive ways of interpreting such scores. Perhaps they are attracted by the very simplicity of the findings, a refreshing change in an increasingly complicated world. Perhaps they do not ask themselves what the
scores really mean, but accept them in blind faith as prompts to action: go or
no-go.

The last of these hypotheses seems the most plausible, because it has not
been unknown in the past for sophisticated advertisers to express unthinking,
albeit temporary faith in philosophers' stones. But to examine these hypotheses more seriously, we should take a look at advertising research in broader
terms than recall alone. We can do this most sensibly if we include in our
discussion some notions of how advertising actually works with recipients of
advertising and consumers of brands. We are going to look in fact at some of
the more visible mechanisms of the small apparatus at the center of the large
machine described in chapter 1.

"Learn-Feel-Do" and "Learn-Do-Feel"

In the process of developing advertising ideas, making them into advertisements, and then exposing these advertisements experimentally before the
expenditure of vast screen-time appropriations, advertising research has two
roles to play. First, it has a mainly diagnostic and generative role, which takes
place before advertisements are prepared in a finished form. Second, it has a
quality-control role, which takes place mainly after the advertisements have
been finished, and normally as a result of experimental exposure.

In its diagnostic role, the best and most widespread type of advertising
research is qualitative, employing groups or small numbers of individual
members of a defined target audience. The research is intended to help generate thoughts, to act as a sounding board for tentative ideas, and to assess the
interest and clarity of communication. The numbers are rarely grossed up;
indeed the research requires careful interpretation and is used in the main to
help creative people in agencies. The sorts of questions the research attempts

to provide answers to include "Is something wrong with this idea?" "Why is it wrong?" and "Is this alternative a way of getting it right?"

On the other hand, in its quality-control role, advertising research is primarily a tool for brand management to ensure that the finished advertising as it is about to be widely exposed meets certain criteria, particularly (if possible) in comparison with the advertising for competitive brands.

To simplify the distinction between roles, creative, diagnostic research tends to be untidy, subtle, and sometimes implicit. Its purpose is to guide judgment. However, quality-control research, in view of its primary function as a management tool, is tidy, ordered, simplified, and standardized. Shirley Young is particularly perceptive in her discussion of this point: "No other type of research, whether product testing, package testing, penetration studies, or strategy research, suffers from the burden of having to provide uniform techniques and simplistic scores to determine a course of action."[15]

If there is a realistic role for advertising research in this quality-control function—something we do not dispute—then it is not a good idea to be inflexible about our systems. We should rather give some thought to the problems that the systems can help solve. This can only be done by analyzing and planning how our advertising is going to work in the marketplace.

Advertising can only work if it is received, comprehended, and responded to in some way. Response, on which we shall now focus, is partly a matter of psychology. It concerns learning, attitudes, and, more importantly, behavior. In consumer goods marketing, behavior generally means buying, for the first time, or more frequently than before, or as frequently as before.

Learning, attitudes, and behavior are all influenced in some way by advertising, but to understand how advertising works, we need to know the order of events, so that we can employ research to help us progress from stage to stage. Here there is no shortage of opinions. As usual, what is lacking is empirical validation.

The earliest theory was based on a simple chain of causality described by Charles Ramond as "learn-feel-do."[16] In this theory, people receive factual knowledge about a brand. As a result, their attitudes toward the brand change and they develop a preference for it. Then they buy it. The phrase "hierarchy of effects" has been coined to describe the sequence[17]; it has also been titled the "learning hierarchy."[18] The theory is an old one, the germ of which can be found in Starch's writings in the 1920s.[19] Over the years it has been presented in at least sixteen different forms.[20]

The theory, however, has been constantly disputed for a variety of reasons, the most serious being the following:

- There is substantial evidence that communication also works in the reverse direction. Behavior influences attitudes, as people strive to reduce cognitive dissonance.[21] Indeed, probably the greatest single influence on attitudes toward a brand is people's use of it. Behavior also influences learning, as a result of selective perception. In particular, users of a brand are normally those most conscious of the advertising for it.

- The theory concentrates exclusively on change (increase in learning, improvement in attitudes, first purchase) and gives no attention to stationary patterns of consumer behavior connected with repeat purchasing. As we saw in chapter 5, such stable patterns are so common as to be the normal situation in real markets.
- It fails to enlighten us about certain well-established phenomena in the real world, such as the high failure rate of new brands, and the continued existence of minor brands with small market shares and advertising budgets.[22] If change is so simple and sequential, why does it not happen more often?

Perhaps most seriously, there have been only limited attempts to validate it empirically, with results falling far short of being conclusive.[23] In the opinion of Michael Ray, who has been responsible for almost all of the empirical work in this complex field, the learning hierarchy may possibly operate in cases in which "the audience is *involved* in the topic of the campaign and when there are *clear differences* between alternatives."[24] Our own feeling is that this hierarchy is more likely to operate with print than with television advertising, and especially with direct response, which, when it works at all, does so as a complete stimulus (because a direct-response advertisement works on its own on a one-exposure basis); it must therefore embrace change of knowledge and attitudes.

A more subtle and pregnant theory than the learning hierarchy is the "low-involvement hierarchy" first propounded in the mid-1960s by Herbert E. Krugman. This has been described by Ramond as "learn-do-feel."[25] The notion hinges on the concept of low involvement, as it applies to people's relationships to products, brands, and media: relationships that are generally associated with a lack of emotional commitment because of the essential triviality of the purchase decision. Low involvement is something that, "while perhaps more common in response to commercial subject matter, is by no means limited to it."[26]

The theory was developed from Krugman's impressions of the impact of television communication, based on work in the psychological laboratory, and from an extrapolation of ancient and well-known investigations by the German experimental psychologist Hermann Ebbinghaus. But although Krugman's starting point seems remote from a strong empirically based theory of advertising communication, the theory as it has been developed has an undeniable plausibility. The core of the argument is that in television advertising, there is a lack of consumer involvement in either brand or medium, and, as a consequence, "perceptual defense may be absent . . . persuasion as such, i.e. overcoming a resistant attitude, is not involved at all," and commercials are only received and responded to as simple descriptions of brand attributes. Decisions about buying are made simply as a result of consumers being subjected to "shifting [of] the relative salience of attributes." This hierarchy proceeds therefore by changing awareness and knowledge of brands, which in turn leads directly to a relatively casual purchase decision, which in turn leads to more knowledge and the development of attitudes stemming from brand use—a chain (in the words of the psychologist) of cognition–conation–affect. "With low involvement one might look for gradual shifts in perceptual structure, aided by repetition, activated by behavioral-choice situations, and *followed* at some time by attitude change."[27]

This theory is distinctly better than the learning hierarchy in two ways. First (and most important), it is compatible with the well-known fact that even if attitudes toward brands influence people's buying of them, people's experience of brands (following purchase) has an equally important if not more important influence on attitudes. In other words, the interaction between attitudes and behavior is two-way and resonant.

The second advantage of the Krugman theory is that it has at least some empirical basis, albeit a rather flimsy one. From experiments in an artificial environment carried out by Michael Ray and his colleagues among a reasonably large sample of respondents, using purchase-intention and not direct behavioral measures, "it is clear that the 'Low Involvement' hierarchy occurs somewhat more often than the 'Learning' one. . . . In all, the involvement variable seems to explain hierarchy effects more clearly than does any other single mediating variable."[28]

Krugman himself carried out a limited program of experimental work, with the use of a piece of apparatus that calls for the most heroic assumptions to make it approximate even remotely to a publication that might be read by any human being: "a fourteen-page hard-cover portfolio that contains seven stop watches within the back cover of the portfolio. A complex of unseen pulleys permits the opening and closing of seven of the pages to be precisely timed."[29] There seems from these curious experiments to be evidence of a higher level of involvement in magazines than in television with high-involvement products (but not much difference with low-involvement products). These points are all general confirmation of Krugman's theory.[30]

An extension of Krugman's hypothesis is the notion that the two hemispheres of the brain store different impressions and carry out different mental functions. The right hemisphere is supposedly concerned with pictorial impressions. The change in the salience of attributes (without the emotions being committed), which is characteristic of low-involvement learning as described by Krugman, is essentially a right-brain function. On the other hand, verbal processes including reading and speaking, are supposedly the function of the left brain; high involvement is concerned with the left brain. (The distinction between these two discrete areas of activity is not irrelevant to the question of recall testing.)

Whether these two types of mental process have different physical loci has not been established with absolute certainty, although perhaps this aspect of the problem is not of material importance. But at least one practical attempt has been made (by Sidney Weinstein and colleagues Valentine Appel and Curt Weinstein) to establish levels of brain wave activity for magazine and television advertising. Their work provides at least directional evidence that magazine advertising generates more brain wave activity than television advertising; that magazine advertising tends to generate more left-brain activity; and that *the more brain wave activity, the higher the brand recall.*[31] (We are quite unable to resist the richly comic image of these three researchers, clipboards in hand, solemnly observing a group of bewildered housewives with wires attached to their heads as they read a popular magazine!)

In contrast to the learning hierarchy, which works with an involved consumer and clear differences between brands, the low-involvement hierarchy works with uninvolved consumers and where there are few obvious differences between the brand alternatives. But what of the cases where the functional differences between brands are of less importance than those based on *added values* that (as we saw in chapter 2) were built over time by advertising? In these cases, which almost certainly represent the majority of brands in real marketplaces, the low-involvement hierarchy does not tell the whole story. But it does lead to a modification of the concept that has, we believe, widespread validity, and has been developed and explored with considerable intellectual rigor by Andrew Ehrenberg.[32] This hypothesis is the notion of trial and reinforcement, embracing the idea of advertising addressed to existing users of a brand and aimed at reinforcing their preference for it, so that it will remain at least in its present position in their repertoires, and perhaps be upgraded from being a minor to a major brand (in exceptional cases from a major to the sole brand). The reader who has followed the argument in this book will realize that this notion of trial and reinforcement is entirely compatible with everything we have said, and in particular with the primary role of advertising in providing nonfunctional added values.

As the theory might have been described by Ramond, it is "do-feel-do," or an interaction of the conative and affective processes among existing users of a brand. A word borrowed from natural science, *resonance,* is an evocative way of expressing this continuous interaction of behavior and feelings. In

Krugman's terms, this process might encompass the use of advertising to increase the degree of consumer involvement in a brand.

This theory is the only one of those considered so far that explains the way advertising operates as a contribution to the maintenance of essentially stable patterns of consumer behavior. Krugman's original low-involvement hierarchy explains only a minority of cases: new brands, sharply growing brands, and sharply declining brands. (We have scrutinized his writings carefully with this point in mind and have found repeated emphasis on *changing* patterns of learning, behavior, and attitudes.) It is Ehrenberg's extension of the theory that explains the rest.

The Limited Circumstances When Recall Testing Can Be Useful

The purpose of attempting to analyze people's mental and behavioral responses to advertising is that the increased understanding will, it is hoped, lead to increased efficiency in advertising planning. In particular, if indeed three types of processes (cognitive, conative, and affective) are at work, then separate types of research can be carried out to isolate the contribution of advertising to each of these processes. This point (which is by no means obvious until someone makes it, at which point we all react "Of course!") was to the best of our knowledge first put forth and illustrated in a short paper by William R. Swinyard and Charles H. Patti based on a real-life case.[33] Their paper explains clearly and simply why three different techniques provided different results when they were used to research a single series of commercials. The three techniques were measuring different things; judgment on the relative importance of learning, doing, and feeling in the particular marketing situation was needed to choose the most *relevant* research technique to apply to the commercials. Bearing this important point in mind, let us consider the three processes and the appropriate research techniques to help us understand how a particular advertising situation is likely to influence our choice of which to use.

It is not difficult for the advertising generalist—let alone the research specialist—to understand that in monitoring the "learning" process, recall testing should in theory be useful, despite such formidable difficulties of measurement. In monitoring the "doing" process, there are measures of purchase intention and more reliable measures of actual marketplace buying. (See the section below, "Pretesting Based on Simulating Consumer Behavior," pp. 154–156.) In monitoring the "feeling" process, there are a number of ways of evaluating, once or repeatedly, people's attitudes toward brands, including particular as well as general attitudes and the strength of all of these attitudes relative to other brands. The reader will note that of these three processes, recall testing is concerned only with learning. The relevance of recall testing to a particular campaign depends therefore on the importance of learning in the role that has been (or should be) established for this campaign.

Let us now return to those hypotheses for how advertising works. Let us also make the reasonable assumption that the advertising for some brands works in one way; in a second way for other brands; and in a third way for still other brands. Note the suggestion here that the determining factor for the way in which advertising will work in particular cases is the state of the *brand* and the role of advertising for that brand at that particular time.

1. "Learn-feel-do" (the learning hierarchy)

The theoretical framework of this hypothesis makes a seemingly good case for using research in a hierarchical format involving

- recall testing to evaluate learning,
- attitudinal and persuasion measures to evaluate feelings,
- purchase-intention or actual purchase measures to evaluate behavior.

Much research has been carried out with the use of this framework without any noticeable increase in the efficiency with which manufacturers have been able to launch successful new brands. The system has not worked on many occasions because it suffers from two faults.

First, individual manufacturers have not evaluated with sufficient care whether advertising in their particular cases is going to be working in the way in which the learning hierarchy postulates. As suggested, it seems only to work in exceptional cases in the real world, where involvement and functional discriminators between brands are both relatively high. Second, although the learning hierarchy may work in isolated circumstances, and factual learning about a campaign (or about a brand) may be a desirable quality as a foundation for an argument directed at improving attitudes as well as building preference and eventually purchasing, *there is no direct link between factual knowledge on the one hand and attitudes and behavior on the other.* This conclusion has been established as a result of considerable empirical study and is one of the things we know about factual recall with virtually complete certainty.

We can conclude, however, that in those relatively few cases in which advertising works by means of the learning hierarchy, recall testing may be of some value. There is, however, a simpler and more reliable testing mechanism available for direct-response advertisements (which may be the most important examples of the learning hierarchy at work), the sort of testing that direct-response practitioners have used for 100 years. They simply expose the advertisement a couple of times and count the coupons! This is a far more complete and reliable mechanism than recall testing, and in many cases a cheaper one.

2. "Learn-do-feel" (the low-involvement hierarchy)

As Krugman's various writings imply, the theory of a low-involvement hierarchy is relevant to the vast majority of packaged goods *in their introductory phase* (before a body of regular users has been built, a period that can vary from six months to two years). As we have discussed in the context of the learning hierarchy, there is a seemingly good case for monitoring recall (at least of a brand's functional characteristics) on the assumption that recall is a basic first ingredient for a working campaign. If for no other reason than to establish brand identity in oligopolistic markets, a manufacturer of a new brand will still insist that potential customers be taught *precisely* and vividly that it fights cavities or dandruff, is easy to apply, or tastes of strawberries; or that the pack is large; or that the product is liquid; or whatever. The reader will note that we have concentrated on facts about the brand. It is not so easy to make a case for communicating campaign slogans or claims, although Rosser Reeves, a distinguished advertising man and former chairman of Ted Bates, published a best-selling book making just such a case,[34] one that is essentially fallacious.[35] Reeves was a powerful thinker and dialectician, but he seems to have striven to propose a general theory for how advertising works, with no exceptions. Our own inductive approach is quite different and by its nature admits of exceptions. But if we are going to use recall testing as part of a research program for a new brand of packaged goods, we shall need to be conscious of all of the qualifications in interpreting the data.

In the first instance, we must remember the many measurement problems described earlier in this chapter. There is no certain way to avoid the various factors contaminating the data, but one useful although expensive procedure is to average out their effects by taking multiple measurements, for instance, by checking twenty-four-hour recall in a number of different cities and in more than one television show of the same type in each city. There is evidence from Yuspeh's study that this avoids many of the eccentricities of individual recall scores.[36]

A second point is that we should judge carefully whether one type of claim will influence the level of recall. As already mentioned, research has provided at least directional evidence that mental activity concerned with verbal processes (the supposedly left-brain variety) generates higher recall levels than activity concerned with pictorial impressions. This is essentially our earlier point that recall testing discriminates in favor of explicit copy and against implicit copy.

A third point is that we should never lose sight of the proven lack of connection between advertisement recall and attitudes and behavior. The communication of factual points is only the beginning of what is required for effective advertising. Much more is needed for an effect. In particular, an advertisement must evoke some type of emotional response from the target consumer.

It is possible, by using qualitative techniques, to determine how well an advertisement communicates, how it reflects consumer perceptions of a brand, and how well consumers empathize with it. This is not a matter of rational persuasion. The essence of the low-involvement hierarchy is the *absence* of hard persuasion (overcoming a resistant attitude) in the initial purchase process. We consequently find it difficult to understand the value of measuring the ability of a commercial to persuade directly in this way.

A delightfully fresh perspective on the measurement of advertising attention value and its connection with buying is provided by a well-known paper by Leo Bogart and his colleagues.[37] Their evidence confirms all the other research: "[T]here is almost no relationship between an ad's sales performance—when compared with other ads—and its comparative readership performance, as measured either by recognition or recall."[38] But the researchers also published most interesting data on the abilities of eighty-three advertising decision makers in leading advertising centers in the United States to judge the effectiveness of particular advertisements. This investigation demonstrated that the experts have a good general ability to judge before the event an advertisement's attention value, but that is about all. "The experts did very well in predicting readership performances, their record in predicting attitude change was mixed, and they could not predict which ads would sell more of the brand." It would not be stretching the case too far to deduce from these findings that recall studies are not only inadequate; they are also unnecessary.

3. "Do-feel-do" (the reinforcement hypothesis)

"Do-feel-do" is the way in which advertising probably works in most cases in the real world. The hypothesis embraces behavior and feelings exclusively, so that factual learning and, as a result, recall testing as a way of measuring consumer knowledge should normally play no part in the process.

There is one minor exception. When a brand is restaged with some dramatic change in its formula, packaging, or advertising claims, it is important to measure once and for all how well the consumer recognizes these changes. In one unpublished case, a brand in a weak fourth place (5 percent volume share) in a highly competitive market was restaged with a dramatic change of campaign. It was important for the manufacturer and agency to know that the advertised brand attributes had been communicated quickly, so as to know when the campaign should be taken to its next stage. But advertising changes as radical as those used for this brand's relaunch are unusual, and in this case they were only implemented because of the brand's weak position, which had indeed become worse immediately before the restage.

The normal research procedure for ongoing brands in stable markets and with established campaigns is to monitor campaign effects by means of tracking studies, a process of continuous monitoring. The reader should note that in this, we move from measuring the effect of a single advertisement exposure to monitoring the effects on a brand of a total advertising campaign (together with other marketing variables). These studies are common and are often extremely useful. But there can also be problems. Tracking studies are discussed in the penultimate section of this chapter.

Pretesting Based on Simulating Consumer Behavior

Although for fifty years recall testing was by far the most popular pretesting system used in the United States, during all this time many advertisers successfully employed a pretesting system focused on one simple but important question—whether a single screening of a commercial will stimulate consumer purchasing of the brand advertised. The most experienced organization carrying out this research in the United States employs a system identified by the acronym ARS (Advertising Research Systems).[39] The manifest problems with recall testing—which are not shared by the ARS system—have led to a continued and increasing use of the latter.

The ARS research system is proprietary and is described technically as a laboratory method, which means that typical consumers are invited to view a one-hour entertainment program in a cinema. There are also commercials for various brands, including one for the brand being tested (although the audience is not told this). The program is preceded and followed by a lottery for a quantity of brand-name goods, in which the brand whose commercial is being tested is included.

The ARS measure is based on a pre/post shift in brand choice obtained in a secure, off-air environment where it is possible to simulate purchase. The measure is calculated by subtracting the percentage of respondents choosing the advertised brand over the competition *before* exposure to the television material from the percentage choosing it *after* exposure. This captures the net effect of retention and attraction as a result of the advertising stimulus. In the United States, the ARS sample consists of 500 to 1,000 respondents, aged 16 or older, randomly recruited by mail from four geographically dispersed markets.

What is being measured is the effect of the advertising stimulus on its own. Testing on the basis of a single exposure means that media weight and advertising repetition play no part in boosting the strictly creative power of the advertising itself in generating immediate sales. As described in chapter 7, a single exposure of an advertisement is quite capable of generating sales, so that a research technique based on one exposure of a commercial offers a realistic structure based on real-world experience.

The ARS method can be described, rather cumbrously, as one based on a "pre/post preference shift." With most repeat-purchase packaged goods, the stimulus to buy is no more than a reminder—an evocation of previous brand experience—which triggers the purchase of a brand that in most cases is already in the consumer's repertoire. This is certainly not persuasion in the sense of overcoming resistant attitudes. But although the purchase is a low-involvement decision and little thought goes into it, the advertising simply does not work unless it says something important about the brand. The most effective advertising maintains a subtle balance between the rational and the emotional. This enables it to resonate with what the consumer believes and feels about the brand advertised.

The ARS system does not discriminate in favor of either rational or emotional advertising. And—most importantly—the predictive value of the system has been demonstrated extensively. In some hundreds of cases, the pretest score achieved by a commercial has been compared with sales measured by scanner research immediately after the advertisement's exposure. As a general rule, the ARS system will predict success or failure; and the *size* of the pretest score will in most cases predict the measurable degree of success or failure actually achieved.

Many advertising agencies and some clients have always been skeptical about the value of the technique. But opponents of the system seem curiously reluctant to study objectively the plentiful facts demonstrating its efficiency.

Tracking Studies

Tracking studies are of two main types: those measuring consumer knowledge of advertising and those measuring knowledge of the functional properties and image attributes of brands (which is, of course, a measurement with strong affective overtones). Of the former, the commonest type is proven advertising recall. It has been widely practiced by Leo Burnett in the United Kingdom, where the data have been extensively analyzed, and general patterns have been described and published.[40] The word *adstock* is used to describe the measure of advertising recall at the end of a period, representing the effect of advertising from previous periods. The term *half-life* is used to describe how long it takes to reduce the *adstock* by half, in the absence of extra advertising to "top it up." The rate of decay can be measured and modeled. When a newly exposed campaign arrests (or increases) this decay, its effect can be isolated and quantified in terms of its ability to augment (or attenuate) the adstock.

The procedure is plausible; and the use of continuous measurement probably eliminates the effect of contaminations in the data. Nevertheless, in the circumstances in which the measure is used as a surrogate for the behavioral effect of a campaign, its users cannot refute the argument that there is no identifiable relationship between recall and sales. Indeed, in the cases in which increases in advertising awareness have been related statistically to increases in sales, the direction of causality has not been established. It can be strongly argued that the progression actually goes from sales to recall, rather than the other way around, since the strongest influence on awareness of (and attitudes to) a brand is normally whether the consumer uses it or not.[41]

A greatly more useful type of tracking study is the continuous monitoring of image attributes. Such studies often reveal subtle relationships that are capable of providing unusual insights. In one real case of a premium-priced brand, the main desired response to the brand was value for money. The advertising did not mention value for money specifically, but was concerned with related brand values, not just physical features. Homemakers were aware of the premium price; when it was discovered through continuous image measurement that they were beginning to believe increasingly that the brand offered both the explicit attributes and good value for money (a point they had to work out for themselves), it became obvious that the campaign was working in terms of buyer psychology. There was also confirming evidence of effectiveness from econometric studies isolating the results of the advertising from the other marketing variables.

Not many studies of this sort have been published, because of the proprietary nature of the data. But two reliable ones have been published in simplified form: those dealing with Listerine in Canada[42] and Andrex bathroom tissue in the United Kingdom.[43]

In these published studies (and in the many proprietary ones that we have worked with over the years) the interacting variables are changes in buyers' beliefs in specific image attitudes of the brand and their purchasing of it. Such changes tend to be quite small in the short term, so that mutations may be a better way of describing them.

As with the continuous tracking of advertising awareness, it is unclear from this research whether the mutation in attitude precedes the change in behavior or vice versa. But since the essence of the reinforcement hypothesis is mutual interaction or resonance between the variables, the exact order of events is not materially important here.[44]

There have been some academic investigations of the relationship between attitude measures and sales, but these do not add much to what has been learned by manufacturers from a long-term study of their brands.[45] One of these studies, after examining a number of cases with the use of a fairly complex mathematical model, concluded, "The findings have consistently demonstrated that the affective dimension is significantly more effective [sic] in explaining variance in market share than the cognitive or usage dimensions."[46] In other words, this work tended to support the direction of operation from attitude to behavior, rather than mutual interaction. If this research provides a true picture of the direction of causality, it reinforces strongly the operational validity of tracking studies of image attributes.

The Argument in Brief—and a Footnote on Aggregated Data

Even when we give recall testing the benefit of every doubt, the most serious uncertainties remain. It is not easy to accept uncritically a measure contaminated with such methodological distortions. Nor is it easy to appreciate the relevance of a measure that applies only to fairly exceptional advertising circumstances. At its best, recall testing is only reliable if used in conjunction with other measures because of the proven lack of connection between recall, and attitudes and sales. There is even sketchy evidence that recall testing is hardly necessary if a campaign is scrutinized by experienced judges of advertising.

Recall tests were nevertheless for many years the most widespread type of advertising research. They were and sometimes still are a standard operating procedure of many successful companies, whose very success robs academic criticism of much of its plausibility, at least in the eyes of people unacquainted at first hand with large, successful companies. But some of us believe that no company is so successful that it can ignore scrutiny of *all* of its operating procedures; there might be some surprises.

The facts described in this chapter show that recall testing is only relevant to a minority of advertising situations. There are three such situations. First there are cases where the learning hierarchy applies (although in many of these, direct response may be a simpler and more reliable testing system). Second, there is the introductory phase of a new brand, a period of six months to two years, when the brand is building its body of regular and occasional users. Third is the rare occasion when an ongoing brand reaches a situation requiring radically new advertising that puts special emphasis on functional benefits. This is generally when the brand is losing occasional users, and the role of the advertising is to encourage them to reappraise the brand by reconsidering its salient physical attributes. It follows from these points that recall testing should only be used for the examination of factual, product-related advertising claims.

There are also strong indications that recall testing should not be employed in isolation. In particular, it should be used in conjunction with the generally more reliable and sensitive mechanism of continuous image measurement. In most advertising situations (for ongoing brands sold to existing regular and occasional users), image measurement should be a basic tool for advertising research. It should also not be forgotten that the in-theater technique of measuring pre/post preference shifts is an extensively validated system of assessing a commercial's selling ability.

There is great emphasis on multiple measurement in the 1982 PACT (Positioning Advertising Copy Testing) recommendation (or "Consensus Credo") of twenty-one leading advertising agencies in the United States.[47] This document makes a number of sensible general recommendations concerning advertising research, although surprisingly it does not comment on individual techniques such as recall testing.

It is also necessary to use a large data base for recall testing. For twenty-four-hour recall, a number of cities and more than one television program in each city should be employed. The greater the number of recall readings that are averaged, the greater the possibility of eliminating the factors contaminating individual measures. But naturally the cost goes up in direct proportion.

It is also important to use the data *comparatively,* not absolutely. Norms for product categories provided by the major research services are reasonably useful, although care is needed when we compare recall of specific commercials with these norms.

Even Starch, with all of its imperfections, can be enlightening if used on a broadly aggregated basis, in comparison with norms. For instance, one measure from among many that could have been chosen—an examination of the following findings from 250 tests of magazine color page advertisements—indicates clearly the superiority of advertisements containing recipes over those not containing recipes.[48] The large data base averages out the effect of many of the statistical contaminations discussed in this chapter. What matters is the comparative interpretation here (see Table 6.2). The precise meaning of this table is *not* that in representative cases 57.5 percent of people noticed before and therefore recognize now an advertisement with a recipe, as opposed 40.6 percent of people who noticed before and therefore recognize now an advertisement without a recipe or end results. Nevertheless, there is no doubt that the data are an unambiguous indication not only that food advertisements containing recipes are more valuable than food advertisements without them, but that the ratio of preference for recipes compared with no recipes is at least on the order of the "noted" ratings (and maybe even the "read most" ratings). By this process of using aggregated data *comparatively,* we have avoided precise explanations of what the Starch data mean and have focused attention on what matters in this analysis: the relative values of food advertisements that contain recipes and those that do not. The Starch information is being used similarly to how a catalyst is used in a chemical process: as a means of making other things happen (in this case a comparison of advertising techniques) without itself entering directly into what is happening.

Table 6.2

Aggregated Reading and Noting Data

	Median "noted" ratings		Median "read most" ratings	
	Rating	Index	Rating	Index
All 250 ads	51.7%	100	13.4%	100
Ads containing recipes	57.5	111	21.3	159
Ads without recipes but showing end results	51.4	99	11.4	85
Ads without recipes and without end results	40.6	77	7.4	54

It would not be a bad objective for us to use advertising research universally in this particular way.

Notes

1. For example, a research report we recently received from a major university in the Midwest included an analysis of responses from a sample of ninety-four individuals. These responses were percentaged to one decimal place, which created an entirely spurious impression of accuracy within narrow limits.

2. The main recall system was provided by Burke Marketing Services, which had a turnover of over $66 million in 1984, according to *Advertising Age,* May 23, 1985, p. 17. Among a sample of thirty-seven of the largest users of television advertising, twenty-six were found to be users of day-after-recall in 1980. Barbara Coe and James MacLachlan, "How Major TV Advertisers Evaluate Commercials," *Journal of Advertising Research* (December 1980): 51–54. From many discussions with manufacturers and advertising agencies, we believe that the technique is still occasionally used, although it is most employed in conjunction with other types of advertising research.

3. Charles Ramond, *Advertising Research: The State of the Art* (New York: Association of National Advertisers, 1976), p. 2.

4. Darrell B. Lucas, "The ABCs of ARF's PARM," *Journal of Marketing* (July 1960): 9–20. Although Lucas was the first investigator to publish his thoughts on this subject, he was not the first to examine it. See also Valentine Appel and Milton L. Blum, "Ad Recognition and Respondent Set," *Journal of Advertising Research* (June 1961): 13–21.

5. Lucas, "The ABCs of ARF's PARM," p. 16.

6. W.A. Twyman, *The Measurement of Page and Advertisement Exposure—A Review of Progress of the ARC* (London: Agencies Research Consortium, 1972).

7. D. Morgan Neu, "Measuring Advertisement Recognition," *Journal of Advertising Research* (December 1961): 17–22; Lyman E. Ostlund, "Advertising Copy Testing: A Review of Current Practices, Problems and Prospects," in *Current Issues and Research in Advertising*, J. Leigh and C. Martin Jr., eds. (Ann Arbor: University of Michigan, 1977), p. 99.

8. J.S. Karslake, "The Purdue Eye-Camera: A Practical Apparatus for Studying the Attention Value of Advertisements," *Journal of Applied Psychology* 24 (1940): 417–440; J.J. McNamara, "A New Method of Testing Effectiveness Through Eye Movement Photographs," *The Psychological Record* (Bloomington, IN) (September 1941): 399–460. The importance of these pioneer studies is discussed by David R. Aitchison, "Some Thoughts on the Readership of Advertisements," in *Admap World Advertising Workshop,* 1970.

9. The experimental work preceding the validation is discussed in Twyman, *The Measurement of Page and Advertisement Exposure,* pp. 22–25; see also Robert Fletcher and Bill Mabey, "Reading and Noting Revived!" *Admap* (December 1971): 422–428.

10. Art Shulman, "On-Air Recall by Time of Day," *Journal of Advertising Research* (February 1972): 21–23.

11. Shirley Young, "Copy Testing Without Magic Numbers," *Journal of Advertising Research* (February 1972): 3–12.

12. Sonia Yuspeh, "The Medium Versus the Message: The Effects of Program Environment on the Performance of Commercials," in *Tenth Attitude Research Conference,* Hilton Head, SC (American Marketing Association, 1979).

13. Young, "Copy Testing Without Magic Numbers," p. 6.

14. John B. Haskins, "Factual Recall as a Measure of Advertising Effectiveness," *Journal of Advertising Research* (March 1964): 2–8.

15. Young, "Copy Testing Without Magic Numbers," p. 3.

16. Ramond, *Advertising Research,* pp. 14–22.

17. Kristian S. Palda, "The Hypothesis of a Hierarchy of Effects: A Partial Evaluation," *Journal of Marketing Research* (February 1966): 13–24.

18. Michael L. Ray, Alan G. Sawyer, Michael L. Rothschild, Roger M. Heeler, Edward C. Strong, and Jerome B. Reed, "Marketing Communication and the Hierarchy of Effects" in *New Models for Mass Communication Research*, Peter Clarke, ed. (Beverly Hills, CA: Sage, 1973), p. 151.

19. Daniel Starch, *Principles of Advertising* (Chicago and New York: A.W. Shaw, 1923), pp. 159–160.

20. Ramond, *Advertising Research,* p. 15.

21. This notion was introduced by Leon Festinger, "Cognitive Dissonance," *Scientific American* (October 1962): 93–102.

22. These arguments are developed by Andrew Ehrenberg in "Repetitive Advertising and the Consumer," *Journal of Advertising Research* (April 1974): 25–33.

23. Henry Assael and George S. Day, "Attitudes and Awareness as Predictors of Market Share," *Journal of Advertising Research* (December 1968): 3–10; Terrence O'Brien, "Stages of Consumer Decision Making," *Journal of Marketing Research* (August 1971): 283–289; Ray et al., "Marketing Communication," pp. 147–176.

24. Ray et al., "Marketing Communication," p. 151.

25. Ramond, *Advertising Research,* p. 18.

26. Herbert E. Krugman, "The Impact of Television Advertising: Learning Without Involvement," *Public Opinion Quarterly* 29 (1965): 350–356.

27. Ibid., p. 355.

28. Ray et al., "Marketing Communication," pp. 158–164.

29. Herbert E. Krugman, "The Measurement of Advertising Involvement," *Public Opinion Quarterly* (Winter 1966–67): 586, footnote.

30. Ibid., p. 587.

31. Sidney Weinstein, Valentine Appel, and Curt Weinstein, "Brain Activity Responses to Magazine and Television Advertising," *Journal of Advertising Research* (June 1980): 57–63.

32. Ehrenberg, "Repetitive Advertising."

33. William R. Swinyard and Charles H. Patti, "The Communications Hierarchy Framework for Evaluating Copytesting Techniques," *Journal of Advertising* (Summer 1979): 29–35.

34. Rosser Reeves, *Reality in Advertising.* (New York: Alfred A. Knopf, 1960). In a nutshell, his theory is predicated on the notion that knowledge of advertising claims determines brand purchase. This ignores, among other things, the reverse influence:

as is widely known, users of a brand pay more attention to advertisements because of selective perception.

35. This point has been nicely demonstrated by Kim B. Rotzoll in "The Starch and Ted Bates Correlative Measure of Advertising Effectiveness," *Journal of Advertising Research* (March 1964): 22–24.

36. Yuspeh, "The Medium Versus the Message."

37. Leo Bogart, B. Stuart Tolley, and Frank Orenstein, "What One Little Ad Can Do," *Journal of Advertising Research* (August 1970): 3–13.

38. Ibid., p. 12.

39. The ARS system is proprietary to the research organization, *rsc* THE QUALITY MEASUREMENT COMPANY. The ARS technique is discussed in detail in John Philip Jones, *The Ultimate Secrets of Advertising* (Thousand Oaks, CA: Sage, 2001), chap. 3. (*rsc* is an acronym for Research Systems Corporation.)

40. Simon Broadbent, ed., *The Leo Burnett Book of Advertising* (London: Business Books, 1984), pp. 86–98; Stephen Colman and Gordon Brown, "Advertising Tracking Studies and Sales Effects," *Journal of the Market Research Society* 25, No. 2 (1983): 165–183.

41. Ehrenberg, "Repetitive Advertising," p. 29.

42. Stephen A. Greyser, *Cases in Advertising and Communications Management,* 2d edition (Englewood Cliffs, NJ: Prentice-Hall, 1981), pp. 148–167.

43. Stephen King, *What Is a Brand?* (London: J. Walter Thompson Company, 1978), pp. 5–9.

44. See the general discussion on this point in Roy H. Campbell, *Measuring the Sales and Profit Results of Advertising: A Managerial Approach* (New York: Association of National Advertisers, 1969), pp. 61–63.

45. Joel N. Axelrod, "Attitude Measures that Predict Purchase," *Journal of Advertising Research* (March 1968): 3–17.

46. Assael and Day, "Attitudes and Awareness as Predictors," pp. 3–10.

47. The Positioning Advertising Copy Testing Agencies, "Positioning Advertising Copy Testing" (January 1982).

48. Data from *Ladies' Home Journal,* July 1959. The Starch readings relate to reading-and-noting figures for 250 four-color page advertisements that appeared in sixteen issues of the *Ladies' Home Journal.*

7

How Advertising Influences Sales

Chapters 7 and 8 should be read and considered together. Chapter 7 is concerned strictly with sales effects; chapter 8 is devoted to the broader matter of how advertising can enrich and strengthen brands. There is a time dimension. Advertising's influence on sales is immediate (i.e., it is generally felt within seven days of an advertisement's exposure). A repetition of such effects, measured at the end of a year, amounts to a medium-term effect. But, in addition, extending beyond a year and reaching into the future are additional advertising-related effects that work slowly to augment a brand's added values, with a measurable influence not only on sales but on a brand's profitability and durability in the marketplace.

Readers will remember from chapter 4 the detailed description of the Dynamic Difference/MAP model, which demonstrated the influence of year-by-year increases and decreases in advertising expenditure on the sales of a brand, effects measured (in the phrase used in this present chapter) in the medium term. The point was made in chapter 4 that in 70 percent of cases there is an incremental effect on sales from variations in advertising expenditure. This is of course only possible because there is some fundamental advertising effect in the first place; logically it could not be otherwise.

But the analysis in chapter 4 does not allow us to conclude that the 70 percent of effective campaigns are all *equally* effective in stimulating sales. This chapter will demonstrate a wide spectrum of effectiveness. And, in addition, there are the 30 percent of campaigns that have no effect at all.

We start with the short term. But as will be explained, a short-term effect does not automatically lead to a medium-term effect or a long-term effect.

Conditions apply, and to understand these, we shall introduce four important points that will form much of the agenda for this chapter.

1. The immediate influence of advertising on sales acts as a gatekeeper to all further effects. Without it there will naturally be no medium-term effect (i.e., a repetition of short-term effects); nor will there be any long-term effect. This point sounds to some people like common sense. It is derived, however, from the observation of facts, since common sense is a dangerous guide to understanding the rather slippery relationship between advertising's three orders of effect. For many years, some practitioners' and academics' common sense led them to believe that although some advertising may be devoid of immediate effect, its influence could be slowly building so that it eventually produces some dramatic happening, in the same way that a dam wall may burst as a result of the buildup of water pressure; and the longer the delay, the greater the eventual bursting of the pent-up waters. This view was once fairly prevalent, although it is now rare, since its believers have given up the search for empirical validation. The "dam-bursting" hypothesis is now generally regarded as a chimera because no one can find any facts to validate it.

2. If an advertisement causes immediate sales (i.e., if it is in the 70 percent "effective" group), it need be exposed only *once* in order to generate its effect. Extra exposures produce very few additional sales. To understand the importance of this point, we must consider two important aspects of a brand's media strategy. First, to be effective, the advertisement must be exposed to a substantial proportion of a brand's target group during any finite period during which advertising is intended to influence sales; and a brand's media schedule is composed of a number of such periods over the course of a year. Media planning today is normally composed of one-week periods. The second point is that members of the target group need be reached only once during each short period. Some duplication must unfortunately be accepted because media vehicles provide a very imprecise demographic match with the target groups for most brands, which means that no matter how carefully the media vehicles are chosen, some members of the target group will not be reached at all, some will be reached once, and some will be reached more than once. But if the strategy is to concentrate on people once only, this can generally be executed in a crude but practical fashion. The principle of maximum reach combined with minimum frequency is at the heart of the doctrine of Continuity planning, an operational procedure discussed later in this chapter.

3. A logical inference of the fact that one exposure is enough for a short-term effect is that the means of engineering more than one exposure—budgetary weight and media deployment—are relatively unimportant in the short term. The power of advertising lies in the advertisement itself, in the creative idea within it, and not in repetition.

4. Since the medium-term effect of advertising comes from a repetition of short-term effects, the only way in which the short-term effect can be maintained at its initial level is by repeating the advertising every week. The problem is that, with few exceptions, even very large advertisers can afford to be on the air for only about half the year. Fifty-two-week coverage is virtually unknown. The doctrine of continuity planning almost always means a reduction in weekly weight below the level dictated by the type of concentrated media scheduling that used to be prevalent. Continuity planning therefore offers the great advantage of helping advertisers spend less money per week, *but to be present on the air for more weeks than before,* which means a measurable improvement in the economic efficiency of deploying media dollars.

The four points described above have an important bearing on a brand's overall advertising strategy and especially on its media strategy. They are all based on sound research, and the rest of this chapter is devoted to describing how this research was carried out and what findings emerged.

Advertising's Short-Term Effect and How It Is Measured

It took a long time before researchers learned how to measure the short-term effect of advertising, because the basic method of measuring sales, the Nielsen retail audit mechanism (described in chapter 3), works by measuring sales over a two-month time span. As was discovered with dramatic clarity during the 1980s, sales of all brands are in fact extremely volatile; a brand's sales in any week of a year are different from its sales in every other week. *And advertising is capable of influencing the sales during any week.*

The flaw in the Nielsen system was that during any two-month research period, sales of a brand can advance and retreat, in some cases repeatedly, so that the end result—the estimated overall sales level over the whole two-month period—will show a substantial total, normally not much different from that of the two months preceding. This is the very stability that encouraged Ehrenberg to develop his ideas about stationary market conditions (described in chapter 5). But there is one thing missing from Ehrenberg's analysis.

Beneath the smooth surface—a real enough phenomenon at least when sales are measured over long periods—there is unexpected ferment. A brand's sales move restlessly week by week, although the ups and downs will tend to even out over time. If advertising influences these movements, which it certainly does, then this effect can be captured only if we measure sales accurately week by week. During the 1980s the scanner system was devised to make this measurement possible. Scanners are used by researchers sometimes at the checkout counter of supermarkets, sometimes in the home. The system that pioneered the accurate measurement of the immediate effect of advertising was based on in-home scanners. The research organization that carried out the work was, not surprisingly, A.C. Nielsen, and the technique is described technically as Pure Single-Source research.[1]

The Nielsen system of Single-Source research was based on Nielsen's ongoing Household Panel, a properly drawn sample of 40,000 households across the United States, in which every purchase of regularly bought brands was logged with hand-held scanners. In each home, the shopper uses the scanner to read the Universal Product Code (UPC) on each pack bought and thus records details of brand name, variety, and pack size. The shopper also punches in manually the date, the price, simple details of any promotional offers, the name of the store, and the identity of the individual doing the shopping. The information that has been fed into the scanner is sent to Nielsen by a simple automatic process over the public telephone lines. The data gathering is continuous—longitudinal, to use the technical language of statistics. The scanner system was data collection of a highly sophisticated type. Nevertheless, it represented only one of three pieces of information needed for Pure Single-Source research.

The second process of data collection covered television viewing. This initial Nielsen study concentrated on television alone, although later studies by other research organizations also covered magazines. Nielsen selected a representative subset of 2,000 homes from their Household Panel and attached a meter to every television set in each home to record when it was switched on and the channel to which it was tuned. The viewing of individual family members was not recorded, but "People Meters" permitted this to be done for the A.C. Nielsen Single-Source research in Germany.

The third piece of research tackled the immense diversity of television viewing patterns: the large number of different channels viewed in each of 150 cities and regions in the United States. Nielsen used a system called Monitor Plus, which employs a series of television receiving stations that log all of the advertising that appears, at 15-second intervals, in the 23 largest Designated Market Areas (DMAs) in the United States, covering more than half the total population. Information is collected from all of the main stations in these areas, both network and cable. The system is called *Pure* Single-Source research because the buying of a brand is related rigorously to the presence or absence of advertising *for that identified brand* during the seven days before purchase.

There were thus three different streams of information—on household purchasing, television viewing, and the identities of the advertised brands. A "window" of seven days was determined as the period during which a short-term advertising effect is assumed to be felt. Since the date when the brand was purchased was collected in the scanner, it was relatively easy to identify whether advertising for that same brand had entered—or had *not* entered—the household during the preceding seven days. Nielsen took immense pains to devise the computer programs to generate the information specified.

The basic idea behind the research was the concept of "ad households" and "adless households," illustrated in Figure 7.1.

A subtle but important characteristic of these two collections of households is that the groups were different *for every single purchase occasion.* With each purchase of any brand, the 2,000 households in the panel formed themselves into unique combinations of ad households and adless households, plus a third group that had not purchased the brand at all at this time. For the next purchase of a brand, the groups were mixed totally differently.

The tabulation of the data was extremely complicated, but this was a vital part of the process. We were examining constantly changing combinations of the same collection of 2,000 households. The advantage of this system was that it guaranteed the homogeneity of the subsamples. The presence or absence of advertising was the sole variable distinguishing the subsamples on every occasion the brand was bought. Here are examples of what this meant in practice.

Buying took place at different times of the year, during various seasonal highs and lows depending on the product category. In the high season, both

Figure 7.1 **Ad Households and Adless Households**

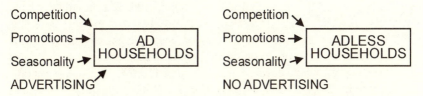

Purchases in ad households *minus* purchases in adless households = purchases driven by advertising.

the ad households and adless households were buying a lot, and the only difference between them was the presence or absence of advertising before-hand. This worked in a similar way in the low season, when people were buying less. Buying was also accompanied or unaccompanied by sales pro-motions. When promotions were in operation, they attracted both ad house-holds and adless households; and again the only difference between them was the presence or absence of advertising before the purchase. The same was true of purchases unaccompanied by sales promotions.

The constantly changing grouping of ad households and adless house-holds was a system totally different from one based on a matched pair of permanent, geographically separated subpanels, the method used by the American research company Information Resources Inc. (IRI) for their BehaviorScan panels. Single-Source research in France also employed the latter method.

The measure of advertising effect developed was based on a brand's mar-ket share *measured in purchase occasions* and not purchase volume. The former is a sharper way of signaling advertising effects. The name given to the system is Short-Term Advertising Strength (abbreviated STAS); it has three elements:

Baseline STAS: The brand's market share in the households that had re-ceived no television advertising for it during the seven days before the purchase took place.

Stimulated STAS: The brand's market share in the households that had received at least one television advertisement for it during these previous seven days.

STAS Differential: The difference between the Baseline STAS and the Stimulated STAS. This is normally indexed on the Baseline, which has a value of 100. The STAS Differential Index is the measure of the short-term sales gain (or loss) generated by a brand's advertising. It is a math-ematical expression of Figure 7.1, which demonstrates the difference in purchases between the ad households and the adless households.

A brand's STAS Differential is an average for all of a brand's separate purchases across a year; the research was mostly based on the twelve months of 1991. The research measured a total of seventy-eight advertised brands (with purchasing data for an additional sixty-four unadvertised ones). Twelve product categories were covered, with a total of 110,000 purchase occasions, an average of about 1,400 per brand. The STAS measures for a real brand, coded AL, are described in Figure 7.2.

Figure 7.2 **STAS Measures for Brand AL**

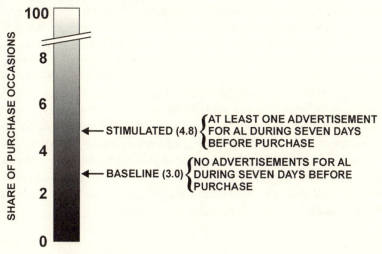

The simplest way to show the sharp and wide-ranging effects of advertising is by dividing the seventy-eight brands into a number of more or less equal groups and calculating the average STAS Differential for each. All of the brands were ranked by the size of their individual STAS, then divided into ten separate blocks (of 7–8-8-8-8-8-8-8-8–7 brands), known technically as deciles. The STAS for each decile was then averaged; the results are shown in Table 7.1.

Table 7.1

Decile Analysis of STAS (Seventy-eight Nielsen Brands)

Rank	Average STAS Differential
Top	236
9th	164
8th	139
7th	121
6th	116
5th	108
4th	103
3rd	97
2nd	89
Bottom	73
Average	124

Table 7.1 does not need much comment. At the top end of the sample of brands, the effect of advertising is very powerful. The most effective 10 percent of advertisements boost sales by an average of 136 percent; in fact 30 percent of campaigns show a strong effect. A further 40 percent show a positive but generally rather weak effect. Thirty percent of advertisements are associated with a *reduction* in sales. We do not believe that these advertisements at the bottom end actually cause sales to go down because they are so positively awful. The better explanation is that the advertising is not strong enough to protect the brands from the more powerful campaigns of competition when the brand and the competition are advertised at the same time.

The research has been replicated in the United States and in a number of different foreign countries. The general spread of STAS scores is everywhere reasonably similar. See Table 7.2, which compares the STAS deciles in the United States, the United Kingdom, and Germany.

Medium-Term Effect as a Repetition of Short-Term Effects

There are huge numbers of potential buyers at all times for all established brands in every category. And in every category, the pattern of buying shows a constant interchange of brand shares, the "ups" for a specific brand reflecting its advertising at the time—provided, of course, that the campaign has a positive STAS. If only one brand is advertised, this will directly attract customers from all others. If more than one is advertised at the same time, the brand whose campaign generates the highest STAS Differential will do best.

Table 7.2

Three-Country Decile Analysis of STAS Differentials

Rank	United States, 1991 78 brands Nielsen	Germany, 1993 28 brands Nielsen	Britain, 1986–90 67 brands *Adlab*
Top	236	154	184
9th	164	127	129
8th	139	116	119
7th	121	108	114
6th	116	106	110
5th	108	101	107
4th	103	100	102
3rd	97	98	98
2nd	89	92	93
Bottom	73	83	73

The gaps in a brand's schedule will therefore cause losses of business because millions of potential buyers have been missed. This process is illustrated in Figure 7.3, a hypothetical picture, although the lesson it contains is real enough. Each short-term sales increase represents the size of the STAS Differential. The net gain at the end of the year represents the sum of short-term gains minus the sum of short-term losses.

The end result is as we see in Figure 7.4, which describes a real German brand, ZAA, whose STAS Differential index (B minus A) showed a rise of 50 percent, but whose medium-term sales improvement (D minus C) was only 14 percent. The difference between the two numbers was the result of the gaps in ZAA's schedule, when consumers were responding to the advertising for competitive brands.

Figure 7.3 **Schematic Diagram of Sales Gains and Losses for Brand AAA over the Course of a Year**

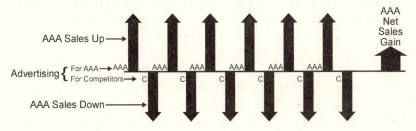

Figure 7.4 **STAS Differential and Medium-Term Sales Effect For Brand ZAA**

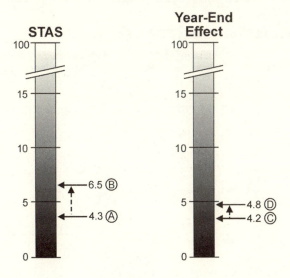

The performance of brand ZAA, despite the drop from 50 percent to 14 percent, is actually good. The losses of business below the STAS Differential are greater for most other brands. In many cases the effect of a positive STAS completely disappears as a result of the stronger campaigns for competitive brands, which means that the brands that lose their STAS end the year in negative territory.

Returning to the 78 brands on which Tables 7.1 and 7.2 were based, we can see the general application of the end-year drop if we look at the medium-term effect of advertising for these brands. Table 7.3 is a decile analysis comparing the range of STAS effects and that of medium-term effects.

The figures describing the medium-term growth of the brands are much smaller than the STAS Differentials. The medium-term figures show weaker effects from the most strongly growing brands, and there are more brands that are declining. The obvious explanation is that, over the course of a year, the increases shown in the STAS figures have been tamed by consumers' responses to competitive advertising. The STAS effect has been repeated over a year, but there has been a countervailing force. With inevitable gaps in the advertising schedules, consumers have responded to competitive advertising during these gaps.

All the brands taken together show a net growth of 6 percent. Since this measure is based on market shares, this increase demonstrates that the advertising of brands is not a totally zero-sum game (i.e., with pluses balanced by minuses). What has happened is that the advertised brands have managed to grow in the aggregate, at the expense of store brands and price brands, which

Table 7.3

STAS and Medium-Term Effects Compared

Quintiles	Average STAS Differential index	Average medium-term Growth index
Top	236	182
9th	164	121
8th	139	113
7th	121	109
6th	116	104
5th	108	98
4th	103	95
3rd	97	90
2nd	89	84
Bottom	73	69
Average	124	103

receive no advertising support. This conclusion provides an interesting general endorsement of the value of consumer advertising.

Table 7.4 examines brand growth. It is a matrix relating two influences on this: STAS Differential and Advertising Intensity (i.e., a brand's advertising investment related to other brands in its category, allowing for differences in brand shares). With both of these the data have been split into two groups: (a) average and above and (b) below average. The average STAS Differential was 124, with twenty-four brands average or above, and fifty-four below.

Table 7.4 demonstrates a number of interesting points:

- The twenty-four brands with the top STAS measures (average and above) grew by 22 percent.
- The fifty-four brands with the below-average STAS measures showed no growth.
- Of the twenty-four brands with the top STAS measures, only eleven combined their high STAS with high advertising intensity, and these achieved an average growth of 35 percent, which is spectacular in the field of repeat-purchase packaged goods.
- For the brands that generated a below-average STAS Differential, high advertising intensity makes little difference to their performance. In sales terms, the brands with heavy advertising were 4 percent in the black; those without it were 4 percent in the red. Extra repetition has very little influence on a basically ineffective campaign.

The two important points revealed so far—the key importance of STAS as gatekeeper and the role of the media budget in prolonging sales growth by engineering a repeated short-term effect—support the proposition that *the short-term effect of an advertisement determines whether or not that adver-*

Table 7.4

Matrix Relating STAS Differential to Advertising Intensity

	Adv. int. below average	Adv. int. average and above	Total
STAS Diff. average and above	13 brands Av. growth index 112	11 brands Av. growth index 135	24 brands Av. growth index 122
STAS Diff. below average	36 brands Av. growth index 96	18 brands Av. growth index 104	54 brands Av. growth index 99

tisement will have a medium-term effect. A repetition of short-term effects over a period (normally twelve months)—effects felt exclusively during the periods when the brand is advertised—adds up to a medium-term effect.

The STAS Differential and advertising intensity are of course natural partners. They work together for the simple reason that advertising intensity determines (in conjunction with the brand's media strategy) whether or not the advertising will be exposed often enough to prolong the short-term effect of the campaign over a longer period.

The two measures should therefore be knitted together, quantity being added to quality. This can be done quite simply, by multiplying the STAS Differential index for each brand by its advertising intensity. The resulting calculation is called the index of advertising effort.

The analysis in Table 7.5 is in the form of another matrix: this time relating advertising effort to promotional intensity (i.e., a brand's expenditure on sales promotions related to other brands in its category, allowing for differences in brand shares). The average figure for advertising effort is 283; twenty-five brands exceeded or equaled this average and fifty-three were below it.

The conclusions from Table 7.5 are striking:

- Medium-term growth is exclusively associated with above-average advertising effort (22 percent growth for the twenty-five high advertising effort brands, compared with no growth for the fifty-three brands whose advertising effort was low).
- Among the brands with above-average advertising effort, *promotional intensity provides a significant extra stimulus to sales.*
- With low advertising effort, promotional intensity, whether high or low, makes little difference to a brand's progress.

Table 7.5

Matrix Relating Advertising Effort to Promotional Intensity

	Promotional Intensity		
	Below average	Above average	Total
Adv. effort av. and above	12 brands Av. growth index 111	13 brands Av. growth index 132	25 brands Av. growth index 122
Adv. effort below av.	32 brands Av. growth index 96	21 brands Av. growth index 101	53 brands Av. growth index 98

This analysis generates an important concept. At the higher levels of advertising effort, sales promotions work synergistically to boost the already strong influence of the advertising. *Sales promotions can add to the effect of advertising; such synergy is strongest when promotions coincide with the most powerful advertising campaigns.*

We now return to the five top deciles of brands. These all had a strong STAS Differential and all made progress in the medium term. (Since we are confining this analysis to five deciles—all of the campaigns that posted end-year growth and ignoring the failures—it becomes simpler to rename these five group quintiles.) Table 7.6 relates the medium-term sales growth of these top brands to the average advertising effort and promotional intensity in each quintile. The figures in the table are plotted in Figure 7.5.

The direction of the figures is unmistakable. The two combinations of marketing inputs succeed in predicting marketplace performance.

The trajectory of the input figures—the steepness of the curves—is more pronounced than the final out-turn in brand growth. The input figures start lower and end higher. But there is no break in the series, and it can be seen that the fit of the curves is good. There is actually some advantage in producing input curves that are steeper than the out-turn, because the operational lessons from the analysis become clearer.

This analysis is made with the aim of helping advertisers boost their brands in large, competitive, and often stagnant markets. Here are four guidelines:

1. The competitive functional performance of their brands must be good enough to support advertising investment. In the eyes of consumers, the brand must justify repurchase.

Table 7.6

Growing Brands: Medium-Term Growth Compared with Combined Marketing Stimuli

Growing quintile	Growth index	Adv. effort index	Adv. effort plus prom. intensity index
Top	209	260	306
4th	139	199	167
3rd	130	139	123
2nd	125	105	109
Bottom	120	79	72
Baseline: average of all declining brands	100	100	100

Figure 7.5 **Quintile Analysis of Thirty-nine Brands Showing Medium-Term Growth**

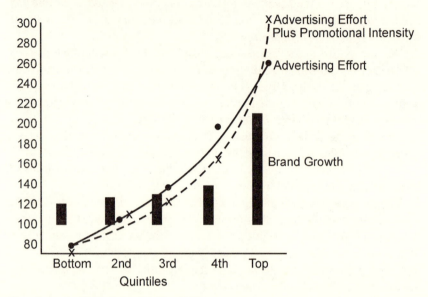

Note: Index on 39 declining brands = 100.

2. Manufacturers should make sure that their brand's advertising generates a high STAS Differential. If not, they must persist until they produce a campaign that does, otherwise the campaign should not be allowed through the gate.

3. A brand's budget will inevitably be governed by its present and/or anticipated profitability. Within these limits, above-average investment is strongly recommended for those campaigns that generate a high STAS Differential. This must certainly be the case for new brands, which must invest at a high level to become established.

4. It is less desirable to boost consumer promotions in view of their uneconomic cost. However, pressures in the marketplace will force manufacturers to promote, and when this happens there is merit in concentrating the promotional support on those brands with a high STAS Differential plus high advertising intensity. In all events, advertising and promotions should coincide in time to maximize synergy.

The Advertising Response Function

The response function is an example of a theory with a directly practical application. It describes the amount of advertising needed to trigger buying. In particular, it illustrates the sales effect of additional amounts of advertising and whether they generate increments of sales at an increasing or diminishing rate. These points will become clearer by comparing Figures 7.6 and 7.7.

Figure 7.6 **Advertising Response Function with Threshold** (S-Shaped Curve)

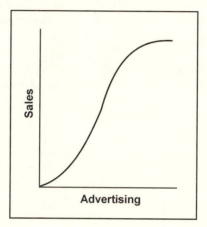

Figure 7.7 **Advertising Response Function without Threshold** (Concave-Downward Curve)

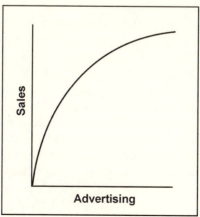

In Figures 7.6 and 7.7, the horizontal axis plots equal "doses" of advertising. These can be measured in a number of ways: in dollars, in television Gross Rating Points, or in consumer impressions ("Opportunities to See"). The vertical axis plots the *incremental* sales that are generated by the progressive doses of advertising. We see therefore *varying* amounts of sales output that have resulted from *equal* amounts of advertising input.

In Figure 7.6, extra advertising causes sales to increase at a growing rate, building up to a threshold shown by the bend in the curve (known as the inflexion point), where the increasing sales increments change to diminishing ones. The amount of advertising that produces the greatest sales effect for the advertising dollar is measured at the inflexion point: where the marginal— or additional—dose of advertising produces greatest return.

In Figure 7.7, all doses of advertising produce sales results, but the increments decline from the beginning. The first advertising generates the most sales; the second produces extra volume, but less than the first; the third produces more still, but less than the second—hence diminishing returns.

These alternative theories are used to support two different ways of deploying advertising money. Figure 7.6 underpins a once-popular belief that a fixed number of advertisement exposures (generally considered to be three) has to be received by the consumer before the advertising will seriously influence his or her purchasing behavior. This number of exposures was considered to be the threshold representing maximum effect. The result was the popular policy of compressing the advertising into confined periods to obtain an "effective frequency" of three.

With the alternative theory of diminishing returns shown in Figure 7.7, the first dose of advertising is seen to be the most productive one, and extra doses produce increases that become progressively smaller. These are less economic because each diminishing sales increment costs the same advertising budget as the one before. The way to exploit diminishing returns is to create during each week a strong effect by covering a large audience *once* and no more. We can then move on to the next week, when the advertising can be used to stimulate fresh sales, again with a single strong exposure. This is a broad description of Continuity planning.

As suggested, the theory embodied in Figure 7.6 once received wide support. This meant that the advertising schedules of the majority of brands in most countries around the world were for many decades made up of two-, three-, or four-week periods of advertising (periods chosen for no logical reason), each concentrated to achieve "effective frequency." These periods were separated by intervals during which there was no advertising. The gaps were of course unavoidable because advertising budgets could not run to year-round exposure at a heavy rate. The pockets of concentration in such schedules are known as "flights" in the United States and "bursts" in Europe.

Until the 1990s the shape of the advertising response function was not a subject of great interest to the advertising business. The majority of media plans employed flights, a policy that was of course tacitly based on the S-shaped response function shown in Figure 7.6. It was unlikely that media planners, who are practical people, were much concerned with the theoretical basis of the strategy of media concentration, which was automatically—and perhaps unthinkingly—applied in virtually all circumstances.

The influential research study *Effective Frequency: The Relationship Between Frequency and Advertising Effectiveness,* sponsored by the Advertising Research Foundation and published by the Association of National Advertisers in 1979, gave academic support to a flighting strategy. The main piece of evidence in this book came from Colin McDonald's pilot study carried out in Britain in 1966, which explored for the first time the possibilities of Pure Single-Source research. This showed an S-shaped curve of a very extreme type. Unfortunately this was a result of the way in which McDonald analyzed the data. He used an incomplete method because he measured the response of purchasing to increments of advertising solely by the amount of switching from brand to brand. This tells us only half the story, since it ignores repeated purchase of the same brand, which can be as influenced by advertising as brand switching can.

The first major piece of Pure Single-Source research, described earlier in this chapter, used a more straightforward method of analyzing all of the data from the first large-scale piece of such research in the United States. It measured the change in purchasing caused by advertising—both in absolute and in incremental terms—by a simple change in market share. This method has not been disputed since the work was first published in 1995. When McDonald recomputed his 1966 figures with this simpler method, his findings echoed the Nielsen ones—a straightforward pattern of diminishing returns. McDonald's results can be seen in Figure 7.8; the Nielsen results, in Figure 7.9.

The Nielsen research was planned to measure the sales response to any amount of advertising for a brand during the seven days before it was bought. It was reasonably simple to isolate the sales response in the homes that had received a single advertisement. As can be seen in Figure 7.9, the average share of market for all seventy-eight brands was 7.8 percent in the adless households, the level of the baseline. The share in the ad households that had received only one advertisement was 8.4 percent; in the ad households that had received any number of advertisements it was 8.7 percent.

Figure 7.8 **Response Function: McDonald's 1966 British Pure Single-Source Data Recomputed with the Jones Method**

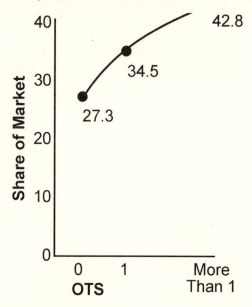

Figure 7.9 **Response Function: Nielsen 1991 American Pure Single-Source Data from Seventy-eight Brands**

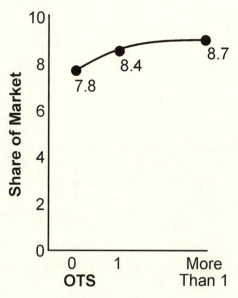

This research demonstrated a sharp pattern of diminishing returns, with 73 percent of the short-term business generated by a brand's advertising accounted for by households that had received a single advertisement. An additional 27 percent came from households in which a larger volume of advertising for the brand had appeared on their television screens. This finding, of a 73:27 ratio between the effect of one exposure and subsequent exposures, had some remarkable effects on American advertising practice. The research was also replicated, and subsequent studies have confirmed broadly what had been found.

The first repeat of the American research was in Germany. This showed quite clearly that a single advertisement can be effective—often highly effective. This conclusion has also been confirmed by other American data from, among others, Lawrence Gibson, and by British data, both from Andrew Roberts and from Colin McDonald's large-scale *Adlab* study. McDonald makes an important point by emphasizing propinquity. The greatest sales effect comes from advertising one day before purchase. Fewer sales come from advertising two days before, and fewer still from three days before. McDonald had found the same thing in his 1966 investigation.

The count of published response functions shows more than 200 brands whose campaigns show diminishing returns, and slightly more than ten—mainly new brands—whose campaigns show S-shaped thresholds. The logic of media concentration—at least on a temporary basis—for new brands is that new product concepts and new advertising campaigns need a degree of repetition before consumers can understand them. However, even in this exceptional circumstance, it can be shown that the most efficient plan is a single weekly exposure.

Continuity in the Marketplace

The size of the medium-term effect is determined not only by the creative content of the campaign, but also by the budget and its media strategy. Budget and media are devices to engineer the advertising continuity needed to protect the brand from competitive assaults.

The most effective media strategy for a brand can be described simply. However, it is not easy to implement such a strategy, because of the complexities of the media marketplace:

1. Aim to cover a substantial proportion of the brand's target group once every week with as little duplication as possible. "Substantial proportion" is a judgment call based on the size of the brand, its

   target group, and knowledge of the effectiveness of defined levels of
   reach achieved in the past.
2. To attain this minimum reach, determine the optimum number of
   weekly gross rating points (GRPs) and establish the best types of
   day parts and television programs to use to minimize audience
   duplication. These procedures are again judgmental, and they require expert knowledge of the television audience and of the fast-
   changing field of programming.
3. Run the weekly advertising pattern for as many weeks as the budget
   will allow. Any inevitable gaps in the schedule should occur during
   the low season.

These recommendations call for redeploying advertising budgets to achieve
a greater continuity than many schedules achieve at present, and of course
this means less short-term concentration—an economically favorable outcome because of the way it manages to reduce the effect of diminishing returns. Regional test programs are also a good idea as long as these can be
carried out efficiently and economically. (This is discussed in chapter 12.)

These thoughts, which would at one time have been considered highly
unorthodox, are not falling on deaf ears, in either the United States or Europe.

In the late 1970s, at J. Walter Thompson, London, the client and agency
commissioned an econometric study of the advertising response function for
Andrex, a very powerful brand and market leader in the bathroom tissue category. This response function—although it came in the form of a rather weak
regression—seemed to show a pattern of diminishing returns. This was nevertheless good enough to persuade the client and agency to plan and run a
pattern of continuous advertising in a number of typical television areas. A
careful analysis of sales at the end of a year showed significantly stronger
sales in the test areas than in the rest of Britain, which acted as the statistical
control.

As a result of this test, the national advertising was changed to a pattern of
continuous advertising. This was a very unusual thing for an important national brand. However, it has been acknowledged by both client and agency
to have benefited the brand enormously over the years. It did this by maintaining the brand's already high penetration and purchase frequency, and indeed by preserving Andrex's comfortable market leadership, as the agency
subsequently reported:

   [J. Walter Thompson] believe[s] that this high level of carry-over and behavior maintenance is in some measure attributable to the disposition of

advertising weight within and between sales periods. Andrex has, for many years, disposed advertising weight continuously. It is not clustered in bursts.

Such an unprejudiced, experimental mind-set has also been adopted by many American advertisers—an attitude that must be welcomed by the research community. During the course of 1996, at least eight major advertisers, with an aggregate national billing of more than $4 billion, were seriously experimenting with Continuity scheduling on an area basis, and in some cases were producing demonstrably positive results.

We possess full details of the media experiments carried out by one of these organizations—an extremely prominent advertiser and a company with nine major marketing divisions whose brands are all household names. In 1995, the average number of weeks of advertising across all of these divisions was sixteen, at an average weekly advertising weight of ninety-seven GRPs. As a result of successful experimentation during the course of 1996, eight of the nine divisions adjusted the distribution of their advertising funds. In 1997, the average number of advertised weeks in all nine operating divisions had increased to twenty-two, and the average weekly GRP level had been decreased to eighty-four. The company has taken—after good research and careful deliberation—a major step toward Continuity scheduling. The plans also accommodated a good deal of detailed media innovation aimed at stretching the net reach of the schedules and reducing wasteful duplication.

During 1996, the level of interest in Continuity scheduling increased. By December, 53 percent of major clients and 70 percent of senior media executives in agencies were aware of the research into single-exposure effectiveness and the value of continuous advertising. Similar numbers also claimed to be either implementing or considering implementing plans to advertise more continuously than before. Interest was particularly strong among packaged goods and automotive advertisers.

In 1999 the celebrated *AdWorks2* study was released to subscribers, and selected extracts were published. This was a cooperative enterprise between Media Marketing Assessment Inc. (MMA) and Information Resources Inc. (IRI). It was a econometric study of more than 800 brands in 200 separate categories, using sales data from 4,000 grocery, drug, and mass merchandiser stores over the two years 1995–96. This research compared the effectiveness of Continuity and Flighted media plans and reached an unambiguous conclusion:

> Continuity plans are more effective than Flighted plans. This supports findings from other studies that point to the importance of Recency. Brands that are planning to increase weight should first consider adding weeks

instead of adding weight to existing flights. Brands with high levels of GRPs delivered per week should consider shifting some weight across additional weeks.

This conclusion was derived from a special calculation of the relative effectiveness of different schedules, based on the average (indexed at 100) for all television schedules covered by the *AdWorks2* research. The relative effectiveness of three mixes of Continuity and weekly weight are as shown in Table 7.7.

The greater effectiveness of high Continuity scheduling over low Continuity is a manifestation of diminishing returns. The high Continuity schedule benefits from operating every week on a lower—more productive—part of the advertising response curve. In contrast to this, the low Continuity (concentrated) schedule soon hits diminishing returns.

Another way of expressing this same point is that if two brands with the same budget, size, media costs, and advertising elasticity choose to raise their GRP support by, say, 20 percent, we would be able to see very different volume returns as a result of different patterns of continuity. With additional weeks but no change in the weekly concentration of GRPs, the extra budget would generate extra sales. But if weekly GRP levels are lifted drastically and weeks on the air not increased, we would consistently and quickly see saturation, and overall television effectiveness would not be improved in line with the budget increase. The extra money would be essentially wasted.

As if to write *finis* to this debate, the Advertising Research Foundation (ARF), which had sponsored the 1979 *Effective Frequency* study, formally announced at the end of 1997 the termination of its support for the doctrine of effective frequency. Using a slightly macabre metaphor, the ARF declared: "We agreed to amputate the rule of thumb. And like any amputation, it was painful."

Table 7.7

Relative Effectiveness of TV Schedules Based on Different Combinations of Continuity and Weekly Weight

	Weeks on air	Maximum GRPs[a] per week	Index of sales effectiveness
Low Continuity	9	240	61
Medium Continuity	22	163	106
High Continuity	38	193	132

[a]GRPs = gross rating points.

Medium-Term Effects Measured Econometrically

Econometrics provides a valuable tool, regression analysis, with which it is possible to calculate the medium-term effect of advertising. It does this by estimating in any year the value of a brand's sales that can be directly attributable to the advertising. (Similar calculations can also be made for trade and consumer promotions.) Regression analysis does not explain *how* the medium-term effect of advertising is actually achieved—by a repetition of short-term effects (which support the logic of a media strategy based on Continuity planning).

But regression analysis provides a hard number to describe advertising's medium-term effect, and this is an important step toward estimating the profit and loss yielded by advertising investments. As a general rule,

1. Advertising contributes between 3 percent and 8 percent of a year's sales value for most brands of repeat-purchase goods.
2. However, in virtually all cases, this sales value falls short of the annual cost of advertising.

Nevertheless, we cannot draw the operational lesson that a manufacturer can always increase his profit by stopping his advertising. Advertising is a means of maintaining sales at a level that generates scale economies. These in turn lower the manufacturer's cost; and because of competition much of this benefit is passed on to the consumer in the form of lower prices. Advertising therefore plays an integral role in enabling the manufacturer to make volume sales at a profit. An elimination of advertising would mean a smaller sales volume at a higher cost per unit.

There is another important point. The long-term effect of advertising (discussed in chapter 8) can often be quantified, and it can in turn be added to the medium-term effect. When we do this, we discover that for many brands the advertising cost is more than covered by the value of incremental sales when the medium-term and long-term effects of advertising are aggregated.

The Argument in Brief

During the 1980s, as a result of an important development in the technique of collecting research data, it became possible to measure accurately the immediate effect of advertising with a method that became known as Pure Single-Source research. The first broadscale research based on this method was carried out by A.C. Nielsen in the United States, and it has been replicated both in the United States and in a number of foreign countries.

The research demonstrated that advertising for a brand of repeat-purchase packaged goods can have a strongly positive effect on the sales of that brand in a period of up to seven days following an advertisement's exposure. In this interval, a single advertisement exposure does most of the work, and additional media weight beyond this does not have much additional effect on sales. Therefore budgetary and media factors are not particularly important in determining whether advertising will achieve an immediate effect. The determining factor is the advertising itself—the creative idea embodied in it.

Not all advertising has a positive effect in the short term. About 30 percent of campaigns have a strong effect. About 40 percent have a positive but rather weak effect. About 30 percent are associated with sales declines, because the advertising is unable to defend the brand from creatively stronger campaigns for competitive brands. As a general rule, the short-term effect of advertising is sensitive to creative differences between campaigns, and these vary widely.

An extremely important aspect of the short-term effect is that it acts as a gatekeeper to longer-term effects. If the advertising has no immediate effect, it will have no further influence on sales, no matter how much extra money is spent on the campaign.

A repetition of short-term effects across the course of a year produces a medium-term effect, measured by advertising's contribution to a brand's annual sales. The medium-term effect is invariably less than each individual short-term effect, because the medium-term effect is an aggregation of effects solely from the periods when the brand is advertised: these might be described as advertising "ups." No brand is advertised during every week of a year, and when it is not advertised, it suffers from the negative effects of advertising for competitive brands: for the brand in question, these represent "downs." The medium-term effect is therefore the aggregation of the brand's advertising "ups" minus the aggregation of its "downs."

The need to reduce the number of weeks during which the brand is unadvertised (so as to reduce the number of "downs") is the basic idea behind the doctrine of Continuity planning. This lays down that during each week, advertising weight should be reduced to the minimum necessary for an impact on sales of the brand, and this weight should be deployed for as many weeks as the advertising budget will allow.

An important device for reducing the weekly weight is to cut back the frequency of a weekly advertising schedule in order to reach as large a target group as possible *once,* with minimum duplication. This involves some difficulties in the tactics of media buying, but serious steps can always be made in this direction. The emphasis on a single exposure is derived from analysis of the short-term advertising response function (which examines the effect on sales of extra amounts of advertising). As a general rule, the response of sales to increasing advertising shows a pattern of diminishing returns, the greatest quantity of sales coming from one advertisement exposure. Additional exposures, beyond one, generate sales increases at a diminishing rate, a pattern that demonstrates the wastefulness of excessive media concentration. The media strategy for most brands should be to plan media exposure weekly, to maximize reach each week, to achieve one-exposure frequency per week as far as possible, but to cut back frequency above this rate, using the money saved to extend the number of weeks on the air. This is the essence of Continuity planning, a doctrine now successfully followed by many major advertisers in the United States in many fields, including repeat-purchase packaged goods.

Note

1. The findings from the first major piece of Pure Single-Source research were published in John Philip Jones, *When Ads Work. New Proof That Advertising Triggers Sales* (New York: Simon and Schuster, Lexington Books, 1995). These findings have been consolidated and extended in John Philip Jones, *The Ultimate Secrets of Advertising* (Thousand Oaks, CA: Sage, 2001). This chapter represents a synthesis of chapters 2, 4, and 5 of *The Ultimate Secrets.* (These chapters also contain extensive notes referring to additional sources.)

—— 8 ——

How Advertising Builds Brands

Advertising's full effect can only be appreciated if we take account of its long-term influence as well as its short- and medium-term effects on sales.[1] Aggregating all three orders of effect should make it possible to evaluate the productivity of an advertising campaign: to measure whether the campaign shows a financial return on the investment and is therefore accountable.

The notion of accountability is derived, as the name implies, from the practice of balancing the financial outlays and receipts from business or personal affairs. It is impossible to do this without establishing a finite period— a week, a month, a year. The time frame for the analysis must resemble a snapshot. We must in fact find a way of freezing advertising effects so that we can do our counting and balancing, using data relating to a defined period.

The periods selected for measurement are as follows:

- *Short term:* Generally one week but occasionally (for methodological reasons) one month.
- *Medium term:* One year.
- *Long term:* One year.

Although the medium-term and long-term measurements use the same accounting period, the difference between them is that in the medium term, we are measuring effects generated strictly within the twelve months. On the other hand, the long-term effects embrace changes that have taken place over many previous years, but are *measured from data that cover one year at a time.* The medium-term effect is calculated by econometric techniques. The long-term effect is measured by applying a weighting to the medium-term measure, a weighting derived from the long-term effects of a brand's advertising.

This system is different from the use of continuous tracking studies. Although these are often very useful, many of them focus on the long term exclusively and disregard other effects. Some analysts go so far as to deny the very existence of short-term effects and look only at a gradual and progressive strengthening of the effectiveness of a brand's advertising, starting from a very low base. As argued in chapter 7, advertising must generate a positive short-term effect (which dips), which is repeated to produce a medium-term one; and a medium-term effect is in turn a precondition for further incremental effects. Thus the beneficial things that advertising can accomplish in the long term are predicated on its ability to sell the brand—in the first instance inside a week, and in the second instance inside a year.

Six Measures of the Long-Term Effects of Advertising

Six measures of advertising's long-term effects are shown in Figure 8.1. The four measures on the outside of the diagram are described as the peripherals; the two in the middle are the core advertising factors. The six measures are grouped in this way for an important reason. Although all six can be calibrated with reasonable precision, only the core advertising factors measure the advertising itself. They are, in other words, the only tools available to provide advertising accountability without the use of surrogate measures.

The long-term effects of advertising are manifested by a strengthening of the brand. It is easy to see this process in action in connection with the four peripherals in Figure 8.1:

Figure 8.1 **Long-Term Effects of Advertising**

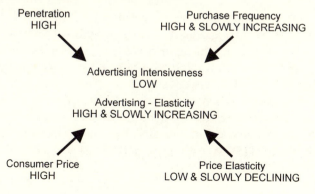

- *Penetration:* Increasing penetration directly drives share of market (as described in chapter 5). Penetration generates breadth of usage, and large brands are generally strong brands. Penetration is normally directly influenced by advertising, and this is a particularly important process during the early years of a brand's life.
- *Purchase Frequency:* Brands with a high share of market have significantly above-average purchase frequency (as explained in chapters 5 and 7). Purchase frequency provides depth and staying power to a brand. Advertising, working in combination with consumers' satisfaction with the functional performance of the brand, strongly influences purchase frequency. Purchase frequency is a centrally important dynamic for a mature brand.
- *Consumer Price:* The largest brands in any category usually command the highest consumer prices. High prices provide a double benefit to manufacturers. First, they signal high personal valuation of the brand on the part of consumers and therefore build a strong franchise. Advertising influences this. Second, high price generally means high profit. Another way of making this point is that manufacturers of large, strong brands are not compelled to undertake orgies of self-destructive sales promotions.
- *Price Elasticity:* A long-term benefit of successful advertising is that it gradually engineers a reduction in a brand's price elasticity of demand. This makes it possible for a manufacturer to maintain sales volume when he increases price in order to boost his profit. One of the most important roles of advertising is to reduce the substitution of other brands for the advertised brand if the price of the latter goes up, and this is what brings about the reduction in the price elasticity of the advertised brand.

The four peripherals are the most important indicators of a brand's health and growth. If the advertising is successful, its influence will inevitably be felt by these four measures. However, a number of readers will immediately think of something important that has been omitted from this list. Is not raw share of market the first and most obvious measure we should look at in appraising an advertising campaign? None of us needs to be reminded that advertising evaluation before the 1960s was based on this simple measure to the exclusion of everything else.

Penetration, purchase frequency, consumer price, and price elasticity are all direct or indirect expressions of share of market. But since they are measures of consumer behavior, they are more relevant to evaluating advertising than share of market (SOM) on its own, since the latter can be influenced by stimuli other than advertising, such as retail distribution and out-of-stock. All four peripherals are based on studying the people to whom advertising is aimed. They therefore have the great merit of monitoring advertising directly rather than indirectly.

This brings us finally to the two core advertising factors, advertising intensiveness, and advertising elasticity. These are not linked to consumer behavior in as straightforward a fashion as the four peripherals are. But the idea that the long-term effects of advertising bring about a strengthening of the brand means that effective advertising reinforces the four peripherals. This is a process that can be efficiently and clearly measured through changes in the two core advertising factors.

The connection is quite logical. If the four peripherals are powerful and as a result the brand has a strong marketing impetus, the advertising does not have to work particularly hard to do its job. This means a lower advertising intensiveness and a higher advertising elasticity. On the other hand, if the four peripherals are weak, the advertising has a harder job to do, hence a higher advertising intensiveness and a lower advertising elasticity. Since the core advertising factors are both measured in terms of the advertising itself, *they provide the key to accountability.*

Penetration and Purchase Frequency

A brand grows by gaining new users; and penetration—the measure of the size of the user base—drives SOM.

We shall now look at four SOM/penetration relationships. Three of these examine complete packaged goods categories: cold breakfast cereals, regular domestic beer, and laundry detergents; the fourth example covers seventy-eight brands in twelve different categories, which were researched in 1991 by the Pure Single-Source technique.

The data are presented in Tables 8.1 through 8.4. The SOM/penetration relationships are plotted diagrammatically in Figures 8.2 through 8.5.

We can draw four inferences from the four groups of brands described here.

1. There is a direct relationship between penetration and market share. As penetration builds, so does SOM—more users mean more sales. This is a basic truth and can be taken as a formal rule describing all brands except the largest ones, mostly the top 20 percent. For these there is a more subtle point, to be discussed in paragraph 3, below.

Table 8.1

Average Share of Market and Penetration, Cold Breakfast Cereals, 1991

	Number of brands	Av. SOM (%)	SOM index	Av. 6-month penetration (%)	Penetration index
All brands	95	1.1	100	4.6	100
Top quintile	19	3.1	282	11.3	246
4th quintile	19	1.0	91	5.6	122
3rd quintile	19	0.6	55	2.9	63
2nd quintile	19	0.3	27	1.4	43
Bottom quintile	19	0.2	18	1.4	30

Table 8.2

Average Share of Market and Penetration, Regular Domestic Beer, 1997

	Number of brands	Av. SOM (%)	SOM index	Av. 6-month penetration (%)	Penetration index
All brands	36	2.8	100	1.6	100
Top quintile	7	9.5	339	4.3	269
4th quintile	7	2.5	89	1.7	106
3rd quintile	8	1.2	43	1.1	69
2nd quintile	7	0.7	25	0.8	50
Bottom quintile	7	0.3	11	0.4	25

Table 8.3

Average Share of Market and Penetration, Laundry Detergents, 1998

	Number of brands	Av. SOM (%)	SOM index	Av. 6-month penetration (%)	Penetration index
All brands	39	2.6	100	4.1	100
Top quintile	8	6.6	254	9.5	232
4th quintile	8	2.9	112	4.8	117
3rd quintile	7	1.8	69	2.9	71
2nd quintile	8	1.0	38	2.3	56
Bottom quintile	8	0.4	15	1.1	27

Table 8.4

Average Share of Market and Penetration, Brands in Twelve Categories, 1991

	Number of brands	Av. SOM (%)	SOM index	Av. 6-month penetration (%)	Penetration index
All brands	78	6.8	100	11.9	100
Top quintile	16	18.7	275	26.9	226
4th quintile	15	6.8	100	18.6	156
3rd quintile	16	3.9	57	11.0	92
2nd quintile	15	2.8	41	7.7	65
Bottom quintile	16	1.8	26	6.3	53

Figure 8.2 **Share of Market and Penetration Relationship: Cold Breakfast Cereals, 1991**

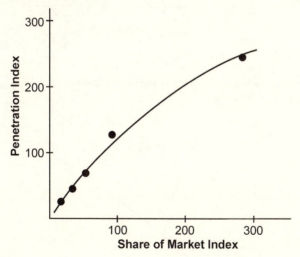

Figure 8.3 **Share of Market and Penetration Relationship:**
Regular Domestic Beer, 1997

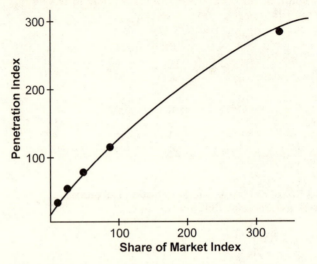

Figure 8.4 **Share of Market and Penetration Relationship:**
Laundry Detergents, 1998

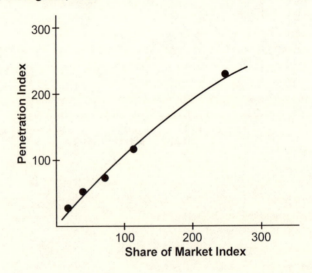

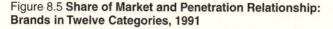

Figure 8.5 **Share of Market and Penetration Relationship: Brands in Twelve Categories, 1991**

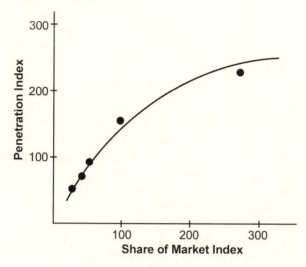

2. There is a large gap separating the top quintile from the remaining four quintiles; the top-quintile brands are *very much larger.*

3. Where the top quintiles have a high market share (Table 8.4), this is accompanied by a flattening of the penetration curve (Figure 8.5). There is also a commonsense reason for this. The larger a brand grows, the more it runs out of potential users. Original-formula Listerine finds it difficult to attract new users who will accept the brand's strong medicinal taste, despite the brand's widely understood efficiency at killing bacteria—a functional benefit that to some users is actually signaled by the taste. Tide finds it difficult to find new users who will accept the brand, because it is regarded by some people as hard on fabrics, despite its ability to wash clothes with maximum efficiency. And Budweiser, despite the fact that its American sales volume alone makes it the widest-selling beer in the world, finds that some potential users regard the brand as too downmarket for their (perhaps snobbish) taste.

4. The relatively small number of big brands tend of course to be the oldest established ones—those that have had years to build and reinforce a loyal franchise. It is rare for a new brand to join this group of large players because the latter have the strength to block serious competition. The big brands are generally made by very large manufacturers, to whom they offer two benefits: (a) the market strength of

the big brand itself; and (b) the resultant scale economies, which provide funds for new brands in the same or different categories. However, these scale economies occasionally produce a negative effect. A manufacturer is often so enthusiastic about new brand ideas (most of which fail) that he neglects his own large brands. In the bar soap category, Dial lost share of market for a few years in the 1970s, and Ivory suffered more permanent damage in the 1990s.

When a brand becomes a very large player in a category, penetration reaches a plateau, with very little potential to grow and increase sales *pari passu.* Nevertheless, some brands have a larger SOM than others despite similar penetration levels. Some large brands grow larger over time, and they do this despite a relatively stable penetration. The dynamic force driving large brands upward is clearly the *loyalty of their users*—their depth of purchase.

Summarizing what has been said so far, it is clear that there is something especially important about the largest 20 percent of brands that sets them apart from the majority of brands in their category. What makes them so special is less their large penetration than their depth of purchase. The large brands not only have greater breadth than the small brands, but—more importantly—they also command greater loyalty. This quality, which is at the heart of strong brands, will now be described.

Table 8.5 sets out in compressed form a large amount of information on depth of purchase. The four groups of brands that have been described in this chapter are compared with one another in this one table. The actual figures are indexes based in each case on the category average, and the quintiles are ranked according to the average size of the brand in each quintile (as in Tables 8.1 through 8.4). The data for the four groups of brands are plotted diagramatically in Figures 8.6 through 8.9. The meaning of these four data sets is clear, and their findings are consistent.

Table 8.5

Depth of Purchase by Quintiles

Quintiles ranked by SOM	Breakfast cereals, 1991	Reg. dom. beer, 1997	Laundry detergents, 1998	Twelve categories, 1991
All brands	100	100	100	100
Top quintile	133	137	127	125
4th quintile	91	124	109	97
3rd quintile	100	110	112	92
2nd quintile	91	63	80	94
Bottom quintile	86	63	71	84

Figure 8.6 **Purchase Frequency by SOM Quintiles:**
Cold Breakfast Cereals, 1991

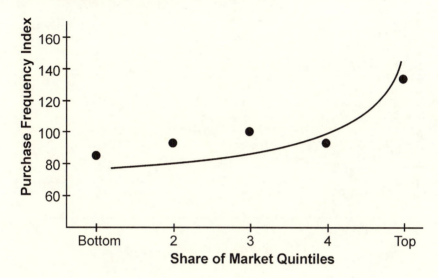

Figure 8.7 **Purchase Frequency by SOM Quintiles:**
Regular Domestic Beer, 1997

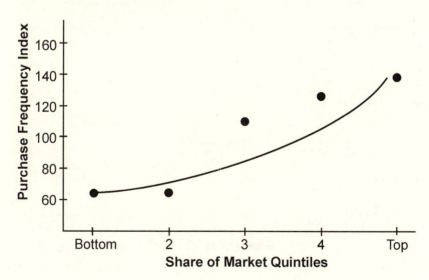

Figure 8.8 **Purchase Frequency by SOM Quintiles: Laundry Detergents, 1998**

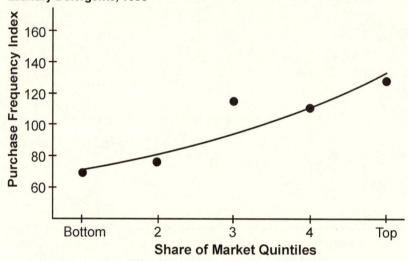

Figure 8.9 **Purchase Frequency by SOM Quintiles: Twelve Categories, 1991**

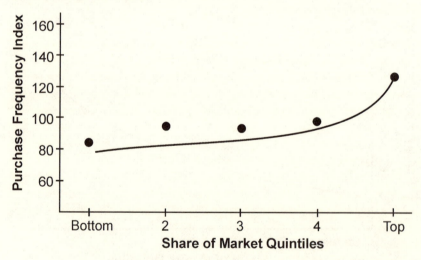

1. The SOM of large brands is the end product of significantly enhanced loyalty/purchase frequency.
2. Looking at brands on a continuum ranging from smallest to largest, we can see that greater loyalty/higher purchase frequencies are related to larger shares of market, with very few discontinuities in the ranking.
3. Finally and most importantly, loyalty/purchase frequency kicks up sharply in the top quintile of brands, opening up the generally large distance that separates this quintile from the remaining four-fifths of brands on the continuum.

These findings are effectively a reprise of those presented in chapter 5, where the phenomenon of high purchase frequency associated with high-penetration brands is described as the Penetration Supercharge. There is a tendency for such brands to underinvest in their advertising, as described below in the section titled "Advertising Intensiveness" (see pp. 207–210). Such underinvestment is harmonious with advertising's long-term effects in reinforcing brands by boosting purchase frequency, with a consequent relaxation of pressure on the advertising budget. The advertising has a less arduous job to do, therefore less money needs to be spent.

Price and Price Elasticity

It is a well-established phenomenon that the largest brands—those that are generally strong because they have benefited from a positive long-term advertising heritage—can command significantly higher consumer prices than the average brands in their categories. The rather obvious reason for this is that the largest brands represent greater subjective value to the consumer, who will therefore pay the premium price.

One example describing a range of brands, from a number of such examples that could be chosen, is to be found in Table 8.6. This is derived from the Pure Single-Source research carried out by A.C. Nielsen in 1991 and described in chapter 7. The price of each of the 142 brands in the table is compared with those of all the others in its own category. The prices of all of the brands, calculated in relative terms, are therefore comparable with one another.

The higher prices of the stronger brands are higher *effective* prices (i.e., real marketplace prices rather than list prices). In most cases the higher prices represent high profitability, stemming from the fact that the brands are less heavily promoted than weaker brands. As will be demonstrated later in this section, promotions tend to suck out a brand's profit.

Table 8.6

Marketplace Prices of 142 Brands in Twelve Product Categories, 1991

All brands	100
Largest 10 brands	114
Second-largest 10 brands	110
Remaining 58 advertised brands	99
64 unadvertised brands	97

Note: Indexes are compared with category average.

As stated, the premium prices of the larger brands represent their subjective value to consumers. The elasticity of demand was discussed in chapter 5, and it is worth looking again briefly at this important topic. We refer again to Gerard J. Tellis, who in 1988 published a summary of the price elasticities of 367 different brands. The calculation was made for each brand by averaging the response of sales to changes in price on a number of occasions. Tellis's average figure was −1.76, which shows (as we shall shortly see) a vastly greater raw response of sales to reductions in price than to increases in advertising. The phrase "raw response" is used deliberately, because the effect of price reductions on the *profitability* of brands is a different story, which will be described later in this chapter.

Sales promotions are essentially devices to reduce temporarily the prices charged by manufacturers to the retail trade and the end consumer. The high average price elasticity provides a powerful reason for why promotions are so popular with manufacturers: price reductions can shift merchandise. Manufacturers are less conscious, however, of what promotions cost them in profit foregone.

Table 8.7 describes the sales increases generated respectively by a 10 percent price reduction for four hypothetical brands, each of which has a different price elasticity clustered around Tellis's average.

Table 8.7

Effect of 10 Percent Price Reduction on Sales

	Brand FAA	Brand FAV	Brand FAC	Brand FAD
Price elasticity	−1.6	−1.8	−2.0	−2.2
Initial volume (m. units)	100	100	100	100
Initial NSV	$100m	$100m	$100m	$100m
Volume from price reduction (m. units)	116	118	120	122
NSV from price reduction	$104m	$106m	$108m	$110m

We can fully judge the effect of price reductions only by estimating the influence of the price reduction on a manufacturer's *profit,* because his costs will also go up when he sells more merchandise. Various alternatives are worked out in Table 8.8. The cost estimates have been rounded to nearest whole numbers.

Table 8.8 does not paint an optimistic picture of the value of price reductions. It is only at the lowest ratio of direct costs and at the highest levels of price elasticity (marked *) that they break even or yield a profit. The reason for this is that price reductions take a large bite out of a brand's net sales value (NSV). Added to this, the substantial increase in volume sold has to be paid for in direct costs, perhaps also by an increase in indirect costs, since the volume increase is so much larger than that brought about by, for instance, an increase in advertising expenditure. (We have not factored this possibility into our calculations.)

Remember also that price reductions have only a temporary effect; there is generally no hope of a further, lagged effect to generate more revenue to balance the increase in cost. Price reductions also encourage competitive retaliation, and they often have a negative influence on consumers' image of the brand.

We are most concerned here with the long-term influence of a brand's advertising on its responsiveness to price changes. The most interesting type of response is to price *increases.*

Table 8.9 describes three brands that cover a rather extreme range of price elasticities. Each has an NSV of $100 million and a 40 percent ratio of direct costs. As can be seen, a 5 percent price increase causes a slight reduction in NSV despite the increased price per unit. But direct costs are also slightly increased.

The important point about this analysis is that *the profit picture improves with reductions in the brand's price elasticity.* The reason for this is that brands'

Table 8.8

Profit and Loss from 10 Percent Price Reduction

	Brand FAA	Brand FAV	Brand FAC	Brand FAD
Price elasticity	−1.6	−1.8	−2.0	−2.2
Extra NSV from price reduction	+$4m	+$6m	+$8m	+$10m
Extra costs at different ratios of direct				
40%	+$6m	+$7m	+$8m*	+$9m*
50%	+$8m	+$9m	+$10m	+$11m
60%	+$10m	+$11m	+$12m	+$13m

*See explanation in text.

Table 8.9

Price Increase and Profit

	Brand FAZ	Brand FAB	Brand FAD
Price elasticity	−1.4	−1.8	−2.2
Original NSV	$100m	$100m	$100m
New NSV	$98m	$96m	$93m
New direct & indirect cost	$97m	$96m	$96m
Change in net profit	+$1m	No change	−$3m

Note: Price, +5%; direct cost ratio 40%.

low elasticity indicates low substitution. Following a price increase, low-elasticity brands hang on to their sales to a greater degree than is the case for brands with a high price elasticity.

Successful advertising, by its ability to reinforce a brand's uniqueness in the minds of its users, impedes substitution and thereby reduces the brand's price elasticity. Data from eighteen typical brands analyzed by Media Marketing Assessment (MMA)—data confirmed from other MMA databases—confirm that brands with high advertising expenditure have a lower price elasticity than brands that spend less (see Table 8.10).

We can therefore conclude that successful advertising, by its ability to reduce a brand's price elasticity, restricts the amount of substitution if the brand's price is increased, and this progressively enables the brand to profit from price increases despite the reduction in sales volume that results.

Advertising Elasticity

The most direct measure of advertising effect is made by calculating a brand's advertising elasticity, which means the precise response of sales to a given increase or decrease in advertising expenditure.

Table 8.10

Price Elasticity Compared with Advertising Expenditure: Eighteen Typical MMA Brands[a]

	Average Annual GRPs	Price Elasticity
Total, 18 brands	2300	−1.2
Nine brands with high advertising	3400	−1.0
Nine brands with low advertising	1200	−1.4

[a]MMA, Media Marketing Assessment.

The calculation is carried out by regression analysis of many individual changes in advertising expenditure alongside their effects on sales of an individual brand. The end product of the calculation is *an estimate of the percentage rise in sales that results from a 1 percent increase in advertising expenditure,* the extra sales having come from advertising alone, since the effect of the other influences on sales has been allowed for.

Any estimate on these lines is of course predicated on the basic assumption that the campaign is creatively strong enough to produce some degree of short-term effect. As we saw in chapter 7, a third of campaigns do not fulfil this condition.

The complicated calculations of advertising elasticity have been made with hundreds of brands. In 1984, three American analysts, Gert Assmus, John U. Farlet, and Donald R. Lehmann, published a summary of the advertising elasticities of 128 separate advertising campaigns. The elasticity varies according to the product category, the brand, and, most of all, the campaign itself. The average published figure was +0.22. If we round this to +0.2, we see an approximate 5-to-1 relationship. A 1 percent increase in advertising produces a 0.2 percent boost in sales; a 5 percent lift in advertising will generate 1 percent extra sales; a 10 percent advertising increase boosts sales by 2 percent; a 20 percent advertising lift will increase them by 4 percent. Increments in advertising are normally in minimum amounts of 10 percent; 20 percent is common for brand restages. A 5 to 1 relationship is a fairly low response rate, but we shall show that the sales return can sometimes be economic (i.e., the value of the extra sales *can* exceed the outlay).

Some elasticity calculations are made with a year's data, which means that the results are likely to be diluted because the period will be so long that the effect of the advertising will be contaminated by the influence of competitive activity. This analysis will be confined, however, to short-term effects, and all of the figures in the following tables refer to notional quantities during the relatively short period when the brand is advertised. This period is not necessarily uniform, but in many cases it would be a month.

We have also found that +0.2 is rather a high figure. This is confirmed by data from Media Marketing Assessment Inc., which show typical elasticities in the range of 0.06 to 0.09, varying according to the level of advertising investment behind a brand. This general experience, together with appropriate caution about interpreting statistics, has led us to concentrate on the lower range of elasticities, with +0.2 at the top of the range and not the average. We have examined the following levels: +0.05, +0.1, +0.15, and +0.2. In Table 8.11, these elasticities are applied to four hypothetical brands whose net sales value (NSV) is a uniform $100 million. The table examines the immediate sales results of a 20 percent increase in advertising expenditure.

Table 8.11

Effect of Extra Advertising on Sales of Four Brands with NSV of $100m, During the Advertised Period

	Brand EAA	Brand EAB	Brand EAC	Brand EAD
Advertising elasticity	+0.05	+0.1	+0.15	+0.2
Additional advertising	+20%	+20%	+20%	+20%
Additional sales	+$1m	+$2m	+$3m	+$4m.

Each of the brands shows a sales increase in accordance with its advertising elasticity. However, this table tells us nothing about whether the sales increases are economic. To do this, we must see how costs have been affected. There are three separate expenses that must be factored into the calculation:

1. The dollar cost of the extra advertising. The amount depends on the advertising:sales (A:S) ratio for the brand.
2. The increase in direct costs (raw material, packaging, etc.) for the extra volume of output sold. This depends not only on the amount of extra sales, but also on the share of a brand's total cost that is accounted for by direct costs.
3. The increase—if any—in indirect costs.

Tables 8.12 through 8.15 use a grid for each of the four brands described in Table 8.11. Each table looks at two variables: the brand's A:S ratio and its ratio of direct costs out of total NSV. With such relatively small sales increases, 1 percent, 2 percent, 3 percent, and 4 percent for the four brands, we are making the realistic assumption that these will not cause indirect costs to

Table 8.12

Incremental Costs for Brand EAA ($m)

Direct cost ratio	A:S ratio		
	4%	6%	8%
40%	A 0.8	A 1.2	A 1.6
	D 0.4	D 0.4	D 0.4
	T 1.2	T 1.6	T 2.0
50%	A 0.8	A 1.2	A 1.6
	D 0.5	D 0.5	D 0.5
	T 1.3	T 1.7	T 2.1
60%	A 0.8	A 1.2	A 1.6
	D 0.6	D 0.6	D 0.6
	T 1.4	T 1.8	T 2.2

Note: Advertising elasticity, +0.05; incremental sales, $1m.

Table 8.13

Incremental Costs for Brand EAB ($m)

Direct cost ratio	A:S ratio		
	4%	6%	8%
40%	*A* 0.8	*A* 1.2	*A* 1.6
	D 0.8	*D* 0.8	*D* 0.8
	T 1.6*	*T* 2.0	*T* 2.4
50%	*A* 0.8	*A* 1.2	*A* 1.6
	D 1.0	*D* 1.0	*D* 1.0
	T 1.8*	*T* 2.2	*T* 2.6
60%	*A* 0.8	*A* 1.2	*A* 1.6
	D 1.2	*D* 1.2	*D* 1.2
	T 2.0	*T* 2.4	*T* 2.8

Note: Advertising elasticity, +0.1; incremental sales, $ 2m.

Table 8.14

Incremental Costs for Brand EAC ($m)

Direct cost ratio	A:S ratio		
	4%	6%	8%
40%	*A* 0.8	*A* 1.2	*A* 1.6
	D 1.2	*D* 1.2	*D*1.2
	T 2.0*	*T* 2.4*	*T* 2.8*
50%	*A* 0.8	*A* 1.2	*A* 1.6
	*D*1.5	*D* 1.5	*D*1.5
	T 2.3*	*T* 2.7*	*T* 3.1
60%	*A* 0.8	*A* 1.2	*A* 1.6
	D 1.8	*D* 1.8	*D* 1.8
	T 2.6*	*T* 3.0	*T* 3.4

Note: Advertising elasticity, +0.15; incremental sales, $3m.

Table 8.15

Incremental Costs for Brand EAD ($m)

Direct cost ratio	A:S ratio		
	4%	6%	8%
40%	*A* 0.8	*A* 1.2	*A* 1.6
	D 1.6	*D* 1.6	*D* 1.6
	T 2.4*	*T* 2.8*	*T* 3.2*
50%	*A* 0.8	*A* 1.2	*A* 1.6
	*D*2.0	*D* 2.0	*D* 2.0
	T 2.8*	*T* 3.2*	*T* 3.6*
60%	*A* 0.8	*A* 1.2	*A* 1.6
	D 2.4	*D* 2.4	*D* 2.4
	T 3.2*	*T* 3.6*	*T* 4.0

Note: Advertising elasticity, +0.2; incremental sales, $4m.

go up. The assumption is made that the firm's general overhead has enough slack in it to cover these modest sales increases. We are therefore estimating only the extra advertising cost and the additional direct costs.

In Tables 8.12 through 8.15, the additional advertising cost is signified by A, the extra direct costs by D, and the total of the two by T.

In the cases in which the extra advertising is profitable (i.e., the value of the incremental sales exceeds the extra costs), we have put an asterisk (*) in the appropriate box.

The above four tables contain a total of thirty-six statistical cells representing varying advertising elasticities, A:S ratios, and proportions of total cost accounted for by directs. In sixteen cases, the extra advertising is profitable. In four cases, the extra advertising breaks even. In sixteen cases—generally those with the low elasticities—the advertising does not pay for itself.

With twenty positive and sixteen negative examples, the odds are better than even that, in the short term, advertising expenditure will lift sales and keep the brand in the black. With advertising run as a more or less continuous series of exposure periods (as recommended in chapter 7), there is a better chance of such advertising running profitably than if it runs intermittently over twelve months. This is due to the fact that, with the latter alternative, the advertised brand will suffer from the marketing activities of competitors. Continuity planning will therefore not only maintain sales at a higher level than a schedule with interruptions; it is also *likely to be an economic rather than a loss-making activity.*

Although econometric estimates show that the medium-term effect of advertising is generally uneconomic (with costs greater than receipts), elasticity calculations often demonstrate that advertising can pay for itself in the very short term. This confirms the value of planning media to achieve a repetition of short-term effects, with maximum continuity.

The profit or loss for each level of advertising for our average brand is plotted in Figure 8.10. This diagram also suggests that advertising produces an incremental, long-term effect, and that one way of evaluating this is by measuring increases over time in the brand's advertising elasticity.

A progressive increase in advertising elasticity in subsequent years is a signal of advertising's ability to generate measurable long-term effects. The increase may be partly due to the extra, lagged effect on buying behavior that follows the initial sales increase. The effect may be coming to some extent from increased purchase frequency from the new consumers triggered by the initial advertising stimulus. There is a well-known published example of this process. This describes the leading British brand of toilet tissue, Andrex, which had a short-term advertising elasticity of +0.06 and a boosted elasticity of +0.15 when the added effect of repeat purchase was included in the calculation.

Figure 8.10 **Profit and Loss for Brands with Different Advertising Elasticities**

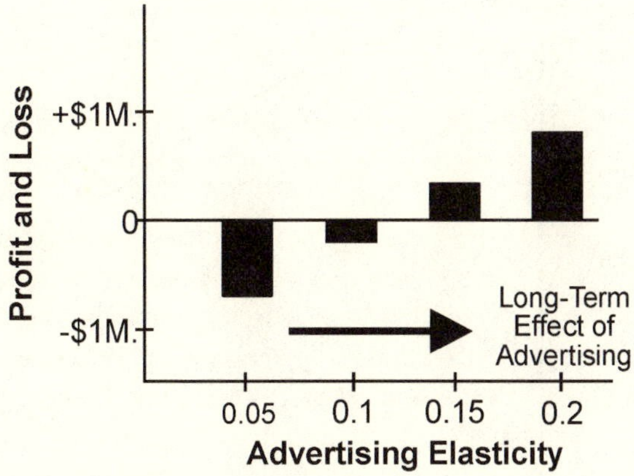

Note: A:S ratio, 6%; direct cost proportion, 50%.

Advertising Intensiveness

The concept of advertising intensiveness is derived from the relationship between a brand's share of market (SOM) and its share of voice (SOV), the latter describing its share of all media advertising in its product category.

Since the cost structure of every brand in a category will be approximately similar to that of its direct competitors, it can be expected that as a theoretical rule, SOM should equal SOV for any brand. But this relationship represents no more than an approximation because a study of brands in many countries has shown that small brands tend to overspend (with SOV exceeding SOM), whereas large brands tend to underspend (with SOV consistently below SOM). This demonstrates a scale economy for large brands—those that have benefited from long periods of successful advertising—a scale economy that can be quantified by the relative degree of underinvestment in the advertising support put behind them. The advertising does not have to work so hard because the brands are still receiving some reward from earlier advertising.

Figure 8.11 plots the SOV–SOM relationship for 666 brands from 23 different countries. Three-quarters of the data come from the various fields of repeat-purchase packaged goods, and the rest come from other types of advertising. The regression in Figure 8.11 was first published in 1989, and it has been replicated in many additional investigations, with substantially similar results. The link between SOM and overinvestment/underinvestment is called the Advertising-Intensiveness Curve (AIC).

Figure 8.11 **Share of Market and Share of Voice: Advertising-Intensiveness Curve**

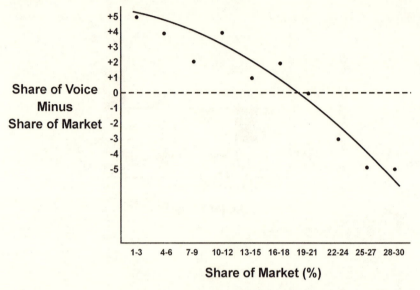

Share of Market (%)

The AIC is valuable to marketing practice in helping us determine the advertising budget for any brand. This is because the SOM–SOV relationship tells us the average level of expenditure for a brand of any particular size. An AIC should ideally be constructed from specific brands in the category in which our brand is operating.

The AIC also helps us evaluate the sales-generating ability of the advertising for a brand of any size. Consider a selection of the brands in Figure 8.11.

- A small brand, with a SOM of 9 percent, will overspend in advertising by 3 percentage points above SOM; it will thus account for a total of 12 percent SOV. This means that each percentage point of SOM must be supported by 1.3 percent of SOV. Another way of looking at the same relationship is that *1 percent SOV will support 0.8 percent SOM.*
- A medium-sized brand, with a share of market of 20 percent, will spend at the category average on advertising, or 20 percent SOV. Each SOM will be supported by 1 percent SOV. And *1 percent SOV will support 1 percent SOM.*
- A large brand, with a share of market of 26 percent, will underspend on advertising by 5 percentage points below SOM; it will therefore account for 21 percent of SOV. This means that each percentage point of

SOV can be supported by 0.8 percent SOV, and *1 percent SOV will support 1.2 percent SOM.*

What this arithmetic shows is that the advertising investment behind large brands is more productive, dollar for dollar, than the investment behind small brands. This difference is robustly quantifiable, and if we are able to understand the reasons for this phenomenon, we shall receive valuable clues to measuring the long-term effects of advertising.

Making the assumption that we are comparing equally effective campaigns, a dollar spent behind a large brand will provide higher sales than a dollar spent behind a small brand. There are at least five reasons for this:

1. The large brand has a bigger consumer franchise, or user base, than a small brand. Since people tend to pay at least some attention to the advertising for the brands they use themselves, this means that the attentive (or semi-attentive) audience produced by a given amount of advertising for a big brand is larger than that for the same amount of advertising for a small brand.

2. The average user of a large brand will buy that brand slightly more often in a defined period than the average user of a small brand. This extremely important point was demonstrated in detail earlier in this chapter.

3. A large brand, because of its substantial user base, will occupy a higher "share of the mind" of more consumers than is the case with a small brand. The ubiquity of a large brand can be a valuable asset. For instance, if any particular brand is out of stock at the store where the consumer is shopping, there is almost a 60 percent chance that she will buy another brand in the product field. This is more likely to be a large than a small brand because of the high display level for the major brands in any category.

4. A large brand is valued more than a small brand by the consumer, and this justifies the generally higher-than-average prices that large brands can command. This point was also examined earlier in this chapter.

5. Most advertising acts as a reminder, or an evocation of previous brand experience. However, some advertising goes beyond this, and the advertising message itself and how it is communicated can leave traces in the memory of the consumer. Such high-profile advertising has a greater overall effect for large than for small brands for the simple reason that the large brands have bigger budgets, measured in absolute terms. It must not be thought, however, that high-profile

campaigns are always better at generating sales than low-profile campaigns. It all depends on the endemic characteristics of the brand and its position in the market. But in the cases in which high-profile advertising is particularly effective, the memorability of the campaign favors large brands.

These five factors add up to what can be described as the *marketing impetus driving large brands*. And there is no doubt at all that previous advertising for the brand—by its ability both to encourage repeat purchase and to build psychological added values in the minds of consumers—contributes to a very large degree to this. The marketing impetus is therefore substantially a description of the contribution made by previous advertising.

Accountability

The six measures described in the above sections provide accurate bearings for locating a brand's strengths and in particular show how advertising influences each of these strengths. Advertising elasticity is the most complete indicator of advertising effect. Advertising Intensiveness can be used to dissect the influence of the long term when this is added to the medium term. The method for calculating these twin effects is as follows.

First estimate with the use of regression analysis the medium-term influence of advertising, by calculating the sales return to advertising in cents per dollar invested (as described in chapter 7). This financial estimate is called the medium-term payback. The second stage is to examine the Advertising-Intensiveness Curve. This indicates, for strong brands, the amount of money by which each underspends on advertising below the category norm (this norm being where SOV is on a par with SOM). This underspending, computed as a percentage of the category norm, can be used to weight the estimate of medium-term payback, for example, if the brand spends 20 percent below the norm, the medium-term payback can be inflated by a similar proportion. The logic of this system is that advertising can be seen to yield a particular payback at a low level of expenditure; what would the payback therefore be with normal spending?

Table 8.16 describes seventeen brands analyzed econometrically by Media Marketing Assessment Inc. With each of these brands, an estimate is made of the absolute amount of television advertising investment after deduction of the total payback (covering both medium-term and long-term effects). As can be seen, four of the seventeen brands produce a positive payback. With these brands—which are likely to be typical of large, well-established successful names—advertising can be shown to pay its own way.

Table 8.16

Medium-Term Plus Long-Term Effects of Advertising: Seventeen MMA Brands, 1997

Brand	(Medium-term) TV percentage payback (cents per adv. $, rounded)	(Medium-term TV-plus long-term) Weighted percentage payback (cents per adv. $)	TV advertising budget ($)	TV advertising deficit (cents per adv. $)	TV absolute advertising deficit ($)
22	93	Over 100	10.9m	Nil	Nil
11	22	81	0.3m	19	0.1m
7	(60)	Over 100	(10.8m)	Nil	Nil
25	72	Over 100	21.4m	Nil	Nil
18	37	62	6.0m	38	2.3m
1	31	44	3.0m	56	1.7m
16	84	Over 100	14.4m	Nil	Nil
19	53	58	2.2m	42	1.9m
10	31	29	5.5m	71	3.9m
21	95	81	(11.4m)	19	2.2m
5	57	47	21.2m	53	11.2m
15	68	48	7.4m	52	3.9m
27	43	29	11.4m	71	8.1m
17	41	26	6.0m	74	4.5m
26	19	11	6.5m	89	5.8m
35	19	11	0.4m	89	0.4m
30	30	15	10.4m	85	9.3m

Note: Figures in parentheses represent averages for a number of years.

The Argument in Brief

The long-term effects of advertising are felt through the ways in which advertising strengthens and enriches brands, in particular, by reinforcing the bond between a brand and its users.

Six such effects can be accurately measured:

- *Penetration:* Advertising can build the user base of a brand, and, as a general rule, a brand's penetration drives its SOM. For all brands, penetration grows, peaks, and then flattens, a process that represents the probability that most people eventually learn about a brand, but many potential users do not like it enough to become actual users. No brand offers everything to everyone, and the strongest brands are often sharply polarized.
- *Purchase Frequency:* Brands of different sizes in any product category have an approximately similar purchase frequency. But there is an exception to this rule: the largest brands (usually the top fifth by share of

market) build a significantly higher purchase frequency than the category norm, as a result of enhanced consumer loyalty. This represents a scale economy for large brands, and it shows the way in which large brands can grow: not only by the process of attracting new users, but also by attracting new business from existing users. Advertising can directly influence this process.

- *Consumer Price:* It is a well-established characteristic of the largest and strongest brands that they can command a price premium 10 percent or more above their category average. This premium represents the above-average value with which such brands are perceived by their users. In the majority of product categories, high (effective) consumer price is the result of a low level of promotional price reductions; such reductions are more common with weak brands, and these have the effect of draining profit from such brands.

- *Price Elasticity:* The price elasticity of a brand is a mathematical measure of the degree to which other brands will substitute for it if its price is increased. Low price elasticity indicates that a brand is perceived as unique, and this results in little loss of business in response to a rise in price. Consumer advertising is much concerned with demonstrating a brand's uniqueness, and there is evidence that highly advertised brands have a lower price elasticity than less advertised brands. Low price elasticity lies at the heart of the higher prices that successful brands can command in the marketplace (as described above).

- *Advertising Elasticity:* This is the most direct measure of the improvement over time in the selling power of a brand's advertising (i.e., the long-term influence of advertising on sales). It is measured by the percentage increase in sales that results from a 1 percent boost in advertising investment. Since to calculate this the effect of advertising must be isolated from the other stimuli influencing sales, the job has to be done with the use of regression analysis. The average advertising elasticity is small, but it can be shown to improve over time. Most importantly, such improvements can transform the upward increments in a brand's advertising budget, changing it from an unprofitable to a profitable undertaking.

- *Advertising Intensiveness:* Although the advertising budget for a large successful brand will invariably be greater than that for a small brand when both are measured in absolute terms, the large brand's budget is generally proportionately smaller (e.g., if it is calculated in terms of its advertising-to-sales ratio, or by its SOV). This budgetary phenomenon means that large brands are, relatively speaking, underspenders. This gives a clue to how to calculate whether advertising is a profitable activity for such brands. We start by estimating the medium-term, end-year return on advertising investment (calculated in terms of the number of cents return on the advertising dollar investment, as explained in chapter 7). With large brands, the advertising investment will almost invariably be below the category norm. It is therefore a feasible procedure to inflate the figure for the medium-term payback by the extent to which the brand underinvests. By doing this we are aggregating the medium-term and long-term return on advertising expenditure. When we do this, it can be shown that a proportion of advertising investments—perhaps for a quarter of all brands—produce a positive payback in terms of sales generated by these investments.

Note

1. Chapter 8, like chapter 7, is based on important research carried out since the publication of the first edition of *What's In a Name? Advertising and the Concept of Brands*. This research is described in John Philip Jones, *The Ultimate Secrets of Advertising* (Thousand Oaks, CA: Sage, 2001). Chapter 8 is based on a synthesis of the main conclusions from chapters 7, 8, 9, and 10 of *The Ultimate Secrets*.

9

Giving a Brand Legs: Brands as Collectible Entities

As discussed in chapter 8, brand loyalty is a powerful force in driving a brand's sales. Brand loyalty is central to how much the consumer values the brand—how important the brand is in his or her daily life. This valued relationship is reinforced through the brand's advertising and the consumer's experience with the brand itself.

Today's competitive marketplace makes it more difficult than ever to keep the consumer loyal. Explanations for consumers' lack of loyalty include some of the following:

- Consumers are smart and experienced shoppers, and many are price-conscious. While they may be willing to pay more for a nationally advertised brand in some product categories—computers, cigarettes, cosmetics, clothing—other categories do not seem to warrant additional spending for a "name brand." Examples are floor cleaners, ketchup, and bathrom tissue.
- Product proliferation provides consumers with more choices and perhaps more confusion. Supermarkets stock upward of 20,000 products. In addition, thousands of new products are introduced each year for supermarket distribution. According to Mediamark Research, there are 38 cat food brands, 57 brands of soft drinks, 57 brands of beer, 53 brands of shampoo, 25 brands of toilet paper, 36 brands of laundry detergent, and 103 brands of ready-to-eat cereal overflowing supermarket shelves.[1]

- In addition to the nationally distributed brands, grocers and mass retailers add to the fray by developing their own brands of soft drinks, margarine, toilet paper, and cereal to compete on the store shelf. Store brands lure price-conscious consumers away from nationally advertised brands, predominately at the point of purchase.
- Thousands of new products are introduced every year, providing consumers more alternatives to currently purchased brands. Heavy promotional spending on the new introductions helps to encourage trial.
- Marketers have shifted above-the-line advertising dollars to below-the-line promotions. This focus on brand switching with price deals and incentives does little for brand loyalty.

Nevertheless, brand loyalty is key to market leadership in mature categories. As the brand reaches its strongest position, penetration and purchase frequency are maximized. The best advertising opportunity is to employ a defensive strategy focused on the retention of existing users and the maintenance and increase of their purchase frequency. To accomplish this, the brand must continue to reinforce and enhance the association between the brand and the consumer.

As discussed in chapter 8, advertising does have an impact on retaining this loyalty. In recent years, however, another brand strategy has emerged that deepens the bond between consumer and brand: brand collectibles.

Manufacturers are extending brands into lines of collectible merchandise such as Christmas ornaments, dolls, figurines, plush animals, glassware, and the like. This merchandise not only heightens brand loyalty, it extends exposure to the brand message. Today, this collecting activity has been associated with some of the most recognizable brands in the world.

The Case for Collectible Brands

Brands are most often thought of as products that are consumed or used. But brand collectibles are acquired and removed from ordinary use.[2] Brand collectibles are big business. Mattel currently manufactures a collectible line of Barbie dolls, some in designer clothing from Donna Karan, Ralph Lauren, and Calvin Klein, as well as brands such as *Got Milk?* Barbie, Oreo Barbie, Harley-Davidson Barbie, Coca-Cola Barbie, and The Gap Barbie. Hallmark has a line of collectible Christmas ornaments, the Keepsake Ornament line. McDonald's is selling Ronald McDonald cookie jars on QVC and hand-beaded designer evening purses in the shapes of burgers and fries on Rodeo Drive for $2,000.

Franklin Mint, a leading creator and direct marketer of collectibles, forged partnerships with a variety of brand marketers such as Coca-Cola, Walt Disney, Planter's Peanuts, Pillsbury, LifeSavers, Ralston Purina, McDonald's, Harley-Davidson, and Campbell's Soup to create collectible products.[3] These mass-merchandising efforts have extended individual brands by making them collectible. And the companies are using marketing strategies to attract new collectors and increase purchase frequency among current collectors—two classic strategies for building a brand's business, as we discussed previously.

When we review the collectible brands listed above, identified by *Advertising Age* as entering the collectible market, certain similarities are immediately evident:

1. All are relatively old brands, ranging from forty to over 100 years in production.
2. Each brand is the leader in its product category: soft drinks, soup, entertainment, fast food, greeting cards, etc.
3. Each brand is in a mature product category, meaning that there is little opportunity for extensive primary market growth.
4. Each brand has distinctive added values.

As defined in chapter 2, while all brands are products, not all products are brands. A brand is imbued with personality characteristics; a brand is unique; a brand is timeless. Consumers purchase a brand not just because of what it will do, or how it will taste, but how they feel about the brand, what emotional or psychological reward is gained from using the brand.

Most consumers purchase brands because of some superior functionality, that is, whiter wash, moister cake, lower calories, less fat, quicker delivery, better gas mileage. In addition to these tangible deliverable benefits, consumers also purchase a brand because of the feelings or emotional attachment or psychological rewards gained by its use, that is, feeling better about themselves, providing for the family better, or simply having fun. These added values that were discussed in chapter 2 form the most important part of a brand's definition.

A collectible brand strategy may be viewed as a brand extension, which capitalizes on the added values of these brands and strengthens the relationship with the consumer by making the brand collectible in itself. Extending the brand is a key ingredient in maximizing the value of the brand in terms of profit, as well as brand loyalty.[4]

Brand collecting becomes a unique form of consumer behavior. In the context of consumer behaviorists, consumption is a means of acquiring, using, and discarding a product.[5] We buy a Coca-Cola to drink, we purchase a Lexus to drive, and we buy a McDonald's Happy Meal to feed the children.

But with collecting, the primary focus is on the acquisition and possession of the brand and seldom, if ever, involves discarding the brand. Russell Belk, a sociologist whose research on collecting has been extensive, believes collecting to be "an intensely involving form of consumption."[6]

Collecting Coca-Cola or McDonald's is a more highly involving form of consumption than simply buying a soft drink or a Big Mac. As a result, according to Belk, collectors tend to feel attached to their collections in ways that may seem irrational if viewed in terms of the normal functions of consumption. The brand collector has a stronger relationship with the brand than a normal brand consumer does. By building lines of collectible goods, brand manufacturers strengthen the association between the brand and the collectors, which enhances brand loyalty. To prove this point, case studies have been conducted on two prominent collectible brands, Coca-Cola and Hallmark.[7] These brands were chosen for a number of reasons:

- Both brands are producing or licensing extensive lines of collectibles.
- Both brands have active and relatively large collector's clubs.
- Both brands have been in the collectible market for almost twenty years.
- Both brands fit the profile of being market leaders and mature brands with significant added values.

These cases will be discussed here as a means to show the strength of the relationship between the brand and the collector.

Collecting Coca-Cola: It's the Real Thing

Chronologically, Coca-Cola comes first. The history of this American icon is a textbook case study in building, managing, and maintaining a brand. Since its beginning in 1886, Coca-Cola has built a powerful brand image. The brand is imbued with added values: the discriminating benefits that extend beyond the functionality of a refreshing soft drink. The brand is seen as traditional, patriotic, friendly, and American. Bill, a Coca-Cola collector for thirty years, describes the brand as follows: "Because it has been so ubiquitous, it's in everybody's past. You put it together with Mom, apple pie, the American flag, and Coca-Cola. Around the world—this is America. This is the symbol of America."

Although the brand is more than 110 years old, the basic brand proposition—Coca-Cola satisfies, Coca-Cola is a delightful, refreshing beverage—has remained virtually unchanged, as has the brand name and its distinctive logo. In its early days, the company developed a strong support system for the brand by building life-long partnerships with its distribution franchises and by creating a distinctive personality that appealed emotionally to consumers. Furthermore, the company has consistently supported the brand and its identity with powerful advertising messages and substantial investments, along with distinctive package designs.

The story behind Coca-Cola, a product that is 99 percent sugar and water, and its ascent to a $20 billion business marketed in 195 countries, is an American phenomenon.[8] But what is also remarkable is the Coca-Cola Collector's Club, which boasts 7,500 members in twenty-three countries who collect Coca-Cola memorabilia, from bottles and cans to delivery uniforms, old advertisements, vending machines, and coolers. The club is independent of the Coca-Cola Company. It is completely governed and financially supported by its members.

Coca-Cola is not only one of the largest brands in the world; it is also the largest brand collectible in the world. From the time the secret formula for Coca-Cola was first used, the Coca-Cola Company has been producing a wide range of promotional materials to encourage consumption of the drink. From its first ad budget in 1901 of $100,000, to its recent $100 million investment in the 2002 Winter Olympics campaign, Coca-Cola has been heavily advertised through virtually every possible message channel.[9]

Long before today's mass media, the Coca-Cola Company used millions of promotional items to advertise and sell its product to the masses. These items ranged from utilitarian merchandising items such as bottles and coolers to traditional, familiar advertising items such as signs and print advertisements, from point-of-purchase items such as trays and calendars to complimentary novelties such as toys and bookmarks.[10] Today these items are considered rare and extremely valuable antiques and form the basis for today's collections of Coca-Cola memorabilia.

The considerable interest in collecting older Coca-Cola memorabilia has created a secondary level of new collectibles manufactured strictly to be collected. These new lines of products, such as polar bear ornaments, glassware, trays, posters, kitchenware, and so forth, have been developed to feed the appetite people have for collecting Coca-Cola.

The Coca-Cola Company became interested in the memorabilia craze as the nation was engulfed in a nostalgia wave during the 1970s. Before this time, Coca-Cola paid little attention to items being manufactured with the company logo but without company approval. But the 1970s nostalgia movement changed all that. People were frantic for any piece of Coca-Cola merchandise that reminded them of their childhood or of simpler times, and the company took advantage of the situation so as not to disappoint these loyalists.

Today, more than 250 companies worldwide are issued licenses to manu-facture over 10,000 different products bearing the Coca-Cola trademark. More than 50 million Coca-Cola items were sold in 1997 in various mass-mer-chandising retail outlets, as well as in the Coca-Cola Catalog and via Coca-Cola.com. The Coca-Cola Company receives annual licensing fees from the manufacturers of the collectibles as well as an estimated 8 to 10 percent of the manufacturer's gross sales value, according to company archivist Phil Mooney. So, while Coca-Cola's main business remains soft drinks, the in-come generated from collectibles and the added financial return the collectibles provide add to Coca-Cola's bottom line while enhancing brand loyalty.

Hallmark Collecting: When You Care Enough

According to independent research provided to Hallmark, "When You Care Enough to Send the Very Best" is one of the most trusted and believed slo-gans in America because it associates the product with the experience of Hallmark. Not only has the "When You Care Enough" advertising slogan been in use for more than fifty years, it is the philosophy of the Hallmark company as well. Founder Joyce C. Hall wrote in 1979, "While we thought we had only established a good advertising slogan, we soon found out we had made a business commitment. The slogan constantly puts pressure on us to make Hallmark cards 'the very best.'"[11]

Hallmark Cards, Inc., founded in 1910, claims to be "the world's largest manufacturer of greeting cards and other personal expression products."[12] The "personal expression" line of products includes cards, ornaments, mugs, t-shirts, gift wrap, and stationary items. The cards and ornaments are, respec-tively, the two top sales-producing product lines, and Hallmark is considered the domestic market leader in both categories. Hallmark's sales of $4 billion in 2001 put the company among the ranks of Forbes' list of the largest pri-vately held U.S. companies.

In 1973, Hallmark introduced the Keepsake line of Christmas ornaments. At the time, the company was seeking to expand its product line while con-tinuing to manufacture what it did best—"personal expression" items. The first offering included six decorated balls and twelve yarn figures as Christ-mas decorations. Today, Hallmark manufactures over two hundred fifty or-naments per year under the Hallmark Keepsake Ornament umbrella. All Hallmark Keepsake Ornaments are limited editions, dated and available at retail for one season only. In this way, Hallmark enhances the collectibility of the ornaments. Destroying unsold stock maintains the ornament's value by limiting availability; it also keeps the secondary market from becoming saturated. This strengthens Hallmark's relationship with the collector by protecting both the emotional and financial investment in the ornament.

According to industry experts, ornament collecting has grown quickly since Hallmark introduced its line to the marketplace. Total annual sales value of the ornament industry was $624 million in 2000, much of which was fueled by Hallmark, according to industry research. Today Hallmark's research estimates that more than 31 million Americans collect ornaments, and more than half of those households collect Hallmark Keepsake Ornaments.[13]

Because of this interest in collecting, the company launched the Hallmark Keepsake Ornament Collector's Club in 1987, which is now the largest collector's club in the nation. There are more than five hundred local clubs nationwide. With a membership of more than 275,000, it is one of the few clubs, if not the only one, that are completely managed and maintained by the manufacturing company. Most collectors' clubs are volunteer organizations with no company affiliation, such as the Coca-Cola Collector's Club. At Hallmark, a full-time staff of eight manages the membership, communications, and events for the Collector's Club. This puts Hallmark in complete control of the collecting activity.

According to Hallmark research, joining the national club is the first step. A buyers' study conducted by Hallmark showed that a noncollector purchases one to three ornaments per year. A person begins to call himself/herself a "collector" when purchases grow to thirteen ornaments a year. Buying jumps to an average of forty ornaments per year when the collector joins the national club and doubles to eighty per year when the collector then joins a local club. Therefore, club membership does indeed increase purchasing. Estimating national membership fees, event fees, event purchasing, and annual collector purchasing, the Hallmark Collector's Club generates approximately $118 million annually.[14]

Hallmark's marketing strategy, including products, events, and communications to collectors, serves to enhance a strong brand association with this special group of consumers. This translates into the retention of a consumer/ collector over a long period of time, and this relationship provides Hallmark with a competitive advantage in the marketplace.

The Loyal Relationship with Collectible Brands

David Aaker, an academic who has specialized in studying brands, has defined brand loyalty as "a measure of the attachment that a customer has to a brand."[15] While loyalty is often seen as a barrier to substitutability, most consumers are not loyal to just one brand, but most often have a repertoire of brands, usually three in any one product category. With brand collecting, this does *not* seem to be the case.

Hallmark and Coca-Cola have extended not only the brand, but the brand's relationship with the consumer beyond the store shelf. The power of this extension deepens the consumer's feelings for and associations with the brand, and the impact of the collection on the collector provides a very positive and powerful experience with the brand. This experience breeds brand-loyal collectors, which translates into sales of both the brand and the line of collectibles. To understand this more thoroughly, we will first discuss the collecting strategies employed by these two brands and then explore the relationship that each has built with collectors.

The key element in any successful brand extension is obviously a strong brand. Hallmark and Coca-Cola have tremendous brand strength. Hallmark intentionally expanded its brand name into the line of Keepsake Ornaments. However, it was not until long after the introduction of the ornaments that the company realized this was an extension into the collectible market as well. Their original plan of destroying after-season inventory backfired when the company realized that people from the Midwest were doing the most extraordinary thing: they were actually digging up the leftovers that had been taken to a local landfill. Thus, the collectibilty was determined by the consumers.

About the same time, Coca-Cola realized that the marketplace was littered with unlicensed Coca-Cola merchandise, and people could not get enough of it. The company took advantage of the situation and developed a licensing program that allowed them to control and profit from these collectibles.

Although Hallmark will not release sales figures for their ornaments, the calculation earlier in this chapter shows that the membership dues and purchasing power of the club add more than $118 million to the company's volume. This income is just from collectors. Hallmark's research reveals that noncollectors purchase one to three ornaments per year, and collectors who are not yet club members purchase thirteen ornaments a year. Using Hallmark's data on the number of households that collect Hallmark ornaments, this estimated purchasing power generates approximately $1.9 billion in ornament sales *from non-club members alone.*[16] This being the case, ornament sales account for almost half of Hallmark's $4 billion in overall sales. This is an amazing proportion.

Coca-Cola has licensing agreements with over one hundred twenty-five companies in the United States alone. The licensing fees generate more than $20 million. In addition, Coca-Cola receives a royalty based on sales of licensed merchandise, estimated at between 8 and 10 percent of the sales value of each item. For example, when Coca-Cola teamed with Mattel to create a collectible vintage Coca-Cola Barbie, Mattel paid a licensing fee as well as providing Coca-Cola with 8 percent of the sales value from the doll. Ten thousand dolls were sold for $130 each, garnering Coca-Cola more than $100,000. It was estimated that three more dolls in the series would generate even more sales, making Coca-Cola Barbie worth half a million dollars. This is an example of just one licensed product; Coca-Cola licenses hundreds more. And while the licensing fees for these collectibles may pale in comparison with the $20 billion in sales of beverages by the company, collectibles do add to the strength of the company in terms of loyalty to the brand.

Building Brand Loyalty

As we pointed out in earlier chapters, the key elements in brand growth are penetration and purchase frequency. Once the consumer has tried the brand, the next step is to get him or her to repurchase and eventually buy more. This same strategy is apparent in the collectibles market—first, get the person to buy a collectible, then get him or her hooked by buying repeatedly.

People start collecting for various reasons. Clara, a Hallmark collector who owns every ornament the company has ever made, connected an ornament with the memory of her husband. A metal serving tray intrigued Bill and Randy, who are credited with the largest private collection of Coca-Cola. Pete, who houses his Coca-Cola collection in three garages, bought a knife. Nora, who owns 3,000 ornaments, was buying gifts for her children when she started her collection. And Luann, whose collection of ornaments tops 5,000, received a Hallmark ornament as a gift. The first purchase is driven by something internal: a desire, a want, a need. But the next purchase and those that follow are driven by something external as well as internal. Pete, a collector for almost twenty-five years, talks about what drove him:

> I bought a Coca-Cola pocket knife for $3. I don't know why. I didn't carry a pocketknife. Never owned a pocketknife. And I didn't even drink Coca-Cola. But something interested me and I bought it. Then I began to buy a bit more. I had 30 or so Coca-Cola pieces, but I didn't consider myself a collector. Then I read about a group of collectors getting together, and I went. I was like a kid in a candy store. I was hooked.

Pete's experience would explain what psychologist Werner Muensterberger calls "replenishment," and this emotional need causes the collector to be in a "constant replenishment" mode. There is no rational need for anyone to have

2,000 Christmas ornaments, when the average Christmas tree holds perhaps 100; or a need to have sixty metal Coca-Cola serving trays that are never used to serve anything. These types of behavior have all been observed while researching these cases. Yet, emotional needs are being met through the collecting of Hallmark ornaments or Coca-Cola metal trays. Muensterberger relates this to a recurring state of hunger: "[R]egardless of how often and how much one ingests, within a few hours hunger returns and one must eat again." So it is with collectors. In the words of many of the collectors interviewed, they call it the "collector's mentality." As one collector admitted: "It's like a mistress, or a habit like drugs. Every so often, you have to have a fix." Hallmark and Coca-Cola capitalize on that "collector's mentality" to build brand loyalty.[17]

These brand collectors are drinking Coca-Cola, talking about Coca-Cola, reading about Coca-Cola, buying Coca-Cola, displaying Coca-Cola, and investing in Coca-Cola. Coca-Cola is a part of their lives. They are immersed in the brand experience every day. The same is true with Hallmark. Although there is some built-in seasonality to the ornaments, Hallmark extends the buying activity through most of the year. In January, the ornaments for the year are previewed on Hallmark.com. In February, members of the Collector's Club receive the Dream Book, the catalog of ornaments. In March, members can begin pre-ordering ornaments for delivery in July, when the ornaments are actually in retail stores. The line of Keepsake ornaments is issued at select times from July through November, creating great anticipation in the six months prior to Christmas.

One interesting aspect of Hallmark and Coca-Cola is that the company name and the products they sell are the same. This is not universal, but the potential for creating and sustaining brand loyalty is thought to increase when this is the case.[18] This allows the consumer (or collector, as the case may be) the opportunity to have positive associations with the product as well as with the company. The brand image is created by sets of these positive associations. The strength of these associations links the collector to the brand, building a relationship of loyalty.

Linking the Collectible to the Company

Linking the product and the company is especially important for these collectible brands. However, the relationships that are created with collectors are very different, depending on how the companies structure the collecting activity.

Coca-Cola

Whereas Hallmark's club is company driven, Coca-Cola's club is collector driven. Since its inception in 1975, the latter has been organized and managed by collectors. This arrangement is very different from Hallmark's control model. The Coca-Cola Collector's Club is controlled and supported by collectors. They have created a volunteer structure that allows for elected representatives from various regions, as well as elected officials and board members. No one appoints officers; candidates campaign for the offices and ask for the votes of fellow collectors. These volunteers publish a monthly newsletter, plan and coordinate the annual national convention, create retail opportunities, and develop collectible merchandise. The company does not sponsor any event or provide any underwriting; nor does it have any input in the planning. It is a collector's convention. As former Coca-Cola CEO Roberto Goizueta explained, "The brand does not belong to us. We're just the custodians."[19]

Indeed, this model is about brand ownership. Coca-Cola collectors feel they own the brand. They not only use the brand, they live with it every day. Pete not only has three garages full of his collection; his house is decorated with Coca-Cola items. Guests eat on Coca-Cola dishes and drink from Coca-Cola glasses. Cold Coca-Cola is kept in a Coca-Cola refrigerator behind a Coca-Cola bar. His license plates tout Coke, and his phone number uses four digits that stand for the letters COKE. But his prized possession is his parrot, Cokey, whom Pete has taught to say "Drink Coca-Cola" over and over again.

The brand belongs to them. These collectors work tirelessly to protect the brand, market the brand, and advertise the brand. They invest in the brand by buying stock (most of the collectors are stockholders). They are part of the brand's history. Because they collect historical pieces, they believe their knowledge about the brand is unparalleled.

They are the voice of the brand. Coca-Cola collectors drive the company to produce collectibles. They are vocal—through the club, the convention, the newsletter, and their purchasing—about what they want from the company and, perhaps more importantly, what they do not want. Collectors share concerns regarding saturation of the marketplace with new Coca-Cola items that are not necessarily collectible. These include the products that are produced in mass quantities and sold by mass merchandisers with no limitations. From conversations with these collectors, the Coca-Cola Barbie was recognized as one of the few limited-edition collectibles licensed by the company in recent years. This is not to say that Coca-Cola allows the collectors to determine what is licensed; that is certainly not the case. However, it is important to note that the company does listen to collectors. As Phil Mooney claims, "These are a powerful group of consumers." Nowhere was this more evident than during the introduction of New Coke.

Nothing tested the loyalists more than New Coke. "It was the ultimate testimony to the power of this brand," according to Mooney. The collectors hated New Coke. They felt betrayed and confused. The real issue was betrayal of their feelings (in the words of collector Nate), like "losing an old friend." Pete never tried New Coke. "I just thought this can't happen. It was like a death in the family," he said. Ross, an avid collector and Coca-Cola drinker, was disappointed they had had no warning. "We felt we had a strong relationship with the company. A lot of collectors felt betrayed. In addition to not liking the flavor, we didn't like the way it was done."

Dissent grew among collectors. They were the most vocal of critics, writing letters to newspapers, talking to reporters, and protesting to the company. As the 1985 Coca-Cola National Collector's Convention date drew closer, company officials grew concerned that coverage would only increase as several hundred brand loyalists gathered in Dallas. When the company decided to reintroduce Classic Coke, the first delivery truck was sent to Dallas to deliver the Real Thing to the collector's convention.

These collectors are not only masters of the brand, they are highly visible in the marketplace, making the brand more visible as well. Coca-Cola collectors are written about in magazines devoted to antiques and travel, in newspaper articles, in collecting magazines, and in newsletters. They often appear on television programs that spotlight collectors and collections, including *QVC* and the *Home Shopping Network*. Collector conventions and local club activities are covered by the local media, and collectors are often invited to special events sponsored by the Coca-Cola Company, such as anniversary parties and retail store openings. Each collector is considered a specialist in his or her own collection, affording each one the opportunity of being an authority on Coca-Cola. Many collectors are considered experts in Coca-Cola collectibles. Their advice and insights are sought after by other Coca-Cola collectors, the collecting industry, the media, and even the Coca-Cola Company. They write articles and books, give lectures, and conduct workshops, lending much visibility to the brand and establishing enormous credibility as its spokespersons, much like an owner. Coca-Cola is theirs. They possess it. They possess the collectible, they own the brand. According to Coca-Cola archivist Phil Mooney, "These collectors are very, very brand loyal. No other brand has this kind of loyalty. These people not only consume the product, they acquire it, save it, and totally immerse themselves in the brand. These collectors are Coca-Cola."

Hallmark

The Hallmark Keepsake Collector's Club is company-driven. Hallmark started the club, markets the club, and basically controls the club and reaps the profits the club generates. Furthermore, the collectors are dependent on the company for replenishment each year. The Hallmark model is to put the collector closer to the brand, with the use of events, exclusive products, and communication tactics. Rewards are offered for joining or renewing membership. Exclusive products are offered at member-only events. Ornament artists are the focus of special events where collectors can collect autographs of those who designed the collectible ornaments. And the magic of the ornament is enhanced by Hallmark sharing information about how it is made and what is being planned for next year. Finally, Hallmark infuses its correspondence with emotional references to tradition, holidays, family, and the "Hallmark experience," which embodies the company's image. This tone infiltrates all communication efforts, whether in mass-media advertising, the *Dream Book*, the guide to starting a collection, or the quarterly newsletter. The purpose is to create an additional emotional attachment to this already emotionally charged brand. All the while, Hallmark is driving the collectors to buy what it provides. The collectors in turn are obedient.

It is no surprise that this emotional attachment creates a strong brand relationship. But this relationship goes beyond brand loyalty; it reaches brand intimacy. These collectors are more than just loyal; they are faithful, devoted, obedient, and steadfast. They love Hallmark, they love the ornaments. Marie, a long-time Hallmark collector, spoke of the company as likable, warm, friendly, comfortable to be with—almost like a companion. "I like Hallmark," she said. "They make me feel important."

Nora speaks of Hallmark with even more emotion. "I love Hallmark. Hallmark is like fireplaces, a cup of tea, sit around with scrapbooks, that kind of nostalgia. It feels like—pull up a chair, have a bite to eat—even if it's peanut butter and jelly, we'll sit around the table and talk."

When Clara discusses her collection, she speaks of her ornaments in a very personal way. The collection is the outcome of a tragic personal loss. By using the activity as a means of emotional and spiritual comfort, the meaning of what she has collected is no doubt strengthened. When asked about her Hallmark ornaments she says, "My favorite ornament is every ornament I have. My ornaments are truly like my children. There's not a one that I want to do without."

To these collectors, Hallmark is like a lover: dating, seducing, and tying the knot on an enduring and dependent relationship. As consumer behaviorists suggest, this relationship is similar to the "marriage metaphor assumed in traditional loyalty definitions." However, these Hallmark loyalists have a passion and emotion about that brand that provides an intimacy. While such a relationship is indeed possible with one brand, what may be occurring in the case of Hallmark is a progression of the relationship—intimacy and then marriage.[20]

The process of dating is very similar to how Hallmark attracts and hooks collectors. First comes the introduction. The consumer is already a Hallmark customer, although not a member of the Collector's Club. Throughout the retail environment many opportunities exist to introduce the consumer to the club. The ornaments are meticulously displayed in the store, membership kits are available, the *Dream Book* displays all of the ornaments and extols the benefits of collecting, and the *Get Hooked on Collecting* book can get you started.[21]

Next comes the seduction. The key here is finding something in common, and Hallmark has no problem with getting the conversation started with 250 ornaments; one of them has to spark an interest. Hallmark has done the research. The ornament line consists of some of the most popular cartoon characters, movie stars, and sports heroes, while using brands, hobbies, religion, and family themes to attract a broad collector base. Certainly, something catches the eye—the holiday Barbie, the Coca-Cola Santa, the Star Trek ships, the rocking horse, the teddy bear, the Christmas stamp, the car, the angel. The seduction occurs when the membership dues are paid.

At that point, the courtship begins. The brand and the collector become more intimate through the constant correspondence. The brand reassures the collector that it is trustworthy, comforting, warm, caring, and steadfast. The collector becomes more familiar and comfortable with the brand, leading to more involvement. Here, the brand arranges dates in public places, such as the ornament premiere at the local Hallmark store. This allows the collector to relax in an informal yet familiar setting and to meet some of the brand's friends. Gradually, the dates move to exclusive events outside the retail environment, and, as more friends are made, the comfort level and the intimacy increase.

Eventually, the collectors are hooked. They fall in love with Hallmark and believe the brand is important in their lives. Furthermore, they are dependent on the brand for their life as collectors. Hallmark is everything desired in a brand or a spouse. Hallmark is always interested, does not take the collector for granted, and is a good communicator and an even better listener. Hallmark will take care of them; they are a family. Hallmark and the collector are married.

The Argument in Brief

There is no question that brands are under siege. Supermarkets house more than 20,000 products; hypermarkets stock more than 30,000. Product proliferation, the tendency for brands to copy one another, price-conscious consumers, mature product categories, and overall saturation make it very difficult for old brands as well as new brands to survive in the marketplace. Brand loyalty is the ultimate prize, while brand infidelity has become the norm. Yet, a collectible strategy has proved successful for mature brands such as Coca-Cola and Hallmark, as a means of retaining a core base of devoted loyalists.

Both Hallmark and Coca-Cola have contact with these collectors beyond the retail shelf. By extending the brand as a collectible, Coca-Cola and Hallmark have created *a marketing environment of multiple contacts.* According to Larry Light, a longtime student of brands, this type of environment positions the brand as a "trustmark" instead of a trademark—one that becomes the point of differentiation for the brand in the marketplace. Therefore Coca-Cola is not just a big company that manufactures a refreshing soft drink. It becomes a prized possession. The Hallmark Keepsake Ornament is not simply a resin decoration for the Christmas tree. It is an intimate part of life. This strategy changes a typical "transaction mentality" (sell the product off the shelf) to a "relationship mentality" (building an affinity for the brand that is positive and long lasting).[22] The collectible strategy, as employed by Coca-Cola and Hallmark, not only serves to maintain brand loyalty, but elevates it to a more powerful level. The affinity these collectors have for the brand is beyond loyalty. These collectors have taken possession of these brands; these brands are an important part of their lives.

Notes

1. Mediamark Research (1998).
2. Russell W. Belk, *Collecting in a Consumer Society* (New York: Routledge, 1995).
3. Laura Loro, "Nostalgia for Sale at Franklin Mint," *Advertising Age,* May 15, 1995, p. 33.
4. David A. Aaker, *Managing Brand Equity* (New York: Free Press, 1991).
5. Russell W. Belk, Melanie Wallendorf, John Sherry, and Morris B. Holbrook, "Collecting in a Consumer Culture," in *Highways and Buyways: Naturalistic Research from the Consumer Behavior Odyssey* (Provo, UT: Association for Consumer Research, 1991), pp. 178–215.
6. Belk, *Collecting in a Consumer Society,* p. 67.
7. This work was originally published in Jan S. Slater's dissertation, "Trash to Treasures: A Qualitative Study of the Relationship Between Collectors and Collect-

ible Brands" (Syracuse University, 1997). Findings from this research have previously been published in various forms. These include Jan S. Slater, "Collecting Brand Loyalty: A Comparative Analysis of How Coca-Cola and Hallmark Use Collecting Behavior to Enhance Brand Loyalty," *Advances in Consumer Research* 28 (2001): 362–369; Jan S. Slater, "Collecting the Real Thing: A Case Study Exploration of Brand Loyalty Enhancement Among Coca-Cola Brand Collectors," *Advances in Consumer Research* 27 (2000): 202–208; Jan S. Slater, "A Case for Collectible Brands," in *How to Use Advertising to Build Strong Brands,* John Philip Jones, ed. (Thousand Oaks, CA: Sage, 1999), pp. 251–266.

8. *Coca-Cola 2001 Annual Report.*

9. Frederick Allen, *Secret Formula* (New York: HarperCollins, 1994).

10. Randy Schaeffer and Bill Bateman, *Coca-Cola: A Collector's Guide* (London: Quintet Books, 1995).

11. Joyce C. Hall, *When You Care Enough* (Kansas City, MO: Hallmark Cards, 1979).

12. Hallmark press release, July 1, 1995.

13. Hallmark press release, July 10, 2001.

14. Based on membership fees of $25 for 275,000 members; ten special collector events, sold out at 2,000 each for $10 registration; purchase of 2,000 special event ornaments at all ten events at $60 each; and the average collector expenditure of $400 annually.

15. Aaker, *Managing Brand Equity*, p. 39.

16. Hallmark estimates that of the 31 million households that collect ornaments, half collect Hallmark ornaments. Deducting club membership from that figure, it is estimated that nonmember collectors total 15.2 million households. Hallmark's research estimates that nonmembers who collect buy, on average, thirteen ornaments a year. The average Hallmark ornament costs $10; therefore the spending would be approximately $130 annually. Multiplied by 15.2 million households, these nonmember collectors generate $1.9 billion in ornament sales per year.

17. Werner Muensterberger, *Collecting, an Unruly Passion: Psychological Perspectives* (Princeton, NJ: Princeton University Press, 1994).

18. Larry Light, *The Fourth Wave: Brand Loyalty* (New York: American Association of Advertising Agencies, 1996).

19. Telephone interview conducted by Jan S. Slater with Coca-Cola archivist Phil Mooney, April 3, 1997.

20. Susan Fournier and Julie L. Yao, "Reviving Brand Loyalty: A Reconceptualization Within the Framework of Consumer-Brand Relationships," *International Journal of Research in Marketing* 14 (1997): 451–472.

21. The *Dream Book* is published annually as the brochure for the line of ornaments available that year. This is available at Hallmark.com in January, and the hard copy is sent to members of the Collector's Club in February. By April, these are also available to the general public at all Hallmark Gold Crown Stores. The *Get Hooked on Collecting* book is part of a collector's starting package sold in the Hallmark Gold Crown Stores.

22. Ryan Matthews, "Branding the Store," *Progressive Grocer* 74 (November 1995): B-4; and Light, *The Fourth Wave: Brand Loyalty.*

— 10 —

The Contribution of Advertising Strategy to Brand Building

We have made a case in previous chapters that long-term advertising effects strengthen a brand and its relationship with the consumer. What we intend to focus on in the next two chapters is the development of effective advertising, which ultimately is the key to long-term effects. As we saw in chapter 7, there is a wide spectrum of effectiveness in terms of advertising's impact on sales. Remember that 30 percent of the advertising campaigns researched showed no effect on sales. This does not make a great case for the general effectiveness of advertising.

What is effective advertising? How do we define something that to most people is quite subjective? People unacquainted with the business will answer that question based on the creativity of the advertisement. Did it make them laugh? Did they like the ad? Was it fun? Many industry professionals will also claim that creativity is the driving force behind effective advertising. To the extent that a big idea is able to connect the brand to the consumer, there is some truth to that statement. It cannot be ignored that the creative element of advertising is a powerful force in gaining attention and delivering a strong sales message. But overall, the strength behind effective advertising is very basic, very fundamental: a solid advertising strategy. The strategy provides the reasoning behind the advertising. Without a strategy there may be no big idea, there may be no creativity. There may be only a chance you can develop an ad that works. Therein lies the definition of effective advertising: advertising that works. It works to do the job as intended—to generate awareness, introduce new brand information, remind the consumer to buy the brand, and encourage the consumer to use more of the brand. When the advertisement delivers the right message, to the right audience, at the right time—there is more than just a chance the ad will do its job. You then have an accountability factor in the advertisement because the strategy provides a benchmark against which to measure the impact of the advertisement.

This is not to say a good strategy will *guarantee* effective advertisements. What we are implying is that the strategy is the first step in the process. Obviously idea generation and the creative execution of advertisements are important in the success of a campaign. In addition, the delivery of the creative message via the media is imperative to success. We will discuss some of these aspects in chapter 11. But this chapter will focus on developing the foundation for effective advertising—the strategy.

Putting Advertising in Perspective

Before we go any farther, it is important to establish some common ground about advertising in general. Advertising cannot solve every problem. We have an arsenal of communications and marketing tools that can be used to strengthen a brand's position. Advertising is just one of those tools. However, because the advertising for a brand has the most visibility, it is often thought to be the most powerful tool. This is not always the case. It is not a miracle drug; advertising has limitations. And it is imperative that those limitations are understood before the strategy is developed. Part of the strategy will be to determine whether advertising can help the brand overall. Therefore, let us look at what advertising can and cannot do.

First, advertising is just one of many communication tools that can be used along the marketing route for a brand. Other tools, such as consumer promotions, trade promotions, product publicity, and direct response, can all be effective in the selling of a brand. But advertising is often the most visible element of a brand. Therefore, much of what people know about the brand they know simply through advertising. For instance, few people know that McDonald's Corporation has 29,000 restaurants in 121 countries, it trains managers and franchisees at Hamburger University in a Chicago suburb, and it owns Boston Market restaurants. But millions of people know Ronald McDonald and the Hamburglar and can recite "You deserve a break today" and "We want to see you smile" because of McDonald's strong advertising presence.

Although advertising may be the most visible part of a brand's business, this does not mean it is always the most effective means of communication.

The first decision that has to be made strategically is whether advertising can help this brand. We are going to discuss how to decide this question later in this chapter. However, it is important to realize that advertising may not be the best or *only* solution for a brand's situation.

Advertising is not all-powerful. Many people, especially advertising critics, believe that advertising has such persuasive powers that it alone can influence consumers and make them buy what they do not want. But this view is grossly optimistic. First and foremost, a brand must meet the needs and desires of the consumer. No amount of research and development, advertising, low price, or massive distribution will sell a product no one wants. But because advertising is so pervasive, many people believe it to be very persuasive. Our discussion of effective advertising campaigns in chapter 7, which showed that only one-third of the campaigns actually helped the brands, contradicts this notion. It must be said that advertising in general has a very difficult job, especially in today's competitive environment. Because of advertising's constant presence, each advertisement has to work exceptionally hard just to engage the consumer's attention amid the clutter.

Furthermore, consumers—especially young consumers—are quite savvy when it comes to advertising. Advertising is totally open. Consumers recognize this and they are skeptical. They know the advertisement's purpose is to sell something. Immediately, the consumer's own psychological barriers rise, allowing the consumer to screen and choose what advertisements are noticed, as well as what advertising information is retained. The consumer is in complete control, not the advertiser.

Finally, if advertising is so powerful, why do so many new products fail each year? Millions of dollars are spent advertising these new products, yet an enormous proportion of them fail. If advertising were as powerful as some people believe, this failure rate would be impossible. This raises key points about what advertising can and cannot do.

What Advertising Cannot Do

1. Advertising cannot make brands with a functional deficiency succeed

In chapter 2 we defined a brand as "a product that provides functional benefits plus added values." Functionality is an integral element in the success of a brand. The term refers to a demonstrable difference in how the brand performs in comparison with its competitors. It might be a better taste, a whiter wash, a moister cake, a faster cooking method, or a no-caffeine soft drink.

This functional point of difference between brands must be one that is easily recognizable to the consumer and one that is desirable.

While advertising may be instrumental in getting the consumer to try a brand, if the product cannot deliver the performance, no amount of advertising will entice the consumer to buy again. This factor is often instrumental in the failure of new product introductions. Most often the functionality is either weak or lacking superiority against entrenched competitors in the market. No matter how strong the advertisements are, they will not be effective if the consumer perceives the brand as not performing well.

2. Advertising cannot succeed without resources behind it

The important relationship between advertising volume and sales has been presented in chapter 8. Advertising intensity is a requirement for advertising success. Indeed, there is a line between overspending and underspending. The most creative, attention-getting advertisement cannot be effective if there is no financial power to support the distribution of the message to the audience at efficient and effective levels. Perfect examples of this are brands such as Lux, Oxydol, Ivory soap—at one time all strong category leaders. When advertising dollars were diverted from these brands the effects were devastating. Lux, a Unilever brand, and Oxydol, from Procter & Gamble, stagnated on U.S. store shelves. Eventually, both disappeared except as price brands when advertising dollars were spent on newer products such as Dove and Tide. With the introduction of Lever 2000, Ivory, one of Procter & Gamble's oldest brands, began losing market share mainly because the brand had not been sufficiently supported. Procter & Gamble has since boosted support for Ivory in both advertising and product development and has regained some of the lost market share. But the brand has yet to return to its previous position in the market.

3. Advertising cannot work if the planning is not logical/vertical

Planning is integral to strategy development and will be discussed later in this chapter. But it is important to see immediately that the planning follows a logical process, starting at the top and working down in a precise manner. Edward de Bono, a well-known writer on thought processes, defines logical/ vertical thinking as selective, directive, analytical, and sequential, moving logically, step by step toward a solution.[1] It is only with this sort of process, when all pertinent brand elements can be analyzed, that a sound advertising strategy can be developed. There is always the danger of jumping to the tactics of creative execution or recommending media vehicles before the strategy is developed. It is not uncommon in the professional world for creative executions or media ideas to be developed before the strategic direction is developed and agreed on. This not only wastes time and energy; it can be financially irresponsible.

4. Advertising cannot work if creativity is not lateral

Whereas the strategy has to be developed by a vertical process, creativity has to be developed by a lateral process. Edward de Bono is the originator of lateral thinking. Lateral thinking encourages generating many approaches to solve a problem, with thought processes jumping about without any set pattern or path. It is this way of looking at the least obvious or most irrelevant approaches, which allows creative thinking to occur and a multitude of advertising ideas to be generated. Logical or vertical thought has no place in the development of creative ideas, because it is so restrictive by nature. Lateral thinking, according to de Bono, "tries to restructure patterns by putting things together in a different way." Accordingly, advertising works when the planning takes a logical direction and the creative ideas do not. De Bono claims that vertical and lateral thinking are complementary. Lateral thinking generates a multitude of ideas; vertical thinking puts them to good use.[2]

What Advertising Can Do

The previous discussion might lead one to believe advertising is a relatively weak force. But that is not to say that advertising cannot be a strong force as well. Again, the key is to understand advertising's abilities and limitations within the marketplace. Much of this book has been dedicated to documenting advertising's strength in building brands. Keeping in mind that certain elements must be in place—the brand, the resources, logical planning, and imaginative creative concepts—advertising can occasionally be a very strong force.

1. Advertising can achieve awareness and trial

At its best, advertising can work to make consumers aware that the brand is in the marketplace, while providing enough information about it to encourage a purchase. Awareness is the first of several components that make up the totality of the brand and its advertising. Other components include brand knowledge, brand image, and brand attitudes. Awareness relates to the consumer's realization that the brand exists. The level of this awareness can then be determined within the component of brand knowledge—what comes to mind when the consumer thinks about the brand.[3]

We see the astounding effects of awareness most often in new product introductions. Heavy advertising is used in the early stages of bringing the product to market mainly for the purpose of building a level of awareness. Although the advertising may drive the consumer to buy the brand for trial, if the brand does not meet the expectation encouraged by the advertisement and the consumer is dissatisfied, no amount of advertising will entice the consumer to purchase the brand again. Advertising's ability to reach the masses with a strong message makes its use very important in establishing brand awareness. It is necessary that the consumer at least think of the brand when considering the product category. Raising brand awareness increases the likelihood that the brand will at least be included in the consideration process—within the repertoire of those brands being considered for purchase. Additionally, brand awareness affects consumer decision-making by influencing the formation and strength of brand associations that directly affect brand knowledge and brand image. Both are necessary conditions for establishing a strong relationship between the consumer and the brand, much of which is established via advertising.[4]

2. Advertising can modify attitudes

Advertising's strength here is much debated. Some people who believe that advertising is a strong force assume that advertising can change attitudes. However, those who believe that advertising is a weak force will only acknowledge that advertising can modify attitudes. Why the debate? Well, while advertising can increase knowledge of the brand, changing attitudes can be a difficult task because of the way in which attitudes are formed. Attitudes are formed through various associations one makes with the brand. These associations can be developed through use of the brand, brand advertising, word of mouth, peer influence, habits, or simply because it was what one's family always used. Attitudes, therefore, are formed through various levels of knowledge and experience the consumer has with or around the brand. These attitudes are thought to vary in strength based on the consumer's relationship with the brand and/or the brand's relevance within the scope of the consumer's needs or desires.

The stronger the attitude, naturally the more difficult it is to change. This is especially true in light of our previous discussion regarding the consumer's general indifference to advertising. It is difficult to engage consumers in something they view as relatively unimportant. Furthermore, most advertising is brief—a thirty-second television commercial does not allow for strong, persuasive arguments. All of these factors contribute to the difficulties advertising must face to change attitudes. Therefore, it is more realistic to expect that advertising can only *modify* attitudes—introducing new information about the performance, personality, or benefits of the brand. But generally advertising is not strong enough to convert people whose beliefs are different from what is claimed in advertising.[5] The source of information creating the strongest brand attitudes is direct experience, not advertising.[6]

3. Advertising can build brand preference or loyalty

Brand loyalty was identified in chapter 9 as the consumer's attachment to the brand. Basically, this is the central construct of marketing—to keep the consumer buying again and again.[7] Therefore, a very large amount of advertising is defensive in nature. This means it is more commonly used to retain existing users, and not so much to bring new users to the brand. Brand knowledge takes over here. Current users are well disposed toward a brand, and advertising merely reinforces this preference.[8] But the advertisement must do more than simply communicate information. Information is of limited importance at this stage. The advertising must *reinforce* what consumers already know and feel about the brand and strengthen their resolve that they consistently make the right choice by buying it. The advertisement strengthens their attachment to the brand by depicting pride, satisfaction, positive experiences, strong user imagery, and strong brand personality. This is how brand equity is built—by retaining the committed user.[9] Brand equity is a set of assets linked to the brand. Loyalty is a factor in the equity equation.[10] Brand loyalty reduces the substitutability factor of switching to another brand. The brand is familiar, comfortable, and reassuring. The advertisements for the brand are just as comforting and reassuring. The consumer relates to the advertisement because she sees herself in the context of the message. Thus, the ad reinforces her judgment; she chose wisely.

4. Advertising can build added values

Perhaps this is advertising at its best—building added values. Brands depend on added values. As discussed earlier, added values form the intangible, discriminating benefits that prompt the consumer to buy one brand over another. There are several means of establishing added values. We will reprise what was said in chapter 2 before we focus on how advertising helps to build them.[11]

- *Added values are established through the consumer's experience with the brand.* A brand is a pact between the manufacturer and the consumer. It is a guarantee of quality, value, and product satisfaction.[12] Based on the experience of using the brand, the consumer develops feelings regarding the rewards received. The consumer then associates the brand with these feelings, and the brand develops a personality based on the consumer's experience of the reliability of the brand. These associations provide a level of differentiation.
- *Added values are established by the type of people who use the brand.* Many consumers relate to others who use the brand. This association, often depicted in the advertising, is an added value. Furthermore, as people become more affluent, added values and brand personalities are likely to become more important to them. They will get more and more of their rewards from nonfunctional brand attributes.[13] User association is an important value in designer fashion, weight-loss programs, automobiles, and luxury items and of course, in cosmetics, beer, and soft drinks.
- *Added values are established by the belief that the brand is effective.* Obviously, the consumer must believe the product will work to buy it. But there is evidence that consumers believe branded products work better than unbranded ones. This is especially true in over-the-counter drugs. This belief also plays an important role in cosmetic brands, where the users feel more beautiful when they use the brand.
- *Added values are established by the appearance of the brand.* Here the packaging is key. This is how the product is presented to the consumer. The package must be attractive and recognizable and must appeal to the consumer. The appearance of the brand is not only important on the retailer's shelves, but is also a key element in advertisements, especially for packaged goods.

Added values are built over time. They are developed by the consumer's satisfaction with the brand and reinforced through advertising. This is the power of Coca-Cola, Kodak, McDonald's, and thousands of other brands. The advertising's focus on added values of the brand helps to strengthen positive feelings about it. Advertising builds these added values by reinforcing positive experiences, providing user imagery that is relevant to the consumer, and demonstrating the effectiveness of the brand as well as its attractiveness. While the brand must have a coherent totality—the totality of what the brand offers to satisfy the consumer's wants and needs, both functional and nonfunctional—advertising is an integral part of building added values and strengthening the appeal of the brand.

The Development of a Strategy

Now that we have established the basis of advertising and its limitations, we can turn our attention to the advertising strategy. What is a strategy? Basically, the word comes from the military. The dictionary definition is "the science and art of military command exercised to meet the enemy in combat under advantageous conditions."[14] There is an obvious analogy between the military and advertising uses of the word. Brands battle in the marketplace, a very competitive zone. Much of the language is similar, with adjectives like "offensive," "defensive," and "aggressive." We discuss "marketing warfare" and refer to category competition as the "cola wars" or "toy wars." The key to winning—or overtaking the enemy—is to plan the attack that provides the strongest competitive advantage. The plan of attack in advertising is the strategy. Therefore, we can define advertising strategy as a method of identifying a plan of action that provides the brand a competitive advantage via advertising. The strategy provides an overview of the situation and direction with respect to which target has the greatest potential, what needs to be said to this audience to influence them, and the basic intent of the advertising.

Why is an advertising strategy so important? There are four reasons.

1. A strategy encourages clear and logical thinking

It is a rational process by which data are analyzed and logical deductions are made. It is quite practical to plan what to do before doing it. A strategy prevents us jumping to conclusions or to tactical solutions, and it enables us to use resources efficiently and effectively.

2. A strategy provides a factual basis for advertising direction and performance

Advertising is part art and part science. The art is obvious in the creation of advertisements. The science is the foundation on which those creative ideas are based. The strategy is part of the science of advertising, a process grounded in facts that aid in decision-making and problem solving. Advertising represents a substantial financial investment in the brand. The decisions made regarding that investment must be strategically sound, working on behalf of the brand, strengthening the brand. The risk is too great for the reasoning behind the advertisements to be based on opinion, general observations, or gut feelings. Strategy is not only about what you think; it is about what you know. Information plays a powerful role in the development of an advertising strategy and thus in the advertising function overall.

3. A strategy encourages understanding and agreement on the situation from the client and the agency

There are many people involved with the brand. Whether those involved work for the manufacturer or for the advertising agency, they are the stewards of this brand. It is their job to protect, maintain, and strengthen it. Therefore, it is extremely important that all involved understand and agree on the direction of the brand's advertising strategy. Without this type of endorsement and agreement, the opportunity for misuse of resources, missed opportunities, or misguided creative executions is greatly increased.

4. A strategy provides a benchmark

Accountability is a very big issue in advertising today. With the spending levels in the business, it is unpardonable not to understand the impact of the investment. A strategy provides the grounding for determining the success of the advertising campaign. It serves this purpose when the campaign is implemented and during the development of advertising executions and their deployment in the marketplace. The strategy acts as the measure of whether the message strategy, the creative executions, and the media plan reflect the target audience, the basic argument, and the purpose of the advertisement.

Formulating the Strategy

The process of developing a strategy involves gathering, processing, and analyzing information as it pertains to the brand. The strategy itself is brief—one or two pages at the most. But to develop the strategy, much work has to be done. This varies depending on the agency's history with the brand. Much can be said about the power of experience. However, it is quite easy to fall prey to the attitude of "we've always done it this way." The process of reanalyzing information is a good one, simply to make certain you are up to date on new developments and are not jumping to conclusions that the facts do not support.

The first step in the process is information gathering and analysis, and from this problems and opportunities can be identified. In agencies, account planners or account executives are responsible for this process, and most have their own formats for organizing the information for the strategy. People learning about the business, however, find the process quite perplexing. When confronted with developing a strategy, beginners have difficulty in determining just what information is needed to make a decision. It takes time to acquire the critical thinking skills needed to sort out the most important information and provide analysis, not just description. We propose below a practical framework that can aid veterans or rookies in the process of analyzing the situation from which the strategy will evolve. This framework is a brand audit.

The Brand Audit

The audit itself includes six components. The resultant advertising strategy immediately follows. The audit is a factual document that provides information from which the advertising strategy will be developed. The audit includes all of the important factors that describe the current situation of the brand: how it got into its current position, how advertising can improve this position, and the most critical elements to address in the advertising. A brand audit should be thought of as a memo, which is short (five to six pages) but concise and totally relevant. In conducting the audit, the following topics should be examined.

1. Company analysis

The company analysis should consist of some basic facts about the company that markets the brand and the company's history. Naturally, this would include sales, profits, and advertising expenditures. It is important to know that the company has the resources to support the brand and whether it has in the past. If the company has recently acquired the brand (e.g., Aurora Foods' recent purchase of Duncan Hines from Procter & Gamble [P&G]), it is especially important to know the company's financial situation. Aurora's financial situation was in turmoil after the purchase. It could not support the Duncan Hines brand in the way P&G had done in the past, and this resulted in a decline in the brand's market share. Another factor here is to make certain that the culture of the company is completely understood. When pursuing opportunities, you must first know whether the company would be willing and able to pursue them.

2. Market analysis

This section provides an understanding of the marketplace in which the brand operates. The first thing is to understand the category and segment. This should include information such as the size of the market; the status of the market, whether it is growing, maturing, or declining; how competitive the market is; and what new trends and developments have affected the market. There are several external issues that may have to be addressed within the analysis. The technological environment may pose problems or opportunities (e.g., the growth of personal digital assistants [PDAs], which pose a threat to the traditional paper personal diary/calendar product line). Franklin Covey, a manufacturer of high-end calendar/organization systems, has taken advantage of this by developing its own PDA software. The political and legal environment may pose problems or opportunities. For instance, tobacco companies have to be well attuned to the new restrictions on tobacco advertising. And the cultural and social environment has to be considered as well. NBC recently withdrew from an agreement to accept hard liquor advertising, because it set off heated social and political debates.

3. Brand analysis

Reviewing the history of the brand is a necessary element because it provides an understanding of the strength of the brand itself. The basic analysis has to center on share of market, share of voice, and elements such as functionality and added values. This analysis should also look at factors such as price, distribution, and promotional activities that may be important in determining competitive advantages or problems. It is also extremely important that the critical components of the brand's equity be identified and analyzed: awareness, knowledge, image, associations, and personality. The strengths and weaknesses of these are important in determining the brand's advertising needs.

4. Competitor analysis

Naturally, this part of the audit focuses on competitors within the marketplace. It should include both direct and indirect competitors. The analysis should include history, product comparisons that relate to functionality and added values, pricing and distribution issues, sales revenues and share of market over several years, share of voice, promotional expenditures and activities, and consumer information. All of this will provide insight into who may be taking business from your brand or vice versa. This exploration does not have to include every brand in the category or segment. Focus on the competitors that constitute a genuine threat. That threat may be coming from store brands as well, so do not disregard these.

5. Consumer analysis

The consumer analysis describes all prospects, current users as well as possible users. This should include information on product usage (light, medium, or heavy), purchase cycles, demographic information that proves to be a factor (i.e., size of household, income, ages of children), psychographic information that relates to the relationship the consumer or prospect has with the brand, degrees of brand loyalty, and geographical differences. It is important to explore many possible consumer groups in this analysis to determine later which target has the most potential.

6. Problem/opportunity statements

Once each brand component has been analyzed, summarize the *key* problems and opportunities the brand faces in its current situation. These should be concise, one-sentence statements that draw conclusions but do not make recommendations. Then set priorities depending on what can be influenced by advertising. Advertising cannot do everything. In the recommendation of a strategy, the focus is on the problem/opportunity that advertising can affect.

The Strategy Itself

First, clearly define the central problem or opportunity that supports using advertising in this situation. Identify the critical factors as they relate to this decision, all of which must be supported by what has been discussed previously. Prove that you understand the brand and its market position, its industry, its competitors, its personality, and its consumers. The strategy is the outcome of that understanding in that you identify whether advertising can help this brand. There are basically three key elements that are addressed within the advertising strategy—target group, proposition, and the role of the advertising. However, as an outcome of the research and analysis from the audit, the key fact or facts that evolve from that process have to be identified as well. This is what directs the strategy. Therefore, the following subjects should be covered in the strategy:

- *Key fact*—Brief description of the problem/opportunity the advertising will solve or exploit.
- *Target group*—To whom should the advertising speak? Identify and clarify all segments of the target group.
- *Proposition*—What has to be said to the target group? Identify the foundation of the message that has to be conveyed. Do not write the copy. Indicate what the consumer needs to know in order to respond to the advertising.
- *Role of the advertising*—How should the target respond to the advertising? Knowing the response expected from the consumer is a key element in creating advertisements.

The strategy document will be brief, one to two pages in length. As stated earlier, it is the end product of the analysis of facts and of a judgment based on their interpretation. Moreover, the advertising strategy is a selective document. An advertisement works most effectively when it is not expected to do too much.[15] This is not a miracle cure for what ails the brand or a quick route to boosting it exponentially.

Knowledge, attitudes, and behavior are key to determining the strategy.

- *Knowledge*—This includes making the audience aware of the brand's existence as well as providing information about the functionality, benefits, and so on, of the brand.
- *Attitudes*—Advertising is not strong enough to change the mind of the consumer—only direct experience can do that. But advertising can modify attitudes and is quite good at reinforcing attitudes of current users.
- *Behavior*—Although few advertisements send the consumer directly to the store, some advertising can encourage immediate action to purchase. Advertising can encourage consumers to buy again and to buy more, so although it does not immediately send them shopping, advertising does affect behavior in more indirect ways.

Target Group

The most important part of the strategy is to define the audience for the advertising. Identifying the target group is central to developing effective advertising and to delivering it. In the deployment of the media budget (where the most money is spent), a well-defined target helps us determine the most efficient and effective media choices for reaching this audience. Perhaps even more important, the description of the consumers allows those creating the advertisement to tailor the message directly for that audience.

The target group must be defined first in terms of brand usage. Many people will attempt to profile the target solely in demographic terms—age, gender, education, income. But this information does not provide the detail required to determine the most profitable and attainable target group. The first question should always be: Where is the business coming from? Understanding this source of business is vital to determining the best audience for the advertising. Answering this question correctly provides the means of building the brand.

1. Source of business

The key source of business for the brand must be determined. While this may sound difficult, it is not, with the use of research and judgment. It is important not just to jump to safe or quick conclusions. Research data become of primary importance in determining the source of business, and syndicated research such as that provided by Mediamark Research Inc. (MRI) and Simmons Market Research Bureau (SMRB) provides reliable information. Within MRI or SMRB, share of market and penetration percentages are available. Remember from chapter 8 that penetration defines the number of households that bought the brand. Increasing penetration directly drives share of market (as shown in chapter 5). Penetration estimates can be found under the heading of *share of users* from the syndicated data. Share of market is indicated under the heading of *share of volume* in the data. In basic terms, share of market equals penetration multiplied by purchase frequency (the number of times that the household purchases the brand). Although there are no purchase frequency columns within the syndicated brand data, some assumptions can be made. If a brand's share of market is higher than the penetration share, the assumption can be made that purchase frequency is high. If the penetration exceeds market share, there is low purchase frequency—the brand is in the household, but usage is minimal. The interpretation of these numbers provides insight into where the brand's business is coming from. Based on the importance of the brand's penetration and purchase frequency, there are only five groups of users that can define where the brand's business can come from. Three relate directly to penetration, which the brand must attain for growth.

- *New users to the category.* The assumption of this source of business is that there must be some growth in the category. Many U.S. categories are mature, and there are not many new users coming in. There are some categories, however, such as retirement housing, that have been stagnant for many years but have recently seen growth. The increasing demand for retirement housing is related to baby boomers reaching retirement, and the population in general is living longer. In addition, there are some categories that gain new users regularly—for example, feminine hygiene products, disposable diapers, razors, and anti-aging cosmetics. If there is growth, is it coming from users new to the category?

- *New users to the segment.* Generally, new users to the segment come from other segments. This can prove interesting because it provides insight into the needs and desires of the users who switch to a new segment or add it to their repertoire. This does not necessarily mean that the new user will stop buying in the other segment. Therefore try to determine why the user is looking for brands in another segment—new uses for the product, perhaps.

  There can be growth in the segments while there is no growth in the category. For example, while the soft drink category was flat with minimal growth over several years, the lemon-lime segment was growing by more than 2 percent annually. This was a factor in PepsiCo's introduction of Sierra Mist, to take advantage of the segment growth and to take business from Sprite and 7-Up.

- *Attracting new users from other brands in the segment.* This pertains to brand switchers and those adding new brands to their repertoire. Therefore, you must identify what brand(s) they currently use. This factor will greatly help in determining how to persuade the consumer to use another brand, in terms of functionality and description of its benefits. After determining the current brands used, you can use MRI or SMRB data to gain demographic information on this group. It should be noted here that targeting this source of business works best for new and small brands. Switching completely is not necessarily the goal here. We are normally adding to the purchase set or repertoire. As discussed previously, it is difficult to change the mind of a consumer. Before determining the most profitable source of business for your brand, determine what your brand offers that the consumer's current brand does not. If there is no differentiation, it may be more difficult and expensive than it is worth to try and take business from it.

- *Increasing purchase frequency among existing users.* There is a justified belief in the advertising industry that gaining more sales from your current users is more profitable than attempting to gain new ones. If penetration of the brand has been maximized, a strategy for increasing purchase frequency should be explored as a viable opportunity. This is generally the case for large brands. However, the question that must be asked is, "How can we get the consumer to buy more?" In answering this, you need to determine whether the consumer can actually use more of the brand he or she is loyal to. For example, Arm & Hammer baking soda had strong household penetration. But the brand was not used often. By presenting new uses of the brand, such as deodorizing refrigerators, freezers, and kitchen sinks, Arm & Hammer was able to increase sales by 193 percent in 1994.[16] Ralston Purina was in the same predicament with strong penetration, but how do you create new uses for dog food? What the company realized is that users were buying Ralston Purina Dog Chow, but that was not the only brand of dog food purchased. The strategy evolved to inform consumers that changing a dog's food is not good for the dog, so it is best to buy the same brand over and over. This increased purchase frequency for Ralston while reducing the frequency of purchase for the other, less expensive brands in the repertoire.

- *Retaining existing users.* Obviously, there are times when the brand's penetration and purchase frequency are maximized. The goal then becomes to maintain current users at their current level of purchasing. A perfect example of this is Coca-Cola. It is estimated that the per capita consumption of Coca-Cola in the United States and Canada is 398 eight-ounce servings annually.[17] Obviously, the opportunity for brand growth is to retain that level of consumption and keep those consumers loyal, reducing the risk of substitution. This is especially important in categories that are in decline (e.g., cigarettes, hard liquor, dairy products, coffee).

2. Demographics

Once brand usage has been determined, it is helpful to profile the users in terms of demographics—age, income, household size, etc. This information can also be garnered from MRI or SMRB syndicated data. The data provide three important demographic measures: the percentage of users who fall within certain demographic groups, the percentage of the demographic population who use the brand, and the measure of the performance of a particular demographic subgroup as compared with the total population. This information can define the audience more clearly and narrowly.

Let us look at an example with Iams/Eukanuba dog food.[18] Of a total 87,017,000 female homemakers, 1,426,000 or 1.6 percent purchased this brand in the last six months. Of those purchasers, 161,000 (11.3 percent) were aged 18–24; 289,000 (20.2 percent) were aged 25–34; 362,000 (25.4 percent) were aged 35–44; and 415,000 (29.1 percent) were aged 45–54. This would give the impression that all age groups were important and that the campaign should target an 18–54 age range. This is a very broad target, and, initially, you might think it difficult to talk to an 18-year-old in the same way as you would to someone aged 54. In addition, delivering the message to such a range might prove difficult and expensive in terms of media vehicles.

By using additional data, you will see a slightly different picture. Within the demographic age segments, you see that 2.2 percent of 18–24-year-olds purchase the brand and only 1.5 percent of those aged 25–34 purchase the brand; within the 35–44 age group, 1.9 percent purchase; and 3.1 percent of 45–54-year-olds purchase. That means that Iams's total penetration of all demographic groups is 1.6 percent, *but among the 45–54 age group, the penetration is 3.1 percent.* The difference is expressed as an index number of 193, indicating that 3.1 percent is 93 percent higher than 1.6 percent; in other words, those aged 45–54 are 93 percent more likely to buy Iams. This age group might need more advertising attention in terms of media delivery or user imagery. Naturally, this exercise would have to be repeated with demographic segments other than age, but it provides a clear example to show that looking at only one variable provides important insights.

3. Psychographics

Demographics seldom tell the entire story. Not all 18–24-year-olds behave the same way or share the same life-styles. This is the insight psychographics can provide. Psychographics put users into groups based on shared interests, life-styles, and attitudes. Psychographics are usually derived from qualitative rather than quantitative data. There are several means of collecting this information—many companies and agencies maintain consumer panels that produce the data. DDB, a division of Omnicom, a large agency group, regularly conducts a major life-style study that is used for its various clients, such as McDonald's and Volkswagen.

One of the most prominent sources of psychographic research originated with the Stanford Research Institute. VALS (Values and Lifestyles) groups U.S. consumers into eight types, based on two main dimensions, self-orientation and resources. Self-orientation refers to how consumers' attitudes, activities, and motivations are related to their social position and self-image. Resources naturally pertain to *all* of the resources consumers can draw from— which may be income, education, health, confidence, and so forth. Each one of the VALS groups demonstrates patterns of decision-making, behavior, and even product/media usage.[19] This type of information is generally more valuable than demographics in understanding the consumer's attitude toward the brand and the purchase motivation.

4. Relationship to the brand

This is a relatively new area of understanding. In our earlier discussion of brand loyalty, we stressed the importance of understanding the relationship the consumer has with the brand—an extension of the brand's added values. But the brand relationship is about the meaning—the importance the brand has—in the life of the consumer. Although this may appear rather grandiose, it is of prime importance for certain brands. Brands can have strong communities of loyalists—such as the Hallmark and Coca-Cola consumers we profiled in chapter 9. This is also the case with Harley-Davidson bikers, Macintosh computer users, Saturn owners, and hundreds of others. There is an emotional attachment that exceeds rational wants. Susan Fournier, of the Harvard Business School, has categorized brand relationships and the means to study them. Foote Cone and Belding, a leading advertising agency, developed its own Relationship Monitor that measures seven different relationship styles.[20] To make the advertising really relevant, understanding the consumer's relationship with the brand is a necessity, not a luxury.

Proposition

The proposition identifies the factors that influence the argument and determine the tone of voice for the campaign. Newcomers to advertising often mistake this as writing copy for the advertisement. Creative ideas are generated *after* the proposition has been determined. The proposition is not about product positioning, or slogans or themes. It is the foundation of what the brand delivers in terms of functionality and added values—qualities that the advertising can exploit to differentiate the brand. The strategy provides strong direction and helps the creative people who will ultimately be responsible for developing the advertisements.

We earlier defined a brand as "a product that provides functional benefits plus added values that some consumers value enough to buy." Therefore, functionality and added values are the main elements of a brand's proposition. However, it must be noted that the proposition is not just a laundry list of brand attributes and benefits. It is an analysis of the brand's uniqueness and how this differentiation can be used in the advertising in such a way as to be believable to the target group. Four subjects are included in the proposition analysis.

- *Brand Functionality:* First you must define the brand's performance abilities and identify what makes it carry out its functional tasks. Obviously, you are looking for some superior functionality, but this is often difficult. Furthermore, the functionality has to be associated with the benefits provided to the end-user. Crest made a strong case for preventing cavities by adding fluoride. While this is a strong attribute, the users were not interested in the fluoride per se; they were interested in fewer cavities. Thus, when Procter & Gamble sought and received the endorsement of the American Dental Association, the benefit was obvious to the consumer—fewer trips to the dentist. The performance features of the brand must be transformed into benefits.
- *Brand Uniqueness:* This element relates directly to functionality—what makes your brand unique. Knowledge of the competition is valuable here in determining what makes your brand different. This is about realistic and credible differentiation. Consumers are savvy shoppers and skeptical of advertising. Do not make claims that cannot be supported. With technology today, it is becoming more difficult to make a preemptive claim. To do so, the brand must have strong research support from double-blind product tests to prove the claim.
- *Added Values:* We have talked extensively throughout this book about added values. These are the nonfunctional qualities of the brand, or the brand's personality. It is important that these added values should be defined in terms of the consumer's perception of the brand. We saw in chapter 9 how the collectors viewed Coca-Cola and Hallmark. The personality that consumers attribute to the brand should be evident in the advertising. This is a key differentiation and reinforces the consumer's relationship with the brand.

Brand personalities are often enhanced through trade characters and spokespeople. The Pillsbury Doughboy, the Jolly Green Giant, Tony the Tiger, and Geoffrey of Toys R Us are trade characters that each epitomizes its brand's personality. Bill Cosby does the same thing for Jell-O and Michael Jordan for Nike, and top fashion models reflect the personality of Revlon cosmetics. These associations have to make sense to the consumer for them to have an impact.

- *Balance:* The next element of the proposition is to determine how best to balance the advertising: between motivators and discriminators, as well as between rational and emotional arguments.

  Motivators provide the reason why the consumer should use the category (i.e., cosmetic creams remove wrinkles, contact lenses make the user look better, dry cake mixes are easy to use, etc.). Discriminating arguments are brand-specific. Claims such as Tide gets out stains, Crest fights cavities, and Listerine kills bad breath are discriminating. These are all rational arguments supported by the functional properties of the brand.[21] "Miller Time," Pepsi's "Generation Next," and Apple Computer's "Think Different" are all nonrational arguments that are supported by the added values of these brands.

  Most advertisements contain both types of argument, but the balance between them varies, depending on the brand's size and position. Determining this balance will set the tone of the advertisements. Hallmark's advertisements, in general, are more heavily weighted to the emotional side, yet the argument is usually quite discriminating in its claim of "caring enough to send the very best."

Role of the Advertising

Whereas the proposition controls the content of the advertisement, the role of the advertising determines how the campaign should work. This is directly related to the target group and the proposition. Stephen King, formerly of J. Walter Thompson, London, formulated a continuum to describe the ways in which advertising should work. There are six roles that range from the most direct to the most indirect, as defined in the King Continuum. The best way to demonstrate the process is to define each role and provide examples.

1. Direct action

Obviously, direct action is the most direct role. This is accomplished by using direct-response advertising where purchasing occurs on the spot. In addition, this can apply to much retail advertising and promotional advertising, and certainly to advertising that strives to gain trial of new brands. Examples of this would be Sunday supplements for Target, or the weekly Kroger advertisement. Most recently, automobile advertisements based on "Zero Percent" financing would be categorized as direct action. Direct action can be used for any source of business. However, the proposition must encourage the consumer to buy now.

2. Seek information

The purchase is not going to proceed directly from the advertisement. This is most often the case with high-involvement or high-ticket items. The advertisement creates curiosity and interest, but consumers need more facts before making the purchase decision. Therefore, this campaign would send them to a showroom or encourage them to send for a brochure or to talk to a dealer or sales associate. NordicTrack sells high-end exercise equipment. Its advertisements include a coupon and a toll-free number that target buyers can use to receive a videotape that explains how the products work and how much they cost. Some of the advertisements send prospects to exclusive NordicTrack stores that are staffed with product experts. Designer cosmetics, such as Estée Lauder, Lancôme, and Chanel, show the products in their advertisements but depend on their own consultants in retail outlets to recommend the appropriate cosmetic product. This role is predominantly used when new users are targeted.

3. Relate to needs/desires

Advertising is working more indirectly here. There is no call to action, as the advertisement's purpose is to connect the brand to the consumer's situation. Obviously, this goal can be one of trial, presenting to new users the reasons why the brand is for them. This can also be the role for users who buy more than one brand in a segment, as one brand may meet certain needs and other brands are bought by the user for different purposes. The key is that the proposition must be focused on relating the brand benefits to user expectations. Therefore, this role of advertising tends to be more rational, supported by discriminating "reason why" arguments.

4. Recall satisfactions

This is a reminder type of role. It may be directed to lapsed users, brand switchers, or infrequent users. The goal here is to help users remember what they liked about the brand in the first place and encourage them to get the brand back into their repertoire. Brand personality can be an important influence, as well as reminding the consumer of what the brand can deliver. This has worked especially well with "nostalgia" brands such as Hostess Cupcakes, Kellogg's Frosted Flakes, and Chevy Trucks.

5. Modify attitudes

As discussed earlier in this chapter, this role is probably the most difficult, because it takes the most time. In this role, advertising must introduce some new information or help target consumers see the brand in a new way. The argument has to be credible and meaningful to the target group. We see much comparative advertising working this way in trying to recapture lapsed users or brand switchers. In the example of Ralston Purina Dog Chow discussed earlier, the role was to inform users that constantly changing dog foods was not good for their dogs. The focus was on modifying attitudes. But this method can also be used to increase purchase frequency, by showing new uses for the brand. Bounce dryer sheets recently depicted ways to use the sheets to freshen clothes outside the dryer—such as in the linen drawer, clothes hamper, or closet. This encourages the target users to rethink and, it is hoped, modify their current use of the product.

6. Reinforce attitudes

A very large amount of advertising takes this role and is directed at existing users. This applies to brands that are established, which advertise continuously, and are regularly purchased. The goal here is to make users feel confident that they have made the right choice. Added values play an important part in reinforcing attitudes, as they pertain directly to how the user feels about the brand. The advertising for Jif peanut butter, a category leader, is a good example of reinforcement. While the advertising mentions the key functional feature of the brand—more peanuts than competitive brands, thus better taste—the real focus is on the brand's added values. A mother and child are always depicted in the advertisement, and the copy relates to the issue of being a good mother. The brand's slogan, "Choosy mothers choose Jif," serves as a positive reinforcement that Jif is the right purchase.

Can an Old Brand Be Reintroduced with a New Strategy?

Successful brands are relaunched every three or four years. Indeed this is one of the reasons for their success. An improved formula, more interesting packaging, and a new advertising campaign with an increased budget all contribute to influencing existing users (and some potential new users) to reappraise the brand. Some will buy more of it; and some will buy it for the first time.

Reintroductions—bringing old brands back on to the market after they have spent a long time without marketing support—are altogether more rare. However, reintroductions occasionally succeed, and this often happens because they follow a totally new strategy. Planning such a strategy is a delicate process, because the manufacturer and his agency will wish to retain some of the brand's past strengths but to graft onto them something radically new.

We will now describe how this process worked for Oxydol, a historic brand from Procter & Gamble (P&G). The brand was reintroduced (as is generally the case) by a new company that had acquired the brand from the original manufacturer.[22]

Oxydol was P&G's first laundry detergent, introduced in 1927. The brand had a long history as a market leader and as a marketing innovator: it was promoted by door-to-door sampling and magazine advertisements featuring "slices of life"; and it was the "soap" behind the soap opera when the brand created this long-lasting genre through its sponsorship of the *Ma Perkins* radio show in 1933. In 1949, P&G introduced Tide, a washing powder based on a totally new nonsoapy detergent (nsd) product formula, which was a measurable advance on anything marketed before. Oxydol's leadership position was challenged. Within three months of introducing Tide nationally, P&G took the brand to market leadership. It remains number one in the $6 billion category today.

By 2000, Oxydol was only on 15 percent of U.S. store shelves, and sales had declined to $5 million from a high of $80 million in 1992. Oxydol did not fit into P&G's global strategy, and the brand was put on the auction block with other brands the parent company had decided to sell. Two former P&G executives bought Oxydol in June 2000, determined to act in an entrepreneurial way to breathe new life into the 73-year-old brand. The new owners, whose company was called Redox, had a superior product but a tired brand. It was in limited distribution and had disappeared from consumers' minds. Redox decided to reintroduce Oxydol as a premium brand with a strongly competitive product story.

The first priority was to determine the source of business. Where was the demand? Originally, the strategy focused on nostalgic baby boomers who remembered the brand as the washing powder their mothers had used. The original bull's-eye box—a familiar icon based on concentric circles of yellow and black—was brought back. A collaboration with the distributor Restoration Hardware put the brand in the retailer's 106 stores as well as in its catalog. But the Redox organization was soon to realize this plan did not go far enough.

In focus groups, regular users of Tide and other top-selling brands were found to be unwilling to use Oxydol. Since the prices of Oxydol and Tide would be similar, nostalgic baby boomers saw no advantage to buying Oxydol. But younger consumers—participants in the 20–30-year-old age group—indicated no loyalty to the leading brands and preferred not to use their parents' detergent brand. Even more encouraging was the issue of price: these young consumers were quite prepared to pay a premium.

Redox felt it important to change the packaging to make it less nostalgic and more exciting and up to date. The strategy was aimed at a younger audience: the 59 million "post-baby boom Xers" who did not enjoy doing the laundry. The proposition speaks to the audience about how to balance their very active life-styles while dealing with the family's grubby clothing. The role of the advertising is to relate to Generation Xers' need for clean clothes— a result that can be achieved with minimal trouble. In brief, they want a brand they can call their own.

Distribution of the brand has been lifted to a weighted level of 70 percent in U.S. supermarkets, drugstores, and mass-merchandisers. The new advertising campaign is under way and the jury is still out on its success. However, the first signals from the marketplace are very strong.

The Argument in Brief

Oxydol provides a good example of how strategy can build brands: in this case a total reintroduction rather than an ongoing brand. It serves to underscore the factors discussed in this chapter. It also demonstrates that advertising does not just happen, it takes homework and good judgment. It takes an understanding of advertising's capabilities and limitations; it takes informed thought, judicious analysis, and insightful judgment. It takes a strategy.

Advertising strategy is a plan of action set to give the brand a competitive advantage. The process of strategy development is a vertical one. It depends on information analyzed within a brand audit, focusing on the various components of the brand. These include the company, the market, the competition, the consumer, and the brand itself. The audit leads to the determination of the problem or opportunity that the advertising will attempt to influence. This key fact drives the strategy.

The strategy incorporates three subjects: the target group, the proposition, and the role of the advertising. The target group is defined in terms of its product usage, demographics, psychographics, and its relationship with the brand. There may be several target groups, but they should be ranked in order of importance, with a realistic estimate of whether each group can be reached and influenced by the same campaign.

The proposition provides the arguments and the tone for the development of the creative idea. The key components include the brand's functionality, uniqueness, added values, and the balance of these within the advertising.

Finally, the role of the advertising determines how the campaign should work. There are six roles that work to affect the knowledge, attitudes, and/or behavior of the target group.

If advertising strategy is used as a necessary process and embraced as the foundation and the benchmark for creating the campaign, the advertising itself can indeed make a strong contribution to building the brand.

Notes

1. Edward de Bono, *Lateral Thinking* (New York: Harper and Row, 1970), pp. 38–45.

2. Ibid., p. 51.

3. Kevin Lane Keller, "Conceptualizing, Measuring, and Managing Customer-Based Brand Equity," *Journal of Marketing* (January 1993): 1–22.

4. Kevin Lane Keller, *Strategic Brand Management: Building, Measuring, and Managing Brand Equity* (Upper Saddle River, NJ: Prentice-Hall, 1998), pp. 46–53.

5. John Philip Jones, *How Much Is Enough? Getting the Most from Your Advertising Dollar* (New York: Lexington Books, 1992), p. 49.

6. Keller, *Strategic Brand Management,* p. 103.

7. David A. Aaker, *Managing Brand Equity: Capitalizing on the Value of a Brand Name* (New York: Free Press, 1991), p. 39.

8. Jones, *How Much is Enough?* p. 51.

9. Keller, "Conceptualizing, Measuring, and Managing," p. 4.

10. Aaker, *Managing Brand Equity,* p. 4.

11. Jan S. Slater, "New Brands: Success Rate and Criteria for Success," in *How To Use Advertising to Build Strong Brands,* John Philip Jones, ed. (Thousand Oaks, CA: Sage, 1999), p. 150; Jones, *How Much is Enough?* pp. 162–163.

12. John N. Murphy, *Brand Strategy* (Englewood Cliffs, NJ: Prentice-Hall, 1990).

13. Stephen King, *Developing New Brands* (New York: Wiley, 1973).

14. *Webster's Ninth New Collegiate Dictionary* (Springfield, MA: Merriam-Webster, 1988), p. 1165.

15. Jones, *How Much is Enough?* p. 128.

16. *Superbrands 1996—Marketers of the Year,* a ranking of the top 2,000 brand names by 1993–94 sales, October 9, 1995, p. 158.

17. Scott Leith, "Coke's Challenge: North American Unit Feeling Pressure to Improve," *Atlantic Journal and Constitution,* March 31, 2002, p. 1G.

18. Mediamark Research Inc., Spring 1998, p. 137.

19. William F. Arens, *Contemporary Advertising,* 7th edition (Boston: Irwin/McGraw Hill, 1998), pp. 154–155. Stanford Research Institute, Consulting Business Intelligence, http://www.sric-bi.com/VALS.

20. Susan Fournier, "Consumers and Their Brands: Developing Relationship Theory in Consumer Research," *Journal of Consumer Research* 24 (March 1998): 343–373; Cara Beardi, "Revved Up to Relate: FCB Finds Brand Loyalty Mirrors Interpersonal Relationships," *Advertising Age,* November 6, 2000, p. 86.

21. Jones, *How Much is Enough?*

22. Information about Oxydol used in the case study was obtained from various sources. These include Richard Curtis, "The X Factor," *Business Courier,* July 9, 2001; Matthew Swibel, "Spin Cycle," *Forbes,* April 2, 2001; "Redox Brands, Inc. Buys Procter & Gamble's Oxydol Brand," *Business Wire,* July 6, 2000; and Mark Winterhalter, Director of Marketing, Redox Brands, personal communication.

11

From Advertising Strategy to Advertising Campaign

The focus of this book has been on describing the influences advertising can have on brands. We have argued in each of the previous chapters how important advertising can be in strengthening brands. We have also discussed how advertising, if not planned or supported properly, can actually have no effect, or in some cases even harm the brand. We have discussed the function of advertising and how it works, but we have yet to discuss the end product—the advertisements themselves.

This chapter describes, in minimal detail, the process of moving from strategy to final advertising executions. This is a topic that really requires a book in itself. It is appropriate, however, for reasons of completeness, that the process should at least be outlined here.

We have started the planning process by formulating an advertising strategy. The target has been identified, as well as what must be communicated about the brand, and the role of the advertising has been determined. This strategy must now be expressed in the form of advertisements that will present the brand to the audience in a noticeable and memorable fashion.

Taking the strategy to this next level can be difficult, demanding, and often frustrating; but it is also exciting. This chapter will focus on the process by which it is accomplished.

First, we need to look at the process in light of the elements that drive effective advertising. There are three key elements: the *budget, the campaign,* and the *media.* All elements are equally important; and all three must work together to make the advertising effective. In chapter 8, we identified the importance of budgeting and the need to provide the budgetary resources for implementing the campaign; there must be enough weight to deliver the message. In chapter 10, we focused on strategy development and determining the purpose of the advertising. This provides not only the reason for the advertising, but the direction as well: the foundations for the creative process. Now comes the challenge of creating advertisements and exposing them widely and efficiently in the media.

This chapter will not attempt to provide a set of rules for developing successful advertisements. Rules often lead to predictable solutions, and effective advertising cannot be developed if it suffers from the handicap of predictability. And we will not attempt to dissect every element of the creative process. There are a number of exceptional sources that bear on this and will enlighten curious readers. These are the published writings of David Ogilvy, William Bernbach, Leo Burnett, and many other practitioners, which provide insights into how those who create successful advertisements view the process.[1] What we will provide in this chapter is practical and relatively simple guidance for how to move forward.

The Campaign

An advertising campaign consists of a series of advertisements that are scheduled in various media over a period of time. A campaign can work in one medium or across various media. What is crucial is that the concept can stand up no matter where it is exposed. The "milk moustache" campaign created by the Bozell agency for the National Fluid Milk Processor Promotion Board appeared only in print for the first years of its implementation. The "Got Milk?" campaign originally developed for the California Milk Processor Board by Goodby, Silverstein, and Partners included television, print, and outdoor advertising from the beginning. The point is that a campaign is more than a single advertisement. It includes a number of different executions developed from a single unifying theme.

The campaign should have staying power. This means that the concept must be strategically strong so that a variety of executions can be employed over time. Multiple advertisements are necessary to reinforce the concept in different ways so that the consumer does not tire or get bored with the advertising. In addition, the campaign enhances the memorability of the concept, which helps attract the consumer's attention to the brand. Although these factors make the campaign valuable, they also make the development difficult, because each expression of the campaign must be related to every other one.

There are three elements governing the creative process—the strategy, the creative leap, and the creative execution. The strategy is consumer-driven, based on the most profitable target consumers for the brand and their perceptions of it. This was discussed in detail in chapter 10. The creative leap is strategy-driven: using the strategy to develop the concept or the big idea that will convey the strategy to the public in a striking and original manner. The execution is idea-driven and is the means through which the idea is converted into actual advertisements. Using the strategy as the starting point, we will discuss the two other pieces of the creative process separately while relating each to the totality of the campaign.

The Creative Leap

The leap, the discovery of the campaign idea, is a type of mental process that is quite different from formulating a strategy. It requires a type of thinking that is different from what was discussed in chapter 10. The essence of the process is the ability to discover directions that are sometimes totally unexpected and/or to generate ideas that strike an intensely personal chord with the audience and will therefore evoke emotional as well as rational responses. This is a process of idea generation best described as a leap. The strategy can be compared to the diving board over a swimming pool. The leap from the board is the discovery of a creative idea.

The leap itself is difficult to explain or comprehend; and many people believe that it cannot be taught. We believe that it can be described reasonably well and that techniques are available for teaching it.

The process of discovery requires freedom but also discipline; it calls for risk taking, unconventional thinking, and insight into human nature. The process involves at different times both vertical and lateral thinking. Most importantly, intuition and imagination play a part. Luke Sullivan, a distinguished copywriter formerly with the Fallon McElligott agency, states, "It's the imagination disciplined by a single-minded business purpose."[2]

Keep in mind that the purpose is to have advertising solve a problem. Jeremy Bullmore, former head of the London office of J. Walter Thompson, claims this is the answer to the argument about advertising being an art or a science. He believes advertising is the latter. In the creation of pure art, there is no problem to solve. The artist creates to please himself or herself. In scientific thought—as in advertising—there is a problem to be solved, an objective to be reached.[3] The idea therefore begins with a hypothesis that stems from the strategy. The job of the idea is to deliver the strategy within the concept of an advertisement. It is unexpected, it is different, it is unusual. In the words of William Bernbach, probably the most distinguished creative figure in the advertising business during the period after World War II, "The truth isn't the truth until people believe you, and they can't believe you if they don't know what you're saying, and they can't know what you're saying if they don't listen to you, and they won't listen to you if you're not interesting, and you won't be interesting unless you say things imaginatively, originally, freshly."[4]

There are techniques and exercises that can be used in the process. However, not everything will work in the same way for everyone. Each person must try various techniques and find what works for himself or herself.

It is important for those people developing the advertisements to create a state of mind and an environment that nurtures the idea generation process. The person writing an advertisement must first encourage himself or herself. The belief that "I'm just not creative" is almost a self-fulfilling prophecy. But the creative process is hard work. The environment has to be such that success is possible. Creative people require encouragement and help. Deadlines must not always be threatening, although deadlines do of course exist in the real world.

Most importantly, creative people must be motivated. In their work the content is more important than the form, so this is where the time must be spent. They are *always* required to give their best.

It is helpful to be guided by a practical process. Edward de Bono, the specialist in mental processes, once claimed plausibly that free-ranging minds tend to drift toward predictable patterns of thought. On the other hand, James Webb Young, a historically important creative figure who worked for decades for J. Walter Thompson, wrote a modest book in 1940 titled *A Technique for Producing Ideas,*[5] which shows that *discipline can lead to originality.* This book has stood the test of time, it has repeatedly been republished, and it is still widely quoted in other books that focus on the creative process. Young's technique is simple yet provides structure to what would otherwise be a confusing process.

Young said that an idea is nothing more or less than a combination of existing ideas. Bringing old elements into new combinations depends largely on the writer's ability to see past the everyday, to see past the brief, and see new relationships and associations. It also requires two separate types of thinking—vertical and lateral. While there are five steps in Young's technique, which embrace the two mental processes, these steps are both practical and imaginative.

1. Preparation

This is really the creative work before the creative work. While the advertising strategy is full of information, there still is a need for more. First-hand knowledge is necessary. As Bernbach once said, reasonably: "The magic is in the product. . . . You've got to live with your product. You've got to get steeped in it. You've got to get saturated with it."[6] It is good advice to get to know the brand, to know the consumer, to know the competitors. Use the product; use the competitors' products. Go to the grocery store, or the pharmacy, or the showroom, or the mall. Walk in the consumers' shoes—get an idea of how it feels to be them. "See" the problem or situation, don't just look at it.

2. Frustration

Now that information has been gathered, the creative person must work with it, think about it. The process is about making sense or giving meaning to the information as it relates to the problem and to the consumer. The information does not have to be organized or put in order, although it is helpful to use 3 × 5 cards or other simple *aides-mémoire* to collect the information. Information has to be put into some form that it can be worked with.

It is now time for what the leading advertising agency Young & Rubicam calls the Creative Play Plan. This includes various exercises and methods to look at the information differently. It is important to get a sense of playfulness about the information and begin to formulate scenarios or tell stories about the brand. Make it a person, make it a hero, make it a villain. Make it a star in a soap opera, a documentary, or a situation comedy. Take familiar elements of the brand and make them strange. Then do the opposite. None other than Albert Einstein termed this process "combinatory play": combining two or more thoughts that have not been combined before. Arthur Koestler, author of the most intellectually rigorous book on the creative process, *The Act of Creation,* calls it "bisociation."

Turn the problem into an opportunity. Write the name of the brand on a piece of paper and begin to generate free associations by writing down any word that comes to mind that describes or can be associated with the brand. Do the same with colleagues and have a brainstorming session. Ask "What if?" and ask questions to which you may think the answer is obvious. Think visually and laterally; assume there are no boundaries.

3. Incubation

It is important now to let information sit undisturbed. Get away from the problem; maybe for an hour, or a day. Ideas cannot be forced. Go for a walk, work on another project, read a book, write a letter, see a movie, play bridge. Relax, engage in anything to give your mind a chance to digest and process what you have put into it. What happens is that your subconscious takes over and the ideas begin to ferment, *and finally there is a magic moment: "Aha!"*

4. Illumination

The arrival of an idea, or ideas, is a sudden process. Write everything down. This is not the time to make decisions or judgments. This is the time to let all the ideas flow. Generate as many as possible.

5. Evaluation

Working the idea out into a practical form can be as difficult as generating it in the first place. This is the practical phase, and vertical thinking takes over. The ideas have to be worked out in the form of an execution; concepts have to be formalized and tough questions have to be answered. What works best to deliver the strategy? What idea can have the greatest impact on the consumer? What idea can be executed most effectively? What idea can work across different media? What idea lends itself to multiple executions? What idea has staying power?

The creative leap leads to an idea that expresses the brand in an interesting way. There are multitudes of big ideas that have turned into successful advertising campaigns. Absolut Vodka's unusual bottle shape; the milk moustaches; the Macintosh computer vs. Big Brother; a country called Marlboro; the man in the Hathaway shirt; the Uncola; "Where's the beef?" Most importantly, each of these ideas solved a problem for a brand.

Creative Execution

The final step in the campaign is putting the idea to work. This can be almost as difficult as generating the concept, but the problems are now practical ones, rather than the frustration of an agonizing wait for ideas to arrive. Some ideas are not easily executed in certain formats. Concept testing or creative development research is generally useful in the evaluation of alternatives.

Creative development research is qualitative. It does not attempt to quantify *how many* people responded to the advertisement, but merely whether it generated any response at all, and what sort of response. The value of this type of research is that it helps us understand the reason behind the response and whether there is any room for improvement. Such research at the creative development stage enables us to study concepts and executions at an early checkpoint. Creative development research can be handled within the agency or with an outside organization. The research must be a part of the process and allowed to work accordingly.

This stage of the campaign development requires craftsmanship. Tailoring the copy, designing the video of the commercials and the graphics of print advertising, presenting the brand, and orchestrating actors to act like consumers are all difficult and tedious tasks that take time, talent, and experience. What is important is to ensure that the craftsmanship is as relevant and as original and has as much impact as the idea it is trying to convey.

Developing the campaign is time consuming, costly, and mentally challenging. And the effectiveness of the effort is not realized until the advertisement is exposed. This brings us to the third major component of effective advertising—the media that are employed and how they are selected.

The Contribution of the Media

Whatever the requirements of the product, the creative idea becomes effective only in the appropriate media environment. Although we do not intend to cover much detail of media planning in this chapter, some basic points must be made. Media planning requires an element of creativity if it is to be successful; the thinking must not be too rigidly programmed.

The objective is to put the right message in front of the right audience at the right time: something that is not easy to achieve. The two main issues in media strategy are efficiency and effectiveness. *Efficiency* refers to choosing media that deliver the greatest number of people for the least amount of money.

Using efficiency measures exclusively is insufficient. We must also consider *effectiveness,* which relates to the interaction between consumer and the medium—or how the medium intercepts the consumer. The two have to work together. We start with selecting media (titled, for clarity, media classes) and then selecting media vehicles.

Selecting Media Classes

Part of the media strategy involves determining which media classes to use. These can include both traditional media (radio, television, newspapers, outdoor, magazines, and the Internet) and alternative media (mall kiosks, grocery carts, in-store radio, cinema, car wraps, etc.). To choose the appropriate media, we start by considering all reasonable possibilities. As a result of analysis and discussion within the agency account group, we can progressively eliminate the media that do not meet the objectives.

There are four arguments to be used for determining media classes:

1. *Psychological.* How does the consumer use, interact with, and think about the medium? For instance, television can be quite entertaining, but it is a low-involvement medium. Some target groups use television only for entertainment, other groups use it for information, and still others use it for both. Newspapers are primarily a general information source. Yet some groups, especially teens and young adults, use newspapers only for very specific information—movie listings, concert dates, reviews, and shopping guides. The psychological argument provides understanding of how the medium is used in the day-to-day lives of the target group.

2. *Creative.* Each medium has advantages and disadvantages that will impinge on the creative idea in the advertisement. If the brand calls for a live-action demonstration, television is desirable. If there is long, involved copy, newspapers or magazines will be appropriate. Perhaps the creative idea requires music that lends itself to radio and television. Creative people in advertising agencies invariably have strong ideas about the media requirements of the campaigns they write.

3. *Economic.* This is the efficiency measure based on economic parameters. How much of the target will the medium reach? how often? and at what cost? Television is the most expensive medium in absolute terms, but it also reaches large groups of people. Certain maga-

zines can also be very expensive in dollar terms, but they may cover the target very efficiently.

4. *Myths.* This "catch-all" group of beliefs refers to opinions that are widely held to be true but cannot be supported. These beliefs have usually evolved in the client or agency organization and often factor into the media decision. People in client companies and agencies often say: "We've always used television," or "Newspapers are too local to be effective for a national brand," or "Outdoor is difficult to buy," or "Alternative media cannot be measured." These types of arguments should generally be recognized for what they are—biased thinking. In the end, the people charged with advertising a brand will have a media plan that determines which media classes can deliver the advertising message. Now comes the difficult job of selecting vehicles (i.e., specific television shows, magazine titles, etc.)

Selecting Media Vehicles

To determine which media vehicles can most efficiently and effectively deliver the target, three constants and three variables are involved. The constants are *the budget, the target group,* and *the time frame.* The variables are *reach, Opportunities-to-See (OTS),* and *cost per thousand.*

The budget, the target group, and the time frame remain constant no matter what vehicle or combination of vehicles is selected. Vehicles should be eliminated if the cost makes them prohibitive or if they do not reach the target group or, of course, if the deadlines for placement cannot be met.

In this planning process, the vehicles must be analyzed according to their ability to deliver the three variables—reach, Opportunities-to-See, and cost per thousand. Reach identifies the size of the net coverage. (How many people will be reached at least once by this combination of vehicles?) OTS determines the number of exposures of the audience that can be bought for the money. And the cost per thousand is a simple measurement that assesses the efficiency of the vehicle, determined by the cost of reaching each thousand members of the target audience. Each proposed combination of vehicles can be compared, and the combination that offers the best balance of the three variables will be recommended.

The media function is one of the most demanding jobs in the advertising process, requiring specialist expertise to execute, on an experienced and professional level, the processes that have been outlined here.

These points will be apparent from a single well-documented example.

The Campaign for Louisiana: "Come As You Are. *Leave Different.*"

According to Dr. Suzanne Cook, senior vice president for the Travel Industry Association of America, more than 1 billion people made domestic trips in the United States during 1999. Regardless of the budget size, the challenge for any state in the Union is to depict its territory as unique and create some point of differentiation that provides the tourist with more than just a destination spot. It is simply an issue of branding the state by creating an identity, an image, a feeling about the place and what it has to offer. The state of Louisiana aimed to do just that in developing a branding strategy.

The state hired Mayer and Partners, a consortium of three Louisiana communications firms, to handle the tourism account. Mayer and Partners proposed a new approach to marketing Louisiana. Previously, the focus of tourism had been solely on food. Louisiana has a long history of a varied, specialized, and interesting cuisine that ranges from jambalaya, gumbo, beignets, and meat pies to boiled crawfish and shrimp étouffée. Even the telephone number used to provide tourist information had a food flavor: 1-800-99-GUMBO. But just like the famous gumbo, Louisiana had a lot of everything in it. Mayer and Partners thought the food focus too limiting as a device for branding the state.

Good branding stems from good research, so the partners began by analyzing existing research. While much research had been conducted regarding state tourism, it had not been used extensively. Mark Mayer aimed at "uncovering some unique element that motivated the visitor to choose Louisiana." The research showed that Louisiana offered several unique destinations. And a large-scale syndicated research study indicated that tourists were drawn to Louisiana more than they were to many other states, because its attractions are so distinctive. In addition to the food, visitors identify with the state's scenery, architecture, history, culture, and music. This information generated a new advertising strategy.

The new creative strategy led to the use of various state attractions in creative executions. Initially, the target audience was identified as frequent domestic out-of-state travelers, between the ages of 25 and 54, with incomes of $30,000 or more. Six different campaigns were created and tested in focus groups against this strategy. Then the field was narrowed to three campaigns considered to be strongest; these three rough executions tested against a large panel of potential visitors; and one selected. The first ad to run was called "The Words," using what would become the signature of Louisiana—the red lipstick logo and the 1-800-99-GUMBO telephone number. According to Mark Mayer, "we've run various versions of that campaign, but it hasn't really changed one bit. The focus is still on food, culture, music, scenery, architecture, and history."

In fact, little has changed from the initial campaign developed in 1993, except that a slogan was added to the campaign in 1997. In 1996, more research was conducted to test the advertising and the images generated by the campaign. The research reinforced the point that Louisiana is unique, different from any other destination. Mayer states, "We had a monopoly. What made Louisiana different you couldn't get anywhere else."

The research showed Louisiana was different and provided "the road map" for a slogan: "Louisiana. Come As You Are. *Leave Different.*" This was used in all materials beginning with the 1997 campaign.

As with any strong brand, every point of consumer contact is used to reinforce the brand image. While the brand strategy remains the same, the flexibility of the campaign allows the agency to adopt various themes—food, music, culture, history, etc. Within the current campaign, there is a special emphasis on music to take advantage of Ken Burns's documentary on jazz and the "Satchmo Summer Fest," a planned celebration of Louis Armstrong's 100th birthday. However, the brand image remains dominant in all the communication. The slogan, the lipstick logo, and the overall design features provide strong continuity of the image in every advertisement or promotional piece. Domestic and international advertising convey similar design features.

The official tour guide incorporates the same photography and uses the logo and slogan throughout its 300 pages. The television commercials employ the photography as well and highlight a picture of the tour guide, the logo, and the telephone number. The Web site and newspaper advertisements splash the signature Louisiana logo across the pages, interspersed with distinctive photography of the state. Trade publications targeted at travel agents, visitors' bureaus, and tour operators use similar graphics and design.

The power behind the Louisiana brand has been a substantial advertising budget, well-targeted media placements, and an effective integrated campaign that uses image advertising as its cornerstone.

In 1996, the Louisiana tourism budget was $13 million. The budget for 2001 was $17 million. In 2002 it is likely to be $18–$20 million. This represents an average annual increase of 6 percent (or over 30 percent in just five years). Seventy-five percent of the budget is spent on marketing and advertising efforts.

The current primary target audience for the Louisiana brand is families: adults aged 25 to 54, with children still at home and household incomes of $40,000 or more per year. In addition, secondary targets comprise seniors, adults 55 years old or older; families with no children at home; and African Americans and Hispanic Americans, aged 25–54. These audiences are reached through a combination of print, television, and some radio advertising. Print is the primary media choice and receives approximately 60 percent of the advertising dollars, and 40 percent is allocated to spot television and radio in various regions.

The media plan for Louisiana tourism uses the Brand Development Index (BDI) to rank and index all U.S. markets to determine their value in delivering an audience of potential visitors. This is based on reliable syndicated quantitative research. The top 20 major markets are then identified and used for spot television and radio "Flights." The current BDI areas range from Beaumont/Port Arthur, Texas (number 1), to Huntsville/Florence, Alabama (number 20).

In addition to television and radio, the campaign employs consumer magazines (both regional and national), trade publications, newspapers, and travel directories. The publications include *AAA Tourbook, Better Homes & Gardens, Black Enterprise, Bon Appetit, Family Circle, Gourmet, Harper's, Modern Maturity, National Geographic Traveler, New Yorker, Parade, Texas Monthly, USA Today,* and *Walking.* In total, more than 50 publications have been used in exposing the campaign. All advertisements in these publications include the 1-800-99-GUMBO telephone number for ordering the Louisiana tour guide. Travel directories run with a bound-in business reply card and a reader service listing. Each advertisement is coded so that inquiries can be tracked.

When Lt. Governor Kathleen Blanco unveiled the "Louisiana. Come As You Are. *Leave Different*" campaign on January 15, 1997, she was quoted as saying, "We are hopeful this campaign . . . will help us continue our growth in the tourism industry." At that time, the 23 million visitors to the state produced $6.6 billion of business per annum.

By 1999, 25 million tourists visited the state, spending on average $120 per day per person. Tourism had grown to $8.2 billion, the second largest industry in the state, with 118,000 jobs directly attributed to it. The economic impact of tourism had grown by 24 percent in three years and was showing no signs of slowing down. By 2000, the figure for tourism had grown to $8.7 billion and is expected to reach $9.5 billion in 2004. Furthermore, the number of visitor inquiries (any request for information on Louisiana as a travel destination) surpassed 2.5 million in the year, showing an increase of 150 percent since 1996, and a 344 percent increase since 1993. At the same time the cost of generating those inquiries had been reduced by more than 50 percent. The campaign is not only successful, it is efficient as well—the end result of first-class planning and imaginative execution.[7]

The Argument in Brief

The Louisiana case serves as an example of how all elements work synergistically to strengthen a brand. The creative process is powered by research and a sound strategy that serves to differentiate the brand from other tourist venues. The strategy is focused yet flexible enough to allow various themes within the executions. The big idea is fueled by the slogan—"Come As You Are. *Leave Different*"—which conveys the state's welcoming attitude, allied to multitudes of unique attractions.

Alternative approaches were tested to determine the campaign with the most impact. The budget provided enough media weight to deliver the message efficiently and effectively. And the state of Louisiana continues to track the working of the campaign, changing it as needed.

Moving from the strategy to the creative leap and then to the creative execution is difficult. It requires different levels of thought, disciplined idea generation, and painstaking craftsmanship. It is an arduous task, and a costly exercise if the campaign does not work on behalf of the brand.

There must be a commitment to the process, a commitment to the advertising, and a commitment to supporting the effort with research and financial resources. With such commitment, although there is no absolute guarantee of success, the risks are reduced and there are improved chances of strengthening the brand. All effective campaigns follow this path.

Notes

1. David Ogilvy, *Ogilvy on Advertising* (New York: Vintage Books, 1985); Bob Levenson, *Bill Bernbach's Book: A History of the Advertising That Changed the History of Advertising* (New York: Villard Books, 1987); Leo Burnett, *Communications of an Advertising Man* (Chicago: privately published by the Leo Burnett agency, 1961).

2. Luke Sullivan, *Hey Whipple, Squeeze This. A Guide to Creating Great Ads* (New York: Wiley, 1998), p. 21.

3. Jeremy Bullmore, "The Advertising Creative Process," in *The Advertising Business*, John Philip Jones, ed. (Thousand Oaks, CA: Sage, 1999), pp. 51–60.

4. Levenson, *Bill Bernbach's Book*.

5. James Webb Young, *A Technique for Producing Ideas* (Chicago: Crain Communications, republished 1972).

6. Levenson, *Bill Bernbach's Book*.

7. Jan S. Slater, "Brand Louisiana: 'Come As You Are. *Leave Different*,'" in *Destination Branding*, Nigel Morgan, Annette Prichard, and Roger Pride, eds. (Jordan Hills, Oxford, UK: Butterworth-Heinemann, 2002), pp. 148–162.

—— 12 ——

How to Develop and Expose Better Advertising

This chapter is devoted to agency practice, the field in which we spent our professional careers. If one tries to observe the advertising scene from a detached and essentially technical point of view, it is difficult not to be impressed and not to respect the originality and understanding demonstrated by many of the campaigns for products in advertising-intensive product fields, the fields in which campaign development is the most difficult art. Nevertheless, if one knows how difficult it normally is to develop such campaigns, and if one adopts a broader point of view, it is hard also not to conclude that there are specific ways in which advertising practice could be improved, in both the United States and other countries.

Advertisers and agencies, if they heed the points made in this book, will not be overoptimistic about growth prospects for their businesses. Most major brands of repeat-purchase consumer goods are positioned in stationary markets and occupy substantially stable positions in such markets. Advertising budgets are in many cases not increasing in real terms. New brand activity remains as hazardous as ever, and available scientific tools have been of little help in making it less so. When companies are forced, by need for growth, into areas outside their traditional expertise, failure too often dogs them. Such need for growth has also led to numerous major company acquisitions and mergers. But since most consumer goods markets are already controlled by a sometimes overlapping network of oligopolists, there is clearly a top limit to the possibility of individual firms' further expansion by these means.

It follows that there is a great need for us to increase the efficiency of our marketing and advertising efforts. The most obvious expression of this would be to improve the productivity of campaigns, to maintain or increase their yield despite a lack of growth in the investments behind them. To bring this about, advertisers and agencies need a change of attitude regarding their advertised brands. They need to wean themselves away from the objective of volume growth and to direct their attention to *profit growth from volumes that are not themselves increasing.*

Any pronounced increase in the efficiency of advertising is unlikely to take place without either a change in existing methods or significant growth in what we know about advertising and its effectiveness. Developments of this sort normally take place only rarely in the real world. Nevertheless, we need a quantum increase in both the effectiveness of our methods and the amount of our knowledge, and these are the matters that we shall address in this chapter.

This chapter makes two specific proposals: that we undertake more market experimentation and close the gaps in our knowledge. The first has as its immediate and direct objective an improvement in advertising efficiency. The second suggestion is equally important, but its influence is more indirect and will be manifested only in the long term. But the best clients and agencies—like the best organizations generally—plan for a long-term future.

First Recommendation: The Case for More Market Experiments

By way of background, we shall describe how advertising campaigns are planned and written in agencies today, and—an important separate stage in their progress—how eventually they are exposed publicly. This process tends not to be scrutinized searchingly and critically, probably because it is considered so normal that no alternatives have been thought of, let alone experimented with. The picture we shall paint is impressionistic, because agencies are numerous and vary considerably in the detail of their organization, yet this portrayal approximates the overall situation.

When a new campaign is developed for a brand every three or four years (sometimes more often), the starting point is appropriately an extensive examination of the advertising strategy. This is most often carried out by the agency, but there are substantial client inputs and much debate. On the client side, three or more layers of management may be involved in these discussions, and the most important recommendations have to be processed progressively through all of these groups.

The advertising strategy is generally drawn up on the basis of judgment supported by quantitative and qualitative research, but in some respects it almost always falls short of the ideal. This is due partly to the fact that the research on which it is based is variable in quality, the advertising research in particular relying heavily on recall. At a more fundamental level, the procedure is bedeviled by the large gaps in our general knowledge of how advertising works in both psychological and marketplace terms. As a result, most strategies, although they are neither completely ill-directed nor grossly deficient in detail, tend to be rather jejune and to lack the subtlest insights. As one example of this, target groups are almost always defined in the simplest demographic terms; and demographic measures are the *least* useful way of defining target audiences for creative (as opposed to media) planning.

The unmistakable impression made by most strategies is that they are not so much a critically important tool for the development of campaign ideas as a frame of reference or a checklist drawn up with the intention of helping to sell a campaign. (In chapters 10 and 11 we have given suggestions for improving this situation.)

When the strategy has been agreed upon (although it has not been unknown for the strategy to be at least marginally adjusted *after* the development of the creative ideas), the agency creative group produces a range of different proposals, which are expressed, with television campaigns, in scripts, storyboards, "animatics" (storyboards shot on videotape), or experimental commercials; and, with press campaigns, in layouts of different degrees of finish. Ideas are normally presented in rough form for the first presentations. At this point they are subjected to discussion and qualitative research, sometimes in progressive stages, using the focus group technique to test creative hypotheses by exposing them to groups of consumers. This is done with the intention of homing in on one of the alternatives, which then becomes the agency's recommendation and which is in turn sold to the client.[1]

The final campaign idea is normally converted into finished advertisements that are rich with expensively acquired production values. It is then subjected to simple standardized quantitative research before being widely exposed to the public.

Problems with the Procedure

This way of planning campaigns has been accepted pragmatically by agencies. Much of its efficiency stems from the fact that agencies have adapted their organizations to make it work; to increase the operating efficiency of this whole process of *problem evaluation–idea generation–elimination of alternatives–sale of the favored campaign.* Agencies have accepted the system and encouraged its growth without asking any fundamental questions about it.

It seems to us that the system has five characteristics that are all far short of desirable.

In the first place, despite a superficial appearance to the contrary, the system is not really concerned with generating a wide range of creative alternatives. It is really concerned with finding one alternative; the elimination of the others becomes a tool for selling this selected one. Creative groups in agencies are sometimes cruelly realistic about this procedure when they label the rejected alternatives "client fodder." The reason the agency favors a single creative route may be that the route has been its favorite from the beginning, even before the various stages of qualitative research. Agencies are generally organized to have a single creative group responsible for a brand; and it is a fact of nature that such a group (which normally comprises a pair of people who work together all the time, or—less often—a small, cohesively organized body of people dominated by one individual) will nearly always decide that a single alternative is best. Moreover, the clients, most of whom have a professional orientation toward selling, generally expect that there should be no ambiguity or uncertainty about what the agency is selling *them.*

The effective restriction of serious creative exploration would not matter if the development of creative ideas were more like the evolution of strategy, a vertical process that tends to lead in a single direction. But, on the contrary, the creative process is mentally a lateral and "bisociative" one concerned with the pursuit of entirely unexpected connections, and the number of creative alternatives that can be produced in answer to a given strategic problem or opportunity is often very large indeed. To discriminate between this large number of alternatives is not nearly as easy or foolproof as it might appear. Much bathwater is thrown out. One wonders about the babies that might still have been in it.

With one real brand, the agency produced and presented a total of forty-seven alternative campaign ideas, the work of a number of creative groups in three countries. All of these alternatives were finally reduced in qualitative testing and discussion to *one* single idea, which was actually tested in the market. In fact, the whole project was mainly concerned with demonstrating to the client the agency's enterprise, hard work, and internationalism—considerations that may be important, but have little to do with the brand and its advertising. If the sole object of the exercise had been to find a new campaign for the brand, it would have been at the very least highly desirable to experiment in the marketplace with more than one creative alternative.

The second characteristic of the system is that it is heavily judgmental. The judgment is often supported by methodologically flimsy qualitative research. "Sheer conventional group discussions which often masquerade as qualitative research but are little more than reportage—running the risk of portraying consumers as rational and worthy, and stunting the creative process."[2] In the absence of research, decisions are made on the basis of background knowledge and gut feeling. Our own experience (which is neither narrow nor of short duration) is that such judgment can be extremely fallible. And this is amply confirmed by the investigation of Bogart and his colleagues that experts are not at all good at evaluating the most important aspect of campaigns: their selling ability. A sample of "83 advertising decision makers (company brand and advertising managers, agency account executives, creative, media and research men) in New York, Boston, Cincinnati, Detroit and Los Angeles . . . could not predict which ads would sell more of the brand."[3]

As an aside, we *know* that with direct response there are huge differences in the pulling power of different advertisements, which are normally only different creative expressions of the same strategy; but direct-response practitioners admit that it is highly unlikely that subjective evaluation will detect these differences in effectiveness. This is why they rely so heavily on experimental marketplace exposure.[4]

The imperfections of human judgment are serious in all events, but what makes the matter even more worrying is that campaigns are commonly judged by six or more people, all of whom have strong opinions and are empowered to require or at least request modifications. In few circumstances does this procedure lead to an improvement in a campaign; on the contrary, in many cases it leads to disastrous erosion and distortion of the original concept. Some clients are worse than others; indeed some have such a bad reputation that the best creative people will not work on their business. (We wish we were at liberty to name names!)

The system has become progressively worse over the past twenty or thirty years. Indeed, agencies today are less concerned with idea generation than with idea evaluation, and less involved with creation than with mere dialectic.

These serious criticisms bring us to the third fault with the system. For a complex of interrelated reasons, there has been a gradual change in the internal balance of advertising agencies from the creative function to the account executive function. It is rare today for there to be fewer than four layers of account executives working on major brands. These are people who judge and can demand modifications to campaigns even before they reach the echelons of executives on the client side.

This fattening of the account executive function was partly in response to client requirements. (Agencies commonly believe that they should match each layer of a client's marketing organization to reinforce the overall client–agency relationship by providing a "safety net" if the account executive at one level loses the confidence of his or her client.) It was also much encouraged by the extreme profitability of larger accounts, which stemmed from the size of the agency's commission income from them. This executive loading mostly took place in the prosperous decades following World War II, but there is little evidence that in subsequent periods agencies made many attempts to reduce their executive layers.

There has indeed been a move from another direction to *increase* the number of noncreative people in agency account groups: the widely discussed arrival of the account planner, the specialist in the consumer viewpoint and in consumer research, whose job is to establish within the agency the strategy for a brand. This function is common in British agencies,[5] where it appears to have been set up to compensate for weaknesses in the training of European account executives: "Partly because account men were rarely competent to handle data but more dangerously because, as my own account man experience had shown—clients on the one hand and creative direction on the other hand made one permanently tempted to be expedient. Too much data could be uncomfortable."[6] However, there has been a very slow adoption of the system in the United States, partly because of the financial pressures that have assailed American agencies, and partly because of the greater professional competence of American account executives. The account planning function is a valuable one; the dispute is about who should carry it out: account executives or account planners. To date, separate account planners have been introduced in a number of first-class American agencies of medium size. The larger agencies have been slower to do this (see the foreword to this book).

The fourth problem with the system is that it imposes delays. The lead time from the beginning of the campaign planning to final public exposure is commonly a year. It is also extremely expensive in management time.

The fifth problem dates from the 1990s. The development of large media-buying organizations separate from mainstream agencies has meant that media planning—a centrally important element in the advertising process—is becoming detached from agency operations. Creative planning and media planning are becoming separate processes—a highly undesirable outcome.

A Lesson from Direct Response

There is one centrally important point about direct-response advertising. Since the results can be so easily traced, the *efficiency* of direct response and by extension, the efficiency of the advertising agencies handling it can be easily established and carefully measured. Not only can the results of the advertising be simply quantified, but (with a little more difficulty) so also can the agencies' contribution to the profitability of their clients' businesses. The scientific basis for direct response is so robust that people engaged in other types of advertising cannot afford always to ignore its lessons. Rather they should work on the assumption that they can learn something from direct response unless there are facts to prove the contrary.

Quantification is in the bloodstream of direct-response advertisers and their agencies, and it is their main device in maximizing the effectiveness of their efforts. Measurement here means changing on a test basis all of the main advertising variables (one at a time) and counting and costing the resulting response coupons.[7] This approach has on occasion been transferred to other fields of advertising by experienced practitioners who believe in the principle of marketplace testing. One such exponent is David Ogilvy: "Test your promise. Test your media. Test your headlines and your illustrations. Test the size of your advertisements. Test your frequency. Test your level of expenditure. Test your commercials. Never stop testing, and your advertising will never stop improving."[8]

We should be extremely interested to know how closely this admirable advice is followed today at Ogilvy & Mather. But we are frankly skeptical, for the reason that much if not most of this agency's business is in mainline consumer goods. To test what are in so many cases detailed variations by the use of techniques available in direct-response advertising is easy; but in the world of general consumer merchandise sold via the retail trade, there is the widespread belief that the relentless type of detailed testing of element after element that is the norm with direct response is in practical terms almost impossible.

This view should not be accepted as final, however. In rare cases clients and agencies employ contingency planning—a punctilious process of testing campaign alternatives. In a well-known case describing the British brand Oxo soup and gravy cubes, the client and agency repeatedly exposed in test areas alternatives to the national campaign, so that if the latter showed signs of faltering, a replacement was readily available.[9]

The point made by the Oxo case is that even in the world of repeat purchase, the procedure of market experimentation has great value (and even greater rarity value). Such experimentation is much more difficult than tests with direct response, so the number of tested alternatives must be restricted. But even one is greatly better than none; and six might be six times as good as one, depending, of course, on what is tested and how carefully the testing is carried out.

An Operational Proposal

A properly conducted market experiment requires the following conditions:

1. A significant alternative in the marketing mix (the variable to be tested).
2. A control, which is the normal ongoing marketing mix.
3. A reasonable sized, representative, and self-contained test area.
4. Effective media that are comparable in the test and control areas.
5. Time (in most cases, at least two years).
6. An evaluation procedure, which as a minimum should include (for the tested brand and its competitors):

   • Continuous usage and attitude measures;
   • Continuous consumer panel data, with the routine possibility of tabulating all of the consumer behavioral measures described earlier in this book;
   • Continuous quantitative and qualitative evaluation of competitive advertising.

Such a program is routine for market tests of new brands. It is more unusual for experiments with ongoing brands, although in view of the potential rewards of such procedures, the reluctance (or rather, inertia) of marketing managements to implement or even consider such programs is difficult to understand.

We shall now describe a recommended program for major established brands. The purpose of such a program is twofold: first, to explore in a practical way a number of marketing variables, some of which might be the keys to future protection and growth for the brand; and second, to have creative alternatives prepared and tested in the event of serious problems with the national advertising campaign.

We believe that at any one time, the marketing management of a major brand, if it is properly to exercise its responsibility to that brand, should have in the field at least six programs, each of which should be run for two years

These can be differently phased, so that, for instance, in any single year, three market experiments can be in their first year, while three others are in their second year. Routine experimentation of this sort should be as much in the bloodstream of manufacturers of repeat-purchase goods and their advertising agencies as it has always been in that of direct-response practitioners.

The specific things that deserve such market experimentation will depend on the brand and its competition. A typical program would be as follows:[10]

Area 1:   Campaign A (the ongoing national campaign); 33 percent media downweight.

Area 2:   Campaign A; 10 percent price increase.

Area 3:   Campaign A; 33 percent promotional downweight.

Area 4:   Campaign A (perhaps adapted); improved formulation.

Area 5:   Campaign B; other variables constant.

Area 6:   Campaign C; other variables constant.

The control of all these experiments would of course be the national marketing mix used in all areas outside the test regions. For these, the United States is extraordinarily rich in its size and diversity. Each test area need not in normal circumstances comprise more than four cities, so that the test areas (approximately twenty-four cities in toto) would account for no more than a significantly minor share of the country as a whole.

Although such a procedure offers enormous advantages over the type of hand-to-mouth and opportunistic marketing so widely practiced with even large and well-established brands, a program like this does have two major problems.

The first is that market tests and experiments, which are rather a public activity, invite competitive retaliation. This is a fact of life—nothing can prevent it. But never in the past has this vulnerability invalidated the principle of test marketing, although retaliation can of course increase the difficulties of interpreting the test results. If our recommendation concerning ongoing market experimentation were to be accepted on any scale, this would mean a substantial increase in the total volume of testing and a resultant increase in the difficulty of effective retaliatory activity. Indeed, in the celebrated Budweiser case—an extremely complex and prolonged series of market experiments—published evidence does not reveal any consistent competitive retaliation at all. (This test is referred to later in this chapter.)

The second problem with the sort of experimental programs proposed is obviously their cost, the seriousness of which cannot be minimized. However, we shall suggest a way in which it might be *viewed:* in relation to a brand's aggregates.

The advertising production, market research, and management time costs for market experiments should be estimated and compared with the overall marketing costs for the brand. This will provide a more rational perspective than appears at first glance. For example, if the advertising production costs for two new campaigns to be tested in different areas total $500,000 (or $250,000 for each of two years), this total would account for a significant but not outrageously disproportionate share (2.5 percent) of the overall above-the-line annual advertising budget for a brand with a $10 million advertising budget. Viewed in this way, the costs seem at least to be sensibly evaluated against a broad total picture of the brand.

The reader should not forget that the scale economies of large brands are capable of yielding millions of dollars per year in advertising savings. It is only prudent that manufacturers should plough back some of these savings into their ongoing brands (and not just their new ones), so that planned steps can be taken to continue indefinitely their extreme profitability. Profit is also "seed money" for a prudent company.

Without being privy to any inside information, we are fairly certain that Charmin, Crest, Folgers, Ivory, and Tide enjoy significant advertising-related scale economies. And if we were asked to comment on the remarkable company that manufactures them (and others with similar strength), we should have little hesitation in saying that the efficiency of Procter & Gamble's marketing operation comes, first, from its emphasis on highly competitive functional performance for its brands; second, from its ability to nurture its older brands without any disastrous long-term erosion of their sales and profits, allied to an active response to first signs of such erosion; and third, from its ability to employ the profits yielded by these large brands' scale economies to operate experimentally in the marketplace—both with these older brands and with a continuous stream of new brand introductions.

We believe that the recommendations made in this chapter and implicitly throughout this book will be treated with less skepticism in Cincinnati than in the head offices of certain other manufacturing companies in the United States and abroad. We should also add that we never ourselves worked on Procter & Gamble business, although we have made a consistent effort for many years to study its operations from the outside, by drawing conclusions about its policies from scrutiny of its actions.

The Division of Labor Between Advertisers and Their Agencies

If the proposals in this chapter were to be implemented at all widely, agencies would be forced back to a much greater concentration on constructing advertisements—the sort of role they adopted so successfully for many decades after emerging from media space selling more than one hundred years ago.

As a complement to this, we visualize that clients should adopt the leading role in planning and evaluating market experiments. These would, of course, greatly add to the store of knowledge about their brands, so that marketing would become a more efficiently planned activity. Specifically, these experiments could provide a more scientific basis than is at present available for drawing up a brand's budget and media strategy. The increase in the sharpness of the division of labor between clients and agencies should also provide natural benefits in terms of increased operational efficiency, in the way predicted by economic theory. Market experimentation is likely, however, to bring about some changes in the internal structure of agencies, which may not be popular in some circles.

If the agency of the future will be expected to produce for its client not one campaign, but three or more, all to be exposed in the marketplace, it is unlikely that such a change could be implemented with the old system of one creative group per brand. Agencies' most likely solutions would be to have a much faster rotation of creative groups on individual accounts; to employ more roving troubleshooting groups in addition to the regular ones; or to make much more use of freelance talent than is done at present.

However, in all events, it seems inevitable that agencies' creative staffs should occupy a higher proportion of the total than they now do. This proportion varies at the moment between 25 percent and 30 percent in full-service agencies. Viewed objectively, this is remarkably low, considering the importance of the creative product in any agency operation, especially since this general creative category covers a total of about twenty functions, some of which are peripheral to the central creative process. (For instance, home economics, packaging, and proofreading are often included with the creative process.)

It is likely, of course, that agencies will be able in time to make savings in the size of the client contact departments, especially as the emphasis of agency work changes more toward the production of ideas and away from an endlessly extended evaluation of them. It is also likely that a widespread abandonment of remuneration based on commission, in favor of fees based on time of staff, will force reductions in the layers of account management (as clients are made aware of their cost).

Implications for Agency Compensation Systems

Perhaps a discussion of the commission system of agency remuneration is unnecessary since the system is being abandoned at a noticeable rate. But two of its specific imperfections deserve comment.

First the commission system penalizes efficiency. As the productivity of advertising increases—for instance, as brands benefit from advertising economies of scale—it should be possible to work with smaller appropriations. Advertising can work like a rapier, although it is only too often used as a bludgeon. What is the incentive to an agency working on commission if more effective work on its part leads to a reduction in its income? The commission system is an obvious impediment to operating experimental programs of budget reduction. Indeed, it is a handicap to any form of experimentation involving high costs in agency staff time but low returns in commission income. The agency for Budweiser beer was, perhaps understandably, only prepared to cooperate in the marketplace tests of advertising pressure—tests that were eventually to prove extremely beneficial to the brand—after Anheuser-Busch had made special arrangements to maintain the agency's income.[11]

Second, the commission system is intended, in the last analysis, to ensure that the scale economies of agency operations are retained by the agency. This is frankly resented by many clients.[12] It led, during the prosperous decades after World War II, to a crude overstaffing of agencies, which had long-term ill effects. It has also, in our judgment, led to much abrasiveness in the relations between clients and agencies. Indeed, price competition between agencies might be a more comfortable as well as a more efficient system.

A fee system means that with very large budgets, the client pays the agency less. But if the agency is engaged in extensive labor-intensive experimental programs, the agency is protected against losses. Moreover, by its flexibility, the fee system encourages necessary changes in agency organization. In Sweden, where the commission system effectively broke down in the 1960s, agencies changed their nature in a short period of time. Agencies spearheaded a considerable creative revival, which coincided with a decentralization into small, self-contained units (a trend followed in other countries). A rather dramatic decline in the older full-service agencies was partially brought about by the growing number of younger thrusting ones. We are convinced that these evolutions were encouraged by the change in the method of agency compensation, but this is of course a major reason for established agencies in the United States to resist the complete abandonment of commission.

However, the pressures of change are affecting even the staunchest of the old guard. In fact, inquiries conducted among members of the Association of

National Advertisers show the proportion of advertisers who work with their agencies on a pure or modified commission system to have come down from 83 percent in 1976 to 35 percent in 1997. Furthermore, in 1997, 26 percentage points of that 35 percent departed in some way from the rigidity of the 15 percent level, leaving the proportion of clients who work on an unamended 15 percent commission as low as 9 percent.[13] Fee-based systems are fast becoming the norm. And many clients are also tackling the admittedly more difficult task of building into their remuneration methods incentives for superior agency performance.

Second Recommendation: How to Close Some of the Gaps in Our Knowledge

A recurrent theme in this book is the paucity of knowledge about advertising. It is not that we know nothing, but the gaps in our knowledge are formidable, particularly if we accept the point that there are no absolutely generalizable patterns about how advertising works. (The absence of such patterns is one of the few things we know pretty much for certain.) The amount we know about the extent of the variations and their causes is, however, much flimsier. In the 1980s, an inventory was made of the state of advertising knowledge, with the conclusion that we had reliable knowledge of only about 35 percent of the total corpus of what could or should be known.[14]

The four areas of inquiry with which we have been most concerned in this book are all related in some way to one another:

1. The response to advertising, including short- and long-term effects of absolute amounts of pressure and the effects of incremental pressure (chapters 7 and 8).
2. Advertising and the human mind: how advertising operates on people. Psychological theories are plentiful, but despite their intellectual attractions, they are almost devoid of empirical support (chapter 6).
3. The creative process: idea generation, and why and how some campaign ideas are more effective than others (chapter 10).
4. Ways of researching advertisements and advertising campaigns and, in particular, research techniques to forecast the success of new brands (chapter 6).

We are convinced that advertising will never come close to being a scientific subject, despite the claims of some of its protagonists, unless our knowledge of these relative unknowns is greatly increased in extent and depth. The vast amount of research (much of it subtle and thought-provoking, but much more of it, unfortunately, unidimensional and repetitive) is hardly intended or used to fill these gaps in our knowledge. There are two reasons for this. First, much of it is too similar to what has been done before, in terms of problems tackled and methodology, to push forward the frontiers to any extent; and second (an even more important point), *it is no one's job to synthesize it and use it for the broader purpose of adding to the general store of what we know.* The problem is, of course, compounded by the extreme care taken to avoid the publication of expensively acquired proprietary data.

This situation should be a source of disappointment to everyone in marketing and advertising. In effect it seriously hampers any serious attempts to extend the amount of our general knowledge. Many people do in fact regret this, and unfair criticism is lavishly distributed. For instance, advertising academics are attacked for their seeming inability to carry out fundamental research. (On the other hand, some people believe that academics should concentrate more on practical, day-to-day brand and market problems, much as commercial researchers do.)[15] The critics would be wise, however, to give some thought to the nature of advertising knowledge and the methods of inquiry available to researchers to extend it. A number of people contend, quite wrongly, that the study of advertising resembles the study of natural science, in that basic research is in some way a foundation for applied research. This view, as it applies to various pure and applied scientific disciplines, has been expressed with admirable lucidity by a scientist of distinction, the late J. Robert Oppenheimer:

> Basic research: that is, research that is aimed primarily at increasing our understanding and our knowledge, without too direct a thought of what use this will be in practice. That this is typically a university function is true in the natural sciences; it is true in the mathematical sciences; and I believe it is even more true in those areas, let us say, of anthropology, psychology, and economics which are becoming subject to research.[16]

Despite the authority of this most distinguished observer, we question his conclusion regarding the social sciences. And if by extension a similar conclusion were to be made about the study of advertising, we believe it would be unambiguously wrong.

Our reason for this disagreement is quite simple. Most worthwhile advertising research must in our judgment be inductive; it must be based on the study of the particular, which will help us to understand parts of the marketing process for certain brands and (to quote chapter 1) "provide the hope (although not the firm expectation) that a general theory might eventually be built up to explain the whole." This progress from the particular to the general is of course what McDonald is talking about in his comparison of the study of advertising to entomology.

If this line of reasoning is correct, it would explain why there may indeed be validity in the common view held by advertising practitioners that there has been little worthwhile research into advertising carried on at universities.[17] The reason for this is simple: the only fundamental place in which research into advertising can possibly be carried out is the market. The method of investigation must be the punctilious and extensive examination of specific brands, marketing situations, and advertising campaigns; and the primary (although not the sole) source of data must be the consumers of the brands under examination and their competitors. Universities lack the financial resources to fund studies of this type, which are rightly seen as the province of the custodians of brands: manufacturers and their advertising agencies.

Advertising people know from first-hand experience, as is clear from the cases referred to in this book, that the inductive principle is well established in the advertising field; indeed, it is the method by which researchers have acquired most of their worthwhile knowledge of advertising. The trouble is that the amount that has been done, or rather the amount released for objective study of underlying conditions, is very small in relation to the amount necessary for the formulation of anything like robust general hypotheses, let alone principles.

There are three reasons for this. First, not enough market experiments have actually been carried out, although the pace is increasing. Moreover, if manufacturers listen to what is being said in this book, it will increase more rapidly in the future. Second, not enough experiments have been released for examination, for reasons of confidentiality. Third—an important reason—is that it has been no one's job to carry out what some people would consider the laborious tasks of analysis and synthesis. What has been grossly lacking is a body of people with the skills, time, and interest to begin to build an edifice out of what at the moment is a small number of bricks and then (an even more important task) to persuade people to make many more bricks available.

The reader may by now have guessed what we visualize to be the true role of advertising research as it should be carried out at universities: to take individual brand studies and to evaluate them in the mass to detect, hypothesize, and eventually enunciate general principles; and to examine the extent and the characteristics of variations and exceptions. A certain amount of work of this sort has already been carried out by the various professional organizations in the marketing field, notably the Advertising Research Foundation

(ARF), the Association of National Advertisers (ANA), and the Marketing Science Institute (MSI). But the total amount of such work done to date is tiny in comparison with what needs to be done; and the research that has been undertaken by these important bodies has been done in the main by people who have full-time commercial careers that make extreme demands on their time and energy, so that our comments should not be construed as critical of the work.

The best collection of case study material available anywhere has been and is being assembled in Britain by the Institute of Practitioners in Advertising (IPA) and the World Advertising Research Centre (WARC). However, the efforts of these bodies have been concentrated more on collecting the information than on drawing specific and general conclusions from it.

For reasons connected (but not solely connected) to the lack of other suitable expertise, we believe that universities have a great deal to offer such research programs. In fact, critics of universities' advertising work would be wise to consider four of academia's advantages.

To start with, universities have brain power. There are full programs in advertising in ninety-one state and private universities and colleges in the United States.[18] Each faculty has a number of instructors and often a body of energetic graduate students. The standard of education among the faculties is generally high.

Second, most academics are objective. They are generally not proponents of any single philosophy or method, which can narrow the thinking of employees of many manufacturing concerns, advertising agencies, and research companies.

Third, academics have a priceless amount of time. Research, intellectual speculation, and plain thought are a central part of their job; and the amount of uncluttered time set aside for these activities is the most striking (and delightful) feature of academic life as it is experienced by people who have adopted it after careers as advertising practitioners.

Fourth, and not least, is something more intangible but very important indeed: what Oppenheimer calls "the fructification of the classroom," something that a person who has not experienced it at first hand cannot fully understand:

> The experience of the student is to be puzzled, not to understand, to be confused, and gradually to find some sensible order, to get a new idea, to find out that what he had been thinking was wrong; this is a typical experience for the man engaged in research, and it is a typical experience for the student, and this is one point of harmony. . . . One finds that although it is

not possible to give a theoretical argument why research and education should occur in the same place, a man himself by uniting these two functions will make it manifest that it is a good idea.[19]

Indeed, the relentless demands of advertising research resemble those of the small handful of outstanding students in the academic's classes, especially if the teacher has successfully taught them a healthy skepticism, an unwillingness to accept received wisdom without testing it first.

This chapter's proposal, that manufacturers should greatly increase the number of market experiments they conduct for their brands, must be decided on its own merits—by its perceived contributions to the health and progress of those brands. In our opinion, these contributions are likely to be considerable indeed. The proposal about using cases individually and in the aggregate to add to our store of general knowledge about advertising is a separate but related matter. If manufacturers accept our first proposal, the amount of material available for general study will be greatly increased, and this is our starting point.

The advertising industry is the only body with the interest in and resources to acquire this knowledge and then (an equally important consideration) to release it for analysis and synthesis. A good deal of case-by-case data collection takes place at the moment (although this is far short of what is needed), but there is no evidence that the industry yet realizes what would be gained if there were a first-class series of studies of the existing corpus of information, let alone what could be done if we had many more data to start with.

Our proposal that universities have a real role to play in these studies is made cautiously, but with some knowledge of their intellectual capacity. The work would incidentally involve the industry in little financial outlay over and beyond the marketplace experiments that would naturally account for the most substantial proportion of the cost of any broad empirical evaluation program.

During our years as advertising practitioners and academics, we have been both excited about what we do know about advertising (no matter how little) and frustrated by what we do *not*. From talking to present and former colleagues, we do not think that these feelings are atypical, which makes us optimistic that at least a few of the things said here may not fall on deaf ears.

We began this book with the intention of using it indirectly or directly as a teaching aid. In retrospect, we have also had some fun writing it. But we end this project with an attempt to reach you, the reader, who may have some sympathy with what we have been trying to say and the interest and energy to turn thoughts into deeds. Will you respond to our call to action? Will you realize both your responsibility and your capacity to extend the frontiers of our knowledge? Will you accept our suggestions as constructive, practicable, and relatively inexpensive to put into action? Will you employ your professional authority and your talents to support what we are saying in a practical way? And will you please act now?

The Argument in Brief

This chapter began by emphasizing that advertisers and agencies will probably have to continue to operate with stationary markets, stationary brands, and advertising budgets that may be falling in real terms. It then addressed the fundamental problem of how to increase advertising's productivity—its ability to augment profits, despite static sales and declining (real) advertising investments. The chapter argued that success can only be made possible with changes in the methods of planning advertising and increases in our store of knowledge.

There was an analysis and critique of the general method of campaign development in major agencies in the United States. In brief, the system puts less emphasis on idea generation than on the processes of idea evaluation and the selling of campaigns to clients. A strong recommendation was made to embark on much more creative experimentation than is common at present, with evaluation by more extensive programs of marketplace testing of alternatives. The chapter recommended that, for major brands, there should at any time be at least six ongoing market tests of variations in the marketing mix. Such testing programs will only be enthusiastically endorsed by agencies when they have totally abandoned the media commission system.

A second recommendation relates to the poverty of our knowledge of the various processes of advertising. A formal study has revealed that we have reasonably firm knowledge of a mere 35 percent of the actual or potential corpus. The advertising industry should take serious steps to augment this store of knowledge. Advertisers and agencies should be persuaded to make proprietary market data available to universities for them to analyze and synthesize, with the object of seeking general patterns and generating hypotheses about how advertising works in a variety of circumstances. This would be a practical example of how advertising can be studied using the principles of entomology, a notion introduced in the first chapter of this book.

This book has attempted to sound the tocsin—to alert advertisers and indeed the whole advertising industry to the pressing need to study their profession in a serious way, so that it can begin to justify the scientific pretensions of so many of its protagonists.

Notes

1. Stephen A. Greyser, *Cases in Advertising and Communications Management,* 2d edition (Englewood Cliffs, NJ: Prentice-Hall, 1982), pp. 3–22, 373–401. Two cases in this book dealing with the Northwestern Mutual Life Insurance Company illustrate well the processes of creative development, research, and elimination of alternatives.

2. Two skilled practitioners of qualitative research, Judie Lannon and Peter Cooper, express this view in "Humanistic Advertising: A Holistic Cultural Perspective," *International Journal of Advertising* (July–September 1983): 211.

3. Leo Bogart, B. Stuart Tolley, and Frank Orenstein, "What One Little Ad Can Do," *Journal of Advertising Research* (August 1970): 12.

4. See an excellent empirical statement of this principle by well-known British practitioner of direct response Graeme McCorkell, "When Experts Can Get It Wrong," *Campaign,* February 15, 1985, pp. 55–56.

5. For a detailed description of British practice, see *Account Planning* (London: Institute of Practitioners in Advertising, 1981).

6. Stanley Pollitt, "How I Started Account Planning in Agencies," in *Account Planning* (London: Institute of Practitioners in Advertising, 1981), pp. 24–28.

7. Greyser, *Cases in Advertising and Communications Management,* pp. 447–472. This provides an excellent example of the technique in action. The advertiser was *The National Observer.*

8. David Ogilvy, *Confessions of an Advertising Man* (New York: Atheneum, 1984), p. 86.

9. John Philip Jones, *Does It Pay to Advertise? Cases Illustrating Successful Brand Advertising* (Lexington, MA: Lexington Books, 1986), chap. 8.

10. Many if not most television schedules include spot as well as network transmissions. Media downweighting in an area would naturally involve cutting back the spot advertising exclusively to achieve the necessary overall reduction. With somewhat more difficulty, an experimental downweighting could be implemented with the use of the split-cable TV mechanism. The latter device is also suitable for testing campaign alternatives.

11. Russell L. Ackoff and James R. Emshoff, "Advertising Research at Anheuser-Busch 1963–68," *Sloane Management Review* (Winter 1975): 13.

12. Evidence of this is provided by a number of investigations by the Association of National Advertisers: *ANA Member Practices and Views on Advertising Agency Compensation* (New York: Association of National Advertisers, various years). Such dissatisfaction appeared as long ago as the early 1930s, at least on the part of larger advertisers. James Webb Young, *Advertising Agency Compensation* (Chicago: University of Chicago Press, 1933), p. 156. Evidence collected by the Association of National Advertisers demonstrates that although certain advertisers have moved to reduce their agencies' compensation, others have moved to increase it. In both cases, the fee system was thought to offer greater flexibility. William M. Weilbacher, *Current Advertiser Practices in Compensating Their Advertising Agencies* (New York: Association of National Advertisers, 1983), pp. 38–46.

13. Rana S. Said. "Advertising Agency Compensation Systems," in *The Advertising Business. Operations, Creativity, Media Planning, Integrated Communications,* John Philip Jones, ed. (Thousand Oaks, CA: Sage, 1999), pp. 111–120.

14. John Philip Jones, *How Much Is Enough? Getting the Most from Your Advertising Dollar* (New York: Macmillan-Lexington Books, 1992), chap. 10.

15. Herbert J. Rotfeld, Spencer F. Tinkham, and Leonard N. Reid, "What Research Managers Think of Advertising Research by Academics," in *Proceedings of the 1983 Convention of the American Academy of Advertising* (Lawrence: University of Kansas Press, 1983), pp. 52–57.

16. J. Robert Oppenheimer, "The Relation of Research to the Liberal University," in *Freedom and the University* (Ithaca, NY: Cornell University Press, 1950), pp. 97–98.

17. Rotfeld et al., "What Research Managers Think of Advertising Research by Academics," p. 54. Thirty leading advertising agencies with which we have been in personal contact have confirmed and added to the conclusions of this investigation.

18. Don E. Schultz, "Advertising Education: Where It Is, Where It's Going," in *Advertising Age Yearbook* (Chicago: Crain Books, 1982), pp. 37–50.

19. Oppenheimer, "The Relation of Research to the Liberal University," pp. 101–102.

Index

AAA Tourbook, 268
Aaker, David A., 220, 228, 229, 255
Absolut Vodka, 262
Accountability
  key to, 191
  medium-term payback, 210, 211*t*
  time frames for, 188
  tools to measure, 189–191
Account management, xxii
Account planner, 275
Account planning, xxi–xxii
Ackoff, Russell L., 288
Act of Creation, The, 261
Added values, 9, 32–37, 69, 102, 249
  belief in effectiveness, 33–34
  from brand experience, 33
  building, 236–238
  collectibles, 216
  contribution to consumer choice, 34–35
  definition of, 33
  indirect effect, 40
  and the low-involvement hierarchy
      theory, 149
  nonfunctional, 35
  packaging, 9, 34
  paying extra for, 37–38
  sources of, 22
  user associations, 33
Ad households, 167–168
Adless households, 167–168
Adstock, 156
Advertisements, 16, 257
  accountability factor, 231
  effective frequency, 178, 181
  exposure to, 178, 181, 187

Advertisements *(continued)*
  rational vs. emotional arguments, 250
  writers of, 260
Advertising, 15–16, 104
  arguments, 131
  boosting brands in stationary markets,
      175–176
  building added values, 237–238
  campaigns, 86
  consumer acceptance, xviii
  continuous. *See* Continuity planning
  core factors, 191
  costs, 279
  early types of, 138–139
  economies of scale, 281
  effective, 153, 155. *See also* Effective
      advertising
  expenditures, 87
    large vs. small brands, 89*t*, 90
    measuring by share of voice, 88*t*–89
    for a new brand, 87
    setting econometrically, 87
    short-term adjustments, 87
  as an expense, 26
  and functional properties, 55
  function of, 185
  growth in consumer, 24, 25
  historical growth of, 25–28
  importance of, 38, 86
  influence on sales, 163–165
  investment for large brands, 209
  knowledge gaps, 282
  literature of. *See* Literature
  long-term benefit of successful, 190
  long-term effects, 37, 185, 191, 211–212

Advertising
  long-term effects *(continued)*
    expenditures on large brands,
      209–210
    four peripherals, 189–191
    measures of, 189–191
    time frame, 188–189
  long-term strategy, xvii
  long-term value, 74
  measuring profits and losses from, 185
  media
    magazines. *See* Magazines
    share of voice, 207
    television, 10. *See also* Television
  medium-term effects, 165, 170–176,
    186, 206
    calculating, 210
    factors determining, 181
    growth, 174, 175*t*
    measured econometrically, 185
    time frame, 188–189
  modifying attitudes, 235
  of new brands with umbrella names, 61
  in oligopolies, 24
  origins of, 27–28
  power of, 165
  previous, 210
  and price elasticity, 202
  and the primary growth cycle, 102
  print, consumer expenditures and, 26*t*
  profits, 190
  propinquity, 181
  recall testing, 138. *See also* Recall
    testing
  retaining existing users, 236
  roles of, 190, 234, 255
    direct action, 250–251
    factors influencing, 131
    modifying attitudes, 252
    providing information, 251
    reinforcing attitudes, 252
    relating to consumers, 251
    reminding consumers, 251–252
  and sales promotions, 175
  selective perception, 131
  short-term effects, 186, 206

Advertising
  short-term effects *(continued)*
    and advertising intensity, 174
    data collection, 167
    measuring, 165
    and medium-term effects, 173–174
    time frame, 167, 188–189
  study of, 283
  theories
    do-feel-do, 149
    hierarchy of effects, 146
    learn-do-feel, 147
    learn-feel-do, 146
    learning hierarchy, 146
    low-involvement hierarchy, 147–149
    reinforcement hypothesis, 149–150
  tone of voice, 131
Advertising Age, 9, 17, 18, 216
Advertising agencies
  account executive function, 274–275
  account planner, 275
  account planning, xxi–xxii
  after World War II, 275, 281
  campaigns. *See* Advertising campaigns
  clients, 274, 275, 280
  compensation system
    commission, 275, 280–282
    fee system, 281
  concerns of, 274
  contingency planning, 276
  creative groups in, 273, 280
  and direct response, 276–277
  division of labor, 280
  function of, xxi
  noncreative people in, 275
  organization of, 273
  overstaffing, 281
  possible improvements to, 271
  practices, 270
  process of developing, 271–272
  super marketers and, xvii
  testing, 276
Advertising campaigns, 104, 258–259
  creating synergy, 175
  creative process, 259
  definition of, 258

Advertising campaigns *(continued)*
early, 139
recipes, 139, 159*t*
for Louisiana, 266–268
milk moustache, 258, 262
procedural problems with
account executives, 274–275
creative exploration, 273
judgment, 274
media planning, 275
predicting selling ability, 274
time, 275
proposal, 272
quality of, 93–94
strategies, 272
Uncola, 262
uniformity of response to, 108
Where's the beef?, 626
Advertising effort, index of
calculating, 174
to promotional intensity, 174*t*
Advertising elasticity, 98*t*, 104, 191,
202–207, 210, 212
break-even, 97
calculating, 203
measuring effect on sales with, 98
vs. price elasticity, 97
range of, 203
relation to sales, 204*t*–207*t*
study of, 203
Advertising industry, long-term growth,
xviii
Advertising intensity, 173, 174, 233
Advertising intensiveness, 191, 210, 212–
213
SOV-SOM relationship, 207, 208
Advertising-Intensiveness Curve (AIC),
207–208, 210
Advertising Research Foundation (ARF),
140, 179, 184, 284
Advertising Research Systems. *See* ARS
Advertising response function, 177–181
concave-downward curve, 177, 178
diminishing returns, 178, 179
exploiting, 178
inflexion point, 178

Advertising response function *(continued)*
plotting curves, 178
shape of, 179
S-shaped, 177, 178
use of, 177
Advertisingspeak, xviii
Advertising strategy, 133, 259
account planner, 275
advertisements. *See* Advertisements
attitudes, 243
behaviors, 243
as a campaign tool, 272
capabilities of, 231, 234–238
definition of, 238, 254
developing, 238–239, 254–255
document, 243
drawing up, 272
factors involved with, 129
formulating, 239–240
getting started, 242–243
importance of, 238–239
key elements of, 243
key fact, 243
knowledge, 243
limitations of, 231, 232–234
media, 181–182
"me-too" strategy, 47–48
proposition, 243. *See also* Propositions
rational vs. emotional arguments, 250
role of, 230, 243
target group, 243, 244–248. *See also*
Target groups
word origin, 238
AdWorks2 study, 183–184
Aitchison, David R., 160
Ajax, 32
Albion, Mark S., 17, 18
All-Bran, 123
Allen, Frederick, 229
American Airlines, 31
American Dental Association, 249
American Tobacco Company, xix
Andrex, 182–183, 206
Anheuser-Busch, 281
Appel, Valentine, 149, 160, 161
Apple Computers, 250

Arens, William·F., 256
ARF. *See* Advertising Research
    Foundation
Arm & Hammer, 33, 246
Armstrong, Louis, 267
Arndt, Johan, 71
ARS (Advertising Research Systems), 162
    description of, 154–155
    measure, 155
    predictive value of, 155
    pre-/post-preference shift, 155
Assael, Henry, 161, 162
Assmus, Gert, 106, 203
Association of National Advertisers
    (ANA), 179, 281–282, 285, 288
Atomistic competition, 28, 29, 40. *See
    also* Perfect competition
Aurora Foods, 240
Automobile industry
    direct action advertising, 250–251
    in the 1960s, 36
Axelrad, Beth, 44
Axelrod, Joel N., 162

Backman, Jules, 22, 30, 41, 43
Baker, Samm Sinclair, 106
Bannock, Graham, 41
Barbie dolls, 215, 227
Barger, Harold, 41
Barnes, Michael, 134
Bateman, Bill, 229
Bates advertising agency, 114
Beardi, Cara, 256
Beer, domestic
    market penetration, 192*t*
    purchase frequency, 197
    SOM/penetration relationship, 194
BehaviorScan panels, 168
Belk, Russell W., 217, 228
Bell brand potato chips, 7
Bernbach, Bill, 7, 8, 11, 18, 258, 260, 261
Better Homes & Gardens, 268
Betty Crocker, 33
Birds Eye, 32
Black Enterprise, 268
Blanco, Kathleen, 268

Blum, Milton L., 160
Bogart, Leo, 153, 162, 274, 288
Bon Appetit, 268
Bono, Edward de, 233, 234, 255,
    260
Borden, Neil Hopper, 24, 41, 42
Boston Market, 231
Bounce, 252
Bozell agency, 258
BP (British Petroleum), 122
Brand audit
    brand analysis, 241
    company analysis, 240–241
    competitor analysis, 242
    consumer analysis, 242
    market analysis, 241
    problem/opportunity statements, 242
Brand awareness, 235
Brand collectibles
    behavior analysis, 222–223
    brand ownership and, 224
    Coca-Cola. *See* Coca-Cola Company
    consumer behavior, 217
    determining factor, 221
    examples of, 215–216
    relationship with consumers, 221
    repeat purchasing, 222
    similarities between, 216
    strategy, 216
Brand Development Index (BDI), 268
Brand equity, 236, 241
Brand image, 223
Brand knowledge, 235, 236
Brand loyalty, 214, 228, 236
    building, 222–223
    definition of, 220
    Hallmark, 226–227
    increased, 223
Brand management, 146
Brand names, 59–62
    similar, 60
    using umbrella names, 59–60
Brand personality, 33
    trade characters and spokespeople,
        249
Brand positioning, 56–59

Brands
  added values, 31–37. *See also* Added
    values
  advertising schedules, 171, 178–179
  analysis of, 241
  appeal of, 216
  boosting in stationary markets, 175–176
  in the breakfast cereal industry, 22
  buying, 167–168
  characteristics of, 216
  decline of, 52, 126, 128
    and consumer promotions, 84
  definition of, 32, 237
  determining key source of business,
    244–246
  devaluing, 84, 85
  display of, 81–82
  distinctiveness, 32
  dwindling popularity of substantial, 53
  economic history of, 19
  emergence of, 19, 31–37
  extending, 216
  functional performance of existing, 55
  growing, 79
  growth of, 128–129
    short term vs. long term, 73–74
  GRPs and, 184
  with a higher penetration, 132
  influencing consumer attitudes, 148
  initial growth, 74–78
  large, 195–196
    importance of, 132*t*
    investment behind, 209
    purchase rates for, 123
  leading advertised (1913), xix*t*
  life cycle of, 52, 53
  major, 111
  market reach, 32
  media
    effective strategy, 164–165
    schedule, 164. *See also* Media
      planning
  milking, 53
  with minority appeal, 6
  new. *See* New brands
  primary growth cycle, 76–78

Brands *(continued)*
  and product purchase rates, 132
  purposes of, 19, 28, 31
  recycling, 77
  reintroducing, 253
  repertoire of, 4–5
  restaging with a considerable change,
    154
  substitution of, 125, 190
  survival of, xix–xxi
  testing, 277. *See also* Market
    experimentation
  unadvertised, 172
  word origin, 27
Bran Flakes, 123
Breakfast cereals
  market
    case study of, 20–23
    penetration, 192*t*
    positioning, 56
  presweetened, 117*t*–118
    purchase levels, 122*t*
  purchase frequency for, 117, 197
  SOM/penetration relationship, 193
  standard (unsweetened), purchase levels
    for, 123*t*
British Gallup organization, 138
British Market Research Bureau, 142
Broadbent, Simon, 63, 71, 96, 97–98,
    105, 106, 162
Brooke Bond Oxo, 55, 131
Brown, Gordon, 162
Bucklin, Louis P., 42
Bud Light, 53
Budweiser, 53, 195, 278, 281
Buffet, 46, 70
Bull Durham smoking tobacco, xix
Bullmore, Jeremy, 259, 269
Burke Marketing Services, 143, 160
Burnett, Leo, 11, 156, 258, 269
Burns, Ken, 267
Bursts, 179
Buyers, 4. *See also* Consumers

California Milk Processor Board, 258
Calvin Klein, 215

Campbell, Roy H., 162
Campbell's Soup, 53, 216
Cannibalism, 56–57, 59–60
  names and, 60
  preventing, 60
Caples, John, 11
Cars. *See* Automobile industry
Carter, Peter, 71
Cashmere Bouquet, xix
Cat Chow, 46, 70
Cat food market, study of sales rates,
  45–46, 70
Chamberlin, Edward Hastings, 42
Champion Spark Plug Company, 134
Chanel, 251
Charmin, 279
Cheerios, 125
Cherington, Paul Terry, 41
Chesebrough-Pond's, 134
Chevy Trucks, 252
Clark, Harold F., Jr., xxiii
Clark, Paul, 44
Clarke, Peter, 161
Classic Coke, 225
Clayton Act of 1914, 25
Coca-Cola Barbie, 215, 222, 224
Coca-Cola Collector's Club, 218, 220,
  224
Coca-Cola Company, 11, 43, 216, 222,
  223, 228, 237, 246, 248, 249
  brand image, 217
  Classic Coke, 225
  licensing agreements, 221–222, 224
  memorabilia, 218
  New Coke, 225
  success of, 217–219
  trademark, 219
  unlicensed merchandise, 221
  Web site, 219
Coca-Cola Santa, 227
Coe, Barbara, 160
Colgate & Co., xix
Colgate Cold Cream, xix
Colgate Dental Cream, xix
Collectibles. *See* Brand collectibles
Colman, Stephen, 162

Commission system, 281–282
Competitive capitalism, 38
Consensus Credo. *See* Positioning
  Advertising Copy Testing
Consumer base, 74
Consumer behavior, 150, 243. *See also*
  Purchasing patterns
  ads influencing, 235–236
  brand collecting, 216–217, 222–223
  buying new brands, 51
  and continuous image measurement,
    156–157
  link between factual knowledge and,
    151
  low involvement, 148
  patterns, 112
  regularity of, 108
Consumer demand, managing, 36
Consumer expenditure and advertising,
  growth of, 26*t*
Consumer goods markets, 5
Consumer loyalty
  brand collectibles. *See* Brand
    collectibles
  lack of, 214–215
Consumer panel, 49
Consumer price, 190, 212
  of largest brands, 199, 200
Consumers
  acceptance, xviii
  choosing target groups, 129–131
  collectors, 221. *See also* Brand
    collectibles
  diary studies, 109–110
  inertia and habit, 56
  influencing attitudes of, 148
  loyalty of, 101, 125–126, 196, 199
  major brands, 111
  marketplace knowledge, 38–39
  persuading, 38
  and premium prices, 62
  and price reductions, 201
  promotions, 83–85
  purchasing, 113–114
    five key variables, 114
    repeat, 55, 56

Consumers *(continued)*
  repurchasers, 121
  sole purchasers, 121
Contingency planning, 276
Continuity planning, 164, 182, 187,
    206. *See also* Continuity
    scheduling
  advantage of, 165
  broad description of, 178
Continuity scheduling
  vs. Flighted plans, 183–184
  low, 184*t*
Cook, Suzanne, 266
Cook, V.J., 70
Cooper, Peter, 43, 288
Cooperative advertising, advantage of,
    82
Copy testing, 138
Corlett, Tom, 99, 106, 128, 135
Corlett Shift, 99–100
Corn Flakes, 38, 56, 116, 117, 123
Cosby, Bill, 249
Cosmetic changes, 5
Coupons, 84
  advantages of, 85
  counting, 152
Crawford, C. Merle, 72
Creative execution, 259, 263
Creative leap, 259–262
  essence of, 259
  process, 259–260
Creative Play plan, 261
Creative process, 259, 280
  direction of, 273
  environment needed, 260
  execution, 263
  leap, 259
  producing ideas, 260–262
    evaluation, 262
    playing with the information,
      261–262
    preparation, 261
Crest, 32, 249, 250, 279
Crisco, xix, 279
Curtis, Richard, 256
Cyclical decline, 52

Daily Mirror, 143
D'Arcy, MacManus, and Masius, 97
DART (day-after-recall test), 143–144
Data
  collection, 132, 240, 285
    demographics, 246
    determining source of business, 244
    psychographics, 247
    television viewing, 166
    using scanners, 166
  percentaging, 138
Davidson, J. Hugh, 7, 17, 43, 54, 62, 67,
    71
Davis, John, 66, 71, 78, 105
Day, George S., 161, 162
Day, Ralph L., 43
DDB, 247
Delsey (Kimberly-Clark), 85
Demand
  elasticity of, 39
  predicting, 39
  and price, 39
DEMOS. *See* Direct eye movement
    observation system
Depth of purchase, 196*t*
Dhalla, Nariman K., 70, 98, 106
Dial soap, 196
Diary studies, 109–110
Direct action, 250–251
Direct eye movement observation system,
    142, 143*t*
Direct response, 274, 276–277
  advantages of, 276
  quantification of results, 276
Dirichlet model, 115
Discriminating arguments, 250
Displays, 81–82
Distribution, 63–65
  of new brands and increasing sales,
    75–76*t*
  retail, 64–65
  running out of stock, 100–101
  of successful brands, 64
Doane, Robert R., 26
Do-feel-do theory, 149. *See also*
    Reinforcement hypothesis

Dog Chow, 246, 252
Donna Karan, 215
Donnelley Marketing, 80
Dove, 32, 233
Duncan Hines, 240, 241
Duplication coefficient, 123
Duplication of purchase law, 123
Dynamic difference, 90, 91–94, 99

Eastman Kodak, xix, 237
Ebbinghaus, Hermann, 147
Economies of scale. *See* Scale economies
Effective advertising, 244
  defining, 230–231
  key elements of, 258
  media usage, 263–265. *See also* Media
    planning
  predictability and, 258
  strength behind, 230
Effective frequency, 178, 179
  exposure to, 181
*Effective Frequency: The Relationship
  Between Frequency and Advertising
  Effectiveness*, 179, 184
Egyptian Deities, xix
Ehrenberg, Andrew S.C., 12, 18, 71, 111,
  112, 115, 124, 127, 133, 134, 135,
  149, 150, 161, 162, 165
Ehrenberg's models, 114
Einstein, Albert, 261
Elasticity
  advertising. *See* Advertising elasticity
  price. *See* Price elasticity
Electronics industry, xviii
Elliott, Jeremy, 94, 99, 105, 106
Elliott Extension, 94
Emshoff, James R., 288
Ennis, F. Beaven, 105
Eskin, Gerald J., 100, 106
Esso, 122
Estée Lauder, 251

Fairy Liquid dishwasher, 84
Family Circle, 268
Famous Artist Schools, 134
Farlet, John J., 106, 203

Farris, Paul W., 17, 18
Fast-moving consumer goods
  added values, 9
  advertising, 9–10
  brand repertoire, 4–5
  buyers, 4
  competitive brands, 5
  description of, 3
  importance of the field, 10–11
  stimulus to buy, 155
Federal Trade Commission Act of 1914,
  25
Festinger, Leon, 161
Fletcher, Robert, 160
Flights, 179
FMCG. *See* Fast-moving consumer goods
Focus group technique, 272
Foote Cone and Belding, 248
Ford Motor Company, 134
Fournier, Susan, 229, 248, 256
Four peripherals, 189–202
  basis of, 191
  connection to core factors, 191
  consumer price, 190
  penetration, 190
  price elasticity, 190
  purchase frequency, 190
Franklin Covey, 241
Franklin Mint, 216
Frequency distribution, 114, 119t–120
  80:20 rule, 119–120
  and growing market share, 128
  model limitations, 120
Friskies, 46, 70
Froot Loops, 117, 122, 125
Frosted Flakes, 117, 118, 125, 252
Functional performance, 54–56, 232–233,
  249
  competitive, 55
  importance of, 132
  and restaging, 102
Functional superiority, 64, 68, 74

Gabor, Andre, 39, 44
Galbraith, John Kenneth, 35, 36, 41, 43
Gallup, George, 138

Gallup and Robinson, 138, 139, 140
Gap Barbie, The, 215
Gardner, Burleigh B., 43
Gasoline market, purchase levels of, 122*t*
General Foods, 21
General Mills, 21
General Mills Cheerios, 125
General Mills Lucky Charms, 117, 122, 125
General Mills Trix, 117, 118, 125
General Mills Wheaties, 116, 117
General Motors, 43–44
Geoffrey (Toys R Us), 248
Get Hooked on Collecting, 227, 229
Gibson, Lawrence, 181
Gillette, King C., 27
Gillette Company, 27, 134
Gillette Company, The, 42
Goizueta, Roberto, 224
Gold, Jack A., 65–66, 71
Goodby, Silverstein, and Partners, 258
Goodhardt, G.L., 71, 111, 112, 134, 135
Got Milk? Barbie, 215
Gourmet, 268
Granger, C.W.J., 39, 44
Grape Nuts, 123
Greyser, Stephen A., 70, 162, 288
Growing brands, 79

Half-life, 156
Hall, Joyce C., 219, 229
Hallmark Cards, Inc., 215, 217, 222, 228, 229, 248, 249, 250
  Collector's Club, 220
  consumer behavior, 220
  the Dream Book, 223, 226, 229
  enhancing collectibility, 219–220
  income from collectors, 220, 221
  marketing strategy, 220
  ornaments, 219, 220
  slogan, 219
  Web site, 223, 229
Hallmark Keepsake Ornament Collector's
  Club, 220, 224, 226–227
Hallmark Keepsake Ornament line, 215, 219, 220, 221, 223, 228

Hamburger University, 231
Hamburglar, 231
Hamilton, Booz Allen, 72
Harley-Davidson, 216, 248
Harley-Davidson Barbie, 215
Harness, Ed, 7
Harper's, 268
Harris, Ralph, 42
Haskins, John (Jack) B., 144–145, 161
Hathaway, 262
Hatt, Roz, 71
Hayek, Friedrich August von, 29, 42
Heeler, Roger M., 161
Hershey, 61
Hertz, 31
Heyworth, Lord, 43
Hierarchy of effects, 146–147
Higgins, Denis, 18
High Life Beer, 72
Holbrook, Morris B., 228
Home Shopping Network, 225
Homogeneous package goods, 5, 8
Hopkins, Claude, 11
Hostess Cupcakes, 252
Household Panel, 166

Iams/Eukenuba, 247
Induced product differentiation, 5
Inertia and habit, 56
Information, using, xx. *See also* Data
Information Resources Inc. (IRI), 168, 183
Innovation, 51
Instant Postum, xix
Institute of Market Psychology, 142
Institute of Practitioners in Advertising
  (IPA), 285
Ivory, 61, 279
Ivory Shampoo, 34, 59
Ivory Soap, xix, 34, 59, 196, 233

Jell-O, 249
Jif peanut butter, 252
Johnston, Don, xxiii
Jolly Green Giant, the, 249
Jones, John Philip, 105, 134, 162, 187, 213, 229, 255, 256, 269, 288, 299

Jones Method, 180
Jordan, Michael, 249
J. Walter Thompson Company, xxiii, 71, 105, 139, 182

Kaldor, Lord Nicholas, 24, 30, 31, 41, 42, 43
Kal Kan, 46, 70
Karslake, J.S., 160
Keepsake Ornament line. *See* Hallmark Keepsake Ornament line
Keller, Kevin Lane, 255
Kellogg's, 21, 61
Kellogg's All-Bran, 123
Kellogg's Bran Flakes, 123
Kellogg's Corn Flakes, 38, 56, 116, 117, 123
Kellogg's Froot Loops, 117, 122, 125
Kellogg's Frosted Flakes, 117, 118, 252
Kellogg's Raisin Bran, 124
Kellogg's Rice Krispies, 94, 100, 123, 125
Keynes, John Maynard, 17
Kimberly-Clark, 85
King, Stephen, 17, 43, 52, 62, 64, 65, 66, 67, 70, 71, 83, 85, 105, 162, 250, 255
King Continuum, 250
Kipling, Joseph, 18
Klein, Naomi, 18
Knight, Frank Hyneman, 42, 44
Kodak. *See* Eastman Kodak
Kodak cameras, xix
Kodak films, xix
Koestler, Arthur, 261
Kraft General Foods, 11, 61
Kroger, 250
Krugman, Dean M., 44
Krugman, Herbert E., 147, 148–149, 150, 152, 161
Krugman theory. *See* Low-involvement hierarchy
Kuehn, Alfred A., 43

Ladies' Home Journal, 162
Lambin, Jean Jacques, 89, 105

Lancôme, 251
Lannon, Judie, 43, 288
Lasker, Albert, 86
Lateral thinking, 234
Laundry detergents
  market penetration, 192*t*
  purchase frequency, 198
  SOM/penetration relationship, 194
Learn-do-feel theory, 147. *See also* Low-involvement hierarchy
Learn-feel-do theory, 146–147. *See also* Learning hierarchy
  problems with, 151
  theoretical framework, 151
Learning hierarchy, 146–147, 148, 149
Lehmann, Donald R., 106, 203
Leigh, J., 160
Leith, Scott, 256
Levenson, Bob, 269
Lever 2000, 233
Levitt, Theodore, 34, 36, 43
Levy, Sidney J., 43
Lexus, 216
Life, 140
LifeSavers, 216
Light, Larry, 228, 229
Lilt, 7
Line extension, 59
Listerine, 53, 195, 250
Literature
  primary works, 11
  secondary works, 11–12
  tertiary works, 12
Logarithmic series distribution (LSD), 115
Lorillard and Co., P., xix
Loro, Laura, 228
Louisiana, campaign for, 266–268, 269
Low-involvement hierarchy, 149, 152–153
  development of, 147–148
  essence of, 153
  mental processes, 148–149, 153
Lucas, Darrell B., 140, 160
Lucky Charms, 117, 122, 125
Lux, 233

Mabey, Bill, 160
McCorkell, Graeme, 288
McDonald, Colin, 14, 18, 67, 71, 134, 179, 180, 181, 284
McDonald's Corporation, 215, 216, 217, 231, 237, 247
McDonald's Happy Meal, 216
Macintosh, 248, 262
MacLachlan, James, 160
McNamara, J.J., 160
Madell, John, 68–69, 72
Magazines, 148
  brain wave activity, 149
Malt-O-Meal Puffed Rice, 21
Malt-O-Meal Puffed Wheat, 21
Manufacturers, 40
  advertising strategies, 108
  building a consumer base, 74, 83
  of large brands, 195–196
  maintaining the status quo, 107
  problem of, 25
  promotions and, 200
  reputation of, 34
  and wholesalers, 24–25
Ma Perkins, 253
Market concentration
  early studies of, 25
  in oligopolistic markets, 30
Marketers, dominant, xvii
Market experimentation, 276
  clients' role in, 280
  conditions, 277
  cost of, 279
  of established brands, 277
  lack of, 284
  of new brands, 277
  phasing, 278
  problems with, 278–279
Marketing, 15
  myths, 67
  pilot, 66
Marketing-Advertising Pattern (MAP), 90–91
Marketing impetus driving large brands, 210
Marketing Science Institute (MSI), 285

Market research. *See also* Market experimentation
  causality, 137
  early types of, 138
    television, 139–140
  questions, 137–138
  samples, 136–137
    frames, 137
  using percentages, 138
Market Research Corporation of America, 13
Markets
  analysis of, 241
  changes in, 50–51
  increasing share of, 127–128
  myths
    demographic and psychographic positioning, 124–125
    leaky buckets, 126*t*–127
    loyal buyers, 125–126
    promotional and seasonal sales, 127–128
Market segmentation, 56–57, 132
  based on functional differences, 57
  case study of, 57*t*–59*t*
Market share, 190–191. *See also* Share of market
Market testing techniques, 65–67
Marlboro, 262
Marshall, Alfred, 42
Martin, C., Jr., 160
Mattel, 215, 221, 222
Matthews, Ryan, 229
Mayer, Mark, 266
Mayer and Partners, 266
Media Marketing Assessment Inc. (MMA), 183, 202, 203, 210
Mediamark Research Inc. (MRI), 56, 228, 244, 245, 246, 256
Media planning
  detachment from agencies, 275
  effectiveness, 264
  efficiency, 263–264
  objective of, 263
  selecting media classes, 264–265
  selecting media vehicles, 265

Medium-term payback, 210
Mennen, 65
Meow Mix, 46, 70
Miller, 72, 250
Miller High Life Beer, 72
Mobil, 122
Modern Maturity, 268
Mogul, xix
Monitor Plus, 166
Monopolistic competition, 25
Mooney, Phil, 219, 225, 229
Moran, William T., 62, 71
Morgan, Nigel, 269
Moroney, Michael J., 90, 105
Motivators, 250
MRI. *See* Mediamark Research Inc.
Muensterberger, Werner, 222, 223, 229
Multibrand buying, 111, 114, 115,
    121–124, 132
  duplication of purchase law, 123–124
Murad, xix
Murphy, John M., 255

Nabisco, 21
Nabisco Shredded Wheat, 56, 113, 116,
    117, 118, 119*t*–120, 121, 122, 123,
    126, 127
Nader, Ralph, 34
Naples, Michael, 134
National, 122
National Fluid Milk Processor Promotion
    Board, 258
National Geographic Traveler, 268
NBC, 241
Negative binomial distribution (NBD),
    115
Nestlé, 11, 134
Neu, D. Morgan, 160
New (as a word), 103
New brands
  advertising expenditures for, 87
  affecting market growth, 50
  affecting market share, 50–51
  difficulty of, 4, 35
  effective frequency, 181
  failure of, 108

New brands *(continued)*
  favorable response to, 51
  first repurchase, 74–75
  growth of, 74
    through distribution, 75–76*t*
  important factors for, 69–70
  influences on, 54
    distribution, 63–65
    functional performance, 54–56
    name, 59–61*t*, 62
    positioning, 56–59
    price, 62–63
  introduction of, 66
  and low-involvement hierarchy, 152
  maintaining position of, 54
  "me-too" strategy, 47–48
  promotion of, 79
  restaging, 102
  retail acceptance of, 64–65
  success of, 54, 61, 67–69
  testing, 277
  with umbrella names, performance of, 61
New Coke, 225
New Industrial State, The, 35
New Yorker, 268
Nielsen Company, A.C.,13, 34, 36, 41, 78,
    83, 85, 86, 90, 130, 167, 180, 185,
    199
  analyses of primary growth cycles, 78
  on brand loyalty, 101
  data limitations, 49
  data provided by, 48
  duration of tests, 67
  Household Panel, 166
  Monitor Plus, 166
  new brands, 60
  Pure Single-Source research, 166, 179,
    180
  on recycling, 102
  system flaw, 165
  television viewing studies, 166–167
  test market information, 66
  trade promotion analysis, 81
Nielsen Researcher, 71, 106
Nike, 249
Nine Lives, 46, 70

Nordic Track, 251
Northwestern Mutual Life Insurance
    Company, 288

O'Brien, Terrence, 161
Ogilvy, David, 7, 8, 11, 17, 102, 106,
    258, 269, 276, 288
Ogilvy & Mather, 276
Old Jim Young, 33
Oligopolies, 5, 40
  advantages of, 30
  competition in, 40–41
    and branding, 31
    breakfast cereal industry, 22
    consumer benefits from, 30
    and market concentration, 30
    vs. monopolistic competition, 41
    pricing, 29, 81
    reason for, 20
    using functional benefits, 29
  conditions leading to, 24, 28
  and cyclical decline, 52
  economies of scale in, 30
  innovations in, 51
  pressures in, 51, 52–53
  status quo in, 51–52
  views on, 23
Olympics, 2002 Winter, 218
Omnicom, 247
Oppenheimer, J. Robert, 283, 285, 289
Orenstein, Frank, 162, 288
Oreo Barbie, 215
Ostlund, Lyman E., 160
Overland Coupe, xix
Oxo, 276
Oxydol, 233, 253–254

Packaged goods, added values in, 9
Packaging, 9, 54
  as an added value, 34, 237
  case size, 65
  displays and, 82
PACT. See Positioning Advertising Copy
    Testing
Palda, Kristian S., 161
Pall Mall, xix

Palmolive, 61
Pan American, 134
Parade, 268
Parity products, 5
PARM. *See* Printed Advertising Rating
    Methods Committee
Patti, Charles H., 150, 161
Peckham, James O., Sr., 6, 17, 35, 42,
    43, 44, 48, 54, 64, 68–69, 70, 71,
    72, 80, 81, 84, 85, 90–91, 104,
    105, 106, 126, 134, 135
Penetration, 113, 114–115, 116*t*–117*t*,
    190, 211
  and consumer loyalty, 126
  and growing market share, 128
  and large brands, 196
  meanings of, 114
  predicting, 115
  relating to share of market, 191,
    192*t*, 193*t*, 195–196
  and repurchase rates, 121
Penetration supercharge, 119, 121,
    132, 133, 199
PepsiCo., 134, 245, 250
Pepsi-Cola, 43
Perfect competition, conditions for,
    28
Peter's, 45
Peters, Thomas J., 71
Petty, Priscilla Hayes, 18
Pillsbury, 216
Pillsbury Doughboy, 249
Pilot marketing, 66
Planter's Peanuts, 216
P. Lorillard and Co., xix
Polli, R., 70
Pollitt, Stanley, 288
Positioning, 56–59
  demographic, 124–125
  psychographic, 124–125
Positioning Advertising Copy Testing
    (PACT), 158
Positioning Advertising Copy Testing
    (PACT) Agencies, The, 162
Post Grape Nuts, 123
Post Raisin Bran, 124

Post Sugar Crisps, 116, 117, 122, 125
Post Toasties, xix
Postum Cereal Co., xix
Postum Grape Nuts, xix
Prentice, Robert M., 80, 104, 105
Presbey, Frank Spencer, 26
Price, 94–100, 200t
  competition
    forms of, 22–23
    in oligopolies, 24
    promotions, 23. See also
      Promotions
  consumer, 190
  and demand, 39
  effective, 199
  elasticity, 39, 63. See also Price
    elasticity
  establishing, 63
  increases, 201, 202t
  premium, 62
    of ongoing brands, 63
  reductions, 201t
Price elasticity, 96t, 104, 190, 212
  break-even, 97
  compared with advertising
    expenditures, 202t
  definition of measuring, 95
  operational value of, 96
  profitability and, 201–202
  study of, 200
  and successful advertising, 202
Price rebates, 83–84
Prichard, Annette, 269
Pricing. See also Price
  initial, 63
  of new brands, 62
  penetration, 63
  skimming, 63
Pride, Roger, 269
Primary growth cycle, 76–78
  British test market research, 78
  definition of, 77
  length of, 77
Pringles, 7
Printed Advertising Rating Methods
  Committee, 140

Procter & Gamble (P&G), xix, 7, 11, 17,
  53, 54, 80, 84, 143, 233, 240, 241,
  249, 253, 279
Product differentiation
  artificial, 8
  and branding, 31
  in the breakfast cereal industry, 22
Products
  branded vs. unbranded, 37, 237
  convenience, 50
  definition, 31
  functional differences in, 6, 8
  induced differentiation, 5
  life cycle of, 53
  parity, 5
  purchase rates, 122
    for larger brands, 123
  substitution of, 101
Product tests, 6
  matched, 35
Progressive Grocer, 135
Promotional intensity, 174
Promotions, 74, 103, 199
  and advertising synergy from, 85
  consumer, 83–85, 79
    objective of, 83
    price rebates, 83–84
    sales levels, 83
  and diminishing returns, 85
  function of, 200
  myths about, 127–128
  price, 84
    couponing, 84, 85
    direct rebating, 84
    house-to-house sampling, 84
  role of, 131
  and television advertising, 168
  trade, 79–82
    cautions, 80–81
    cooperative advertising, 82
    cost of, 79–80
    data from, 82
    display, 81
    objective of, 79
Propositions, 248–250, 255
  primary elements, 249

Propositions *(continued)*
  role of, 248
  subjects included in, 249–250
Psychographics, 247
Purchase decision, low involvement, 5
Purchase frequency, 114, 117–119, 190,
    199, 211–212
  growth rate, 118*t*
  increasing among existing users, 246
  increasing with collectibles, 216
  and penetration, 118
  predicting, 115
Purchase rates, 123
Purchasing behavior, operational value of
    understanding, 133
Purchasing patterns, 110*t*
  factors involved with, 110
  major brands, 111
  multibrand purchasing, 111
Purdue University, 142
Pure Single-Source research, 166, 167,
    179, 180, 185, 199
Purina, 46, 70

Quaker Cap'n Crunch, 116, 117, 122, 125
Quaker Life, 117, 122, 125
Quaker Oats, xix, 21
Quaker Oats Puffed Rice, xix
Quaker Oats Puffed Wheat, xix
Quaker Puffed Wheat, 21
Quelch, John A., 105
QVC, 215, 225

Raisin Bran (Kellogg's), 124
Raisin Bran (Post), 124
Ralph Lauren, 215
Ralston Purina, 21, 216, 246
Ralston Purina Dog Chow, 252
Ramond, Charles, 146, 147, 149, 160, 161
Rave, 7
Ray, Michael L., 147, 148, 161
Reading-and-noting method, 138
  investigation into, 140–143
    contaminating factors, 141
    DEMOS, 142, 143*t*
    hypothesis of, 141

Rebates, 84, 85
Recall testing, 138–139, 157–159
  adstock, 156
  comparative interpretation of, 159*t*
  DART, 143–144, 158
  data base size, 158
  effectiveness of, 144–145
  half-life, 156
  investigation into, 140
  learn-feel-do. *See* Learning hierarchy
  low-involvement hierarchy. *See* Low-
    involvement hierarchy
  reasons for using, 145
  reinforcement hypothesis, 154. *See also*
    Reinforcement hypothesis
  relevance of, 151, 158
  reliability of, 157
  and sales, 156
  type of claim, 144
  usefulness of, 150–154
Recency scheduling, 183
Recognition testing. *See* Reading-and-
  noting method
Recycling, 77, 101–103
Redox, 253, 254
Reed, Jerome B., 161
Reekie, W. Duncan, 42, 44
Reeves, Rosser, 18, 134, 152, 161
Regular Postum, xix
Reid, Leonard N., 289
Reinforcement hypothesis, 149–150,
    154
Reintroductions, 253
Relaunching. *See* Recycling
Repeat buying, 114, 120–121
*Repeat-Buying: Theory and
    Applications*, 111
Repeat purchase, 55, 56
Repeat-purchase goods, 4, 10
Repeat-purchase packaged goods, 173.
    See also Fast-moving consumer
    goods
Research, 150, 283–284
  data source for, 284. *See also* Data
  image measurement, 158
  market. *See* Market research

Research *(continued)*
Positioning Advertising Copy Testing, 158
pre-testing. *See* ARS
qualitative, 145
roles of
diagnostic, 145, 146
quality control, 146
STAS (Short-Term Advertising Strength). *See* STAS
on television viewing, 166–167
tracking studies
advertising recall, 156
image attributes, 156–157
in universities, 283, 284–285
advantages of, 285–286
role of, 284
use of scanners for, 166
Resonance. *See* Reinforcement hypothesis
Resor, Stanley, 139
Restaging, 139. *See also* Recycling
with a considerable change, 154
Restoration Hardware, 254
Retail, 25
acceptance of new brands, 64–65
audit, 48–49
vs. consumer panels, 49
limitations of, 48–49
and cooperative advertising, 82
running out of stock, 101
sales, expectations for me-too brands, 48
stores, importance of, 46
Revlon, 249
Rice Krispies, 94, 100, 123, 125
Roberts, Andrew, 83, 97–98, 105, 106, 181
Robertson, D.H., 17
Robinson, Joan, 31, 33, 42, 43
Robinson, William A., 104
Ronald McDonald, 215, 231
Rotfeld, Herbert J., 289
Rothschild, Michael L., 161
Rotzoll, Kim B., 162
Rudolph, James, 72

Safety razor market, 27
Said, Rana S., 288

Sales
advertising, additional effects of. *See* Advertising response function
and advertising expenditures, 87–88
advertising influence on, 163–165
calculating in consumer terms, 113*t*–114
and cash cows, 53
in cat food market, 45–46, 70
and consumer promotions, 83
diminishing returns, 179, 181, 186–187
and low Continuity scheduling, 184
theory of, 178
to distribution ratio example, 76*t*
effect of price reduction on, 200*t*
effect of trade promotions on, 80–81
initial, 103
of a new brand, 75
packs on display, measuring rates of, 45–46
pattern, 166
promotions and, 174–175
propinquity of advertising and, 181
recall testing and, 153, 156
relation to advertising elasticity, 204*t*–207*t*
retail. *See* Retail
Sales promotions, 175
Samples, 136–137
frame, 137
Sampling, house-to-house, 84
Saposito, Bill, 17
Saturn, 248
Sawyer, Alan G., 161
Scale economies, 30, 132
advertising, 281
distribution, 64
and manufacturers, 196
penetration supercharge, 119
Procter & Gamble, 279
SOV-SOM relationship, 207
in terms of advertising expenditures, 89
Scanners, in-home, 166
Schaeffer, Randy, 229
Schultz, Don E., 104, 289
Seasonal sales, 131
Seasonal uplifts, 127–128

Seldon, Arthur, 42
Selective perception, 131, 142
7-Up, 245
Share of market (SOM)
  formula for, 244
  of large brands, 199
  and overinvestment/underinvestment,
    207. *See also* Advertising-
    Intensiveness Curve
  relating to penetration, 191, 192*t*, 193*t*,
    195–196
Share of voice (SOV), 207
Shell, 122
Sherman Antitrust Act of 1890, 25
Sherry, John, 228
Short-Term Advertising Strength. *See*
  STAS
Shredded Wheat, 56, 113, 116, 117, 118,
  119*t*–120, 121, 122, 123, 126, 127
Shulman, Art, 160
Sierra Mist, 245
Simmons Market Research Bureau
  (SMRB), 56, 244, 245, 246
Simon, Julian L., 17, 71
Slater, Jan S., 228, 229, 255, 269, 299–300
Smale, John, 18
SMRB. *See* Simmons Market Research
  Bureau
SOM. *See* Share of market
SOV. *See* Share of voice
Special Dinner, 46, 70
Sprite, 245
Stachmo Summer Fest, 267
Standards of living, growth in, 27
Stanford Research Institute, 247
Starch, Daniel, 138, 139, 140, 161
Starch technique, 141, 159
Star Trek, 227
STAS (Short-Term Advertising Strength),
  168, 169*t*
  Baseline, 168
  competitive brands and, 172
  Differential, 168, 170*t*
    relating to advertising intensity, 173*t*,
      174
  Differential Index, 168

STAS *(continued)*
  medium-term effects, 172*t*
  Stimulated, 168
Steiner, Robert L., 42
Steiner Effect, 42
Steward Warner Speedometer Co., xix
Strategies. *See also* Advertising strategy
  long-term, purpose of, xxi
  media, 164–165
Strong, Edward C., 161
Substantial proportion, 181–182
Sugar Crisps, 116, 117, 122, 125
Sullivan, Luke, 259, 269
Super marketers, xvii
Swibel, Matthew, 256
Swinyard, William R., 150, 161

Target, 250
Target groups, 133, 255
  brand relationship, 248
  defining, 244
  demographics, 246–247
  psychographics, 247–248
    vs. demographics, 248
    VALS (Values and Lifestyles),
      247–248
  reaching, 164
  source of business, 244–246
    existing users, 246
    new users, 245–246
Technique for Producing Ideas, A, 260
Television, 10, 288
  brain wave activity, 149
  early use of, 139–140
  low-involvement hierarchy theory,
    147–149
  vs. magazines, 148
  Nielsen studies, 166–167
  and recall testing, 143
Tellis, Gerard J., 106, 200
Tender Vittles, 46, 70
Test market, 65–66
Texaco, 122
Texas Monthly, 268
Thompson Company, J. Walter, xxiii, 71,
  105, 139, 182

3M Company, 70
Tide, 195, 233, 250, 253, 254, 279
  liquid, 53, 59
  powder, 53, 59
Tinkham, Spencer F., 289
Toasties, xix
Tolley, B. Stuart, 162, 288
Tony the Tiger, 249
Toys R Us, 249
Trademarks
  joint, 61
  origins of, 27
Treasure, John A.P., 111, 134
Trix, 117, 118, 125
Twyman, W.A., 160

Ultimate Secrets of Advertising, The, 213
Umbrella names, 59–60
  advantage of, 60
    economic, 61
  success of, 61*t*
Understanding Buying Behavior, 111
Unilever, 134, 233
Unilever marketing companies, 90
USA Today, 268

VALS (Values and Lifestyles) groups, 247–248
Vanden Bergh, Bruce G., 44
Vertical thinking, 233, 234, 262
Victor Records, xix
Victor Talking Machine Co., xix

Victrola Players, xix
Volkswagen, 247

Walking, 268
Wallendorf, Melanie, 228
Walt Disney, 216
Warner-Lambert, 11, 53
Waterman, Robert H., Jr., 71
Wegmans supermarket, case study of, 20–23, 25, 38
Weilbacher, William M., 288
Weinstein, Curt, 149, 161
Weinstein, Sidney, 149, 161
What's In a Name? Advertising and the Concept of Brands, xvii, 213
Wheaties, 116, 117
Wholesalers, 40
  decline of, 24
  and manufacturers, 24–25
Willys-Overland, xix
Winterhalter, Mark, 256
Woman's Own, 143
World Advertising Research Centre (WARC), 285

Yao, Julie L., 229
Young, James Webb, 11, 16, 18, 32, 35, 43, 105, 260, 269, 288
Young, Shirley, 144, 146, 161
Young & Rubicam, 261
Yuspeh, Sonia, 70, 144, 153, 161, 162

ZAA, 171–172
Zubelda, xix

About the Authors

John Philip Jones is an advertising professor at Syracuse University. Born in Britain, he received his degrees in economics from Cambridge University. He has twenty-seven years of professional experience, including twenty-five years in international operations with the J. Walter Thompson Company. Jones has been with the Newhouse School of Public Communications, Syracuse University, for twenty-two years and is an adjunct professor at the Royal Melbourne Institute of Technology, Australia. He is also employed as a consultant by numerous first-rank national and international organizations, mainly advertisers and advertising agencies. He is a specialist in the measurement and evaluation of advertising effects and the originator of two widely used concepts to measure them.

Jones is the author of five books, including *The Ultimate Secrets of Advertising* (2002), and has published more than seventy journal articles. His books have been translated and published in eight foreign languages. He was also the editor and part-author of a series of five major handbooks (published between 1998 and 2000), which cover all aspects of professional advertising practice.

Jones is the recipient of several national awards and recognitions, the most recent of which is the Syracuse University Chancellor's 2001 Citation for Exceptional Academic Achievement.

Jan S. Slater is an associate professor of advertising at the E.W. Scripps School of Journalism at Ohio University in Athens, Ohio. In addition to her sixteen years of teaching experience, Slater has twenty years' experience in the advertising industry, having worked in both private industry and in advertising agencies. Until 1990, she owned her own agency in Omaha, Nebraska. She is a member of the Academic Division of the American Advertising Federation (AAF) and serves as chair of the Advertising Division of the Association for Education in Journalism and Mass Communication (AEJMC). Her research has been published in *Journalism and Mass Communication Educator, Advances in Consumer Research,* and *Journal of Advertising Educa-*

tion. She is a contributing author to a series of advertising handbooks published by Sage. Her primary research focus is on brand relationships involving strategy and media. Slater earned her B.A. from Hastings College, Hastings, Nebraska; an M.S. in advertising at the University of Illinois, Champaign-Urbana; and a Ph.D. in mass communications at the Newhouse School of Public Communications at Syracuse University.